Administering for Quality

Leading Canadian Early Childhood Programs

FOURTH EDITION

Karen Chandler

George Brown College

PEARSON

Toronto

Vice-President, Editorial Director: Gary Bennett
Editor-in-Chief: Michelle Sartor
Editor, Humanities and Social Sciences: Joel Gladstone
Marketing Manager: Ann MacDonald
Supervising Developmental Editor: Madhu Ranadive
Developmental Editor: Cheryl Finch
Project Managers: Marissa Lok and Renata Butera (Central Publishing)
Manufacturing Coordinator: Susan Johnson
Production Editor: Sudip Sinha/Aptara®, Inc.
Copy Editor: Seilesh Singh
Proofreader: Barnali Ojha
Compositor: Aptara®, Inc.
Art Director: Julia Hall
Cover and Interior Designer: Miriam Blier
Cover Image: Getty Images/Martin Poole

Library and Archives Canada Cataloguing in Publication

Chandler, Karen (Karen A. M.)
      Administering for quality : leading Canadian early childhood programs /
Karen Chandler.—4th ed.

Includes bibliographical references and index.
ISBN 978-0-13-211358-8

      1. Early childhood education—Canada—Administration—Textbooks.
2. Child care services—Canada—Administration—Textbooks.   I. Title.

HQ778.7.C3C373 2011   362.71'2068   C2011-904407-2

D 9 8 7 6 5 4 3   RRD–H

ISBN 978-0-13-211358-8

To Olivia and Caitlin, who need educators who are willing to make all the difference in their world.

Brief Contents

Contents

Preface

This fourth edition of *Administering for Quality: Leading Canadian Early Childhood Programs* is designed to facilitate early childhood educators' understanding of administrative, professional, and advocacy responsibilities. Considering that each educator's influence on young children and families is so lasting, it is important to fully prepare oneself for this commitment.

Over many years—as an early childhood specialist working with children, families, and professionals in a wide variety of settings; as a professor of administration, professionalism, advocacy, sociology, and interpersonal communication; as a writer on early childhood topics, including *Administering Early Childhood Settings: The Canadian Perspective and The Whole Child*; and as a senior policy advisor for the Early Learning and Child Development Branch of the Ontario government making recommendations about the ECE's role in Kindergarten—I appreciate that leadership, thoughtful planning, and administration are essential to the success of quality EC programs. This book is built on that conviction. I will note that my role as grandma to Olivia and Caitlin, being personally involved with their parents' quest for high quality learning experiences, as well as witnessing their reassurance from their partnership with knowledgeable, career-committed EC professionals, has reinforced the importance of strong leadership at all levels.

Readers are introduced to a range of types of early childhood experiences. Special attention is given to family child care, as it is the type of care the majority of Canadian parents use—and many ECE graduates, at some point in their careers, work in family child care.

Although primarily written for EC programs at the post-secondary level, this book can also be used as a self-help resource in preparing for credentialing. A rich source of information for practicing directors, it includes up-to-date Canadian statistics, highlights current research, and identifies a variety of resources including vital weblinks.

Terminology

A continued struggle faces our profession: to attain recognition for our important work. In part, we struggle with our identity. This is reflected in an inconsistent use of terminology and nomenclature—the terms we use to describe ourselves and the titles others assign to us. For words such as "doctor," "lawyer," and "nurse," we have a clear set of images about what the profession does and what it stands for. We in the field of early childhood education have long debated what to call ourselves, and at times discussion of the title has been contentious. Among the terms used are "early childhood educator," "child care professional," "developmental worker," "teacher," "caregiver," "child care worker," "home child care provider," "day care staff," and "practitioner." One point of agreement: Don't call us "babysitters"! A task for our profession is to reach consensus on what we are going to call ourselves. In this book, I chose to use the term "early childhood educator." "Director" describes one who acts as an administrator and/or supervisor. I have used the pronoun "she" for directors because it continues to be uncommon to find men in these roles.

I have used the term "early childhood," which acknowledges a broader range of services, including services for children and families that foster health, safety, security, success at learning, and social engagement and responsibility.

New Features

This fourth edition of *Administering for Quality: Leading Canadian Early Childhood Programs* emphasizes Canadian research, resources, and policy, with this edition reflecting some of the significant changes taking place in the early childhood field. One monumental transformation is with the provincial ministries of education taking responsibility for early childhood in most provinces. A second change is taking place in Ontario where ECEs are working collaboratively with teachers in full-day kindergartens, and in Prince Edward Island where ECEs are the primary educators in kindergartens. Unquestionably, there is growing acknowledgement of the importance of leadership and the ECEC director. There are initiatives to develop leadership at all levels through professionalism and mentoring. With these changes, there has been increased focus on the expectations of the early childhood educator with the development of Occupational Standards for both educator and director positions, as well as the emergence of standards of practice and public accountability for performance. In Ontario there is a professional college for early childhood educators and the requirement of meeting standards of practice. As well as being *legally accountable* for their adherence to these standards, ECEs have the ethical responsibility to work in partnership with families to create conditions that foster optimal development for all children.

These educator standards and the use of websites which rate the quality of ECEC programs reflect increased accountability and expectations by governments and families who demand quality learning experiences for their young children whether they are paid for directly through fees or indirectly through taxes that fund the school-operated kindergartens.

The Child Care Human Resources Sector Council (CCHRSC) contributes greatly to the understanding of the EC workforce and conducts research into salaries and working conditions. My work with CCHRSC and CCCF has enabled me to work with First Nations' representatives and SpeciaLink. I have endeavoured to reflect wider values and perspectives in definitions of quality.

These new expectations and broadened perspectives are woven throughout the book. Highlights of these understandings include:

- Chapter 1 "Defining Quality Early Childhood Programs" reflects wider values and perspectives in several definitions of quality; it includes multiple rationales for EC programs: social justice such as children's rights; economic—public investments in young children and families; and human development—preventing a loss of potential for children.

- Chapter 2 "Social Policy and Roles of Government" introduces readers to social policy and roles of the three levels of government and includes:

    - discussion of the complexity of implementing ECEC policy of a larger vision for child and families into education,

    - expanded international comparisons of ECEC policy and children's rights are reflected through the work of the OECD,

    - discussion of initiatives and challenges of the integration of EC and kindergarten into the school system.

- Chapter 3 "Leadership and Governance in Early Childhood Programs" outlines the growth in the number of programs, as well as new partnerships with school boards. It identifies a number of leadership roles in addition to the director, including the school principal and the governance board. The chapter underlines the importance of the role of leadership to creating and maintaining high quality EC programs as well as the importance of the development of leadership at all levels including EC students.

- Chapter 4 "Planning and Evaluating the Program Goals" introduces the readers to a discussion of how program philosophies are linked to the vision of what EC programs want to achieve. Readers are encouraged to define their personal philosophy and examine how it may merge with the employer's. A number of tools are reviewed to assess program quality from a variety of perspectives, such as involvement with schools, inclusion, and greening of EC environments.

- Chapter 5 "Human Resources Management" outlines occupational standards for educators, with an example job description that reflects these increased expectations. The emergence of standards of practice and public accountability for performance, ongoing professional development strategies such as mentorship, performance appraisal, and the developmental stages of ECEs are discussed.

- Chapter 6 "Promoting Professionalism" highlights aspects of professionalism, including the newly released standards of practice and code of ethics from the professional College of Early Childhood Educators.

- Chapter 7 "Managing Safe and Healthy Learning Environments" clearly links quality practices with current research reflected in program policies and practices. The chapter introduces resources to evaluate and improve the environmental quality of programs given the vulnerability of young children to environmental hazards.

- Chapter 8 "Building Partnerships with Families" outlines the complexity of families and the stressors they face, noting considerations in engaging culturally diverse families. Making use of internet-based communication with families, such as classroom websites, to support parents' engagement in their child's learning is discussed.

- Chapter 9 "Financial Matters" describes the iron triangle formula for financial policy, linkages of financial decision-making with quality, and strategies for building financial stability for EC programs.

- Chapter 10 "Advocating for Canada's Children" provides a rationale for rectifying the gulf between the often-touted high quality programs and the much larger number of barely good enough programs experienced by many children. The reader is introduced to advocacy objectives such as working for equality and social justice using new strategies such as social media. The chapter highlights key pieces of research and long-term studies as well as credible partners.

Instructional Features

The following pedagogical features are included in each chapter:

- *Objectives*. At the beginning of each chapter, learning outcomes are suggested. Individual instructors of a variety of courses can adapt these suggestions to their own focus.

- *Exhibits/focus boxes*. Figures, charts, and tables are used to summarize research. Boxes highlight material, provide samples, and help organize, illustrate, and simplify information.

- *Standards*. Samples of quality standards from the Occupational Standards and other sources are provided in most chapters.

- *Key terms and concepts*. These are identified in boldface type on first use, and definitions are located in a glossary at the end of the book. At the end of each chapter, key terms and concepts of particular relevance to the chapter are listed.

- *Activities*. Student activities follow a summary at the close of each chapter. Questions are designed to stimulate the reader to reflect, examine her or his beliefs, and take a look at practices.

- *Recommended readings*. Suggestions for further reading are given for each chapter.

- *Weblinks*. This feature links readers to a whole world of resources pertinent to chapter material.

- *Appendix*. A list of government and professional organizations, including internet addresses, is given at the end of the book.

A special request to readers of this book: Please let me know how you like the book and how I can make it better. I can be reached at George Brown College; School of Early Childhood.

Karen Chandler
School of Early Childhood
George Brown College

Supplements

Instructor's Manual

The Instructors Manual includes Quizzes with Answer Key for Quizzes, Chapter Summaries, Recommended Readings, Weblinks, and Transparency Masters. The Instructor's Manual is available in PDF format from the Pearson online catalogue to instructors who adopt the textbook.

CourseSmart for Instructors (ISBN 978-0-13-607013-2)

CourseSmart goes beyond traditional expectations—providing instant, online access to the textbooks and course materials you need at a lower cost for students. And even as students save money, you can save time and hassle with a digital eTextbook that allows you to search for the most relevant content at the very moment you need it. Whether it's evaluating textbooks or creating lecture notes to help students with difficult concepts, CourseSmart can make life a little easier. See how when you visit www.coursesmart.com/instructors.

CourseSmart for Students (ISBN 978-0-13-607013-2)

CourseSmart goes beyond traditional expectations—providing instant, online access to the textbooks and course materials you need at an average savings of 60%. With instant access from any computer and the ability to search your text, you'll find the content you need quickly, no matter where you are. And with online tools like highlighting and note-taking, you can save time and study efficiently. See all the benefits at www.coursesmart.com/students.

Technology Specialists

Pearson's Technology Specialists work with faculty and campus course designers to ensure that Pearson technology products, assessment tools, and online course materials are tailored to meet your specific needs. This highly qualified team is dedicated to helping schools take full advantage of a wide range of educational resources, by assisting in the integration of a variety of instructional materials and media formats. Your local Pearson Canada sales representative can provide you with more details on this service program.

Pearson Custom Library

For enrollments of at least 25 students, you can create your own textbook by choosing the chapters that best suit your own course needs. To begin building your custom text, visit www.pearsoncustomlibrary.com. You may also work with a dedicated Pearson Custom editor to create your ideal text—publishing your own original content or mixing and matching Pearson content. Contact your local Pearson representative to get started.

Acknowledgments

First of all, I would like to pay tribute to the students at George Brown College, who help me formulate my ideas about the field and who continue to teach me a great deal about life. They support the need for current Canadian materials. The many children, families, and professionals I work with who challenge my thinking and broaden my understanding. I have had endless opportunities to discuss new ideas and strategies with my colleagues at the School of Early Childhood at George Brown College and former associates at the Ministry of Child and Youth Services. One of the most rewarding aspects of the field is the people I work with in a voluntary capacity, including my colleagues at the Canadian Child Care Federation—both staff and participants on member council, the Child Care Human Resources Sector Council, and the ECE Affinity group.

This book could not have been written without the many organizations and colleagues in the EC field who contributed through their research and publications, and recommendations and advice. To them, I proclaim my admiration and gratitude. To gain insight into the real world, I interviewed and shared resources with experienced practicing directors; family child care providers; faculty; former students; leaders of national, provincial, and territorial organizations; researchers; and government officials. Many individuals and reviewers contributed their time and expertise to the development of this book. Special thanks go to Bill Vizard for his valued feedback and ability to translate concepts into the many diagrams throughout the book; Carolyn Ferns of the Child Care Resource Unit; Cynthia Abel, Ministry of Children and Youth Services; Diana Carter, Child Care Human Resource Sector Council; Christine McLean, Government of Newfoundland and Labrador; Marc Battle, Red River Community College; Marni Flaherty and Maureen Hall, Today's Family Early Learning and Child Care; Phil Cowperthwaite, Cowperthwaite Mehta Chartered Accountants; Canadian Child Care Federation; Jennifer Kim and Shani Halfon, graduates of George Brown College; Deb Young, City of Toronto Children's Services; Melanie Dixon, College of Early Childhood Educators; Denise Gilbert, Schoolhouse Playcare Centre; Carol Rowan and Elisipee Inukpuk', Avataq Cultural Institute; Sharon Hope Irwin, SpeciaLink; Joanne Morris, College of the North Atlantic; Fran Dobbin, University of Toronto Early Learning Centre; and Mary Gross-Prowse, Association of Early Childhood Educators, Newfoundland and Labrador.

I thank my family, who lived through the clutter of research reports and articles—particularly Rod, who supported me in meeting each successive deadline. Our cat Mishe provided a welcome distraction and endeavoured to add her own editorial comments while walking on the keyboard.

Thank you also to the reviewers who provided feedback during the early stages of the development: Kathleen Kummen, Capilano College; Dale Long, Seneca College; and Brandy Champagne, Canadore College.

I would like to express my appreciation to Pearson Canada for inviting me to write this edition.

Karen Chandler

Defining Quality Early Childhood Programs

chapter 1

Objectives

- **Outline the benefits of early childhood experiences.**

- **Appreciating multiple rationales for EC.**

- **Identify the principles that guide high quality early learning and care.**

- **Describing an ecological framework.**

- **Define quality EC programs.**

- **Identify the ingredients contributing to effective EC programs.**

- **Provide methods of achieving quality.**

- **Identify the relationship of regulation, accreditation, and program evaluation to program quality.**

The creation and maintenance of effective early childhood (EC) programs is a focus throughout this book. This chapter describes early childhood programs, explains the need for these programs, discusses quality from a variety of perspectives, and reviews the factors generally recognized as indicative of high quality programs. Early childhood education settings refers to child care, kindergarten, nursery schools, regulated home child care, family resource programs, parenting centres, child development programs, and early intervention services. Quality programs benefit all children—those whose parents are in the paid workforce as well as those who are not. Canadian parents from all social, economic, and cultural groups and from all regions seek opportunities for their children to get the best start in life.

The Organisation for Economic Co-operation and Development (OECD) noted that "'care and education' are inseparable concepts . . . the use of the term EC supports an integrated and coherent approach to policy and provision, which is inclusive of all children regardless of employment or economic status ... such arrangements may fulfill a wide range of objectives including care, learning and social support" (OECD 2006).

The Early Years Are Crucial to Healthy Child Development

A child's experiences during the early years have the greatest influence of any time in the life cycle on brain development, learning, behaviour, and health. These experiences shape their brain architecture, and affect their health and well-being throughout their lives. Positive, stimulating learning experiences in the early years contribute to self-confidence and a positive attitude toward learning, exploring, and problem solving. There is overwhelming evidence of the importance of early childhood experiences in determining greater success in school, health, and social success throughout a person's life.

Early childhood experiences nurture, protect, and educate young children and benefit their families, their communities, and the larger society. The *Early Learning and Care Impact Analysis* study and the *Benefits and Costs of Good Child Care* study conclude that for every dollar invested in high quality early childhood development, there is more than a two-dollar benefit to children, parents, and society (Fairholm 2009; Cleveland and Krashinsky 1998). Children who participate in high quality early learning programs are more likely to succeed in school and ultimately earn higher wages. They are less likely to require remedial education, social assistance, or correctional services—all costly publicly funded programs. The potential economic benefit is even greater for children at risk. The social and economic benefits of quality **early childhood settings** reach into every segment of Canadian society—children receive the best nurturing and early childhood experience possible while parents are able to work or attend school.

Significant economic and social changes over the past two decades—including increased global economic competition, a shifting economic base, changing demographics, and an influx of mothers into the workforce—have made the issue of children's early years one of primary importance. Quality early childhood development is crucial to Canada's future economic prosperity (Cleveland and Krashinsky 2001). Quality early childhood development can provide members of the next generation of workers with a solid foundation of skills, competencies, attitudes, and behaviours that will ensure their success in a more technologically based economic environment. This perspective has caught the attention of policy makers.

Even more importantly, we must also recognize that children are citizens with their own rights and deserve a healthy start. The United Nations recently reaffirmed this in the Moscow Framework for Action, calling ECE "part of the right to education and the main foundation for holistic human development" (Kaga et al. 2010). The reasons for investments in early childhood development are numerous. Children are less likely to drop out of school; there is increased workforce participation of both single mothers and mothers in two-parent families, poverty reduction, creation of jobs, and a resulting ripple effect through local economies; produces lower social spending on families, higher tax revenue to governments,

Quality EC programs foster children's confidence and identity.

and increased future economic security for women (Fairholm 2009; Prentice 2008; Cleveland and Krashinsky 1998).

A child's ability to think, form relationships, and live up to his or her full potential is directly related to the synergistic effect of good health, good **nutrition**, and appropriate stimulation and interaction with others. Human development research confirms how important the first five years of life can be for children's lifelong abilities, health, and well-being. This is a crucial time for brain development, when the structure of a child's brains is strongly influenced by the world around her. The quality of care that children experience affects the way they think and learn. Unhealthy physical, emotional, and social environments can have lifelong consequences. The brains of infants and toddlers develop quickly, and children can learn a great deal before kindergarten when they are in environments where they can discover and explore. In fact, children who have been well nurtured have brains that are physically different from those of children who experienced less favourable conditions in their early years.

Early childhood programs are a powerful tool for breaking the intergenerational cycle of poverty. Under the right conditions, these programs have significant economic benefits for all children—most particularly for the poor. But the poor, almost by definition, are unable to pay for the considerable costs of EC programs (Toriman 2008). Poor nutrition during childhood, exposure to unsafe environments, and lack of stimulation may damage children for the rest of their lives. Effective EC programs aim at preventing this damage. Consequently, EC programs deserve a place among the public policies that governments put in place to comprise a just society (Van der Gaag and Tan 2001).

Provincial governments want to reap the benefits of investing in young children and are spending money on EC programs that lay the foundation for healthy cognitive and emotional development. Ensuring healthy child development, therefore, is an investment in a country's future workforce and capacity to thrive economically and as a society.

> There is more to life and ought to be much more to childhood than readiness for economic function. Childhood ought to have a few entitlements that aren't entangled with utilitarian considerations. One of them should be the right to a degree of unencumbered satisfaction in the sheer delight and goodness of existence itself. Another ought to be the confidence of knowing that one's presence on earth is taken as an unconditional blessing that is not contaminated by the economic uses that a nation does or does not have for you.

Access to Universal EC Is Founded on Multiple Rationales

The case for EC is founded on multiple rationales, including:

- Every child's right to care, development, and education
- Ensuring that every child has equal opportunities as a prerequisite for **social justice**
- Recognizing that EC is a critical period for learning and development
- Recognizing that investing in EC brings economic benefits to society

Educational Quality—A Right for All Children

All children, without exception, have the right to quality early childhood education (ECE). The UN Convention for the Rights of the Child (1989) provides the most significant basis for policy development on behalf of young children. It requires that governments ensure that all children be respected as persons in their own right and places an obligation on national governments to make regular reports to the UN.

Respecting children's rights requires a radical shift in public and professional attitudes. Young children can no longer be regarded as passive recipients of services, but rather individuals who should be listened to and contribute to change. This means that education should not be viewed primarily as an investment opportunity, building human capital to achieve strong economic outcomes for society, nor should the rationale of providing early childhood services to enable women to enter the workforces be a primary motivator. These justifications provide a role in policy, but they are not the core rationale for building EC policies and services. Children's rights is a firm foundation for policy, recognizing that children are social actors, entitled to respect, care, education, and comprehensive services in their best interests, and identifying those with the responsibility to secure these rights on behalf of young children (Friendly 2006).

Social Justice—All Children Should Have Access to Quality EC Experiences

In Western democracies, a commonly held view is that social justice provisions should be based upon equality of opportunity, recognizing that some degree of inequality of outcomes is inevitable. For most individuals, the government has a role in securing justice and providing a level playing field where individuals are protected from disadvantages such as poverty. In many countries, EC is not achieving its full potential to promote equity and to change the lives of many disadvantaged children. Many disadvantaged children are the least likely to access an EC program, and when they do, the program is often of poorer quality than that accessed by children from more affluent families. In the absence of proactive EC policies, there is a risk of perpetuating intergenerational poverty and inequalities.

Research evidence from longitudinal studies such as the High Scope Perry Preschool as well as from neuroscience has shown that the children's earliest learning experiences are the most significant in determining their future progress in education and subsequent successes in life. In order to level the playing field, decision makers must take into account the impact of poverty, ill health, and other adversities as well as the differences in the quality of the EC experience. The social justice requires basic equity and demands that adequate provisions should be made.

Economic Case—Public Investments in Young Children

The economic wealth of countries rests with the capabilities of their population. The loss of human potential and economic wealth can be the result of inadequate investments in human development. Today, investments in human development are the least adequate for young children in both developed and developing countries. In a recent UN *Human Development Report 2010—20th anniversary* looking at human development trends across four decades, Canada dropped to eighth place in global rankings due to less investment. Political leadership at the federal level remains quiet about the issue of EC vulnerability despite prioritizing child and maternal health in international meetings.

The immediate consequences for underinvestment in young children are well known: malnutrition, impaired motor, language, cognitive, social, and emotional development; and death and disease. In Canada, these early risks have long-term consequences: school failure and lower achievement, poor physical and mental health; lower workforce productivity; and crime and delinquency.

Increased public investments in the nurturing and education of young children make a difference and produce large economic returns. *The Early Learning and Care Impact Analysis* study on the economics of early learning found that investing in EC provides the greatest economic benefit of all sectors of the Canadian economy. Economist Robert Fairholm of the Centre for Special Economics concluded that the provincial governments' decision to provide four- and five-year-olds with full-time schooling will do more than raising the children's academic achievement; it will result in a big boost for provincial economies. The returns on investment can far exceed the original costs of the program. He summarizes that investing in young children is:

- *A job creator:* Investing $1 million in EC would create 40 jobs: at least 43% more jobs than the next highest industry and four times the number of jobs generated by $1 million in construction spending.

- *A strong economic stimulus:* Every dollar invested in EC increases the economy's output (GDP) by $2.30. This is one of the highest GDP impacts of all major sectors.

- *Beneficial to the society:* Increased earnings lead to improved health outcomes and reduced social costs.

Some other findings are:

- Positive child outcomes and benefits, as illustrated in Figure 1–1, are strongly related to the quality of the EC service. However, parents have a difficult time judging quality.

FIGURE 1–1	Good EC Provides Savings/Reduced Costs
Effect on Child Outcome	**Benefits (or Costs) to Government**
Reduced child maltreatment	Lower costs to child welfare system
Reduced child accidents & injuries	Lower costs for emergency room visits & public health care
Reduced grade repetition	Fewer years spent in K-12 education
Reduced use of special education	Lower costs for special education
Increased college attendance rate	More years spent in postsecondary education
Increased labor force participation & earnings in adulthood	Increased tax revenue
Reduced use of welfare & other means-tested programs	Reduced administrative costs for social welfare programs; reduced welfare-program transfer payments
Reduced crime & contact with criminal justice system	Lower costs for the criminal justice system
Reduced incidence of smoking & substance abuse	Lower costs for public health care system and from premature death

Adapted from Lynn A. Karoly, M. Rebecca Kilburn, and Jill S. Cannon, Early Childhood Interventions: Proven Results, Future Promise, Santa Monica, Calif.: RAND Corporation, 2005.

- Low rates of pay and poor working conditions have led to high turnover among EC staff. This has contributed to immediate workforce shortages of EC staff, averaging more than 5000 per year in the recent years.

- The social benefits—and the government revenues—from more EC staff are greater than both the costs of professional education and current subsidy levels.

- The net national economic cost of these immediate shortages is estimated at over $140 million for the period from 2001 to 2007. The shortage of EC staff also held back parents from entering the workforce. In total, it meant a loss of almost 50 000 person years of employment for EC staff and parents during this period.

High quality EC programs are necessary for large economic returns, but existing public programs are often of meagre quality and, therefore, are likely to be less effective. The lesson is clear. Ensuring quality must be an essential component of a public program investment.

Human Development Case—Preventing the Loss of Potential

The case for EC is not just about the years before school. Development begins before birth and is multifaceted. Globally, the Van Leer Foundation estimates that more than 200 million children under five years are not reaching their full potential in mental and social development due to extreme poverty and poor health and nutrition. The environment in EC affects brain development. Many factors such as parental care, stimulation, stress, nutrition, and environmental toxins can all have long-term effects on brain development and function.

Interventions at this time can have long-term benefits, and are more cost-effective than interventions at a later age. The graph by Carneiro and Heckman (2003) in Figure 1–2 illustrates the importance of investing in quality early learning programs for children aged zero to six years. An investment in the early years reaps more long-term rewards than an investment at any other period in human development including further education and job training.

FIGURE 1–2	Heckman Returns on Investment

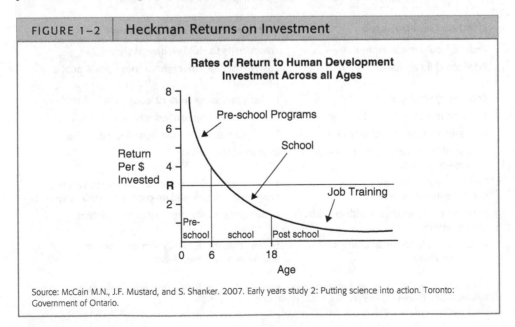

Source: McCain M.N., J.F. Mustard, and S. Shanker. 2007. Early years study 2: Putting science into action. Toronto: Government of Ontario.

Low levels of educational attainment lead to poor employment opportunities and reduced income during adulthood. Poverty is transmitted to the next generation. Through maximizing this developmental potential, society can interrupt the cycle of poverty and help to promote equity in society.

Strong Evidence for Early Childhood Program Effectiveness

Experimental longitudinal studies evaluating EC programs offer compelling evidence of improved school experience and outcomes, as well as more positive life-long outcomes. Reviewing a range of experimental and national public programs such as Head Start, economists concluded: Investments in early childhood development programs easily pay for themselves by generating high rates of returns for participants, the public, and the government. Good programs produce three dollars or more in investments for every dollar of investment. While children and their families get part of the total investments, the benefits to the rest of the public and the government are larger and, on their own, tend to outweigh the costs of the programs.

Heckman and Carneiro's work shows that the benefits of increased investments in young people lead to improving both cognitive and non-cognitive skills. Although preschool can have an impact on improving cognitive skills, later on these interventions can improve non-cognitive skills such as perseverance and self-control. According to Heckman, the Perry Preschool experience did not lead to a lasting boost in IQ scores. The children exposed to the preschool got an initial bump in general intelligence; however, this gain had dissipated by the second grade. Of interest, the preschool experience seemed to improve performance on a variety of non-cognitive abilities, such as self-control and perseverance. Heckman argues that these non-cognitive traits are often more important. Dependability is a trait highly valued by employers, while perseverance, dependability, and consistency are important predictors of success in school. Heckman and Carneiro's work notes that the sustained investments in disadvantaged children have dramatic results to improve the children's school performance as well as their social skills. The children who perform better in school would likely complete more education and not become involved in crime or dependent upon welfare. With no early childhood investments, only 41% of the students would finish high school, and more than 22% would be convicted of crime or on probation. Just 4.5% would enrol in college. The study also showed:

- With early childhood intervention, high school graduation rates would increase to 65% and college enrolment to 12%. Participation in crime would decrease.

- With skill-building investments in high school, graduation rates also would be 65%, while convictions and probation for crime would fall dramatically.

- Combining early childhood intervention with high school intervention would increase high school graduation rates to 84% and college participation rates to 27%.

- Disadvantaged children who received balanced additional attention throughout childhood would fare even better. More than 90% of those students would graduate from high school and 37% would attend college, while conviction and probation rates would fall to 2.6%. The additional investments throughout childhood could include extra enrichment and tutoring in school as well as opportunities provided by parents and institutions other than schools.

There is growing global evidence of the benefits from EC programs from small- and large-scale studies in various countries. These studies demonstrate that the most effective interventions were comprehensive (health, nutrition, and development) providing services to children, and including an active parenting and skill building component is a more effective strategy.

Greater Demand for EC Programs

Growing numbers of parents are aware of the research on brain development and the impact of effective EC experiences on healthy child development. As a result, the demand for quality EC services has grown. Many parents rely on EC programs for their child while they are at work or school. With more parents working (more than 70% of mothers with children under age six were in the paid workforce in 2008—up from 32% in 1976), the demand for high quality, afford-able early learning and care services has increased. For newcomers, EC experiences provide a valuable way for children of different cultures to integrate into Canadian society and learn English or French.

The demand for EC experiences has also grown from parents who are not in the paid work-force. Experience in all provinces and territories shows that when kindergarten, nursery school, preschool, and child care centres are available and affordable, families enrol their children. For example, when Québec opened its publicly funded early learning and care system to all young children—regardless of whether parents were in the paid workforce—programs were hard pressed to respond to all the families who applied. As a result, 436.1% of Québec children aged 0–12 have access to a regulated child care space, compared to 18.6% Canada-wide (Beach et al. 2009).

In reality, a range of services is not available in most communities across Canada. Many families are struggling to balance work demands with their family's needs. A critical component is family-friendly policies. Many working parents of all income levels experience the challenges of balancing work and family responsibilities, although there are some settings where employers are family sensitive and appreciate that family-friendly environments lead to greater retention and productivity. These approaches may provide support for employees' involvement with their children's learning. However, many parents' work environments are not supportive of family obligations. This is compounded when parents must work on weekends or shifts.

The supply of early childhood programs is inadequate. Virtually no EC opportunities exist in some areas of the country, and where there is an adequate supply, quality is uneven. Rural areas and Aboriginal communities are particularly poorly served (Bronwell 2000; Ball 2008). Often children between the ages of 5 and 12 are at home alone after school because working parents cannot establish stable care arrangements. Parents may not be able to afford or find a regulated space. They may even have difficulty making satisfactory arrangements in the unregulated sec-tor. Children who care for themselves are at increased risk for injury, loneliness, and unhealthy eating habits (Canadian Institute of Child Health 2000).

There is little evening or weekend care for children of shift workers. There are few services for mildly ill children, and since family-friendly policies are absent from so many workplaces, many parents often face loss of income if they take time off from work. Parents of **children with special needs** often find few settings that are inclusive. Where a full range of quality EC services exists, many parents are barred by the high cost. The report *Early Childhood Education and Care in Canada* (Beach et al. 2009) reported that 6 million children from birth to 12 and only 867 194 attended regulated child care spaces.

As early as 1999, a study by Canadian Policy Research Networks (Jensen and Mahon 2001) found that three-quarters of Canadians want a system that provides economic supports for chil-dren in their first three years of life. In 2006, a public opinion poll found that 77% of Canadians felt that a lack of affordable child care was a serious problem in Canada (Environics Research Group 2006). Recognizing the compelling evidence, several provincial and territorial governments are undertaking a variety of initiatives. There is a variation in the governments' visions from a well-funded, integrated, child development and parenting programs to full-day kindergarten.

What Should Comprise an Early Childhood System?

Friendly and Prentice (2009) echo three decades of Canadian child care advocacy when they call for a publicly funded ECEC system made up of programs that seamlessly blend care and ECE . . . available for all parents and for children aged 0–5 years and for school-age children up to age 12 outside of regular school hours'. Peter Moss, a European early childhood expert, advocates that every country should have a comprehensive early-years policy that provides flexible, coherent, and high quality services with equality of access for all children, whether or not their parents are employed. Keating and Hertzman (1999) adds that an early childhood strategy should be comprehensive, universally available and accessible, integrated, community-driven, accountable, and of high quality, incorporating early learning, child care, and parenting support. McCain, Mustard, and Shanker believe that effective EC programs can deliver additional outcomes such as enhanced maternal employment, gender equity, less family poverty, better parenting skills, and greater family and community cohesion (Pascal 2009). Principles to guide such a system are found in the box on the next page.

All families should have the opportunity to participate in EC programs in their community that demonstrate these principles. These programs should be sustainable, adequately resourced, and publicly supported. There would be parent fees, but they would be affordable, and programs would be accessible to those who choose to use them. Attendance at early childhood programs should be by choice rather than required.

For years, advocates called for a public infrastructure (such as school boards and/or local governments) to operate programs rather than relying on parents or volunteers to initiate and operate programs. At the same time, programs would continue to be responsive to and involve parents and would be shaped and delivered at the local level. The Toronto First Duty Project, a research project with OISE and the City of Toronto, the Toronto District School Board, and partnering community agencies piloted such a blend with an integration of early childhood, kindergarten, and family support programs. The reports *With Our Best Future in Mind: Implementing Early Learning in Ontario* and *Moving to a System of Integrated Early learning and Care in BC* reflect these comprehensive visions. This model has influenced a number of the provincial initiatives occurring in British Columbia, Ontario, New Brunswick, and Prince Edward Island.

PRINCIPLES GUIDING HIGH QUALITY EARLY LEARNING AND CARE

- All children have the right to live and learn in a society that supports their early development, health, and well-being.
- All children are entitled to participate in programs that enable them to reach their full potential regardless of family income, language, ability, cultural background, parents' employment status, geographic region, or other potential barriers to access and participation.

(continued)

- All parents are entitled to resources to support their role as parents, to make choices that optimize their children's healthy development and to be active participants in their children's early development and learning.

- All EC settings are inclusive and share a commitment to meet the needs of all children in the community, including children from diverse backgrounds and children with special needs.

- EC practitioners deserve appropriate compensation, working conditions, respect, and opportunities for ongoing professional education and career development.

- EC practitioners deserve appropriate compensation, working conditions, respect, and opportunities for ongoing professional education and career development.

- All communities benefit from EC programs delivered by a diverse, knowledgeable, skilled workforce that contributes to the quality of daily life of young children and their families.

- Governments have a responsibility to develop a policy and regulatory environment and provide stable, adequate public funding in order to give all children and families access to high quality early learning and care services.

Need for a New Vision

In many provinces, service fragmentation and chaos exist (see Figure 1-3). Bennett (2008) writes that early childhood education and care systems are governed in one of two ways, integrated either through one ministry or through split management in two or more ministries. Historically, care and education policy have developed separately. In welfare states, care was often assigned to health or social services ministries, while early education (kindergarten) was assigned to education ministries. The cultures and the mandates of these different ministries made it difficult to achieve coordinated policies necessary for the optimal development and education of young children. Families often struggle to find and coordinate the services they need. Although there have been a number of initiatives to coordinate services, progress is often hampered by legislation and funding through various ministries. The continuing split in EC systems owes more to traditional divisions than to the developmental needs of children and practical concerns of families.

In Canada, an impetus to tackling this chaos came from the work of the Organization for Economic Cooperation and Development (OECD), which identified a number of key elements for successful EC policy. One of the elements was governance, and the second concerned the integration of care and education. The OECD team recommended that Canada:

- Build bridges between child care and kindergarten
- Conceptualize and deliver care and education as one seamless program
- Have a single responsible department in each province and territory

Policy makers and educators increasingly recognize the benefits of offering a school-based, blended, universally accessible EC program. Many countries put coordination, leadership, and

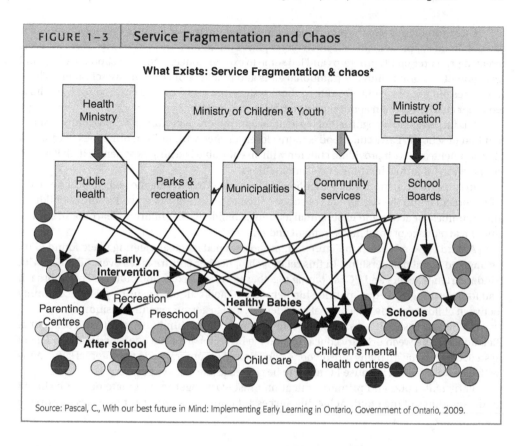

FIGURE 1–3 | Service Fragmentation and Chaos

What Exists: Service Fragmentation & chaos*

Source: Pascal, C., With our best future in Mind: Implementing Early Learning in Ontario, Government of Ontario, 2009.

accountability under one ministry—generally education. In Canada, over the past 10 years, ministries of education in several provinces and territories have demonstrated an increased awareness of and interest in ECE. In some provinces, policy makers are removing the split between EC that has been unproductive for children, families, and society. Ministries of education in most jurisdictions across Canada are increasing their roles in the provision of various forms of early care and learning.

Research suggests that universal public school EC programs are effective in improving child outcomes. Yet across the country, the debate continues whether to establish EC programs in primary schools rather than to strengthen existing community-based EC programs. There is concern about retaining the unique culture of EC programs with its enhanced parental involvement and greater focus on play and play-based learning.

Toward Strong and Equal Partnerships

Growth in EC programs is driven by the compelling evidence of the potential benefits of effective, quality programs for children and families as noted earlier in this chapter. One rationale is to ensure that children are more able to adjust to the expectations of school. Quality programs in the early years can help children make a successful adjustment to primary school. However, for many young children, the discontinuities between early education and primary school may create new challenges. Some EC programs do a better job of facilitating the transition to school than others.

One prominent policy approach has emphasized the role of EC in preparing children for school. In this approach, there is often an emphasis on literacy and numeracy. This emphasis created pressures on EC programs and led some to express concern about "schoolification" and bringing EC programs into the traditional aims and practices of compulsory schooling. These pressures did not come only from the school system, but also from parents themselves whose goals for children is often about the mastery of school learning.

It is important to recognize that the general atmosphere or culture of EC programs is different that of schools. Early childhood is more closely aligned with holistic principles of care and development, and with providing children with an enjoyable learning experience, than it is with preparation for formal learning and school settings.

In some models, some policy attention has been given to carrying the pedagogical strengths of EC practice into the first grades of school, such as attention to the well-being of children, opportunities for active and experiential learning, confidence in children's learning strategies, and the avoidance of child measurement and ranking.

A third view, as shown in Figure 1-4, proposes a pedagogical meeting place founded on strong and equal partnerships. In this relationship, neither culture takes over the other, with kindergarten teachers and ECEs coming together to create a common culture. This approach can form a strong and equal partnership between EC and schools, ensuring greater continuity between children's early educational experiences, and foster successful transitions.

To be successful, it is essential to redefine the relationship between EC and schooling. Relationships between primary education and the EC sector are often one-sided with the school system dominating. In many jurisdictions, schools and EC programs do not interact sufficiently with each other, often because EC tends to be viewed as the weaker partner.

Early childhood and primary education must work together to create new and shared understandings of the child. Achieving successful transitions requires new ways of working

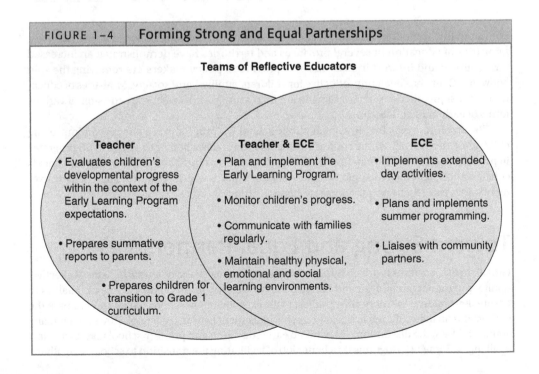

FIGURE 1-4 | **Forming Strong and Equal Partnerships**

Teams of Reflective Educators

Teacher
- Evaluates children's developmental progress within the context of the Early Learning Program expectations.
- Prepares summative reports to parents.
- Prepares children for transition to Grade 1 curriculum.

Teacher & ECE
- Plan and implement the Early Learning Program.
- Monitor children's progress.
- Communicate with families regularly.
- Maintain healthy physical, emotional and social learning environments.

ECE
- Implements extended day activities.
- Plans and implements summer programming.
- Liaises with community partners.

together such as creating a curriculum and pedagogical continuity, home to school continuity, and professional continuity.

The transition from preschool to school is important for young children. It can be a stimulus to growth and development. However if it is handled without care, it carries—particularly for children from disadvantaged backgrounds—the risk of regression and failure. Going to school has highly positive connotations for most young children and families. Educators should use these transitions in children's lives positively and not see them as problematic for every child.

Curriculum and Pedagogical Continuity

One strategy is supporting pedagogical curriculum for children as they move from one educational setting to another. These linkages can build on the strengths of both pedagogical approaches found in EC and kindergarten. This integration of pedagogy is the approach in Ontario as shown in Figure 1–5. Central to an effective early learning curriculum is an "emergent" approach that builds on a child's curiosity, intrinsic interests, and self-discovery. In 2006, the Ontario government's Expert Panel developed a curriculum framework for early childhood settings—ELECT (Early Learning for Every Child Today).

This province-wide curriculum framework complements a variety of pedagogical approaches and recognizes that through play, young children discover the basics of learning. The Continuum of Development is a component of ELECT, which includes descriptions of growth and learning organized into developmental domains representing the unique timetable of children's development. Under the leadership of the ministry of education, ELECT was merged with the Revised Kindergarten Program, creating a hybrid Full-Day Learning-Kindergarten Program—blending the best of Kindergarten with elements of early learning as well as introducing the basics of language, math, science, arts, physical activity, and personal development

FIGURE 1–5	Merging of Pedagogy	
ELECT, Early Learning for Every Child Today	**Full-Day Kindergarten Program**	**Kindergarten Program Revised**
• Province wide curriculum framework for preschoolers • Through play, young children discover the basics of learning • Continuum of development- description of growth & learning	• Builds on ELECT, Kindergarten Program Revised & Summary of Evidence • Introduces basics of language, math, science, arts, physical activity & personal development through activities rooted in play.*	• Province-wide curriculum for 4/5 year olds • Introduces basics of math, science, arts, physical activity

through activities rooted in play. The Early Learning-Kindergarten Program contains learning expectations and descriptions of play-based learning and outlines the roles of the teacher-early childhood educator team.

It is important for both EC environments and primary schools to focus on the continuity of pedagogy and methods across the EC age span. Closer linkages can build on the strengths of both pedagogical approaches. For example, primary schools can become more child-centred and expand the role of families. EC programs can focus more on fostering the skills children need to succeed in school. Both ECEs and kindergarten teachers can bridge their unique understandings of how young children learn by learning from one another as each group brings specific skills.

Kindergarten teachers bring:

- Knowledge of curriculum development/purposeful learning;
- Understanding how the kindergarten program connects to later school expectations;
- Have more experience in assessing children and reporting to families.

ECEs bring the use of observations and assessments to:

- Meet the needs of children individually and in groups,
- Plan for enriched learning through play,
- Guide behaviour and facilitate self-regulation,
- View child holistically (nutrition/health),
- Understand and address the priorities of their families, and
- Appreciate the importance of the continuity of learning between home and centre.

Planning for pedagogical continuity goes beyond ensuring institutional and curriculum coordination. Teachers and ECEs need to take into account the differences within any group of children, their family circumstances, prior experiences, and abilities.

Professional Continuity

Children benefit when ECEs and primary school teachers work together. When staff members communicate and collaborate well, they are more likely to develop compatible program philosophies and broaden their understanding of children's trajectory from preschool to school. Joint professional development can facilitate a common knowledge base and common practices which build partnerships. To transform practice, the team needs opportunities to work collaboratively and to build understanding of each other's roles.

It is important to create a supportive infrastructure by providing opportunities for professional development; joint time for curriculum planning, observation, and documentation; time to dialogue and problem solving. This infrastructure also needs resources and materials, access to pedagogists, professional development opportunities, and time for educators to reflect on their own practice through documentation/learning stories. When educators have opportunities to feed on each other's expertise, they can contribute pedagogical approaches unique to their education and individual teaching styles.

Another key aspect to achieving professional continuity is achieving comparable status and compensation. This is necessary to equalize power relationships. EC educators have traditionally lower status and less professional education compared with primary school teachers. Long-term harmonization is desirable. In the short-term, all who work with young children should be respected as equal members of the team who bring different and valuable skills, knowledge, and experiences.

What Are the Ingredients Needed for Effective EC Programs?

The long-term effectiveness of model EC programs appears to have the following features:

1. *Equitable access.* All children have the right to participate in programs that enable them to reach their full potential regardless of family income, language, ability, cultural background, parents' employment status, or other potential barriers. They include children living in low-income families or otherwise at risk of school failures.

2. *Training and ongoing professional development.* There are enough well-qualified teachers and who are provided with ongoing support such as professional development opportunities. Being qualified is taken to mean having post-secondary education in child development, education or a related field. In addition to receiving ongoing opportunities for professional development, staff also receive curriculum-based supervision.

3. *Suitable programs.* Programs need a clear, explicit, and relevant educational program in which the general principles are appropriate for all participants. The educators use a validated, interactive child development curriculum in which both children and adults have a hand in designing children's learning activities. Children take an active role in their own learning through play. The curriculum focuses on all areas of children's development—cognitive, language, socio-emotional, motivational, artistic, and physical—not only on reading and mathematics. Implementing such a curriculum requires serious interactive education, reflection, and practice for teachers.

4. *Quality adult–child relationships.* The quality of interaction among all participants, and especially in adult-child relationships, is important for children both emotionally and cognitively. Positive relationships are essential for the development of personal responsibility, capacity for self-regulation, for constructive interactions with others, and for fostering learning and mastery. In order for children to receive sufficient individual attention, highly effective EC playrooms have two qualified adults for every 16 to 20 children aged four, and smaller numbers for younger children.

5. *Involvement of families.* The contribution of parents to EC programs is important in terms of children's emotions and for ensuring consistency of educational issues at home and in the EC environment. Staff need to spend adequate amounts of time with families, engaging them in discussions about their children's development and how they can extend their children's learning experiences at home, as well learning about parents' perspectives, knowledge, and goals.

6. *Monitoring and evaluation systems.* There are monitoring and evaluation systems for the program and for children's learning. The results of this are taken into account when planning educational practice. Decision makers need to confirm the effectiveness of EC programs through continuous assessment of program quality.

7. *Stable and adequate funding.* Governments have the responsibility to develop a policy and regulatory system and provide stable, adequate public funding to give all children and families access to effective EC services.

Internationally, there is an ever growing body of evidence that EC programs are a wise social and economic investment. Although many governments are moving forward on integrated systems of early learning and care, it is recognized that plans are not guarantees. It is necessary that interested stakeholders are vigilant and actively engaged to ensure that these visions come to full fruition.

Defining Quality Early Childhood Environments

Defining quality in ECE is a complex task. Definitions of quality in education vary throughout the world. The educational quality of early childhood experiences is a frequently occurring educational issue for professional ECEs as well as decision-making agents, especially those in the political and economic sectors and, in some cases, the "users"—the families and the children. Moss (1994) claimed that "quality is a relative concept" and that definitions of quality reflect the values, needs and agendas, influences, and authorities of various decision-making groups that have an interest in EC services. In the early 1990s, the concept of quality as an inherent attribute, some universal and knowable entity waiting to be discovered and measured by experts, was being increasingly questioned. How could quality take into account the context and values, subjectivity and plurality? How could it accommodate multiple perspectives, with different groups in different places having different views of what quality was or different interpretations of criteria? This problem became more acute as stakeholders began to talk about the importance of the process of defining quality and how this should include a wide range of participants, not only academic experts but also children, parents, and educators.

The central problem is how to reconceptualize quality taking into account the subjectivity, diversity, views of various stakeholders, and wide range of special and temporal contexts, without losing sight of the factors that contribute to a good learning experience.

Quality EC settings promote children's physical and psychological safety, health and their physical, emotional, social, communication, cognitive, ethical, and creative development. They support the family in its role as the child's primary caregiver and maintain collaborative relationships with other community professionals. In a quality setting, each child feels accepted, understood, supported, and respected by knowledgeable adults; enjoys positive relationships with children; and finds activities interesting, engaging, and satisfying.

The term "quality" refers to the extent to which settings meet more than the minimal **standards**. No single issue related to early childhood is as complex or important. Over the past 25 years, the discussion has moved beyond debates about whether EC programs help or harm the development or which types of EC services are best. The current focus is—how can we make them better?

Ecological Framework for Early Childhood Environments

Children and families are affected by the neighbourhoods where they live, their parents' workplaces, and the nature and scope of available support services such as schools and health care facilities. These aspects of family life are directly affected by government social policies and funding. In assessing early childhood environments, many researchers use an **ecological** approach: They look at the interactions among children, parents, and educators and the relationships of each with the environments in which they live, work, and play. They consider not only how to structure EC environments to foster children's growth but also how these environments interact with influences outside the setting. Earlier efforts to improve early childhood programs viewed each program as a self-contained unit and concentrated on internal changes—such as adapting the curriculum or buying new equipment. However, knowledgeable educators have come to understand that if a setting fails to consider the wider environment within which its programs take place, the positive impact of such changes is limited.

FIGURE 1–6	Ecological Framework for Early Childhood Environment

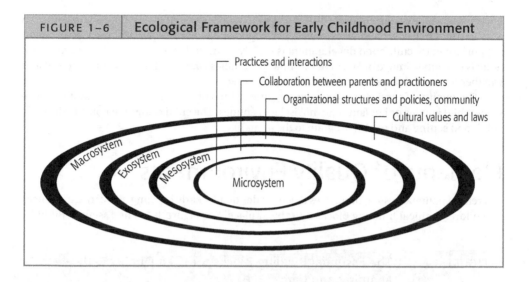

Many writers incorporate the framework for looking at EC settings provided by Bronfenbrenner (1986) in his **ecological model** of human development as illustrated above in Figure 1–6. His model is adapted to provide a framework for understanding the influence of contextual factors on a child's daily experience. Bronfenbrenner thinks in terms of four systems, each embedded within the next. His model provides a way of considering the layers of influence acting on the developing child, along with the impact of the early childhood experience on the family, community, and society.

At the heart of this ecological model, the **microsystem** is centred on the developing child within his or her immediate settings—the family, the early childhood environment, or the peer group. The microsystem is made up of the physical environment; the resources within it; the curriculum; the relationships between the parent, educator(s), and child; and the interactions among the children.

The second level is the **mesosystem**, where different microsystems are linked together through relationships—such as the educator-parent interaction—or through employment practices that affect the family—such as parental leave benefits. Here, for example, one would consider the relationship between the early childhood environment and the home. These interactions will be influenced by how different adults view the child as well as parenting beliefs; a critical factor is the need for the environment to be welcoming to all those who use it—the child, the parents, and the staff. In a second instance, if an employer changes a parent's work schedule to one that does not conform to the hours of the EC setting, this impacts on the lives of the parent as well as the child. The parent may have to find and pay additional child care costs, and the child may sense increased stress.

Outside the mesosystem is the **exosystem** which represents the social structures, both formal and informal, that influence the settings the child experiences. In this dimension, one must consider the roles and influences of parents' jobs, government policies for child and the family, the local economy, the media, the workplace, and the immediate community. Families are strongly affected by government policies regarding how programs are funded or whether educators receive adequate compensation that promotes staff stability. As another example, to provide program quality, directors need to be aware of community services to refer families for support; it is also essential that they keep abreast of government initiatives.

All these sets of relationships are located in a **macrosystem** encompassing the ideologies and patterns of culture such as the economic, educational, legal, and political systems. Included here are attitudes toward the family and the role of mothers and community definitions of environments for young children. The macrosystem defines what is possible. For example, in a society that believes children are solely the responsibility of their parents, then government support for early childhood development is greatly restricted. An example of a macrosystem issue is the public image of EC services—how the families who use the services are viewed and whether the staff is valued and respected or patronized.

The quality of services depends on the interactions of these four dynamic systems. The young child and his or her family are not isolated entities. The child brings the home to the early childhood setting and the EC program to the home.

Elements of Quality Environments

To create a national system of services that provides quality early learning and care experiences for children, critical building blocks must be in place. See Figure 1-7. The Essential Building

FIGURE 1–7	The Essential Building Blocks for High Quality Early Learning and Care

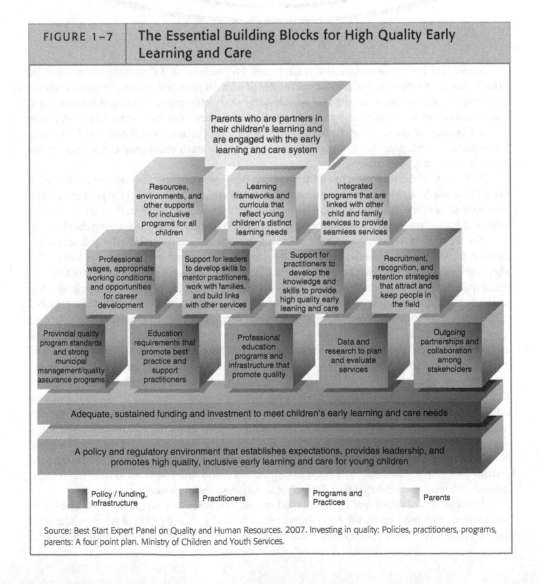

Parents who are partners in their children's learning and are engaged with the early learning and care system

Resources, environments, and other supports for inclusive programs for all children

Learning frameworks and curricula that reflect young children's distinct learning needs

Integrated programs that are linked with other child and family services to provide seamless services

Professional wages, appropriate working conditions, and opportunities for career development

Support for leaders to develop skills to mentor practitioners, work with families, and build links with other services

Support for practitioners to develop the knowledge and skills to provide high quality early leaning and care

Recruitment, recognition, and retention strategies that attract and keep people in the field

Provincial quality program standards and strong municipal management/quality assurance programs

Education requirements that promote best practice and support practitioners

Professional education programs and infrastructure that promote quality

Data and research to plan and evaluate services

Outgoing partnerships and collaboration among stakeholders

Adequate, sustained funding and investment to meet children's early learning and care needs

A policy and regulatory environment that establishes expectations, provides leadership, and promotes high quality, inclusive early learning and care for young children

Policy / funding, Infrastructure   Practitioners   Programs and Practices   Parents

Source: Best Start Expert Panel on Quality and Human Resources. 2007. Investing in quality: Policies, practitioners, programs, parents: A four point plan. Ministry of Children and Youth Services.

Blocks for High Quality Early Learning and Care. Each building block is essential to support a high quality EC system.

Quality depends on:

- effective policies, appropriate and sustained funding and infrastructure
- knowledgeable and committed educators
- evidence-informed, age appropriate programs and practices
- parents who are partners in their children's early learning

The quality of a program is critical in determining how developmentally beneficial it is to children. Research has identified a number of discrete elements of quality. Many of these indicators are interrelated, and their mutual impact ultimately affects the child's well-being.

There are various ways of conceptualizing quality. Researchers discuss quality in terms of structural quality and process quality. **Structural quality** generally refers to variables that can be enforced through legislation or regulations. Structural requirements defines the physical environments for children, including buildings, space, outdoors or pedagogical requirements, the quality and training of the teaching staff, adult:child ratio, and **group size**. Structural factors are concrete and relatively easy to assess objectively and accurately. Typically, a selection of structural standards forms the substance of provincial/territorial licensing requirements. Structural variables are so interconnected that to speak of them separately as unique contributors to overall development is difficult. Historically, when researchers focused on quality, they highlighted three critical elements: the **adult:child ratio**, the group size, and the staff's professional education in child development. The experts have called this trio the "iron triangle" because these elements exert so much influence on quality, particularly when they are clustered together. For some time, they have been considered the foundations of quality EC programs.

Process quality refers to the warmth and quality of the relationship between adults and children, the quality of the interaction between the children themselves, and the quality of the relationships among the adults. The pedagogical relationship between the children and educators is most effective when it includes concern for the children's learning as evidenced through the provision of a **developmentally appropriate** curriculum. Process variables have a direct influence on children, and because they require interpretation by knowledgeable educators, these variables are more difficult to regulate. Some process quality elements are connected to structural elements. We may consider the example of adult consistency, which encourages the development of trust and provides an environment in which children feel free to explore; this approach supports learning. In this case, structural quality and process quality are related—and structural quality can be regulated. In another example, however, most people would agree that educators must be sensitive to each child in their group. But a process quality element such as sensitivity is not easily measured: It is difficult to imagine how an employer could, through either a hiring process or a performance appraisal, ascertain an individual's level of sensitivity. Research findings show, though, that educators with more years of formal education are more likely to offer high quality environments that provide better outcomes for children (Barnett 2003). Therefore, a requirement of professional education is intended to ensure that educators are more likely to be sensitive.

Woodhead (1996) proposed organizing quality criteria in ECE using the three broad headings:

1. Entry indicators that establish the base for regulating quality standards. These reflect the areas in the program that are the easiest to define and measure, previously labelled structural quality elements. They include:

    - The buildings and surroundings (amount of space per child, heating, lighting, toilets, washing facilities, etc.)

- Materials and equipment (furniture, learning materials, play equipment, etc.)
- The staff (qualifications, experience, wages and working conditions, adult:child ratios, etc.)

2. Process indicators that reflect the relationships and what happens on a day-to-day basis. As mentioned earlier, these elements can be the most difficult to identify and standardize. Some examples are:
   - Children's experience (variety, way it is organized; choices provided; patterns of activity; play, rest, meals, etc.)
   - Approach to teaching and learning (support for children's activities, sensitivity to individual differences, control, etc.)
   - Style of interactions (whether adults are available to the children, ability to respond, consistency, etc.)
   - Approach to guidance and discipline (setting limits, rules, managing the group, strategies for guiding behaviour, etc.)
   - Relations among adults (day-to-day communication, cooperation, etc.)
   - Relations among staff, parents, and others (greetings, opportunities for discussing the children, mutual respect, cooperation, awareness of differences, etc.)

3. Exit Indicators, which deal with the impact caused by the experience. This falls into the realm of efficacy and cost benefit and can include:
   - Children's health (monitoring growth, record of illnesses, etc.)
   - Children's skills (motor coordination, language, cognitive aspects, social relations, etc.)
   - Children's adjustment to school life (transition challenges, progress through grades, school achievements, etc.)
   - Family attitudes (supporting children's learning, parental competencies, etc.)

While research has helped answer many questions, others remain unanswered. Those interested in the improvement of quality in early childhood experiences must consider the setting's relationship with the external environment. The exploration of this relationship needs to be further explored.

Provincial/territorial licensing and regulatory systems that are well designed and effectively administered help assure the provision of early childhood programs that will nurture, protect, and educate young children. Regulation by itself does not ensure quality: It is designed to prevent programs from harming children rather than to promote programs that enhance development. Although regulation does not ensure quality, it is an important factor in safeguarding it.

In addition, while quality is a requirement that is subjected to ongoing evaluation, it often lacks sufficient technical and financial support (sometimes referred to as infrastructure) in the form of consultation and training to improve implementation.

A huge gulf exists between the high quality model programs and the larger number of mediocre and poor quality programs experienced by many children. Some may argue that high quality EC programs are unaffordable or unattainable. Providing an EC program does not ensure an effective learning experience. Too often, governments concentrate on enrolments that most children have access. But without the resources to ensure quality, some children suffer silent exclusion from worthwhile learning experiences and are missing out on opportunities to achieve their potential.

In addition to the perspective of the experts in the field regarding quality, there is a need to consider the points of view of children, parents, educators, and the community and society at large. The child's perspective derives from her or his actual experience. For example, does the child feel welcome and protected by adults and accepted by other children? Families may look at the extent to which the service meets their needs and priorities. Educators' definitions of quality may be influenced by their perceived support and working conditions, such as having paid planning time or opportunities to collaborate with the team. Various communities have distinct perspectives. A quality early childhood experience may be one that reflects and supports the **values**, beliefs, and needs of the people served. Understanding and ensuring quality involves a continuous process of merging the perspectives of different **stakeholders**.

Elements of Quality Environments for Young Children

Research highlights the following as the most influential factors to measure effective EC environments listed in order of their impact:

1. The **contribution of families** to the design and implementation of programs is vital in terms of children's emotions and for ensuring consistency between home and the EC setting. Quality programs are characterized by collaborative relationships with families. Families are the first and most powerful influence on children's early learning and development. Relationships between early childhood settings and families benefit children when those relationships are respectful of family structure, culture, values, language, and knowledge. Children benefit when parents and staff share a common commitment to acting in their best interests, communicate openly, and have mutual respect; in particular, open and regular communication between educators and families has a very significant impact on positive outcomes for children. For example, when parents and staff communicate about practices such as discipline and routines, potential conflicts and confusion for the children are minimized, and some continuity can be achieved. Chapter 8, "Building the Partnership with Families," provides more examples of how to achieve family-centred programs.

2. The **quality of interactions** between all participants, but especially in adult-child relationships. Positive relationships are essential for the development of personal responsibility, capacity for self-regulation, for constructive interactions with others, and for fostering learning and mastery. Warm, sensitive, and responsive interactions help children develop a secure, positive sense of self and encourage them to respect and co-operate with others. Positive relationships also help children gain the benefits of learning experiences. Children who see themselves as highly valued are more likely to feel secure, thrive physically, get along with others, learn, and feel they are part of a community.

Keating and Hertzman state, "The quality of the social environment in which children are brought up—especially through interaction with peers and adults—is a major influence in early life and therefore on competence and coping skills in later life" (1999). Young children also develop through peer interaction. Here again, adult support and guidance are crucial. Capable educators support children's beginning friendships. The program should accommodate a variety of play levels where children play with and beside other children. Interactions between children and staff should provide opportunities for children to develop an understanding of self and others characterized by respect, affection, freedom from bias, and humour.

From a child's point of view, EC experiences are a joint enterprise of parents and educators. Since young children's learning and development are integrally connected to their families, to support and promote children's optimal learning and development, educators need to establish relationships based on mutual trust, respect, and support; involve families in their children's growth; and fully participate in the program.

Quality of interaction is also affected by the ratio of adults to children, teacher education, group and program size, and **continuity** of care. Fewer children per adult is one of the strongest indicators of quality. Frequent supportive, individualized interactions between adult and child are required to foster development in young children. An adult who is responsible for too many children can do little more than attend to their basic physical needs and safety. The adult is also likely to feel stressed in such situations, and this increases the probability of harshness and restrictiveness.

Optimal ratios vary with the age of the child and appear to be especially important for infants to children under the age of three. In this age group, ratios lower than one adult to four children have been observed to result in increases in child apathy and distress. For older children as well, the more children per adult, the more time staff must spend simply managing and controlling activities, and the less time they have to interact with the children.

Group size—the total number of children in a group—is typically considered in conjunction with adult:child ratios. For children older than the toddler stage but under age five, adult:child ratios may be less significant than group size. Where groups are smaller, educators spend more time interacting with the children and less time simply watching them. As well, because moderate-sized groups permit children to have a choice of playmates while protecting them from overstimulation, peer relationships may also be enhanced. In smaller groups, children are more verbal, more involved in activities, and less aggressive, and they make the greatest gains in standardized tests of learning and vocabulary.

Maximum group size should be determined by the distribution of ages within the group, the developmental needs of the children, the activity, and the **inclusion** of children with special needs. The group must be small enough to permit educators to facilitate both individual and group needs effectively. This will encourage the appropriate development of independence, self-assertion, problem-solving skills, co-operation, and friendliness. Health officials also recommend group-limiting strategies—that is, keeping small groups of children consistently together—to reduce the spread of infection.

3.   An **explicit, clear, and relevant educational program** in which general principles are fitting for all participants. A curriculum is an organized system of intentions and plans to promote children's development and learning. Educators implement a curriculum that is consistent with its goals for children and promotes learning and development in a variety of domains. Educators with professional education in child development use their skills of observation and assessment to plan appropriate experiences to facilitate the development of the whole child. The term "curriculum" includes such items as program goals, planned activities, the daily schedule, and the availability of materials and equipment.

A planned curriculum with goals for children's learning and development impacts on the quality of early childhood experiences. It begins with an informed understanding of what children are capable of learning and how they learn effectively. It has specific goals for children that support self-regulation (behaviour, emotion, and attention), identity, social inclusion, health and well-being, language and thinking skills, and physical skills as well as the foundation knowledge and concepts needed for literacy and numeracy. It provides structure and direction for early childhood educators who support the development of capacities and skills while respecting a child's interests and choices.

Children need choices and opportunities to explore their own interests. EC educators who are guided by the principles of developmentally appropriate practice ensure that the curriculum enhances the development of the whole child in all domains—including social, emotional, aesthetic, moral, language, cognitive, and physical—and that activities are individually, age-group, and culturally appropriate. Curriculum planning is based on an educator's observation of each child's interests and developmental progress. Children need adequate amounts of uninterrupted time in which to pursue self-chosen tasks and activities.

Cultural relevancy must be an integral and continuous part of the program, which should reflect the diversity of the wider society in which the child lives. Culture is a fundamental building block of identity, and a setting must be sensitive to the backgrounds of families served. Early experiences should be in harmony with the culture of the home. Different cultures have unique ways of viewing the world, preferred ways of social organization, and unique language patterns, learning styles, and concepts of acceptable behaviour. Demonstrating respect for diversity, equity, and inclusion are prerequisites for optimal development and learning. At the core of respecting diversity is the flexible creation of curriculum that is responsive to individual children. It reflects the cultures of the families served.

Using imported educational practices and programs may undermine the culture and alienate children by threatening their sense of belonging. In some communities, EC programs ignore traditional values and norms of shared child care and participatory education. EC programs must focus on an approach that fits the community context and integrates characteristics of successful EC development.

Linguistic continuity is an essential component. When children can read and write in their mother tongue, the skills are transferable to other languages. Linguistic continuity is promoted by instruction in their home language and by bilingual programs. Children who learn in their mother tongue for the first six to eight years perform better in terms of test scores and self-esteem than those who were taught exclusively in the official language. While recognizing the benefits of linguistic continuity, schools are often under pressure to introduce the dominant language. Parents themselves are sometimes strong supporters of early teaching of the dominant language. As much as possible, educators should convey the message that home languages are important and valued.

In an **anti-bias curriculum**, the EC educator models and conveys respect for differences and encourages children to recognize the many options open to them regardless of gender, age, ability, race, ethnicity, or culture. Children and their families are encouraged to share aspects of their culture and lifestyle with the other children. To help make the program more familiar and meaningful to the child, educators should incorporate culturally responsive practices into the early childhood environment, including:

- Recognize the rights of children.
- Create a sense of belonging and acceptance where each child experiences a feeling of being valued by others. Model acceptance, respect, and flexibility in interactions with all learners.
- Create learning environments for the full participation of all children that include adaptations for children with special needs.
- Set up a learning environment with books, print materials, and other artifacts in French, English, Aboriginal, and other home languages that respect and promote language and literacy learning, and that reflect diversity in unbiased ways.
- Accommodate the needs of children who are learning French or English in addition to their home language.

The BC Aboriginal Child Care Society developed standards for culturally responsive EC programs. Following is a selection from its standards, Elements of Quality Child Care from the Perspectives of Aboriginal Peoples in British Columbia:

> *Keeping of Aboriginal Languages:* Key element of maintaining our identity and heritage. The continuation and revival of Aboriginal languages are urgent priorities. EC programs have a critical role to play in preventing further loss of Aboriginal languages.
>
> *Elder Involvement:* A defining feature of Aboriginal cultures is the special respect given to elders. We look to our elders for guidance and we include them in important decision making. We ask our elders to help us learn the traditional teachings of our cultures. Elders play valuable roles in our communities, and we turn to them for their knowledge and wisdom (BC Aboriginal Child Care Society 2004).

To create a program that is culturally and linguistically appropriate and incorporates the values and traditions of the Inuit community, the Avataq Cultural Institute in collaboration with Kativik

Elders provide traditional teachings.

Regional Government developed materials based in Inuit culture (Avataq Cultural Institute 2004). Wide consultation was held with the Inuit communities of Nunavik, and an elder leader was hired to provide elder guidance, expertise, and advice. Twenty-six story sets, including handcrafted dolls, videos, and materials, were created in order to promote Inuktitut language and Inuit culture through the use of timeless legends and stories of Inuit life. These materials support practitioners to provide geographically relevant and culturally and developmentally suitable curriculum in their work with young children in the Far North. These two initiatives illustrate some of the work being done to support cultural continuity.

Different curriculum approaches emphasize different aspects of child development. In general, highly structured programs emphasizing cognitive and language development are particularly effective with children from disadvantaged backgrounds. In programs structured by adults, children show less independence and initiative, but do better on intelligence and achievement tests. In open, or **child-centred**, programs—which facilitate the selection of activities by the children themselves—children are observed to be more independent and persistent. Children in moderately structured programs appear to fare best overall, demonstrating gains in creativity and self-esteem as well as in cognition and achievement. Whatever the approach, a program's success is related to how clearly its **philosophy** is defined as discussed in Chapter 4.

4. **Monitoring and evaluation systems for the program** and for the children's learning, the results of which are taken into account when planning educational practice. Decision makers need to confirm the effectiveness of EC programs through continuous assessment of program quality. To achieve positive results for children, decision

makers must systematically monitor results, access, quality of programs, and outcomes. Governments are accountable to the public and citizens need to understand the returns on their investments.

5. **Adequate and organized physical environments,** with access to materials that enable children to explore, discover, and transform. It is more important to have a variety of materials, produced by the creativity of the educators and the community, than expensive ready-made items. Whether indoors or outdoors, the environment must be appropriate; well-maintained; and include facilities, equipment, and materials to facilitate child exploration, learning, and development. The physical environment affects both the level of involvement of children and the quality of interaction between adults and children. Children demonstrate more advanced cognitive skills and greater social competence in environments that are safe and orderly, contain a wide variety of stimulating material, and are organized into learning centres. There are four basic needs for children to be considered in designing physical space: (1) encourage movement (2) support comfort (3) foster competence, and (4) encourage a sense of control.

In examining the impact of the environment, educators must consider:

- indoor and outdoor space;
- overall size, design, and layout of space;
- availability of materials and equipment; and
- health and safety needs of the children.

Early childhood environments must ensure a minimum number of square metres per child. Studies have found that, as the number of children in a space increases, so do aggressiveness, destructiveness, and apathetic behaviour. The OECD identified the importance of outdoor space as a critical element of quality, especially adjoined outdoor space to minimize unnecessary transitions.

Equipment and learning materials are difficult to quantify, since many types of equipment contribute to the objectives of quality programs. Equipment should be designed to develop skills in children of various ages. Materials should be available in sufficient quantities to allow choices by children and avoid unnecessary competition.

Stable routines that organize children's days into regular periods, but without becoming monotonous. One of the most obvious environmental elements is health and safety, including such factors as personal safety, the inclusion of nap/rest times, and nutritious meals and snacks. Health and safety are central aspects of government regulations, which specify such things as the number of fire exits, the presence of first aid kits, and staff health and safety training. EC programs require regular fire and public health inspections as part of the licensing process. (See Chapter 7, "Managing Safe and Healthy Learning Environments," for more information on this aspect of quality.)

Ongoing professional development and preparation for the EC team and leadership. After parents, EC educators have the greatest influence on the quality of children's early learning. The quality of experiences is most importantly associated with the knowledge, skills, attitudes, and stability of the educators. Directors who have higher expectations hire educators with certain skills, knowledge, and performance in classroom practices and child outcomes. The study *Understanding Quality in Context: Child Care centres, Communities, Markets and Public Policy (2010)* found higher quality in programs where directors had high expectations and a high degree of confidence in their staff.

Education in early childhood development sensitizes practitioners to each child's needs, abilities, disposition, and response to new ideas, people, and challenges. Young children learn

in different ways than older children. To
thrive during their childhood and become
competent adolescents and adults, young
children need strong attachments with
significant adults in their lives. They need
educators who:

- Are knowledgeable and demonstrate sensitivity about early child
  development and young children's
  learning styles and needs.

- Understand the impact that culture,
  race, ethnicity, language, gender,
  family environment, and developmental abilities have on learning—
  and have the knowledge and skills
  to address the diverse needs of all
  children.

When young children have educators with post-secondary education in
early childhood development, who are
well compensated and supported in their
work, the children are more likely to:

- be involved in stimulating, developmentally appropriate activities;

- be calmer and more engaged with
  other children in positive ways;

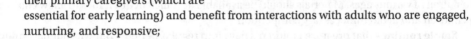

To thrive during their childhood and become competent adults, young children need strong attachments
with significant adults.

- develop stronger attachments to
  their primary caregivers (which are
  essential for early learning) and benefit from interactions with adults who are engaged,
  nurturing, and responsive;

- score higher on various measures of child development and in academic performance in
  the early grades.

Professional education includes pre-service training and ongoing professional development. Educators with more education have less authoritarian styles and more knowledge about
child development. The amount of professional preparation, both pre-service and in-service,
predicts program quality, which in turn is linked to positive child outcomes, especially in language and representational skills—critical areas for school success. In EC programs in schools,
there are requirements for kindergarten teachers who do not have EC knowledge to complete
additional coursework on child development, curriculum and pedagogy, early identification
and parent engagement.

In the integrated model, creating staffing teams of reflective educators is critical. Teams
integrate theoretical frameworks, research findings, and daily experiences to guide their interactions. This new dynamic needs to be built on respect for one another as colleagues. Team
members recognize that their learning is both a continuous and a reciprocal process—learning
from each other, children, and families.

In contrast, experience alone appears to bear little relationship to positive child outcomes.
By itself, experience is not a predictor of effective interactions, and in the absence of other

factors, it has been linked to less cognitive and social stimulation among children and more apathy among infants.

Educators should also have education in meeting the needs of children with special needs and an awareness of the social and political forces affecting EC programs. They must possess the knowledge, skill, and competency to interact sensitively and successfully not only with the children they care for, but also with families, co-workers, and community professionals.

As well as education and ongoing learning, two additional factors are stability and job satisfaction. Educators who are satisfied with their jobs are more likely to provide encouragement and guidance to children. Educators who are dissatisfied tend to be harsher and more restrictive with children and less likely to provide activities that will support and encourage child development.

Studies indicate that salary is the best predictor of job satisfaction: Higher salaries are associated with job commitment, and practitioners with higher salaries are more likely to view early childhood development as a viable career. Staff who are compensated better tend to stay longer in their jobs, forming consistent relationships with the children and fostering the emotional stability necessary for learning and growth. Whitebook et al. (1990) also found that educators earning salaries at the higher end of the range worked in programs of better quality.

Many programs across Canada are struggling with staff recruitment and retention problems. Poor compensation, working conditions, and the devaluing of the early childhood workforce are the main causes of job dissatisfaction. Highly qualified, competent educators have left the profession. In addition to poor compensation, lack of opportunities for career growth is contributing to staff leaving regulated child care. New ECE graduates are also choosing not to work in regulated child care because they can find better paying, more attractive positions in other children's services occupations or other sectors. (Chapter 10, "Advocating for Canada's Children," discusses the need for concerted efforts by professional and advocacy groups to improve the compensation and working conditions as well as perceived public perception of practitioners.)

It is believed that with significant numbers working in EC in schools, this situation will improve by increasing the amount of education required to a degree and by achieving wage parity with elementary teachers. There are concentrated initiatives by unions to organize ECEs and improve wages and working conditions.

Since leaders play a key role in shaping their programs, how they define quality and strive to achieve it is important. Directors who have higher education levels are better able to provide curriculum and pedagogical leadership to staff. Equally important, they need to provide good human resource practices to retain staff. Effective leadership creates a knowledgeable, stable staff team, a supportive workplace, opportunities for ongoing program planning, and continuous program improvement. Strong leaders of quality programs supplemented their budgets by tapping into additional funding sources, initiatives, and maximizing in-kind resources to improve their programs. They made use of external consultants and standards to shape program practices to exceed licensing requirements. Strategic investments in leaders have a trickle-down effect, raising standards and improving quality throughout early learning and care programs.

Principals, directors, and supervisors are responsible for establishing and maintaining quality standards for their programs. They develop the vision and philosophy based on the principles of development and learning, and they communicate the philosophy to families and staff. Effective leaders create organizational cultures and work environments that support quality and ongoing learning. They play a crucial role in implementing age-appropriate learning programs, developing curricula, and building relationships with parents and other services in the community.

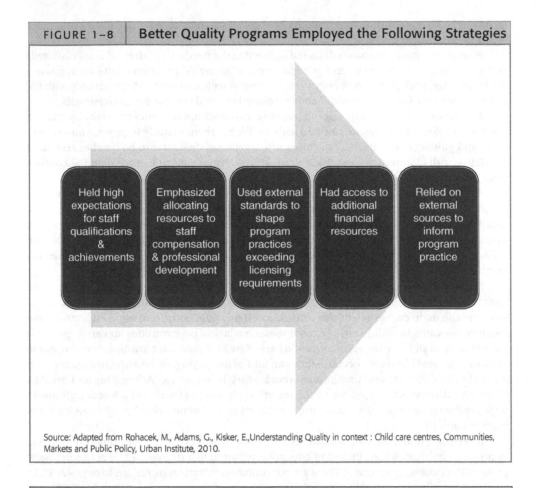

| FIGURE 1–8 | Better Quality Programs Employed the Following Strategies |

Held high expectations for staff qualifications & achievements

Emphasized allocating resources to staff compensation & professional development

Used external standards to shape program practices exceeding licensing requirements

Had access to additional financial resources

Relied on external sources to inform program practice

Source: Adapted from Rohacek, M., Adams, G., Kisker, E.,Understanding Quality in context : Child care centres, Communities, Markets and Public Policy, Urban Institute, 2010.

CONTEXTUAL FACTORS OF QUALITY ENVIRONMENTS

- infrastructure
- funding for EC programs
- government regulation
- wages
- working conditions
- auspice
- relationships with the external environment

"Contextual factors" are variables outside the EC program that influence quality. The following contextual factors associated with quality have been researched: infrastructure, auspice, and government regulation and funding.

Funding for EC Programs   Although sufficient funding does not guarantee high quality EC programs, some of the costs are clearly associated with delivering better quality services. Nearly all program inputs—including staff, equipment and supplies, food and space—are constrained by revenue. Working with young children is a labour-intensive service, with cost depending on the staff:child ratio and the wages and **benefits** paid to the staff. As noted earlier, research has demonstrated that compensation influences the way they behave with a child. Thus, quality requires favourable ratios and group sizes, adequate supplies of appropriate equipment and materials, and reasonable compensation. All of these elements require adequate funding.

Adequate, sustained funding is the key to quality and accessibility. Despite misguided efforts to keep fees low, regulated EC services are beyond the reach of many low- and middle-income families. Small, more remote communities face higher costs to deliver EC services across more sparsely populated geographic areas. Governments provide funding to subsidize early childhood spaces for low-income families as well as grants for wage enhancements and resources for children with special needs. However, there are not enough subsidized spaces to meet the needs of low- and middle-income families or enough funding to support the inclusion of all children with special needs. Both the affordability and availability of regulated care are factors that affect access and **parent** choice. For example, a majority of children are enrolled in publicly funded kindergarten programs. This is not the case with regulated child care, where 50% to 80% of the cost is paid by parents. This approach to funding has led to inequities.

Regulated early learning and care services—like other education for children—should be 100% publicly funded. However, increasing public funding to the level where parents pay no more than 20% to 25% of total program costs will make services accessible to many more families, and bring more children into the regulated system. This change would bring Canadian provinces/territories into line with other jurisdictions, and with the recommendations of the OECD.

Many provinces' low public investment in regulated child care is based on the traditional view of EC programs as the private responsibility of parents who purchase services provided by the private market, rather than the current economic view of quality EC as the most effective way for society as a whole to invest in children's development. According to the 2006 OECD review, weak public funding for services for children under age five is a "fundamental flaw in the early education and care system in Canada."

According to the OECD review, direct public funding of services results in more effective control, advantages of scale, better quality, more effective training for educators, and a higher degree of equity in access and participation. The appropriate level, share, and type of funding for early learning and care should take into account:

- true costs of providing quality programs, including wages and benefits that reflect educators' responsibilities and education, funding for ongoing pay equity adjustments for the predominantly female workforce, and ongoing professional development;
- costs associated with providing quality EC programs for different populations and in different regions (i.e., northern, rural, and remote areas and Francophone, Aboriginal, and newcomer communities);
- costs of quality assurance programs.

Creating the comprehensive, integrated EC and education initiatives has become part of the education system with governments allocating permanent base funding. There is recognition that four- and five-year-old children leaving the regulated child care system has significant financial impacts and that governments should allocate sustainable funds to mitigate this change.

Government Regulations   In Canada, provincial/territorial governments regulate EC programs by establishing standards that must be met in order to obtain a licence to operate. The level of regulatory requirements exerts an influence on quality. Regulation encourages quality by setting standards for structural elements, but it can only be effective when there is both adequate

monitoring for compliance and stringent enforcement of the required standards. Licensing requirements are minimal and measurable.

Steps have been made toward reducing the complexity of the regulatory environment by making one ministry responsible for EC services in many provinces. New legislation has been introduced in come provinces by ministries of education. Additionally, the services are planned and managed by different organizations (e.g., municipalities, school boards, individual boards of directors, and operators) at a local level. This complexity continues to make it difficult to harmonize policies and challenges a truly integrated, high quality system of early learning and care.

Provinces and territories set minimum requirements for EC services. Most regulatory environments focus primarily on child health and safety, rather than on the quality of early learning environments and the qualifications of educators. There is great variation in the stringency of provincial/territorial regulations. Some organizations and jurisdictions have developed initiatives to improve quality, but there are no required national standards for program quality, quality assurance mechanisms beyond licensing inspections. In many parts of the country, the current requirements for teacher education do not reflect the complex demands of practice.

However, policies, regulation, and funding are not enough. A high quality system also requires other infrastructure supports, including:

- program standards that set consistently high expectations for programs/services and mechanisms to monitor program quality and incorporate new knowledge about children and how they learn;
- education requirements that reflect professional standards, promote best practices, and support practitioners;
- supports that develop, coordinate, and provide pre-service and ongoing professional education;
- partnerships and collaboration among stakeholders—including professional associations and unions—to address quality, human resource, and other systemic issues.

Other jurisdictions—including Sweden, New Zealand, and Québec—have faced similar challenges: a lack of policies, funding, and infrastructure to support quality early learning and care; shortages of knowledgeable educators; programs not geared to the way young children learn; and programs that do not recognize parents as partners or meet their needs. Those jurisdictions that have been successful in improving quality and stabilizing their EC workforce have made comprehensive systemic changes through the establishment of a policy and regulatory framework that promotes quality, raising education requirements, and working with stakeholders to develop quality standards and quality assurance programs. They have also supported leadership development, improved wages and working conditions, actively recruited people to the field, and provided the resources, including funding required to deliver quality programs.

Auspice   The term **"auspice"** is used to describe the sponsor of an early childhood service, or the type of **organizational structure** under which a service is operated and/or licensed. In Canada, EC services operate under the auspices of non-profit or for-profit organizations and corporations, municipalities, or schools. A parent group, an organization such as the YMCA/YWCA, a voluntary **board of directors**, a municipal government, or a First Nations band may sponsor non-profit programs. The for-profit, or commercial, category includes owner-operators of one or more programs. The availability of each type of program varies widely across the country.

High quality EC programs are more likely to be found under non-profit than commercial auspices (Cleveland et al. 2007). Non-profits generally hire better-trained staff and encourage them to pursue professional development and renumerate their staff better than for-profit centres. This is not to deny the existence of high quality for-profit programs—or of poor quality non-profit programs.

The differences between the for-profit and non-profit categories may, in part, be the result of the absence of direct government grants to commercial programs. It also may be true that non-profits have more volunteer donations such as maintenance and cleaning services by a sponsoring organization than for-profits. However, the issue of auspice is complex. The differences in the sectors suggest that various factors are at work and that quality depends upon more than a program's auspice.

The Nonprofit Child Care Project analyzed four Canadian studies about quality of for-profit/non-profit status of centres. The average quality difference varies from a 7.5% to a 22% advantage for the non-profit centres (different averages in different studies). In communities with inadequate parental ability to pay for higher quality care, there is no average quality difference between for-profits and non-profits. For policy makers who are anxious to provide quality EC experiences at a reasonable cost, this quality advantage of non-profits is important. However, non-profit status is not, by itself, a magic elixir. The study found that in conditions of inadequate government financial support, efforts to encourage quality can fail. Government policies that support and encourage the development of a higher level of quality in EC services are also necessary to permit non-profits to develop a culture of quality called the non-profit advantage.

Cost of Quality

Many parents consistently report that their greatest concern about the EC arrangements is quality followed by cost (National Association of Child care Resources and Referrals 2010). Parents may want the best they can afford for their children. Parents seeking to support their families should not be forced to compromise on quality or safety. Quality programs are minimally more expensive than poor ones. One American study, *Cost, Quality, and Child Outcomes in Child Care Centers* (Hepburn et al. 1995), found that, while only one in seven of the programs assessed provided care of a quality that promotes healthy development and learning, better quality services cost, on average, just 10% more than mediocre care. States with less stringent regulations had more programs of poor quality. These findings suggest that modest investments, combined with reasonable regulation, could significantly improve the efficacy of early childhood intervention.

This study also confirmed that programs paying higher compensation attract better quality staff. Variations in program quality corresponded to wage levels and the practitioners' level of education and specialized training. Parents were not generally found to be good judges of quality, tending to overestimate the quality of care their children were receiving.

Ongoing Program Evaluation and Change

With increased public investments in early childhood, there are higher rates of accountability for programs such as public websites for families. In determining the level of quality, directors, families, and staff need to be involved in regular program evaluation that measures progress toward the program's goals and objectives. Among the areas that should be included: program quality, quality of children's experience on a daily basis, staff well-being, children's development and learning, family and community involvement, and overall satisfaction. Results benefit children by informing decisions about pedagogy and curriculum. The assessments and evaluations support communication with families and are sensitive to the cultural and community context of children's lives. Assessment, evaluation, and monitoring are conducted in early childhood settings for the following reasons:

- Assessment to observe, document, and support children's development
- Child assessment to identify possible developmental problems
- Program evaluation of quality

Although measures for assessing the quality of children's environments were developed originally for use in research and as self-assessment tools for directors and practitioners, these tools have moved into the arena of public policy. Results are being used to make decisions about the program and inform families about the quality of settings. In fact the results of these measures are posted on websites, some on a room by room basis where parents or potential users of the program can see how the room is functioning against various criteria. The City of Toronto Children's Services website is an example of this growing transparency of program quality.

There are a number of ways to systematically monitor what is going on in a program, including observation and asking parents, staff, and children about their experiences. Leaders will want to create a culture where there is ongoing monitoring of program outcomes experienced by children and parents. As well, there should be regular evaluation of the program's purpose, philosophy, goals, and objectives. (Program evaluation, including sample tools, is discussed further in Chapter 4, "Planning and Evaluating the Program Goals.")

Any effort to assure quality in early childhood programs must begin with an effective licensing and regulatory system. Licensing provides the necessary foundation upon which all other efforts can build. Provincial/territorial government licensing requirements tend to address structural indicators, such as staff:child ratios, even though process dimensions are more indicative of quality. Nonetheless, research indicates that regulatory requirements increase the probability that all children in licensed settings will receive a higher quality of care (Doherty 1999).

Quality levels higher than the minimum licensing standards can be established by professional organizations or funding agencies. Professional standards are the profession's own benchmarks of quality beyond the requirements of legislation, and they contribute to enhancing the quality of early childhood settings. Professional organizations adopt standards of practice to ensure that members apply uniform procedures and principles in response to typical situations using their best professional judgment.

Professional bodies may require that individual staff members meet certain educational levels. Or, such standards may be required as a condition of funding. A funding agency can define the level of quality it is prepared to purchase. For example, a municipal government may require a program in which it is purchasing subsidy spaces to meet higher standards than those set by the provincial government.

Initiatives to Improve Quality

Accreditation of programs is a type of quality control by which a representative body, recognized by both service providers and the EC community, establishes standards that are above the basic requirements of government. Unlike licensing, accreditation is owned and administered by the profession. Programs apply on a voluntary basis for evaluation against these standards and, if found to meet or surpass them, are granted accreditation status. An outside professional verifies, or validates, the accuracy and completeness of program documents submitted as part of the accreditation process. Although accreditation is usually a voluntary process, it can be required by funding bodies. Some governments have tied funding levels to achievement of standards that exceeds licensing requirements. Programs must register and participate in a quality accreditation process such as in Alberta. These types of initiatives require a commitment on the part of the government and EC programs as well as additional funding.

An additional method used to improve program quality is credentialling, or **certification**, where all practicing professionals have a designated level of knowledge, experience, and qualifications. Credentialing is the process of identifying qualifications required to do a particular job. Certification of ECE program graduates can provide validation that the individual is able to translate theory into good practice. Provincial and territorial governments outline requirements for entry to the field. No province or territory requires all educators in early childhood programs to have related post-secondary credentials. Since in most parts of the country it is not mandatory to undergo an accrediting process by a professional organization, some educators choose to forgo this option. While some provincial early childhood organizations have a certification process in place, this process may be viewed as duplicating the role of the licensing authority. In Ontario, the provincial government passed the Early Childhood Educator's Act 2009, which requires that all persons who wish to use the title "early childhood educator" or "registered early childhood educator" are required to be a member of the College of Early Childhood Educators. The college has established professional standards of practice, qualifications, and ongoing professional development for early childhood educators. In Newfoundland and Labrador, it is mandatory to become certified in order to work in a licensed child care setting. Certification is carried out by the Association of Early Childhood Educators, Newfoundland and Labrador (AECENL), funded through the provincial government. (Accreditation and certification are elaborated on in Chapter 6, "Promoting Professionalism.")

Summary

Children's earliest experiences can have substantial and long-lasting effects on their development. While some EC programs do an excellent job, others are inadequate and some may even harm healthy development. Children are not aware that early childhood settings vary in form, function, auspice, or regulatory environment. What makes a difference for them is the quality of their relationships with teachers and peers. High quality EC services for Canadian children and their families depend upon the co-operation and support of all segments of the community.

More and more, policy makers and the general public understand that the achievement of optimal overall development for all children is beneficial not only to children and their families but also to society as a whole. It should be gratifying to educators that many of the principles of developmentally appropriate practice have been confirmed in brain research studies, which are read and heard about with great interest by the general public.

Policy makers move only within the limits of what they believe public attitudes to be. Public perceptions are cultural patterns, part of the macrosystem that defines what is possible. In order to achieve quality in EC settings for all Canadian children and their families, continued changes are needed. An increased valuation of women's work in the home and the work of stay-at-home parents, an increase in the compensation of EC practitioners so that their pay is commensurate with their knowledge and skills, and a change in the common assumption that women (rather than both parents) should expect to be the primary caregivers of their children are all needed. Many beliefs about motherhood, women's roles, the nature of families, and caring for young children need to be revisited since they impede the process of redistributing the costs of quality early childhood education into the public realm.

Key Terms and Concepts

Accreditation, p. 32	Inclusion, p. 22
Adult:child ratio, p. 19	Macrosystem, p. 17
Anti-bias curriculum, p. 23	Mesosystem, p. 17
Auspice, p. 30	Microsystem, p. 17
Benefits, p. 29	Monitoring, p. 30
Board of directors, p. 30	Nutrition, p. 3
Certification, p. 33	Organizational structure, p. 30
Children with special needs, p. 8	Parent, p. 29
Continuity, p. 22	Process quality, p. 19
Developmentally appropriate, p. 19	Social Justice, p. 3
Early childhood setting, p. 2	Stakeholder, p. 21
Ecological model, p. 17	Standards, p. 16
Exosystem, p. 17	Structural quality, p. 19
Group size, p. 19	

Activities

1. Identify barriers to providing quality early childhood services.
2. In small groups, identify and discuss indicators of high quality early childhood settings from one of the following perspectives: families, staff, community professionals.
3. How would you describe the quality of Canada's child care? Cite sources to support your point of view.
4. Assess the quality of an early childhood setting using one of the following tools:
   - Early Childhood Environment Rating Scale (Harms and Clifford 1998)
   - Family Home Day Care Environment Rating Scale (Harms and Clifford 2004)
   - Early Childhood Work Environment Survey (Jorde Bloom et al. 2002).
5. Choose an aspect of your field placement site where you think quality could be improved. Identify a strategy and, if possible, implement it.

Recommended Reading

Doherty, G. National Statement on Quality Early Learning and Child Care, Canadian Child Care Federation, Ottawa, 2007.

National Association for the Education of Young Children. *Accreditation Criteria and Procedures of the National Academy of Early Childhood Programs.* Rev. ed. Washington, DC: National Association for the Education of Young Children, 2005.

Organisation for Economic Co-operation and Development (OECD). *Early Childhood Education and Care Policy: Canada, Country Note.* OECD Directorate for Education, 2004.

Rohacek, M., G. Adams, and E. Kisker. Understanding Quality in Context : Child Care Centres, Communities, Markets and Public Policy, Urban Institute, 2010.

Siraj-Blatchford, I., and M. Woodhead. Early Childhood in Focus 4: Effective Early Childhood Programs, Bernard Van Leer Foundation, U.K., 2009.

Woodhead, M., and J. Oates. Transitions in the Lives of Young Children. Early Childhood in Focus no. 2. The Hague, Bernard Van Leer Foundation, 2007.

Weblinks

www.zerotothree.org
Zero to Three

This site offers a rich array of resources for parents and professionals, including information on brain development, a glossary, and tips. *Zero to Three* promotes the healthy development of infants and toddlers by supporting and strengthening families, communities, and those who work on their behalf. It is dedicated to advancing current knowledge; promoting beneficial policies and practices and community resources; and providing training, technical assistance, and leadership development.

www.cyc.uvic.ca/uccr
Pedagogical Connections

Pedagogical Connections is a publication of the Unit for Early Learning and Child Care Research (the Unit). Located within the School of Child and Youth Care at the University of Victoria, the Unit was created to provide services and resources to EC organizations, agencies, individuals, communities, and governments in the areas of early childhood care and education. The Unit has the Investigating Quality Project to promote active engagement of ECEs in discussions and actions that lead to the formation of innovative environments for young children and families. They have held forums, discussing quality, policy, and innovative approaches to pedagogy.

www.accel-capea.ca
Aboriginal Children's Circle of Early Learning

This site includes a bulletin board, a calendar of events, a database of research, best practices, and links to training and mentorship opportunities. This website is a partnership of First Nations Child and Family Caring Society of Canada and the Canadian Child Care Federation.

www.bernardvanleer.org
Bernard Van Leer Foundation

The Bernard van Leer Foundation is an international grantmaking foundation based in the Hague. Through their grant-making programs, they pioneer innovative ways to improve opportunities for disadvantaged young children. The site has free publications that share learnings with practitioners and policy makers and shape the debate about early childhood care and education. Among them are Early Childhood Matters, Early Childhood in Focus, Practice and Reflections.

www.worldbank.org/children
The World Bank

This site has a section on early childhood development programs that provides synopses of programs around the world, publications, definitions, and links to regional chapters.

Social Policy and Roles
of Government

chapter 2

Objectives

- **Introduce the functions of the three levels of government.**
- **Overview Canadian EC social policy for children and families.**
- **Introduce comparison to international social policy directions.**
- **Outline the roles of provinces and territories in licensing and regulation.**
- **Describe Canadian policy milestones.**

It is important for early childhood (EC) educators to have an understanding of the foundations of government social policy and its implications for Canadian children and families. In the last decade, three things have emerged that have a bearing on public policy. One is the accumulated knowledge pointing to the long-term impact of experiences in early childhood for the strong intellectual and social development of children, and ultimately for society's well-being. The second is the urbanization of Canada and the fact that most of Canada's families live in cities. Lastly, families are running hard to keep up with the pace of modern life. Canadians spend more time engaged in paid employment and work-related activities and less time with family. How governments respond to these changes—what policies they choose to implement or not—will make a difference for children and families; these decisions matter.

EC educators should thus be knowledgeable about the evolving roles of government, and with licensing procedures and other regulations pertaining to the provision of services for young children. Regulations and program policies guide and facilitate the functioning of EC programs—and affect its children, families, staff, and operator (the owner, board of directors or school board). Regulations pertain to many early childhood issues such as staff qualifications and ratios. And the complexity of these issues brings us face to face with the fundamental challenges that impede the delivery of quality systems and the challenges of getting the public support for the sustainable funding necessary for attaining quality.

Overview of Government Roles

In Canada, government funding priorities and policy heavily affect the provision and quality of early childhood programs. In the past decade, Canada has undergone an enormous social and economic transformation. To meet the new challenges and needs of Canadian families, the focus of social policies and programs are ever evolving. Governments express their priorities through funding allocations, such as federal transfer payments to the provinces and territories, direct operating grants, wage enhancements for the EC sector, and child care subsidies and income tax deductions for families. Although our governments are required to respond to the needs of society within a constitutionally and legally defined framework, each administration (federal, provincial/territorial, and municipal) acts on its own political objectives as it sets policy and collects and spends tax revenue.

In Canada, the federal government influences the development of health, education, and social programs through the application of its spending powers. There are specific populations that the federal government is directly responsible for, such as Aboriginal people, military families, and new immigrants and refugees. However, health, education, social services, and the regulation and funding of services to young children are the direct responsibility of the provincial and territorial governments.

Recently, many provincial/territorial governments have taken steps to blend kindergarten and child care, implementing full-day kindergarten and placing responsibility under ministries of education. This vesting of responsibility into one ministry is intended to forge strong partnerships and expand kindergarten to provide universal access.

What happens in Canadian cities has a major impact on society's well-being. Municipal governments enforce local bylaws that set standards in areas such as zoning, building and fire codes, and public health regulations. A few municipalities, primarily in Ontario, have a role in the planning and management of EC services, cost sharing, allocation of subsidized child care spaces, and some directly operate EC services or are involved in the supervision of programs. Additionally, they may have the responsibility for the delivery of child care and associated services such as family resource programs and support for children with special needs.

Snapshot of Canadian Families

The challenges facing Canadian families in their daily lives have changed over recent decades. Today's families are culturally, economically, and structurally more diverse. Most families are running hard to keep up with the pace of modern life. Canadians are increasingly working non-standard hours, and more Canadians are experiencing a high level of "time crunch" now than a decade ago. As a result, many Canadians now spend more time engaged in paid employment and work-related activities and less time with their family (Canadian Index of Wellbeing 2010).

One of the most significant trends is the labour market participation of women (25–54 years) reaching 81.5% in 2009 (Vanier Institute of the Family 2010). Women's involvement in paid work has profoundly changed the economic status of women and the earning capacity of families. Women's earnings are now essential to the economic security of most households. There is now no statistical difference between labour force participation of married women and single or divorced women. The consequences of these changes are numerous, impacting an individual's abilities in carrying out their family responsibilities and obligations, for the women themselves and for employers.

Family life is not what it used to be. Motherhood also does not alter women working. The vast majority of mothers return to the labour force soon after childbirth. Two factors—economic class and the receipt of maternity benefits—were found to be strong predictors of a mother's early return to work after childbirth (Canada 2000b). For example, mothers who did not receive maternity benefits were six times more likely to return to work by the end of their child's first month than were those who received benefits. Since the 1970s, a number of demographic, economic, and social trends have contributed to a steadily increasing demand for child care services in Canada. With most parents of young children working, non-familial child care has increasingly become the norm and an integral part of Canadian childhood. Despite a declining birth rate, increases in the proportion of lone parent families with young children, and increases in non-traditional work hours have added to the demand for non-parental care. With women's increased participation in the paid labour market and the increased mobility of Canadians, women's unpaid care of children, by mothers or female relatives, has declined. In fact, in the last decade of the twentieth century, almost 77% of Canadian mothers with children under age six were in the paid labour force (Statistics Canada 2006).

Impact of Poverty

Canadian economy has seen a shift away from predominantly full-time jobs toward more contract and part-time work, more self-employment, frequent job changes, and ongoing demands for retraining. Additionally, mothers and fathers are working longer hours, and accompanying these longer hours is an increase in reports of work overload and stress (Waldfogel 2005; Canadian Index of Wellbeing 2010). These changes have been particularly difficult for already vulnerable families as the number of low-income families with full-time employment declines. In spite of a relatively healthy economy, the average low-income, two-parent family is living as far below the poverty line as it was in 1994.

Family and child poverty remain persistent social problems, while enormous inequalities of wealth and income continue to separate rich and poor. Lone parent, First Nations, and recent immigrant families, and families led by persons with disabilities are overrepresented among those who are living on low incomes. Poverty is a critical issue for First Nations communities and for urban Aboriginal people, who now comprise more than half (54%) of the Aboriginal population.

Newcomers experience a period of transition upon arrival to Canada—finding a place to live, learning about and adapting to life here, and finding gainful employment. These challenges provide an important public policy issue when the result is a vast underutilization of immigrant workers' skills and heightened levels of income insecurity. Although Canada has been successful in attracting immigrants with high level skills and education, today's immigrants have a rate of low income nearly three times higher than the Canadian-born population (Vanier 2010).

In a recent survey on poverty National Association of Friendship Centres (2009) reported that these very serious issues of poverty and social exclusion affect tens of thousands of children, youth, and lone-parent families in their daily lives and are having a detrimental impact on their health, social, educational, and economic well-being. Low income followed by low levels of education and poor housing was rated as the most crucial factor for those in poverty.

Economic realities are such that the active participation of more than one income earner is necessary to achieve family economic security. For many families, yearly expenditures exceed annual income. Household debt has reached a new high, and if it were divided among all Canadians, each individual would carry over $41 000 in outstanding debt. Debt has become a common feature in many households leaving Canadian families little room to save against job loss, illness, for their child's future education, or retirement.

Poverty is a key determinant of health. The poor living conditions that low-income families experience have a powerful impact on their health. Considerable research identifies the following impacts as a result of poverty: higher infant mortality, shorter life expectancy rates, more risk of poor mental health, more time spent in hospital due to chronic conditions.

What Are Governments Doing about the Impact of Poverty?

To address child poverty, the federal government has a pivotal role to play through its fiscal and social policies, including income security, social programs, and incentives for action. There are legal, economic, and ethical reasons for Canada to be concerned about the impact of poverty. Canada is a signatory to international covenants, including the UN Covenant on Economic, Social and Cultural rights and the 1989 Convention of the Rights of the Child. As mentioned earlier, Canada has much work to do to meet its commitments to ensure a healthy standard of living for all children. Both the federal government and provincial/territorial governments have key roles to play. They can support parental and community capacity, generate and transfer knowledge through funding demonstration programs and research, build societal support on actions on the determinants of health, and foster action among different sectors. The federal government has direct responsibility for many of the children in greatest need: First Nations and Inuit children and youth.

Child Development and Family Work Arrangements

Early childhood programs play a role in meeting a broad range of both national and provincial policy objectives. These include promoting the optimal development of all children, supporting the effectiveness of the current workforce, reducing child poverty by enabling parents to enter the workforce, advancing women's economic and social equality, and promoting social cohesion.

Canada has historically been divided by regional and cultural issues and finding consensus on social policies continues to be a challenge. Canadians worry that the implications of social changes such as increasing demands of work and its impact on the family, job security, and global competition—for the security of their families and their children's futures—have not yet been considered seriously enough.

As noted in Chapter 1, early childhood services are especially critical during the first few years, when fundamental social, intellectual, and physical development takes place. A growing number of parents are aware of the research on brain development and the impact of quality early learning and care programs on child development. As a result, the demand for high quality early learning and care services has grown. Yet, for many parents, the driving force is economic: Parents rely on early learning and care programs for their children while they are at work or school. For recent immigrants, early learning programs provide a valuable way for children of different cultures to integrate into Canadian society and learn English or French.

The demand for high quality early learning and care has also grown from parents who are not in the paid workforce. Experience, in all provinces and territories, shows that when kindergarten, nursery school, and preschool programs are available and affordable, families enrol their young children. For example, when Québec expanded its publicly funded early learning and care system to all young children—regardless of whether parents were in the paid workforce—programs were hard-pressed to respond to all the families who applied. As a result, 36.1% of

Quebec's young children are now in regulated early learning and care programs, compared to a Canadian average of 18.6%. EC programs are increasingly a central influence in the development of Canadian children and are likely to remain that way.

Consequently, government policy with respect to the early years has become a matter of increasing public concern. Over the past decade, children and families have come to be a key focus of public policy and to occupy a prominent place in social policy deliberations. A significant contributor to this heightened interest is the recognition that EC lays a foundation for achieving societal goals, including supporting equity and social justice as discussed in Chapters 1 and 10. However, the absence of a sustained and systematic approach to EC is directly linked to poor accessibility and in many cases, inadequate quality. Many advocates feel that Canadian children and families must fit into narrow eligibility categories, and are segregated into class, income, and lifestyle silos to gain access to EC programs (Campaign 2000, 2010).

Although Ottawa and the provinces have campaigned to improve the circumstances of vulnerable children (with some programs established by both levels of government), and existing ones reformed. Campaign 2000 Report Card found that progress toward building the foundation for a system where every child can have access to an EC program stalled when the federal government terminated funding that was to be provided under the bilateral agreement on early learning and child care (2006). The proportion of children living in poverty differs considerably from province to province as a result of varying public policies on income security, affordable housing, different labour markets, and patterns of economic growth. Quebec is the only province where child poverty rates have been declining since 1997, attributable to the comprehensive social policy the Quebec government undertook (Campaign 2000, 2006). However, no province has reduced child poverty to a single-digit figure despite UNICEF's challenge to do so and some governments vow of poverty eradication!

Canadian families want their children to have a strong start in life. Participation in quality early childhood experiences enhances children's language and social development and their chance of school success. The quality of a child's early childhood experiences is the strongest predictor of success when that child enters the school system. High quality programs have been shown to lower the rate of school drop-out and school failure, reduce the need to admit children into special education programs, lower juvenile delinquency rates, and increase the detection and treatment of health problems. The Early Years Study suggests that 75% of the brain's development occurs after birth (McCain and Mustard 1999). The early years set the foundation for a child's ability to trust, to learn, and to develop the abilities needed to continue learning for a lifetime. Quality early childhood services have the potential to support all families by providing enriching child development while enabling parents to attend school, job training, and work. Yet progress on making quality EC services universal and affordable has been quite limited other than in Quebec.

Although the number of regulated spaces has grown, less than 19% of children aged 0–12, about 1 in 5 Canadian children, have access to a regulated child care space (Beach et al. 2009). Canada lags far behind other industrialized nations in ensuring that all children have access to quality EC programs.

The poor availability, lack of coordination, and high cost of child care cause stress among working parents. Many parents cannot afford the fees that regulated services must charge in order to survive. The number of child care fee subsidies far from meets the need. The 2001 proportion of children in regulated child care who received subsidy was 36%, suggesting limited access to licensed services for low-income families. More recently, fewer than one in three of the children using the regulated system have a **fee subsidy** (Campaign 2000, 2004). In 2011, the subsidy waiting list in Toronto was reported as having more than 18 000 children (Toronto Star, January 11, 2011). Many parents who might prefer to use regulated services are left to make other arrangements because of economic and/or geographic barriers to service.

TABLE 2–1	Comparison of Regulated Child Care Spaces, Provinces and Territories, 2008
Province/Territory	**Number of Spaces**
Newfoundland	5 972
Prince Edward Island	4 424
Nova Scotia	13 711
New Brunswick	15 506
Quebec	368 909
Ontario	256 748
Manitoba	27 189
Saskatchewan	9 173
Alberta	73 981
British Columbia	87 538
Northwest Territories	1 768
Yukon	1 262
Nunavut	1 013
National Totals	867 194

Source: J. Beach, M. Friendly, C. Ferns, N. Prabhu, and B. Forer, *Early Childhood Education and Care in Canada: Provinces and Territories, 2008* (Toronto: Childcare Resource and Research Unit, 2008). Statistics reprinted by permission.

Most parents rely on informal, unregulated, and sometimes unreliable care by family members or neighbours. Exact figures for those in unregulated care are difficult to obtain. Beach et al. (2008) reported that there are 3 057 000 children between newborn and 12 years with mothers in the paid labour force. Table 2–1 shows that the number of regulated child care spaces in Canada at the end of 2008 totalled just 867 194.

Canada's Commitment to the Rights and Well-being of Children

When it ratified the **United Nations Convention on the Rights of the Child** in 1991, Canada recognized that children, by virtue of being human, have rights. These rights include civil and political rights as well as economic, social, and cultural ones. The specific rights are often summarized and grouped as the "three *p*s": provision, protection, and participation. *Provision* means children have the right to possess, receive, or have access to certain things and services, including life, early childhood services, health care, an adequate standard of living, education to develop to their fullest potential, and rehabilitative care. Under *participation,* children have the right to participate in society and in decisions affecting their lives, including "the right to express their views in matters affecting themselves." Included in *protection* is the right of children to be shielded from harmful practices and acts—such as discrimination or separation from parents—and the right to special protection if they are without a family. In addition, by virtue of being young and vulnerable, children have some special rights—to protection from harm, to promotion of their growth and development, and to participation in decisions affecting them according to their age and maturity. Many of these rights affect parents and families. The Convention acknowledges the central role of families in safeguarding these rights and reinforces the state's obligation to help families meet the basic needs of their children.

The United Nations Children's Fund (UNICEF) researches children's rights and examines how societies live up toward their obligations in support of children. Differences of opinion arise between countries and across different political traditions concerning the rights of children. Although the Convention acknowledges limits in resources and services available to countries, it insists that young children are vested with the full range of human rights.

As a signatory to the Convention, Canada needs to do a much better job of fulfilling children's rights and assuring them "a standard of living adequate for physical, spiritual, moral, and social development." Many nations fare better than Canada in tackling child poverty and mitigating the negative impact of unemployment and poor wages through substantial investments in comprehensive family policies that include income security for families, affordable housing, EC programs, and other forms of assistance (Campaign 2000).

Protecting children from poverty during their years of growth and formation is a mark of a civilized society. All countries wishing to improve the development and learning of their children need to reduce national levels of child poverty. Although child poverty has multisectoral causes, its effects can be lessened through family support and children's services. Governments need to attack family poverty through social, housing, and labour policies. Children need access to programs that embrace care and nurturing as well as education.

The UN report *The State of the World's Children 2000* called child care "a moral imperative" and "sound economic service." The report stated that the reason many countries have not yet invested in early childhood development is that it holds no short-term political gain (UNICEF 2008). In Canada, health, education, and social services—the areas in which policies and practices most strongly shape the conditions of childhood—all fall under provincial jurisdiction. However, some decisions made at the federal level, such as taxation and child benefits, have a direct impact on children.

For more information on the United Nations Convention on the Rights of the Child, see the resources cited at the end of this chapter, and visit the Canadian Coalition on the Rights of Children website at www.rightsofchildren.ca.

International Comparisons of ECEC Policy

Canada accepts some responsibility for the protection and promotion of the economic and social well-being of its citizens, through supports such as employment insurance and access to health care and education. Canada, unlike many European countries, is "less generous," relying on the free market rather than extensive government support to families and social programs. The state—Canada—will step in if citizens are in dire need, usually with targeted programs rather than universal social programs such as early childhood. In many parts of Europe, child care is viewed as a citizenship right; early childhood programs are seen as important for young children regardless of the employment status of the parents. Child care is regarded as a societal responsibility, therefore services are publicly funded. Policies that enhance child development contribute to the social and economic security of the country. In most Western European countries, most 3- to 6-year-olds attend ECEC programs for a full school-day. These programs are primarily publicly delivered and publicly funded, although parents usually pay some fees for younger children and after-school hours (**OECD** 2006).

The Organization for Economic Cooperation and Development (OECD) has collected comparative economic and social data for over four decades. In comparing ECEC across economically advanced nations, it identifies a growing need for non-parental care, and such care is seen as a public good. The report Starting Strong (2006) identifies many of the challenges encountered in ECEC policy making and service coordination, compares availability and access to services, and provides a series of recommendations of how to improve the quality of and access to ECEC. Early childhood policy is concerned not only with providing education and care to young children, it is also linked with issues of parental support, women's employment, and equality of opportunity; child development and child poverty issues; labour market supply; health, social welfare, and elementary school education for children.

What is striking is Canada's poor showing, compared with other developed nations. Canada has one of the highest female labour force participation rates in the world, while only 24% of children under the age of six were in regulated child care. Out of the 14 countries compared, Canada rated the lowest in public expenditures as a per cent of the gross domestic product. Additionally, in a 2008 UNICEF published international study to rank the quality, access, financing, and policy of ECEC programs, Canada ranked at the bottom of 25 developed countries.

What this means is that while Canada is among the richest nations in the world, it is also the least generous when it comes to public spending on ECEC. In its 2004 report assessing EC services in Canada, the OECD described the current situation as "a patchwork of uneconomic, fragmented services." It also means that the larger portion of the cost of EC services remains the responsibility of individual families. Parents generally turn to the private market to meet their child care needs. To give some perspective, European Union guidelines recommend annual government expenditures of 1% of total national expenditures for early childhood development, learning, and care. Some countries, such as Denmark, are spending 2%, whereas Canada is reported as spending less than 0.5% (OECD 2006). In some OECD countries, parents contribute as little as 10% to 15% of the child care costs for their young child.

Policy research shows that the recognition of high quality EC for children and families is well entrenched in other countries. These services operate within the context of a comprehensive family policy that includes well-paid maternity and paternity leaves, generous child benefits, and children's health services (OECD 2001). In Belgium and France, 95% of children aged three to school age are enrolled in publicly financed programs (OECD 2001). European nations publicly fund blended early childhood services. France, Denmark, Sweden, Italy, Spain, Belgium, Finland, and others provide services for all children over the age of two-and-a-half years plus fairly broad coverage for infants and toddlers.

Policy Roots of the Federal Government

Government policy defines a broad vision that provides a framework for operational decisions. **Social policy** primarily refers to guidelines and interventions for the changing, maintenance, or creation of living conditions that are conducive to *human welfare*. Thus, social policy is that part of *public policy* that has to do with *social issues*. Policy addresses key issues such as *who* is responsible for programs for children, *what* types of programs should be provided, and *how* these programs should be delivered. At the heart of these discussions is the question of whether ECEC should be a public or a private, family responsibility. An overwhelming majority of Canadians believe that child care is too expensive and not accessible enough to all children and over 90% of the public wants "government to do more to ensure that all Canadians have access to quality child care" (CCCF and CCAAC 2003). These attitudes toward early childhood are consistent with beliefs about public education for children aged 6 to 18. Beginning in the nineteenth century, the policy of providing education for all Canadian children transformed attitudes about public education, which became recognized as a right of all children.

The welfare of children is consistently rated a strong priority relative to other major issues such as taxation, the federal debt, and economic competitiveness. It is generally acknowledged that the impact of childhood experiences lasts for a lifetime and that the government has a critical role to play in providing services and programs that support children and families. This public opinion shift is a critical factor in moving governments toward making significant investments in EC programs. Educators must continuously build their awareness of government social policy as depicted in image below.

With respect to supporting children, the federal government traces its role to the introduction of a tax exemption in 1918 (Canada 1994a). The 1942 Dominion-Provincial Agreement for Wartime Day Nurseries initiated a 50–50 federal–provincial cost sharing arrangement. After the Second World War, with the introduction of the universal Family Allowance Program, federal involvement was expanded. Subsequently, the influence of the federal government became primarily financial, through cost-sharing payments it made to provincial government budgets for child care and related services first through the Canada Assistance Plan in 1966 and now through the Canada Health and Social Transfer.

Canada is governed by a federal system that is the key to how responsibilities for EC are defined. The Canadian Constitution confers legislative and executive powers on two levels of government—the federal government and the provinces/territories. Each level is independent, or sovereign, in its respective areas of responsibility. The 1867 *British North America Act* defines the federal and provincial/territorial responsibilities. Canada's Constitution specifies that the federal government does not have direct jurisdiction over education, health, or social welfare. These are

Educators must use reputable websites to build their awareness of government social policy.

Source: www.childcarecanada.org/

the responsibilities of the provinces and territories. Consequently, the federal government does not have the authority to enact an early childhood program without the agreement of the provinces.

Over 40 years ago, Canada published the findings of the Royal Commission on the Status of Women (1970). The document forcefully declared the need for a universal, affordable child care program. In the decades since then, promises of a national child care strategy have come on and off agendas with few concrete results.

The functions of the federal and provincial governments with respect to EC programs are complex and interrelated. Many issues relating to family policy fall under provincial jurisdiction. While divorce law is federal, marriage laws and the enforcement of child support are under provincial jurisdiction. EC programs fall under provincial jurisdiction, although they receive substantial funds from the federal government. The federal government provides maternity and parental leave benefits, but for most Canadian employees, leave from employment is governed by provincial legislation. There is no federal role in public education, including kindergarten. The federal government does not pay for primary or secondary education (it does pay for post-secondary education through the Canada Social Transfer [CST]), and there is no national department of education. Consequently, Canada does not have a unified, national approach to ECEC.

Today, early childhood services are funded through a patchwork approach combining primarily parent fees and funding from various levels of government (for more details on parent fees, see Chapter 9, "Financial Matters"). In 1994, the Liberal government began a process of reforming Canada's system of social security. Because it provided working parents with the assurance of care for their children and thus provided critical support for employment, child care was seen as part of this agenda.

ECEC Policy Directions

The 1990s brought forward a number of federal/provincial/territorial agreements (excluding Quebec) that have created frameworks, policies, and provide funding to expand rights, benefits, and programs for all families and their children. Efforts were made to better define the roles and responsibilities of the federal and provincial/territorial governments acknowledging the decision-making role the provinces play in providing services.

By the late 1990s, the federal government seemed to be getting out of the business of funding service delivery. Instead, they provided income supplements to individual Canadians via, for example, the 1997 National Child Benefit. The National Child Benefit (NCB) supplement provides additional income support to low-income families with children. Through the National Child Benefit, the federal, provincial, and territorial governments are working to reduce child poverty and promote parents' attachment to the workforce. However, tax deductions or tax credits do not contribute to creating quality EC services that would enable parents to have a greater choice of EC arrangements.

The Social Union Framework Agreement (1999) had a key principle to ensure access for all Canadians to essential social programs and to services of reasonably comparable quality. SUFA committed both levels of government to working in collaboration and accountability as well as to preclude unilateral federal action in areas of provincial jurisdiction without provincial consent.

By the late 1990s, however, the federal government had budget surpluses, and it seemed willing to commit federal funds to some kind of national early childhood development program. They negotiated the Federal–Provincial–Territorial Agreement on Early Childhood Development (ECDA), signed by all provinces except Quebec in 2000. The Agreement provided federal funds in program areas deemed to be part of a "child development" agenda to enable provincial/territorial governments to improve and expand ECEC programs in four areas: healthy pregnancy, birth, and infancy; parenting and family supports; early childhood development, learning, and care;

and community supports. Governments are obliged to be accountable through annual public reports on results based on specific outcome indicators of child well-being. There were concerns among the EC community regarding the reporting of the funding and that many provinces had cut their own funding to these programs.

In 2003, the federal government agreed to transfer $900 million over five years to support specific provincial/territorial investments in child care through the Multilateral Framework Agreement (MFA) on Early Learning and Child Care. The agreement's intent was to promote child development and support parental workforce participation or employment training. The Canadian government extended funding until 2013–14. The funds are primarily directed to services such as regulated child care programs, licensed home child care, and preschool programs. There is an agreement from the EC community that the Multilateral Framework was an important milestone in making the difference in the lives of children and families.

Getting an agreement from the provinces to spend the $5 billion on building a national early learning and childcare system became one of the defining issues of the Martin government. All the provinces, *including* Quebec, entered into bilateral agreements to spend federal government funds under the national umbrella of the agreed-upon QUAD principles (Mahon and Jenson, 2006). Each province and the federal government signed an agreement-in-principle that included a general outline of how funds were to be used. Each province was to develop a more specific action plan for the five-year phase, with a five-year funding agreement. However, when the federal Liberal government fell at the end of 2005, only Manitoba and Ontario had finished the process, with the other provincial agreements in various stages.

By the time of the 2006 federal election, Canada was close to achieving the foundations of a national ECEC system. However, these commitments were short-lived, when the Conservatives were elected in 2006, they ended the intergovernmental agreements and the accompanying development plans. The minority Conservative government came with a very different philosophy, not only of federal involvement in particular policy areas but also in the role of the state more generally. In the place of a national program focused on provinces/territories developing ECEC systems, the Harper government opted for a straight cash payment to parents, as well as a fund to create new childcare spaces.

At the same time, the advocacy groups and activities that kept ECEC a vital public policy subject from the early 1980s to the present time have withered, as groups have lost long-standing public funds and their ability to monitor developments and sustain democratic involvement with policy makers. This loss of resources has affected not only childcare and women's groups but also NGOs working in social policy generally, international development, and health.

Parental Leave

Paid parental leave is essential to gender equity, enabling both women and men to enjoy parenthood while maintaining their attachment to the work force. Maternity and parental leaves are part of the context for EC programs as they determine when parents are likely to return to work and to begin to seek alternative care for children. Canadian maternity/parental leave provisions are shared between federal and provincial governments. Provinces set the length and conditions of leave under employment legislation. The federal government provides benefits under Employment Insurance (EI). In 2001, the maximum length of paid parental leave increased to 35 weeks, making a total benefit covering 50 weeks. This benefit is available to biological and adoptive parents and may be shared by the parents. For biological parents, the combined maternity (17 weeks) and parental benefits are paid for one year. The OECD found that Canada's parental level policy was in the bottom third of 20 effective programs. Fathers and other non-birthing parents also need time to bond with their babies.

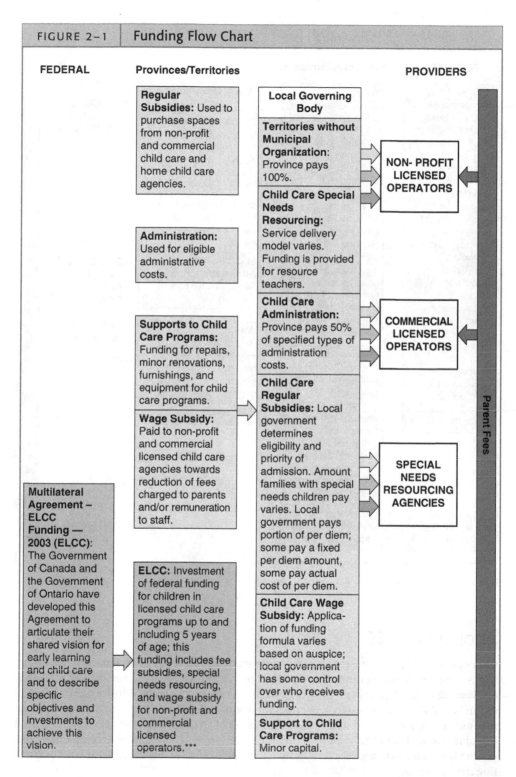

FIGURE 2–1 | Funding Flow Chart

FEDERAL

Multilateral Agreement – ELCC Funding — 2003 (ELCC): The Government of Canada and the Government of Ontario have developed this Agreement to articulate their shared vision for early learning and child care and to describe specific objectives and investments to achieve this vision.

Provinces/Territories

Regular Subsidies: Used to purchase spaces from non-profit and commercial child care and home child care agencies.

Administration: Used for eligible administrative costs.

Supports to Child Care Programs: Funding for repairs, minor renovations, furnishings, and equipment for child care programs.

Wage Subsidy: Paid to non-profit and commercial licensed child care agencies towards reduction of fees charged to parents and/or remuneration to staff.

ELCC: Investment of federal funding for children in licensed child care programs up to and including 5 years of age; this funding includes fee subsidies, special needs resourcing, and wage subsidy for non-profit and commercial licensed operators.***

Local Governing Body

Territories without Municipal Organization: Province pays 100%.

Child Care Special Needs Resourcing: Service delivery model varies. Funding is provided for resource teachers.

Child Care Administration: Province pays 50% of specified types of administration costs.

Child Care Regular Subsidies: Local government determines eligibility and priority of admission. Amount families with special needs children pay varies. Local government pays portion of per diem; some pay a fixed per diem amount, some pay actual cost of per diem.

Child Care Wage Subsidy: Application of funding formula varies based on auspice; local government has some control over who receives funding.

Support to Child Care Programs: Minor capital.

PROVIDERS

NON- PROFIT LICENSED OPERATORS

COMMERCIAL LICENSED OPERATORS

SPECIAL NEEDS RESOURCING AGENCIES

Parent Fees

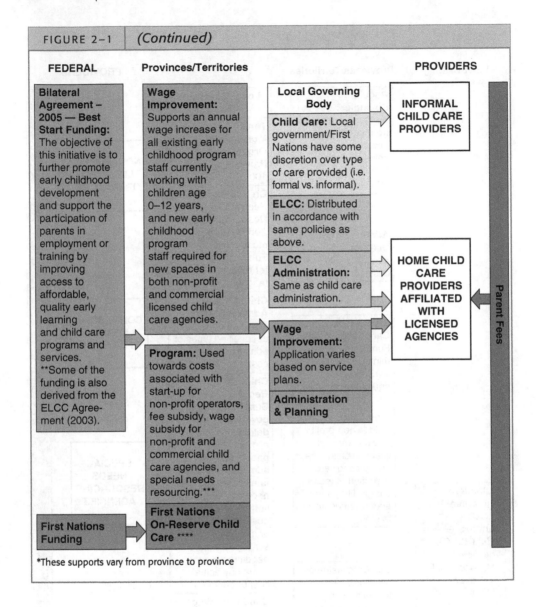

FIGURE 2-1   *(Continued)*

FEDERAL	Provinces/Territories		PROVIDERS

Bilateral Agreement – 2005 — Best Start Funding: The objective of this initiative is to further promote early childhood development and support the participation of parents in employment or training by improving access to affordable, quality early learning and child care programs and services. **Some of the funding is also derived from the ELCC Agreement (2003).

Wage Improvement: Supports an annual wage increase for all existing early childhood program staff currently working with children age 0–12 years, and new early childhood program staff required for new spaces in both non-profit and commercial licensed child care agencies.

Program: Used towards costs associated with start-up for non-profit operators, fee subsidy, wage subsidy for non-profit and commercial child care agencies, and special needs resourcing.***

First Nations Funding

First Nations On-Reserve Child Care **

Local Governing Body

Child Care: Local government/First Nations have some discretion over type of care provided (i.e. formal vs. informal).

ELCC: Distributed in accordance with same policies as above.

ELCC Administration: Same as child care administration.

Wage Improvement: Application varies based on service plans.

Administration & Planning

INFORMAL CHILD CARE PROVIDERS

HOME CHILD CARE PROVIDERS AFFILIATED WITH LICENSED AGENCIES

Parent Fees

*These supports vary from province to province

Aboriginal ECEC

Generally, funding for on-reserve social programs is a responsibility of the federal government, while social programs for other Aboriginal people may be a federal or provincial responsibility. Typically, First Nations and Inuit organizations have the responsibility for administration of funds and developing services. Services for Aboriginal children and families remain fragmented and significantly underdeveloped. Aboriginal groups have larger than average child populations, making ECEC a particularly important issue. The maintenance of indigenous culture is an important concern for Aboriginal peoples, along with a strong interest in controlling their programs.

Future Role of the Federal Government

At a time when Canada is undergoing social and economic change, social policies and programs must respond to the changing needs of Canadian families. A society that is interested in the long-term social and economic security of its citizens and a healthy and prosperous future must be committed to the care and nurturing of children. Canada is one of the few major industrialized nations without a national child care policy.

Many factors, including lack of political will and jurisdictional wrangling, have contributed to a virtual paralysis in the establishment of national EC policies closer to those found in other developed nations. Canada's contribution to early childhood programs lags behind most other OECD countries. When the OECD conducted its study of Canada, it recommended: strengthening the present federal/provincial/territorial agreements and focusing them on child development services; encouraging provincial governments to develop along with key stakeholder groups; an early childhood strategy with priority targets, benchmarks, and timelines with adequate funding; to build bridges between child care and kindergarten programs; and to effectively fund a universal early child care system. Figure 2–2 provides a summary of roles for three levels of government in Canada.

UNESCO (Kaga et al. 2010) notes that Canada's comparatively low public investment rates in early childhood services has negative consequences; the resulting high costs to parents lead to unequal access and the segregation of children by income. Many have contended that Canada's limited support for families, women, and children has negative implications for its future as a nation, as birth rates have slowed; the working-age population is aging; and women, immigrants, and Aboriginal Canadians continue to be impeded in participation in education, training, and the labour force (e.g., McCain and Mustard 1999; Friendly and Prentice 2009).

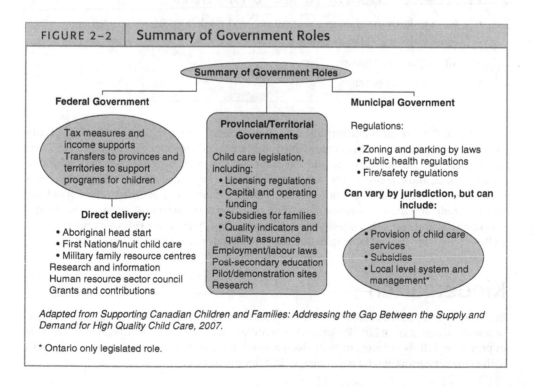

| FIGURE 2–2 | Summary of Government Roles |

Summary of Government Roles

Federal Government

Tax measures and income supports
Transfers to provinces and territories to support programs for children

Direct delivery:

• Aboriginal head start
• First Nations/Inuit child care
• Military family resource centres
Research and information
Human resource sector council
Grants and contributions

Provincial/Territorial Governments

Child care legislation, including:
• Licensing regulations
• Capital and operating funding
• Subsidies for families
• Quality indicators and quality assurance
Employment/labour laws
Post-secondary education
Pilot/demonstration sites
Research

Municipal Government

Regulations:

• Zoning and parking by laws
• Public health regulations
• Fire/safety regulations

Can vary by jurisdiction, but can include:

• Provision of child care services
• Subsidies
• Local level system and management*

Adapted from Supporting Canadian Children and Families: Addressing the Gap Between the Supply and Demand for High Quality Child Care, 2007.

* Ontario only legislated role.

Advocates urge a renewed federal presence in ECEC. Without a federal role to provide the glue and sustainable funding to support provincial efforts, EC stakeholders are not optimistic about the future. Like health care, ECEC falls under provincial jurisdiction where it is under-resourced and underdeveloped as an effective anti-poverty strategy and social determinant of health. All levels of government, federal, provincial territorial, First Nations, and local, need to be engaged to play their role. While as a nation, Canada has a long way to go to reach the commitment of resources, policy, and infrastructure levels of other countries, the focus of EC policy has shifted to the provinces where there are some promising initiatives. Recent trends in Canadian ECEC demonstrate that a number of provincial governments recognize the importance of the early years for subsequent developmental, social, and economic success.

Role of Provincial/Territorial Governments

Currently, each of Canada's 14 jurisdictions—10 provinces, 3 territories, and the federal government—has its own approach to early learning and child care. The provinces and territories hold the constitutional responsibility for education and social policies, where EC programs emerge. Each province and territory has responsibility for setting its own education policy, establishing its own mechanisms for funding and regulating EC, and creating its own set of rules governing relationships with municipalities. Early childhood programs have the common characteristics of education, health, and social services, all of which fall under provincial/territorial jurisdiction (except for the welfare of First Nations children on reserve programs, which as noted earlier is a federal responsibility).

PROVINCIAL/TERRITORIAL RESPONSIBILITIES

- EC standards, policies and procedures, and guidelines
- regulation of child care services
- kindergarten programs
- funding arrangements

Each of the provinces and territories has developed its own program of regulated EC that includes nursery or preschools, centre-based child care, and regulated family child care. These EC programs provide legislative requirements for the operation of services, a variety of funding arrangements, and established systems for **monitoring** compliance of legislated requirements. Government funding and regulations remain fluid and change in response to current politics, new research, and monetary restrictions. Provincial/territorial responsibilities can be divided into financial and regulatory ones. No jurisdiction, except Quebec, provides a comprehensive, well-designed and funded EC system that meets the needs of a majority of families.

Kindergarten

In all cases, every province and territory provides kindergarten as it is part of the public education system, and in most jurisdictions, it is an entitlement. While some kindergarten is part-day or part-time, full-day kindergarten for five-year-olds has become the norm in many provinces, with expanding provision for four year olds in a few provinces.

Government regulations mandated many safety improvements since this 1903 program.
Source: Toronto Reference Library

As noted earlier, generally there has been little connection between kindergarten and EC programs at the policy level, although changes are emerging. EC programs and educators and kindergarten programs and teachers have been regulated under separate pieces of legislation. A number of governments are looking to harmonize policies, regulations, and funding. This is a mammoth task. There are no common education requirements or credentials for the professionals who work with young children across these various programs and services. These differences and disparities make it difficult for early learning and care programs to fully integrate with kindergarten programs.

The availability and quality of early learning and care programs vary enormously. The supply of child care spaces covers only a minority of children, and public kindergarten schedules do not meet the needs of working parents. A number of the provinces have begun to transform their EC approach blending EC with education as recommended by the OECD.

Integration of EC and Kindergarten

Over the past decade, ministries of education in several provinces and territories have shown an increased awareness in ECEC policy and programs. Governments want to reap the social and economic benefits of investing in the learning of young children, resulting in an expansion in the number of regulated CC programs, expansion of full-day kindergarten, and policies to provide space of EC programs in schools.

In part, there was service fragmentation and chaos with services for young children and families in a number of ministries. The cultures and mandates of the different ministries made it difficult to achieve coordinated policies necessary for development and education of young children. A significant number of provincial/territorial governments have taken steps to close the gap between child care and early education by consolidating responsibility for EC from social service ministries to education ministries/departments, and in part by addressing the OECD recommendation of a systematic and integrated approach to policy development and implementation. As with other countries, through integrating ECEC into a single ministry, there are opportunities for more coherent policy, greater equality, and consistency across sectors in terms of:

- social objectives,
- legislation, funding,
- staffing, and
- curriculum and assessment.

This growing involvement with the education sector is in progress, and needs further development.

One of the major barriers to building integrated ECEC systems is the historic divide between education and child care. Separated by legislation, funding, and delivery structures, kindergarten with its own educational roots is viewed as the public good, whereas child care has been mired in its social welfare status (Bennett and Moss 2006). The researchers acknowledge the contribution to ECEC policy and practice made by ministries of health and social welfare, and they advocate for bringing EC into the education system as many provinces and territories did in 2010. Among the reasons for consolidating children's programs under education are:

- The primary focus of education is children.
- Contemporary education theory recognizes children are learners from birth and promotes the importance of lifelong learning.
- Unlike welfare services, education offers universal access and a strong infrastructure (financing, training support, curriculum, data collection, evaluation, and research).
- Education is a publicly recognized and publicly supported system.

Moss and Bennett affirm that consolidation under education improves goal definition, governance, accountability, and results.

Complexity of Implementing Policy with a Larger Vision for Child and Families

ECEC policy is a complex area. As well as being concerned with child care and early education, it is concerned with children's health, nutrition, social welfare, women's employment, equal opportunities, and poverty issues. Numerous studies have documented the importance of establishing comprehensive, flexible, and integrated services capable of providing seamless support to children and their families (Pascal 2009; OECD 2006; McCain and Mustard 1999).

There is concern that integration with education may separate ECEC services from child welfare, health, and other key policy areas for children and families, ultimately undermining attention to the whole child. There is also apprehension about the downward pressure by the school system on young children of narrowly defined standards, leading to an increased emphasis on traditional education methods. There is a fear of overemphasizing curriculum outcomes limiting the offering of child-centred programs based on the needs and interests of the children. An additional challenge is integrating approaches such as emergent curriculum into school systems with more rigid time frames and a subject focus (math, literacy). As well, narrowly defined goals lead to a school readiness focus—and that "real" learning happens at grade one. It is essential for the policy to recognize that each developmental stage of learning is relevant.

The report *With Our Best Future in Mind: Implementing Early Learning in Ontario*, Pascal called for such a comprehensive plan that integrated child and family systems and was hailed by many as a progressive model. This vision provided an opportunity to achieve a coordinated, coherent approach that could optimize each child's holistic development. This comprehensive approach can only occur when the multi-sectoral nature of ECEC forms the cornerstone of the policy.

There is a need to fuse the two disciplines (EC and education), creating an environment where EC can help influence curriculum in schools to be more young child and family focused. In implementing policy, care must be taken to ensure that EC does not become the junior partner. The culture of EC has a lot to offer the education system. In EC settings, relationships with families are valued and cultivated. EC programs promote family engagement, encouraging family participation in decision making related to the child's education as elaborated in Chapter 8. Another well-documented worry is about the ability of ECEC field to influence education pedagogy. Recent reports note, in a number of countries that have integrated CC/Education, there is a failure to bring the enhanced influence of EC pedagogy. *Caring and Learning Together: A Cross-national Study of Integration of ECE and Education within Education* (2010), UNESCO. In countries where this partnership had been established, the emergence of a mutual and equitable meeting place has generally not evolved.

Ontario is in the process of laying a platform and an infrastructure to facilitate a transformation of practice. To transform practice, teams of ECEs and kindergarten teachers need opportunities to build understanding of each other's knowledge and roles. This approach is intended to create a pedagogical meeting place between EC and kindergarten educators. Such a strategy can include resources, materials, access to pedagogists, professional development opportunities, and time to reflect on practice through documentation and the sharing of learning stories.

At the end of its first year of implementation, the government of Ontario announced its intention to amend the newly passed *Education Act* in a bid to address the challenges and concerns around the implementation of the extended day program and the fuller blueprint for a child and family system for children from prenatal to age 12. Some advocates feel the announcement institutionalizes the divide between education and care and the split in the child's day. They believe that this decision undermines the professionalism of early childhood educators, relegating them to part-time workers whether employed in kindergarten classroom or in after-school childcare. Lastly, that impact of the decision adds more complexity to an already chaotic field. While the situation in Ontario is still in flux, there is concern among advocates that provincial government may not follow through with the broad vision set forth in the Pascal report, and may concentrate almost exclusively on full-day kindergarten, leaving the rest of child care unreformed.

In the book *Switch: How to Change Things When Change Is Hard* (2010), Heath proposes that we should not obsess over what will happen during the middle of the implementation when standing at the initial stage. It is best to move forward with the vision and allow each step to define the next. It is key for all stakeholders to define their big, bold goals for children and families. Transforming a comprehensive ECEC system is an iterative process. Implementation is both collaborative among many partners (governments, school boards, community organizations, educators, and families) and incremental. In order for the envisioned EC system to evolve, all must accept that challenges will arise and that stakeholders need to problem solve collectively how they will get there.

Financial Responsibilities

Each province and territory has developed its own system of planning, regulating, and funding EC services. Even under fiscal constraints, total provincial and territorial expenditures for EC services have grown in recent years. A major means of supporting EC is through subsidies for low-income families. Many provinces and territories have also developed grants that provide assistance to EC programs for capital costs, equipment, staff salaries, or other program expenditures. These grants allow for improvements to program quality without an increase in parental fees, thus providing assistance to all families who use the service.

The three main sources of revenue for an EC program—parent fees, fee subsidies, and grants—strongly influence the kind and quality of services a setting can offer and wage levels. The public funding model in all provinces except Quebec relies heavily on fee subsidies targeted to eligible low-income families; and in some provinces, notably Ontario, many eligible families cannot access a subsidy, and large subsidy waiting lists exist. This welfare—rather than universal—approach means that the high user fees for regulated child care that are levied to support most of the cost of program operations are a major barrier to access for modest- and middle-income parents. From province to province, there is a wide variation in the amount of funding provided by each province for a regulated child care space from a low of $195 in Alberta to a high of $1694 in Quebec (see Table 2–2 for more detail). *You Bet I Care!* found that although

TABLE 2–2	Total Provincial Allocation for Each Regulated Child Care Space, 2008	
Province/Territory	**Allocation for Each Child[1]**	**Total Allocation**
Newfoundland	$304	$19 844 115
Prince Edward Island[2]	$313	$6 226 767
Nova Scotia	$313	$37 150 418
New Brunswick	$274	$26 236 200
Quebec	$1694	$1 730 574 000
Ontario	$414	$780 400 000
Manitoba	$606	$105 983 600
Saskatchewan	$326	$47 133 989
Alberta	$195	$105 732 793
British Columbia	$382	$216 740 000
Northwest Territories	$294	$2 542 000
Yukon	$1415	$6 409 284
Nunavut	$272	$2 470 000

[1]Estimates based on total provincial allocation for regulated child care and total regulated number of children 0–12.

[2]For the purpose of comparison with other jurisdictions where kindergarten is in the public school system, this calculation did not include spaces in part-day kindergarten or its spending on kindergarten.

Source: *Early Childhood Education and Care in Canada: Provinces and Territories, 2008* (Toronto: Childcare Resource and Research Unit, 2009). Statistics reprinted by permission.

nationally centres obtained 49.2% of revenue from parent fees, there was heavier reliance in some provinces such as Newfoundland (82.1%) and Nova Scotia (72.7%). Manitoba has the lowest reliance on parent fees.

Among the concerns identified about provincial/territorial funding approaches are:

- Fee subsidies do not cover the actual cost of care.

- Too many parents are on waiting lists for subsidized child care.

- In most jurisdictions, there is a lack of accountability for the use of public funds used by subsidy recipients to purchase unregulated care.

- Public money is used to support commercial care.

As Chapter 1 makes clear, a significant barrier to high quality EC is staff dissatisfaction, usually expressed through high turnover. The most common cause of turnover is inadequate compensation, followed by poor working conditions, which are usually the result of underfunding. Full-time earnings vary considerably by province and territory with a high of over $35 000 for a majority of practitioners in Quebec. The national average for ECEs and assistants in 2000 was $21 519 (CCHRSC 2006). Increasingly, ECE graduates and educators are seeking careers outside of regulated child care and in other areas of the field. This is occurring particularly in education, with the merging of EC and education with ECE's working alongside kindergarten teachers. In other parts of the country, there appears to be little immediate prospect of substantial improvement, and this is a major reason why every practitioner in the field needs to be aware of the routes to public education and advocacy (see Chapter 10).

The gaps between Quebec and the rest of Canada in EC policy, funding, and services are dramatic. Beginning in 1997, the Quebec government undertook a massive reorganization of the child care system transforming it into a component of a new, comprehensive family policy that included improved maternity/parental leave as well. The new act stipulated that *every child is entitled to receive good, continuous, personal child care until the end of primary school* (Government of Quebec 1997). Quebec's broad family policy gave concrete expression to the educational dimension of ECEC services. Half-day programs for five-year-olds were extended to a full day. Four-year-olds had a supplemental half-day program provided at no cost to the parent. By 2001, an additional 85 000 spaces were to be created for children aged from newborn to four, and the new regulations required double the former number of trained staff. In fact, in 2001, 58% of total Canada-wide provincial and territorial spending on regulated child care was spent in Quebec. Its policy was a bold move toward universality whether or not parents are employed and regardless of total family income. Quebec's progressive social policy was regarded as the desired goal by advocates across the country. Observers note that the policy started under the Parti Québécois stagnated somewhat under the Charest government. While Quebec's policy is still pointed to as a great example within Canada, it isn't that progressive when compared internationally as there are issues with access, and programs are often of a mediocre quality.

Regulation through Licensing

The primary benefit from public regulation of the ECEC is its help in ensuring children's rights to EC settings that protect them from harm and promote their healthy development. As noted earlier, the importance of these rights is underscored by a growing body of research evidence that emphasizes the importance of children's earliest experiences to their development and later learning.

Whether related to early childhood education, banks, or broadcasting, regulation is designed to provide specific levels of quality and accessibility for the entire population. Regulation takes place through legislation shaped by the policy priorities of a particular government. The Millward Brown Goldfarb survey found that 96% of Canadians believed the quality of EC programs could be improved by "regulating all child care services to meet quality standards" (CCCF and CCAAC 2003). An effective licensing system minimizes the potential for harmful care.

Each regulation is attached to a piece of legislation and can be enforced by law. Consequently, regulations are powerful tools for establishing basic standards such as health and safety provisions in a physical setting. The term "**standards**" implies degrees of excellence along a continuum, with some regulations only setting baseline standards for acceptability below which quality is unacceptable (possibly leading to sanctions that could be program closures and fines) and other regulations indicating quality when met.

Regulation to do with early childhood is administered by the provinces and territories and takes the form of **licensing** of centre-based programs and family child care agencies or homes. All provinces and territories have licensing standards, although these standards vary widely in scope. **Regulations** include the rules, directives, statutes, and standards that prescribe, direct, limit, and govern early childhood programs. When regulatory systems are well designed and effectively administered, they set a baseline for an acceptable level of care. Directors of **licensed programs** are responsible for understanding licensing and other regulations pertaining to provision of services for young children. Directors, and when applicable with operators/licencees, must ensure that all requirements are fulfilled in a timely manner.

Provincial/territorial regulations should reflect current research findings. Licensing standards ought to result from careful consideration of their value and benefit to children and should positively affect both children and educators. Regulations need to be clear, so everyone can understand them. Programs need to know what is expected of and from them, and government officials need to interpret and enforce standards fairly and consistently. Rigid standards and hazy guidelines are difficult to interpret and enforce. A functioning system of regulation establishes standards of quality and applies those standards to programs across the board. It specifies penalties and procedures for programs that do not meet the standards.

Licensing standards provide a baseline for acceptable care of children. In programs operating below that level of service, a child is actually deemed to be in danger. Regulations cover structural aspects of quality that are readily measurable (staff:child ratios, group size, and floor space,) as outlined in Chapter 1. Licensing standards set forth the public definition of acceptability: Regulated programs must meet at least this level of quality in order to legally operate. While services need to meet regulations, these alone cannot ensure an adequate standard of service delivery. The process aspects of the program, such as educator–child interactions, provide a truer indication of quality. A licence gives a program permission to operate; it does not guarantee quality.

Many parents feel more secure placing their child in a licensed facility. Some agencies or provincial governments provide parents with information, generally through websites, about the standards of quality they should be looking for when placing their child. It is important to note that the majority of children are not in the regulated system with limited measures in place to assure their safety. A large number of settings in some provinces are exempt from regulation. Many children are unprotected because they receive care outside their families in programs that are legally exempt from regulation. Some policy makers may view licensing as unnecessary because they believe that it seeks the ideal or imposes an elitist definition of quality rather than establishing a minimal baseline of protection (NAEYC 1998b).

Although licensing regulations vary greatly from province to territory, most provincial regulations cover most aspects of a program—administration, organization, facilities, personnel, funding, and services—as outlined in the examples below:

- *Staff:* qualifications, medical requirements, and criminal reference checks
- *Building safety:* minimum fire and building safety standards, procedures for evacuation, and procedures for storage of harmful materials
- *Program:* regulations ensure that the daily schedule offers opportunities and activities that promote children's development
- *Physical space:* the amount of space necessary both indoors and outside, levels of light, fencing, and provision of diaper-changing areas
- *Equipment:* the amount appropriate to the ages and numbers served, and specifications for equipment, such as cribs meeting product safety standards
- *Record keeping:* policies and procedures, financial statements, and health records for children and staff
- *Nutrition:* the requirement that children's meals meet *Canada's Guide to Healthy Eating* recommendations and are prepared safely
- *Behaviour guidance:* prohibition of certain kinds of discipline; encouragement of positive guidance strategies
- *Ratios/group size:* the specific number of staff required for the number and age of children served, in order to protect the safety of the children

An operation can be licensed when it meets the basic criteria in these areas. Licensing has traditionally looked after the safety and protection of children, although other important areas such as record keeping, staff qualifications, and personnel policies must also be assessed before a setting can be licensed. Obtaining a licence can be a long and complicated procedure. Delays are not uncommon, and coordination among agencies such as fire and health agencies is often lacking.

The licence must be posted in a conspicuous place. It identifies the name of the operator, the number of children permitted, and the period for which the licence is in effect, usually one to three years. The granting of a licence to a facility means that the province or territory also assumes responsibility for monitoring the centre or home to check compliance with standards. **Regular monitoring of a program** is an essential component of accountability. Families and the public need to be assured that, once a program is given a licence, it must continue to meet or exceed licensing standards. Monitoring can vary from unannounced spot checks to scheduled visits.

Doherty-Derkowski (1995), among others, view a lack of adequate monitoring as a contributing factor to poor quality EC programs. Adequate monitoring involves appropriately trained inspectors with a thorough background in early child development, assessing the quality of care in the EC program. There has been movement by a number of governments, away from experts in EC, toward a more generic inspector who may be less familiar with the nuances of environments and the needs of young children. At its best, the licensing process can go beyond basic checklist inspection to a model that encourages continuous quality improvement.

Enforcement practices range from the granting of conditional licenses and the removal of licences to fines and prosecution. In extreme cases, such as child abuse, flagrant lack of safety precautions, or outright negligence, a centre or home may be closed immediately, and its director, owner, or educator may face criminal charges. The effectiveness of regulations is tied to their enforceability through penalties for non-compliance.

There are issues with enforcement of regulations. Some provinces do not always provide the licensing office with sufficient funding and power to effectively enforce licensing rules. In some programs, untrained or poorly trained staff may be unaware of regulations or of how to meet particular regulations. Very few programs are actually ordered closed if they do not meet standards, since it is usually felt that parents and children are better served if licensing officials work in a consultative capacity to improve weak programs. In such a case, the program is usually given a provisional licence listing improvements that need to be made by a specific date. Up to this time, officials and/or consultants work closely with the director to bring the program up to minimum standards. If a condition is not met, then the operator may lose its licence.

No regulatory system can guarantee quality, and many EC facilities meet only the minimum standards required by their province or territory. Others operate at a higher level exceeding requirements. The minimum standards set by regulation should be considered the beginning of quality, not the end goal. In any case, it should not be forgotten that less than 19% of the total number of children in non-parental care receive care in a licensed or regulated setting (including regulated family child care) (Beach et al. 2009).

McLean (1994) reported that provinces and territories vary in how they apply sanctions, how frequently a program is visited, and the number of programs for which each inspector is responsible. In some provinces, including Nova Scotia, Ontario, Manitoba, and British Columbia, centres and homes are re-licensed annually. In Newfoundland, annual inspections must occur, but relicensing can vary from six months to up to three years depending on the facility. There is a difference between inspections and licensing. Licensing can be more of a paper exercise, whereas regular inspections are vital to the effectiveness of the licensing system. A current trend is for governments to reduce the frequency of licensing and monitoring visits to help cope with funding restraints. Since regulations are only as strong as the system of enforcement, this trend has generated some concern about the effectiveness of the licensing system.

There continues to be much change in provincial/territorial legislation concerning early childhood programs. For current information, consult your provincial or territorial office. Websites are provided in the appendix at the end of this book.

In some jurisdictions, the program director may be required to work simultaneously with municipal and provincial/territorial regulators. The regulations from the various bodies are not always totally compatible. It is the role of the operator to ensure that the program is in compliance. If the program is not in compliance, the operator runs the risk of having to delay the opening of a new program, pay fines, or in rare cases close down a program for failure to meet a licensing requirement.

An effective system of public regulation is the cornerstone of an effective system of ECEC services. But for the regulatory system to be most effective, other pieces of ECEC services system also must be in place, including:

- a holistic approach to addressing the needs of children and families that stresses collaborative planning and service integration across traditional boundaries of child care, education, health, employment, and social services;
- systems that recognize and promote quality;
- an effective system of professional development that provides meaningful opportunities for career advancement to ensure a stable, well-qualified workforce;
- equitable financing that ensures access for all children and families to high quality services; and

- active involvement of all stakeholders—providers, educators, parents, and community leaders from both public and private sectors—in all aspects of program planning and delivery.

---

10 PRINCIPLES FOR EFFECTIVE REGULATION

1. Any program providing care and education to children from two or more unrelated families should be regulated; there should be no exemptions from this principle.

2. Governments should license all facilities that provide services to the public, including all centers, large family or group child care homes, and small family child care homes.

3. In addition to licensing facilities, governments should establish complementary processes for professional licensing of individuals as teachers, educators, or program administrators.

4. Licensing standards should be clear and reasonable and reflect current research findings related to regulative aspects that reduce the risk of harm.

5. Regulations should be vigorously and equitably enforced.

6. Licensing agencies should have sufficient staff and resources to effectively implement the regulatory process.

7. Regulatory processes should be coordinated and streamlined to promote greater effectiveness and efficiency.

8. Incentive mechanisms should encourage the achievement of a higher quality of service beyond the basic floor of quality.

9. Consumer and public education should inform families, providers, and the public of the importance of the early years and of ways to create environments that promote children's learning and development.

10. Governments should invest sufficient levels of resources to ensure that children's healthy development and learning are promoted in early care and education settings.

Regulatory Requirements for Family Child Care Providers

Of the estimated 180 000 family child care providers in Canada, approximately 95% are not licensed or regulated (Goss Gilroy 1998). There are two models of regulated family child care in Canada. Some provinces and territories license agencies to monitor individual providers. Others directly license individual family child care homes. Newfoundland does both—licensing agencies and licensing individual family child care homes. While all provinces and territories currently have some system of regulated family child care, they also permit the provision of care outside the regulated EC system for a specified maximum number of children per home; a license is not required until enrolment exceeds a certain number of children. The ages and number of children permitted in family child care homes, regulated and unregulated, vary by region. All jurisdictions limit the number and ages of children permitted at any one time. Some providers choose to be licensed in order to participate in family child care support programs or enable parents to access subsidies. This process differs from the licensing of group settings where licensing is not optional.

The following provinces/territories license individual caregivers: British Columbia, Manitoba, Saskatchewan, New Brunswick, Prince Edward Island, the Yukon, and the Northwest Territories. Providers in jurisdictions that use the individual licensing model receive home visits from government officials. The number of visits ranges from one to four annually. Ontario, Alberta, Quebec, and Nova Scotia license agencies that monitor homes. Agency staff known as "home visitors" make regular visits to observe the care being provided. The required frequency of these visits ranges from twice monthly in Nova Scotia to four times yearly in Ontario and Quebec.

Provincial/territorial **legislation** concerning family child care may include standards, similar to group settings, covering the physical environment, safety, minimum age and training of the practitioner, health and criminal record checks, limits on age groups, the program offered, and meals and snacks.

The advantages and supports available to family child care providers working within the regulated system include:

- *Resources, training, and support.* Most jurisdictions have a variety of resources available that may include orientation sessions and start-up assistance, workshops, toy and equipment loans, mediation and assistance with problem solving, and playgroups for caregivers and children.

- *Financial incentives.* Some jurisdictions offer operating, equipment, and/or maintenance grants to licensed family child care homes; families that qualify for financial assistance can receive child care subsidies.

- *Administrative assistance.* Many ministries/departments and/or family child care agencies actually contract with parents and forms (e.g., for child's health information, emergency contacts, permission to go on an outing) and other administrative information and assistance to family child care providers.

Funding for Family Child Care

Regulated family child care providers in all jurisdictions can obtain government fee subsidies for eligible children. Start-up grants are available in Saskatchewan, the Northwest Territories, Newfoundland, and Labrador, and Yukon. British Columbia and Ontario fund a network of child care resource and referral programs with a mandate to assist in recruitment, support, and training of both regulated and unregulated providers (Doherty 2000b).

Role of Municipal Governments

Across Canada, EC has emerged on urban agendas. Forty per cent of Canada's population live in 20 cities. This trend toward urbanization is increasing. Early childhood programs, including child care, are a part of urban social/economic infrastructure with local government being the closest to providing services. Service impacts are felt primarily at the local level. The availability of services has a direct impact on the social and economic life of communities. With the exception of Ontario, Canadian cities do not plan, manage, fund, or operate child care. In Ontario, local governments have all four roles in early childhood settings.

Regulation

In some situations, municipalities and provincial governments work together to ensure that provincial requirements are reflective of municipal fire, health, and zoning bylaws. In addition to provincial licensing requirements, an EC program must comply with local ordinances. The local or municipal government generally sets requirements in the areas of fire, safety, health and sanitation, building codes, and zoning through bylaws. A program must meet all these standards before a license can be issued and it can accept children. A different department of the local government may administer each ordinance, and visits from several inspectors may be required.

Building codes and requirements concerning fire, safety, and sanitation have their statutory basis in public safety and health laws. The local fire department will require that an early childhood program have fire extinguishers, alarms, fire escapes, and a procedure in place for fire drills. Local health and sanitation authorities will inspect food handling, water, toilets, sewage disposal, hand washing and diapering procedures, and plans for meeting the needs of children who are ill. Local health departments may also set requirements for immunization and the monitoring of the health of both staff and children. Building codes cover such areas as the type of structure that can be used for a child care centre, and the local department of building safety will be concerned with plumbing, electrical wiring capacity, and other related factors. The local zoning agency will be aware of the building and safety requirements. Zoning requirements restrict the use of land. Each municipality can regulate the use of land and the erection and use of buildings.

Some municipalities have in place bylaws specifically governing family child care. In some communities, a business licence is required to provide family child care. In others, the number and ages of children permitted in family child care are restricted.

Anyone setting up an early childhood program needs to be knowledgeable about these regulations and how to meet them. Often a program hires a consultant to assist them in this area.

Funding

In most provinces, municipal involvement in child care is discretionary. Similar to senior levels of government, the attitudes of local politicians and financial priorities determine families' access to EC programs. Few municipalities have the tax base or the commitment necessary to adequately support social services such as regulated child care. In many cases, local governments do little more than ensure that facilities meet local bylaws. Municipalities may determine the rules for making subsidies available to individual families and administer payment of those subsidies. Income testing, needs assessments, and eligibility will vary from one jurisdiction to the next. Even within the same province, different cities may not be using the same guidelines or income cut-off points in their needs assessments. Thus, a family receiving a subsidy in one part of a province may no longer qualify if they move to another municipality.

Provincial fee subsidy funding may be directed to local governments through a transfer of payments for early childhood services. In some parts of the country, provinces have cut funding significantly. In other regions, regional budgets have been enhanced. Provincial and municipal social services budgets pay for social assistance as well as child care, and with the downloading of other costs, the provision of subsidies for child care has often had to take a back seat. A number of local governments have reduced the amount allocated to child care. When municipalities and provinces cut their funding, expansion of child care services, however necessary, becomes impossible, and it becomes increasingly difficult to maintain existing programs.

Municipally Operated Early Childhood Programs

Some municipalities operate their own EC services. Others enter into purchase-of-service agreements with existing community EC programs. Some local governments do one or the other, some do both, and a few offer no services at all. In Ontario, 47 CMSMs (Consolidated Municipal Service Managers) and DSSABs (District Social Service Administration Boards)—municipal and regional governments—are designated the "child care service system managers" and are legally obligated to manage services and fee assistance for families. As well, they play a significant role in providing direct funds for child care.

When a municipality embarks upon **purchase of services**, it contracts with a community program or agency to provide subsidized spaces. This may mean that the local government enters into an individual contract with an organization, either non-profit or for-profit, to enable parents receiving subsidy to use a certain number of its spaces. Often a local government will purchase services in geographical areas where high parental needs exist. The contracting procedure is analogous to letting a tender for road repair, where the municipality shops around for the best price, although some are concerned with quality as well.

Sometimes, local governments use a purchase-of-service agreement to raise the quality of services for children. **Fiscal monitoring** refers to standards associated with funding. When the government buys or creates a service through a grant or contract, it establishes certain conditions for quality. This can be done by imposing requirements additional to those required by the province, such as that a program must be on a clear licence and not a provisional one, or that all staff members must have particular qualifications. A purchase-of-service agreement may also be directed at specific groups of children, such as those needing infant/toddler care, school-age care, special needs care, or family child care. In Toronto, a community program that holds a purchase-of-service agreement must meet the standards set out in *Operating Criteria for Child Care Centres Providing Subsidized Care in Metropolitan Toronto* (Children's Services Division 2009). There is a similar set of criteria for home child care agencies and regulated family child care homes. These go above and beyond the provincial regulation requirements and help ensure higher quality.

In addition to the mandated municipal role in Ontario, a few other municipalities in Canada have taken it upon themselves to provide directly operated municipal programs. These include Jasper, Beaumont, and Drayton Valley in Alberta and Vibank, Bengough, Carnduff, and Pittville in Saskatchewan.

Milestones in Policy and Legislation

Pages 63–64 describe major social policy milestones in the development of Canadian early childhood programs. It is crucial that EC educators understand social policy, be aware of changes to legislation, and contribute to continuous improvement in early childhood services in Canada. We must ask ourselves:

- What will societal and governmental priorities be for early childhood services?
- What are the goals of the government policies and programs?
- Will new services be funded privately, by government, or through a combination of both?
- Will these new services be accessible and affordable to all parents and children in need of them?
- How can I advocate for quality early childhood services for children and their families?

Milestones in Policy and Legislation

1820s	Infant schools started in Halifax to increase the number of workers available as well as to provide care and education for children.
1850	Earliest crèches are established in Montreal provided by charitable organizations.
1885	Factory work by children under 12 becomes illegal in Quebec.
1887	Ontario, the first province to recognize kindergartens as part of the public school system.
1890	Ontario's first recorded child care centre, The Crèche, in Toronto; also functions as an employment agency for domestics.
1914	Jost Mission Day Care is founded in Halifax during World War I.
1916	British Columbia moves in terms of government intervention and support for child care services when the Crèche, founded in 1910, is placed under the jurisdiction of the provincial Health Department.
1918	First federal Child Tax Exemption introduced.
1920	Introduction of the *Mothers' Allowance Act* of Ontario provides welfare benefits to single mothers, enabling them to stay at home to care for their children.
1926	Dr. Hincks, a leading figure in the early mental health movement, and Dr. Blott, head of the psychiatry department at the University of Toronto, establish the St. George's School for Child Study (later the Institute of Child Study) headed by Dr. Blatz, the founder of Canada's EC movement.
1930	Mother's Allowance is given to two-parent families on relief.
1937	British Columbia licenses child care centres, becoming the first province to do so.
1942	The Dominion-Provincial Agreement for Wartime Day Nurseries enables any provincial interested in establishing child care facilities to cost share with the federal government. Ontario and Quebec are the only provinces to take advantage of this agreement. The other provinces maintain that they have no need for child care.
1945	Quebec closes wartime centres. In Ontario, a substantial public campaign keeps the centres open. The surviving wartime programs primarily serve children in low-income disadvantaged families. The Institute of Child Study (Toronto) develops the *Day Nursery Act*, then administered by the Welfare Ministry. Family Allowances introduced.
1950s	Dramatic rise in nursery schools, which serve as enrichment programs for children.
1960s	Insufficient number of child care spaces and the high cost of child care are issues for parents as more women enter the workforce. Regulated home child care is piloted in Ontario for infant/toddler care.
1966	Canada Assistance Plan (CAP) is passed by Parliament. Child care is included among social services for which the federal government agrees to pay half the cost of provincial subsidies for low-income families.
1970s	Royal Commission on the Status of Women calls for government recognition and expansion of quality child care services, stating that women will not achieve full equality without government involvement.
1981	Census reports that mothers in the workforce outnumber those staying at home. 52% of mothers participate in the workforce, and women make up 42% of the total workforce.
1984	For the first time, all three major federal parties make child care a campaign issue.

(continued)

1987	Statistics Canada reports that the participation rate in the workforce of mothers with children under the age of 16 has increased to 65%.
1988	Non-refundable federal Child Tax Credit replaces the Child Tax Exemption.
1989	Re-elected federal government announces it will reduce child poverty before 2000.
1990	Federal government limits annual increases to 5% on Canada Assistance Plan payments, signalling a withdrawal from the notion of universality.
1991	1989 United Nations Convention on the Rights of the Child is ratified by Canada.
1993	Federal Child Tax Benefit and Work Income Supplement replace Family Allowances.
1996	Federal government announces that the assent of a majority of provinces is necessary for the federal government to embark on any new social programs.
1997	Federal and provincial/territorial governments agree to develop the National Children's Agenda to improve the well-being of Canada's children. Quebec implements its $5 per day child care policy.
1998	National Child Benefit is implemented to build a co-operative approach between the federal and provincial governments to address child poverty.
1999	Federal, provincial, and territorial governments (excluding Quebec) sign the Social Union Framework Agreement (SUFA). SUFA sets the parameters for Canadian social policy.
2000	Early Childhood Development (ECD) Accord, **First Ministers**, with the exception of Quebec's, agree to commit $2.2 billion over five years to support early development of children.
2001	Parental leave benefits extended from six months to one year.
2003	Prime Minister Paul Martin states, ". . . an innovative society rests on strong social foundations. A learning society like Canada understands . . . the fundamental importance of early childhood development and of lifelong learning, which starts in infancy and continues well after the final degree is granted."
2003	Multilateral Framework on Learning and Care, a federal/provincial/territorial arrangement to invest in children under six, is introduced. Child Care Human Resources Sector Council established to address human resource issues.
2004	Federal government announces $1 billion annual federal program to expand EC services. Bilateral agreements signed with all provinces. Two years of funding were transferred.
2006	Election results in a change of government and the termination of all funding agreements related to the 2004 announcement as of March 2007.
2007	Harper government announces a $10 000 per space tax credit to employers or community organizations to create 125 000 child care spaces. This initiative is viewed as poor public policy, as previous attempts of this kind did not result in take-up of the credit.
2008	UNICEF published International study on quality, access, funding, and policy of ECEC. Canada ranked at bottom of 25 countries.
2009	In British Columbia, EC Agency created
2010	All ECEC moved under education in (PEI, New Brunswick, Ontario). Previously, Saskatchewan, Nunavut, and Northwest Territories placed ECEC under education.
2011	Full Day Kindergartens begun in many provinces.

Summary

ECEC policy is a complex area. As well as being concerned with child care and early education, EC policy is concerned with children's health, nutrition, social welfare, women's employment, equal opportunities, and poverty issues. To meet the challenges and needs of Canadian families, the focus of social policies and programs are ever evolving. The accumulated knowledge points to the long-term impact of experiences in early childhood for the strong intellectual and social development of children, and ultimately for society's well-being have a bearing on public policy.

Public investment in quality ECEC programs has been shown to be cost-effective. As a service to children, quality EC programs pay for themselves. James Heckman, a University of Chicago economist and winner of the Nobel Prize in economics, believes that investing in the very young is the most economically efficient investment society can make. That a society reaps a significantly higher return on its investment in EC programs than on its investment in post-secondary education or job training programs. In fact, the return on investment in education declines steadily as people age, while the opportunity cost of providing education remains the same.

There are fundamental challenges that impede the delivery of quality ECEC systems as well as the difficulty of getting the public support for the sustainable funding necessary. Governments express their priorities through funding allocations, such as federal transfer payments to the provinces and territories, income tax deductions, direct operating grants, wage enhancements, and family child care subsidies. Canada, unlike many European countries, is less-generous, relying on the free market rather than extensive government support to families and social programs.

Canada's Constitution specifies that the federal government does not have direct jurisdiction over education, health, or social welfare. All levels of government, federal, provincial territorial, First Nations and local, need to be engaged to play a role. Although there was some progress in the development of a national approach to funding ECEC from the late 1990s, progress stalled after 2006, with the cancellation of the national ECEC program. While as a nation, Canada has a long way to go to reach the commitment of resources, policy, and infrastructure levels of many other countries, the focus of EC policy has shifted to the provinces where there are some promising initiatives. Governments wanted to reap the social and economic benefits of investing in the learning of young children. This resulted in an expansion in the number of regulated programs, expansion of full-day kindergarten.

An estimated 3.5 million children need quality early learning programs while their parents are employed or attend school. When parents entrust such an important portion of their child's life to us, we must be the best that we can be. The provision of good early childhood experiences is an investment in healthy children. It contributes to child development, reduces child poverty, supports parents, and contributes to economic growth. The challenge is to persuade our governments to muster the political will to move the vision to reality.

Key Terms and Concepts

Fee subsidy,   p. 40

First Ministers,   p. 64

Fiscal monitoring,   p. 62

Legislation,   p. 25

Licensed program,   p. 56

Licensing,   p. 56

Monitoring,   p. 50

OECD,   p. 42

Purchase of service,   p. 62

Regulations,   p. 56

Activities

1. Would you make any changes to your province's or territory's legislation for child care? If so, discuss what you would like to see changed and explain why.

2. Construct your own "milestones chart" for legislation and other relevant facts for the last 24 months. Show what has been happening nationally, provincially/territorially, and locally. What changes would you like to see for children during the next 24 months?

3. Outline who in your local government parents should contact to apply for child care subsidies or financial assistance. Where are these officials' offices located? Are they easily accessible to families?

4. Make a list of the steps you would take to license a child care centre in your province or territory.

Recommended Reading

Bennett, J. *Early Childhood Services in OECD Countries: Review of the Literature and Current Policy in the Early Childhood Field*. UNICEF, 2008.

Friendly, M. *Child Care Resource and Research Unit. Canadian Early Learning and Child Care and the Convention on the Rights of the Child*. Toronto: Childcare Resource and Research Unit, 2006.

Beach, J., M. Friendly, C. Ferns, N. Prabhu, and B. Forer. *Early Childhood Education and Care in Canada: Provinces and Territories, 2008*. Toronto: Childcare Resource and Research Unit, 2009.

Organisation for Economic Co-operation and Development (OECD). *Starting Strong II: Early Childhood Development and Care*. Paris: Education and Training Division, OECD, 2006.

Weblinks

www.rightsofchildren.ca
Canadian Coalition on the Rights of Children
This organization is devoted to ensuring a collective voice for Canadian organizations encouraging rights for children. Its website provides resources and an interactive quiz on the United Nations Convention on the Rights of the Child.

www.childcarecanada.org
Childcare Resource and Research Unit
The Childcare Resource and Research Unit (CRRU) is a policy and research-oriented facility that focuses on early childhood education and child care (ECEC) and family policy in Canada and internationally. Its mandate is to promote universally accessible and high quality settings in Canada. It provides public education and policy analysis and publishes papers and other resources on child care policy, many of which are available online.

www.ccsd.ca

Canadian Council on Social Development

Canadian Council on Social Development is a non-profit research and advocacy organization focussing on economic and social policy issues and publishes the annual *Progress of Canada's Children* report.

www.nieer.org

National Institute for Early Education Research (NIEER)

The Institute conducts and communicates research to support high quality, effective, early childhood to policy makers, journalists, researchers, and educators. It explains the costs, outcomes, and economic benefits of alternative policies; develops and analyzes model legislation, standards, regulations, and other policies required to improve quality.

www.oecd.org

Organization for Economic Cooperation and Development (OECD)

The OECD's mission is to promote policies that will improve the economic and social well-being of people around the world. Their work is based on continued monitoring of events in member countries as well as outside. This site provides access to many highly regarded reports on ECEC.

Leadership and Governance in Early Childhood Programs

chapter 3

Objectives

- **Identify a variety of leadership roles.**
- **Describe the qualities that make a successful leader.**
- **Outline the roles and responsibilities of the administrative leader.**
- **Introduce director occupational standards.**
- **Discuss the evaluation of director's effectiveness.**
- **Describe ways in which programs are organized.**
- **Outline the roles and responsibilities of the governing body.**
- **Discuss the relationship of the director to the owner/board of directors.**

The Field of EC Is Changing

As a field, ECE is at a fork in the road. The direction we pursue will have direct impact on whether an effective system of services for young children and their families in Canada will be achieved or not. We need courageous leadership from within the field of EC. Through the past three decades, we have witnessed enormous growth in the number of programs and people working in the EC field. The knowledge base of the care and education of young children has exploded. Working with experts from a variety of disciplines, individuals in the field have widely disseminated the findings that the early years are significant. That EC, not only changes the life trajectories of all children, that effective programs can also fuel economic growth. The importance of child development and information about children's learning capacities are widely available to the public. Policy makers and business leaders have embraced EC and made it part of the national dialogue. Economic cost-benefit studies of high quality EC programs have provoked interest by business, economic, and education leaders in universal kindergarten as a credible way to reduce achievement gaps for children from both low- and middle-income families. As a result, public expectations have risen regarding the educational contributions of EC, accompanied by increased public and private investment. Overtime advocates have successfully increased provincial investments in EC. In fact, in the past few years, education has expanded its role significantly in the policy setting and regulating of EC programs with most provinces putting EC programs under the jurisdiction of Ministries of Education.

Consequently the field of EC has burgeoned into a large and fragmented industry characterized by a dramatic increase in the number of children, educators, as well as the numbers of families using the services. Accordingly, there are numerous challenges to making good the full promise of these EC programs, such as:

- staff recruitment and retention: many of the field's well-educated practitioners are approaching the end of their careers;

- most EC directors are not adequately prepared for their position;

- lack of investments in an infrastructure to support programs such as professional development;

- too often EC programs are mediocre; and

- many staff working directly with children to not have the skills and knowledge needed to achieve the child outcomes touted in the landmark studies referred to in Chapter 1.

In light of these new realities, the field must move beyond a reliance solely on individual leaders toward a creation of a community of leaders.

Leadership comes in many forms—leading a group of children in a new experience, leading a class of ECE students, leading a **board of directors**, ECE students preparing to become the next generation of leaders, being a principal within a school, leading a rally of ECEs to the legislature, and in many other ways. ECEs, like many leaders, don't always recognize this leadership skill within themselves. This chapter discusses the need for leadership at all levels—from EC student to experts at a pan Canadian level. The evolving and expanding role of the EC director is described in depth along with the responsibilities of the governing body.

Developing Leadership at All Levels

There is a need to foster more leadership and encourage all stakeholders to see their individual roles in the leadership process, regardless of their position. Sharing leadership opportunities is an inclusive process that not only makes use of the leadership potential of those around, it also enables the director not to feel solely responsible. No one pathway leads to making a difference in the EC field. Personal motivation, direct service with children, and academic education are among the experiences that guide educators to leadership positions.

In *Building Strong School Cultures*, Kruse and Louis (2009) note the importance building a culture that provides better opportunities for children, moving the former role of principal as heroic leader—a person with all the answers—to one of a facilitating number of staff engaged in leadership roles. What is needed to create this type of community are shared norms and values, reflective dialogue, and collaboration in which educators feel a sense of collective responsibility for children and outcomes. Paula Jorde Bloom in her book *Circle of Influence: Implementing Shared Decision-making and Participative Management* echoes that when more staff are cultivated as leaders, this synergistic effect increases the likelihood of better decision making. As well, the people involved in making the decisions will have a greater stake in ensuring that they are carried out.

Staff should have opportunities to demonstrate leadership.

When staff have an opportunity to demonstrate leadership at whatever level within an EC program, they have the opportunity to hone their leadership skills. At some later date, some of these staff may become administrative leaders. If they wait until they are in an administrative position to practice leadership, they may be set up for failure. A key way to facilitate these opportunities is to delegate leadership by stepping back in order to leave room for educators to step up.

Effective training for nurturing responsibility and leadership begins with those who supervise others—either staff, students, or volunteers. Responsibility in the workplace occurs when individuals feel they have some control over their work. In some environments, there is a strict procedure and process for every aspect of the work. These environments create a climate where there is no need to think—one just follows the highly scripted directions. Effective environments leave room for responsibility and leadership, where leaders step back, enabling others to step up and supporting leadership to happen.

This approach enables the administrative leader to form an effective team that functions well in her absence. An effective leader is intentional in creating stand-in or replacement leadership—whether temporary covering during an absence, or permanent when the leader moves on.

ECE students form another potential pool of leaders and have a variety of valuable skills. Some have demonstrated strong organizational capabilities, and many are leaders through school organizations and have taken leadership training. Involving students in activities that foster leadership and enhance their professional growth is rewarding for all. When interacting with students, mentors experience the passion and excitement they felt when they first entered the profession. Among the strategies to further develop leadership potential in ECE students include:

Encourage joining EC professional organizations and getting involved. Encouraging students to become active and recognizing their efforts when they accept responsibilities can facilitate their continued support. Delegating responsibility is the key to meeting the workload in a member organization. Students can make presentations, and introduce/thank speakers.

Demonstrate the need for advocacy. Some students have the experience of being placed or volunteering with an EC advocacy organization. These opportunities enable them to keep the student body informed about events and actions in the field and thereby develop a broader vision of the profession for both self and peers. Students can develop campus focus groups to lead students in discussing pressing issues, such as quality, funding, implementing standards, or equitable salaries.

Scope of Roles and Responsibilities of the Director

The responsibilities of being an effective **director** of an early childhood program vary depending on the size, type of program, and the auspices under which it operates. Different terminology is used to describe various types of directors. The term "administrator" refers to individuals administering, supervising, and/or managing an early childhood service, be it a private or non-profit early childhood program, a nursery school or university or college laboratory school, a family child care agency, a setting for children with special needs, or a family resource program. Other common job titles are "director," "manager," "supervisor," "teacher-director," "executive director," and "educational coordinator." Because of the broad professional expertise needed to carry out the job, such individuals are more appropriately referred to as "administrators," "directors," or "managers" rather than "supervisors."

Although the legal authority resides with the owner/s, in a non-profit program it rests with the governing body as discussed later in this chapter. This authority is delegated to the individual holding the title of director, who is responsible for the total program and services. In smaller programs, the director may function as both director and educator, regularly spending part of the day working with a group of children. A director of a small program usually handles all the administrative tasks, including record keeping and parental inquiries. Many directors do not work directly with the children, and some are responsible for multi-site operations—which involve travelling between sites and being aware of a variety of circumstances, children, families, staff, and environments. Some directors function as business managers and have other staff, such as an assistant director, administrative assistant, and/or accountant, to whom they may delegate specific tasks. Some directors are responsible to a board of directors or owners, others report to a **corporation**, a school board, a municipality, or a college's board of governors.

Increasingly, EC directors are working in school settings that require working closely with the kindergarten teachers and the principal. Some programs are seamless with kindergarten teachers and early childhood educators working as a team, whereas others are physically located in the school, but operate independently. Directors must be skilled in communicating the goals of early childhood with all levels of school personnel. In these settings, it is important that directors support efforts to develop children's conceptual skills before moving on to

EC directors now work closely with kindergarten teachers and the principal.

the advancement of specific skills and focus on child-centred learning, as well, to support the continuation of the strong parent-teacher relationships.

There is little doubt that directors wear many hats—from **budget** analyst to mentor to pedagogical leader. As elaborated in Chapter 4 "Planning and Evaluating the Program Goals," the director develops the vision and philosophy for EC settings based on principles of development and learning. She communicates the philosophy to families and staff. She builds the capacity of the setting to provide high quality, inclusive programs that consider the developmental needs of all children. Effective leadership creates a knowledgeable, stable staff team; a supportive workplace; opportunities for ongoing program planning and for continuous program improvement. It assures compliance with relevant regulations and guidelines, promoting fiscal soundness, program accountability, effective communication, and positive community relations. Leaders keep abreast of emerging trends in the field and reconcile this learning with the approach and content of the program provided. Providing opportunities for staff to receive **mentoring**, supportive supervision and to participate in ongoing professional development supports that their knowledge reflects the profession's developing knowledge base.

A MORNING IN THE LIFE OF A DIRECTOR

The job of director encompasses all aspects of the program and human resource management. Even with a daily plan, the director responds spontaneously to the ebb and flow of the day. For example, as a director walks in the door, she may learn that one of the staff has called in sick and no substitute has been found. She must call the roofers to repair a leak. A father approaches who is impatient to speak with her before he heads off to work. The payroll must be completed in order for the cheques for the staff to be prepared. There is a long list of "to do's" to get through before a board meeting this evening. With so many daily challenges, it is easy for a director to lose sight of goals and vision for the program.

To perform any of the above mentioned tasks, a director must have knowledge and skills. To perform them effectively requires exceptional leadership and communication skills. This individual must be able to bring out the best in varied groups of people: children, parents, staff, board members or owners, and stakeholders. More typically in small agencies, a director has worked her way up through the ranks from playroom educator can bring to the job a broad perspective on the functioning of the program. Similarly, it is easier to empathize with parenting pressures if one is a parent oneself. Experience in a variety of EC environments can help the director see a broader picture.

SCHOOL PRINCIPALS

With early childhood programs in many parts of Canada moving under ministries of education, there is a significant new player in the field—the school principal. The role of the principal is evolving and is likely to be dissimilar in different parts of the country. In some respects, the principal's role is similar to the governing body described later, while some functions may reside at the level of the school board.

Whatever the governance structure, the school principal plays an integral role and influences the quality of early experience a child undergoes. In *Toronto First Duty's Guide to Childhood Service Integration*, the role of the principal is described as overseeing the development and management of the early learning program by providing leadership, support, and direction to ensure that the goals and objectives are achieved. More specifically, principals set direction and collaboratively demonstrate the vision and values that are evident in everyday practice. As with administrative directors, they build relationships, support professional learning, and develop effective strategies for orientation as discussed in Chapter 5. A key role is building a collaborative learning culture within the school, and working with other schools to build effective learning communities. They provide pedagogical leadership ensuring that learning is at the centre of planning and resource allocation. Finally, they secure accountability ensuring that individual staff roles are clearly defined, understood, communicated, and evaluated.

Kruse and Louis (2009) note the importance of building a school culture that provides better opportunities for children, meaning principals must move from the role of heroic leader—a person with all the answers—to engaging a number of staff in leadership roles. Kruse et al. believe that principals need to move beyond the focus on curriculum and instruction to integrating the fragmented sub-cultures that exist in every school. Of course leadership at the district school boards is required to enable in shift in this leadership to occur through:

- Clarifying expectations;
- Establishing common values and priorities;
- Designing opportunities for communication and mutual learning;
- Building trust and modelling a culture of professionalism; and
- Thinking and planning strategically.

Need for Leader-Manager

This section identifies the differences between **management** and **leadership** and underlines the need for both to be a successful director (Figure 3–1). Mistakenly, leadership is sometimes considered synonymously with management. Traditionally, directors were seen as needing to be effective at implementation and execution of plans. Their role was to monitor, support, and control resources to ensure that tasks were achieved. They were primarily focused on the short term and accepting the status quo. Management involves working through individuals or groups to accomplish the program's goals and objectives. It refers to the day-to-day work required to achieve the program's vision and to make it a reality.

Unlike managers, traditionally, leaders were more focused on the future. The leader's role was to set targets, develop strategies, and communicate the vision—challenging the status quo Figure 3–2). Many directors acquired program management skills, failing to appreciate the importance of the skills of leading people. The EC field needs strong leadership to help programs to adapt and change to this rapidly transforming field.

The success of today's EC directors lies in their ability to be both leaders and managers, knowing when to manage and when to lead. Leadership relates to the broad plan of facilitating a program to clarify and affirm values, set broad goals, articulate a vision, and chart a course of action to achieve that vision as discussed in Chapter 4. Leadership involves motivating people

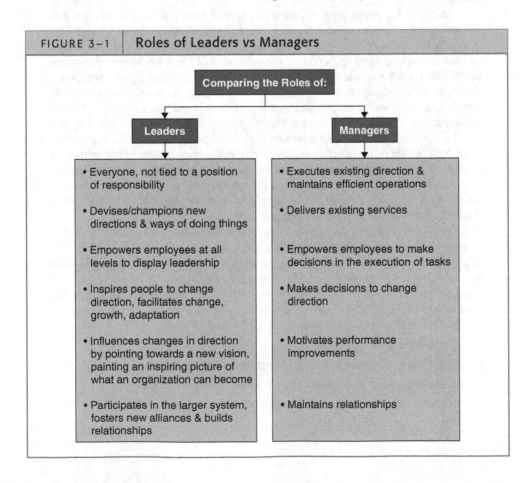

FIGURE 3–1	Roles of Leaders vs Managers

Comparing the Roles of:

Leaders

- Everyone, not tied to a position of responsibility
- Devises/champions new directions & ways of doing things
- Empowers employees at all levels to display leadership
- Inspires people to change direction, facilitates change, growth, adaptation
- Influences changes in direction by pointing towards a new vision, painting an inspiring picture of what an organization can become
- Participates in the larger system, fosters new alliances & builds relationships

Managers

- Executes existing direction & maintains efficient operations
- Delivers existing services
- Empowers employees to make decisions in the execution of tasks
- Makes decisions to change direction
- Motivates performance improvements
- Maintains relationships

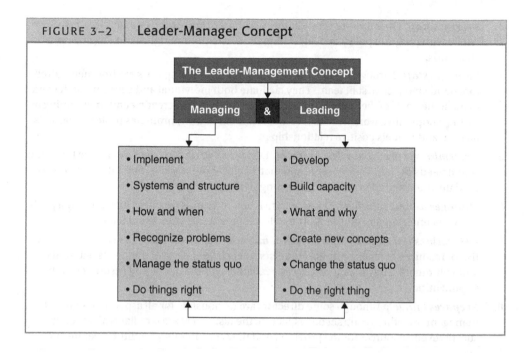

FIGURE 3–2 | **Leader-Manager Concept**

The Leader-Management Concept

Managing & Leading

- Implement
- Systems and structure
- How and when
- Recognize problems
- Manage the status quo
- Do things right

- Develop
- Build capacity
- What and why
- Create new concepts
- Change the status quo
- Do the right thing

to work willingly toward those objectives. It is no longer enough that directors know what needs to be done; it is equally important that they know how to motivate their employees to facilitate the tasks getting done.

Occupational Standards for Directors

There have been a number of efforts to delineate the specific skills and knowledge needed by directors. The Occupational Standards for Directors outlines the broad range of tasks, including the skills, ability, and the core knowledge needed to be a competent director of an early childhood setting. They were developed by the Child Care Human Resources Sector Council in 2006 through an extensive consultation process with directors across Canada. This set of **occupational standards** that follows complements the ones revised for early childhood educators (2010). Competencies should be revisited every four to five years to ensure that they align with changing expectations. People-focused competencies make up about half of the competencies in best-practice organizations. Although a director may perform tasks in most of the areas outlined in the competencies, he or she is not responsible for all areas. Tasks should be delegated to others, for example, a lead educator who makes program decisions.

1. *Develops and implements children's programs.* Directors build the capacity of the setting to provide high quality, inclusive children's programs that consider the developmental needs of the whole child.

2. *Creates child-centred environments.* Directors ensure the environment is physically and emotionally safe for young children as well as non-judgemental, welcoming, and respectful. They support staff to provide an effective learning environment and to protect children's rights.

3. *Recruits staff.* Directors are active in the recruitment and hiring of practitioners in accordance with program policy and legislation related to human rights and employment standards.

4. *Manages staff.* Through the creation of a positive, motivating work environment, directors build an effective staff team. They facilitate both individual and collective staff work to meet the goals of the setting. Directors serve as leaders in creating and maintaining a caring, cooperative workplace that respects human dignity, promotes professional satisfaction, and models positive relationships.

5. *Determines professional development.* Directors secure resources to provide for professional needs of staff. They observe and match staff abilities, skills, and interests to accommodate and respond to individual learning styles.

6. *Manages labour relations.* Directors use labour relations practices that support a positive work environment and support the development of a strong staff team.

7. *Determines requirements for external human resources.* Directors secure the expertise of resource teachers, physiotherapists, speech/language pathologists, students, and volunteers. They match resources available with the needs and resources of the organization.

8. *Prepares budget.* Although some directors are responsible for all aspects of financial management, others contract out aspects of the task. They are familiar with and pursue all revenue sources for the program, and they continuously monitor revenue and expenses.

9. *Manages revenue and expenditures.* In order to deliver the program and maintain stability, directors manage and monitor revenue and expenditures.

10. *Ensures a safe and healthy environment for children and adults.* Directors are vigilant and responsive to health and safety, arrange for appropriate **staff development**, and implement relevant policies and procedures. They ensure that the setting provides a nutritional program that responds to children's dietary and cultural requirements.

11. *Manages facilities.* To comply with municipal and provincial codes and regulations, directors generally work with others on facilities management.

12. *Creates a family-friendly environment.* Directors support families with their child rearing responsibilities. They have knowledge of family systems and different parenting styles, and community resources to support family wellness. They implement program practices to support families of diverse cultural, ethnic, linguistic, and socio-economic backgrounds.

13. *Creates and maintains links with the community.* Directors establish reciprocal relationships with organizations that can aid in achieving the program's goals for curriculum, health promotion, children's transitions, inclusion, and diversity.

14. *Participates in organizational policy development.* Directors ensure that the development of policies in human resources, financial management, and health and safety contributes to the overall effectiveness of program **operations**.

15. *Plans for the organization.* Directors ensure the viability and sustainability of inclusive, quality early childhood settings through the development of plans and strategies based on the needs of the community.

16. *Relates to governing authority.* Directors identify and gather information to inform the organization's stakeholders to facilitate the decision-making process reflecting the philosophy, values, and goals of the organization.

Defining Director Competencies

Research indicates that directors who carry out these multiple roles effectively and succeed in creating a quality EC program and supportive, collegial environment have strong educational and experiential backgrounds. There are several areas in which a director must excel.

Professional Education and Experience

An individual's professional education has been shown to be a strong predictor for high quality practices in both teaching and administration. The director sets the standards and expectations for the EC staff and creates the climate of the program, as a caring and educational environment for children. In fact, the study *Understanding Quality in Context: Child Care Centres, Communities, Markets and Public Policy (2010)* found higher quality in EC programs where directors who have higher expectations hire educators with certain skills, knowledge, and performance in classroom practices and child outcomes. The role requires a solid understanding of child development and the implications for the program. In addition, the director must possess the knowledge and skills to provide leadership, successfully manage resources, and engage in strategic planning. A key role of the director is to create and maintain a collaborative organizational culture. She must be clear on what makes her setting unique and why staff chose to work there.

ECE preservice professional education programs do not prepare graduates for administrative and management duties. Most education and training in early childhood prepares individuals to work directly with young children and families. Their preparation rarely provides them with the management skills, leadership, and knowledge they need to be successful directors. The study *Working for Change: Canada's Child Care Workforce* found that over half of ECE programs did not specify course content on legislation, financial management, or administration (Beach et al. 2004). Among those jurisdictions that stipulate specific training requirements for directors, Ontario requires a two-year diploma or equivalent and two years' experience—the longest period of experience required; Newfoundland and Labrador, Nova Scotia, Prince Edward Island, and Saskatchewan require only a one-year Early Childhood Care and Education (ECE) certificate. Manitoba requires directors to have some education in administration.

The majority of leadership and management training comes from workshops or seminars. Current provincial/territorial regulations have failed to recognize the importance the knowledge and skills of the director position. Few provinces require specific course work in administration and supervision for the licensure of directors.

Recognizing the importance of this leadership role in creating and maintaining quality experiences for children and families, there are now a number of specific degree, post diploma, and distance education programs. In Ontario, an Early Childhood Leadership, Bachelor of Applied Arts Degree is available, whose goal is to prepare EC professionals with program leadership ability in a variety of settings. Graduates are able to:

- guide and lead curriculum and pedagogy in licensed child care, family support programs, early intervention services, and full-day early learning kindergartens;
- design policies related to an emerging EC system;
- participate in applied research initiatives related to early child development and related program delivery.

Experience on the job provides a basis for evaluating both effective and ineffective practices. Experience with different ages of children and different program models can comprise a powerful laboratory for learning. *You Bet I Care!* found that most directors have substantial experience in the field: 64% had worked for 11 or more years.

Early Childhood Knowledge and Skills

Since a director's paramount responsibility is to ensure that settings for children are healthy, safe, nurturing, and provide opportunities for learning, she needs a strong foundation in the fundamentals of child development and educational programming and in practices that promote the inclusion of children with special needs. Directors provide leadership in creating, maintaining, and evaluating quality EC environments that support children's development and learning; promote respect for individual differences; and create a learning community of children and adults that promotes optimal child development and healthy families. The program must promote children's self-awareness, competence, self-worth, resiliency, and physical well-being. Directors need to understand:

- health, safety, and nutrition components necessary to optimize development;
- developmental patterns in early childhood and in school-age children and their implications for the program;
- environmental psychology and the arrangement of the environment to support development; and
- diverse family composition and background—cultural, socio-economic, and religious.

Pedagogical leadership requires a process of planning, implementing, and reviewing what children do and how they are doing. Although in *Investing in Quality: Policies, Practitioners, Programs, Parents: A Four Point Plan* (Best Start Expert Panel on Quality and Human Resources 2007) reported a lack of pedagogical leadership present—meaning the director was neither supporting nor expecting staff members to create, establish, and maintain environments that facilitated young children's learning and development, increased demands on directors for record keeping and documentation related to health and safety requirements and financial accountability often challenge their ability to provide pedagogical leadership.

Pedagogical leadership requires the director to have the ability to explain educational practices to staff, parents, and the public. The pedagogical leader is knowledgeable about, and able to apply current theories and research findings in early childhood education. In order to provide pedagogical leadership, directors need to support and value the development, implementation, and evaluation of a coherent curriculum. They set the stage with program practices that respect all families, provide leadership through the development of a vision and philosophy that guide the setting's curriculum and pedagogy, and create a workplace that values the work of educators through the provision of support and ongoing professional development.

INITIATIVE TO SUPPORT PEDAGOGICAL LEADERSHIP

Supervisors/directors are responsible to provide leadership for the design, delivery, and evaluation of EC programs, their curriculum and pedagogy. The curriculum begins with a clear vision that includes a unified purpose, philosophy, and values. Pedagogical leadership supports turning this vision into action. City of Toronto Children's Services partnered with George Brown College to offer the Curriculum and Pedagogical Leadership course to more than 800 directors. Ontario, like many other provinces, has a provincial curriculum framework, Early Learning for Every Child Today (ELECT), which guides all early childhood programs. During this course, EC leaders use this framework to review the curriculum and pedagogy in their own programs. Participants will integrate knowledge from empirical studies, practitioner research, and reflective practice. Among the topics included:

1. Analyzing the early human development that underpins ELECT and Full-Day Early Learning-Kindergarten Program.

2. Critique strategies to support diversity, equity, and inclusion and prerequisites for early learning.

3. Evaluate how partnerships with families and communities strengthen the ability of early childhood settings to meet the needs of children and families.

4. Demonstrate how curriculum planning supports early learning and development in early childhood settings from infants to school age.

5. Analyze evidence reported in academic journals and practitioner research in order to construct pedagogical strategies that encourage early learning and optimal development.

6. Demonstrate pedagogical leadership skills that cultivate knowledgeable and responsive staff.

7. Analyze observation and documentation tools to assess children's development progress and plan curriculum.

8. Implement program evaluation that complements and supports curriculum and pedagogy.

Management Knowledge and Skills

The effective administration of early childhood settings requires an understanding of business and management practices. Directors must demonstrate effective leadership needed to create environments for high quality EC programs by meeting and ideally exceeding provincial regulations and guidelines, community relations, creation of a learning community, and provision of a supportive workplace; including strategies to maintain stable, knowledgeable staff; and providing opportunities for ongoing program planning and career development as well as for continuous program improvement.

Directors need to administer the organization in a way that is consistent with legislative requirements, such as human rights, provincial regulations, employment standards, and the directions of the organization's **governing body**. Directors need to be knowledgeable about both provincial/territorial and local regulations, as well as professional standards pertaining to the education, care, health, and safety of young children—and they need to be able to develop and implement informed **policies** and **procedures** that promote quality practice.

Directors have the ultimate responsibility of providing the reliable information necessary to make decisions within the program and produce records necessary to aid the preparing of financial statements and reporting. Increasingly, directors are required to ensure that their programs are financially viable; consequently, they must understand accounting terminology and have skills in budgeting and **cash flow** management. They need to set service targets and rates, prepare financial reports, maintain insurance coverage, and know how to secure funding from a variety of sources, including government grant programs and donors. Directors need to develop yearly operating and capital budgets and policies and procedures for monitoring and controlling revenues and expenditures. In addition, directors need to implement procedures to maintain accountability for government funding. Directors must be able to use technology and use budget software.

FIGURE 3–3	Top 12 Director Training Needs

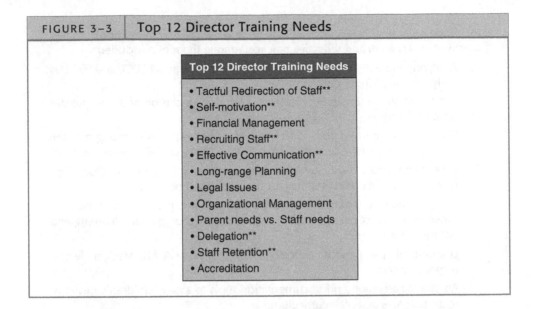

Top 12 Director Training Needs

- Tactful Redirection of Staff**
- Self-motivation**
- Financial Management
- Recruiting Staff**
- Effective Communication**
- Long-range Planning
- Legal Issues
- Organizational Management
- Parent needs vs. Staff needs
- Delegation**
- Staff Retention**
- Accreditation

A central theme that emerged from numerous reports and studies is the "weak culture" of human resource management that exists within the sector. The demands of balancing tight budgets and meeting regulatory requirements occupy director's time, leaving little attention for human resource issues. Directors oversee the systems for the supervision, retention, and professional development of staff that affirm program values and promote a shared vision. To accomplish this, they need expertise in staff supervision, mentoring and performance appraisal and clear policies to guide practices in areas such as conflict resolution, team communication, and employment termination. Directors identified the following areas that they felt they needed more skills and knowledge.

Six out of the 12 of these areas are related to managing people. Figure 3–3 identifies the top twelve training needs of directors. All of those marked with an asterisk are linked with issues related to human resources. These issues are explored more fully in Chapter 5, "Human Resources Management." It is critical that a human resource infrastructure (opportunities for professional development, mentoring, further education) is available to sustain an early childhood team.

Organization and Leadership Skills

Under the direction of the governing body and in co-operation with colleagues, the director is responsible for overall planning, implementing, monitoring, and evaluating the EC program in accordance with provincial regulations, quality standards and the program policies, procedures and philosophy. In the leadership function, directors help the program to clarify and affirm values, set goals, and implement a course of action to achieve the vision. As a manager orchestrates the tasks and sets up the systems to carry out the program's mission, directors need to ensure the many parts that make up the program work together and are part of the larger system. Directors have the ability to translate broad goals into concrete objectives and identify and secure the resources needed. They communicate the vision beyond the organization.

Directors are able to:

- develop, implement, maintain, and evaluate a vision, philosophy, and values;
- assist the governing body with strategic planning and the development of the program philosophy and policy;

- monitor and evaluate program effectiveness in meeting program goals and requirements;
- provide leadership in recruiting, selecting, orienting, supervising, and motivating staff to high levels of performance;
- support staff to create responsive environments;
- build and maintain a cohesive team; develop a work environment and culture with staff that supports the program mandate;
- utilize strategies of mediation and problem solving;
- translate program goals into well-written policies and procedures;
- understand leadership styles and group behaviour; and
- be aware of changing demographics, social and economic trends, and developments in the field.

Governing Body, Parent, and Community Relations Skills

Directors provide leadership creating a welcoming environment for all families and create collaborative partnerships with families. They set the tone for the program in establishing and supporting the family's role in their child's learning. This must include outreach to recent immigrants and newcomers and reflect the cultural, ethnic, and linguistic diversity of the population served. Directors promote the communication, cooperation, and collaboration between family and staff in ways that enhance the child's development. In addition, they need to maintain good relations with a broad range of **stakeholders**, including licensing authorities and community agencies, health, fire, subsidy, and school personnel in a way that enables representatives to articulate their needs, further the objectives of the program, and improve the quality of services.

Specifically, directors need to be able to:

- understand the dynamics and diversity of family life;
- interpret child development for parents and others in the community;
- respond to parents' questions and concerns;
- support educators in their work with families;
- utilize community resources that can support families;
- articulate a rationale for program practices to the board of directors, owner, or sponsor;
- work with professional organizations, legislative representatives, elementary schools, the media, and community organizations; and
- provide information to members and the general public to increase awareness of the field and the role of early childhood educators.

The roles and duties of directors are as varied as early childhood programs. Clear job descriptions can reduce conflict and uncertainty and provide a baseline from which to assess performance. Job descriptions should also identify the type of preparation required for the position.

JOB DESCRIPTION—DIRECTOR

JOB SUMMARY
Under the direction of the board of directors and in co-operation with colleagues, is responsible for overall planning, implementing, monitoring, and evaluating the ECEC program in accordance with provincial regulations, Toronto Operating Criteria

(continued)

and program policies, procedures, and philosophy. In the leadership function, helps the program clarify and affirm values, sets goals, and implements a course of action to achieve the vision. As a manager orchestrates the tasks and sets up the systems to carry out the program's mission.

QUALIFICATIONS

- Early Childhood Education Diploma
- Degree in ECE or related credential and/or post diploma certificate in Management of ECE, minimum 5 years experience
- Current registration with the College of Early Childhood Educators
- Maintains a current CPR and First Aid Certificate. Clear Police Reference check.
- WHMIS training, annually
- Verification of medical suitability of the successful candidate will be required as specified in the Day Nurseries Act

KNOWLEDGE & ABILITIES

- Demonstrates effective leadership needed to create environment for high quality ECEC programs by assuring compliance with relevant regulations and guidelines, community relations, creation of a learning community, and provision of a supportive workplace; including strategies to maintain stable, knowledgeable staff; providing opportunities for ongoing program planning and career development as well as for continuous program improvement
- Demonstrates understanding of mentoring and coaching skills, and knowledge of adult learning
- Establishes/maintains partnerships with program staff, families, board members community professionals, civic leaders, and other stake holders to design and improve services for children and families
- Demonstrates a solid foundation in principles of organizational management
- Establishes systems for smooth program functioning and managing staff to carry out the mission of the program
- Demonstrates understanding of emerging trends in child care sector and ability to relate to program administration
- Actively involved in local ECEC community
- Builds and maintains effective community resources
- Demonstrates awareness of sector-wide trends and issues
- Displays good understanding of the ECEC supervisor role and has knowledge of the Occupational Standards for Child Care Administrators
- Displays problem solving by using judgment and ability to analyze and respond to situations effectively; timely decision making
- Demonstrates leadership, flexibility, creativity, and innovation
- Knowledge of bookkeeping, accounting; skill in budgeting, cash flow, grant writing and fund-raising

- Advocates on behalf of high quality ECEC services to meet the needs of children, families and staff
- Contributes to team cohesion through demonstrates effective team building skills; provides clarity in team goals

JOB RESPONSIBILITIES

1. Provides leadership in creating, maintaining, and evaluating high quality ECEC environments
    - Develops, implements, maintains, and evaluates a vision, philosophy, and values
    - Creates a learning community of children and adults that promotes optimal child development and healthy families
    - Provides pedagogical leadership to ensure that curriculum meets standards for quality programming
    - Monitors and evaluates program effectiveness in meeting program goals and requirements
    - Provides direction to staff in setting, implementing, and evaluating curriculum goals appropriate to program mandate
    - Assesses program effectiveness for children's learning and identifies supports needed
    - Manages environment requirements and specifications based on children's strengths and needs
    - Uses administrative practices to promote/support the inclusion of children with special needs
    - Collaborates with team and families, recommends the referral of children to community agencies
    - Incorporates intervention programs, such as speech therapy, to meet the individual needs of children
    - Participates in educational assessment conferences with community agencies
    - Uses knowledge of nutritional and health requirements for food service; ensures children have adequate nourishment and any special dietary requirements (culture, allergies, and so on) are met
    - Monitors the quality of the work and guides the improvement process
    - Ensures activities are aligned with the programs strategic directions
    - Develops a work environment and culture with staff that supports the program mandate
    - Uses effective methods to facilitate team behaviours through creating team agendas, keeping notes, maintaining schedule of upcoming meetings/ agenda items

(continued)

- Maintains files/uses effective time management/project management/ evaluation strategies
- Facilitates team meetings to discuss the implementation of the overall program, share information, and discuss progress of individual children
- Collects accurate enrolment statistics and tracks monthly statistics
- Uses effective marketing and enrolment strategies; manages wait list
- Processes enrolment of children, at all times is aware of license capacity, staff ratios and administrative details (registration forms, medical records, and permission forms)
- Maintains legal, financial, children, and personal records in accordance with policy and the required legislation
- Recognizes, documents, and takes action in cases of suspected child abuse, illness, or accidents, and demonstrates knowledge of the laws pertaining to child abuse

2. Oversees systems for the supervision, retention, and professional development of staff that affirms program values and promotes a shared vision
   - Provides leadership in recruiting, selecting, orienting, supervising, and motivating staff to high levels of performance
   - Interacts and collaborates with colleagues and other professionals in ways that demonstrate respect, trust, integrity, and accountability
   - Builds and maintains a cohesive team
   - Reviews communication and log books, monitoring consistent use by staff
   - Appoints a designate as needed
   - Keeps staff informed of changes affecting the program
   - Employs strategies to maintain stable, knowledgeable staff through providing a supportive workplace
   - Prepares job descriptions for each position
   - Plans and carries out a comprehensive staff orientation in collaboration with program coordinators
   - Supports staff involvement in professional development and community activities
   - Maintains personnel records and personnel handbook
   - Facilitates team focus on their goals, manages relationships
   - Creates a learning community; supporting career development and learning
   - Reviews and provides feedback on written communications and prepared materials, checking for reflection of ECE principles, policies as well as for accuracy and content
   - Creates an environment where the team is motivated and productive
   - Monitors the quality of work and guides the improvement process
   - Inspires and motivates excellent performance in ECERs

- Arranges, plans, and conducts regular staff meetings, which update and educate
- Uses a variety of supervisory and group facilitation styles
- Demonstrates knowledge and application of group dynamics, communication strategies, and techniques for conflict resolution
- Resolves performance problems
- Inspires acquisition of new skills
- Uses individual coaching strategies
- Participates as a resource and/or mentor through sharing professional experiences, resources, and role modelling best practice
- Determines requirement for, screens, orients, and monitors external human resources
- Ensures feedback provided to ECE students that supports their theoretical training.

PERFORMANCE MANAGEMENT

- Participates in establishing job requirements and goals
- Provides staff with the opportunity to discuss all aspects of their work performance in a confidential manner
- Provides continuous assessment of staff development needs; identifies competencies of overall team
- Facilitates probationary and annual reviews; utilizes probationary periods with clear and fair expectations
- Uses documentation tools to chart performance and goals
- Evaluates team and plans for improvements; identifies need for, develops, implements in-service training
- Adapts leadership style to individual staff/students
- Demonstrates effective team building and group facilitation skills; provides clarity in team goals
- Models and facilitates reflective practice in others
- Demonstrates confidence in managing interpersonal conflict
- Consistently uses conflict resolution and group dynamic understanding skills
- Manages problem performers
- Recommends to board and/or provides discipline when necessary in accordance with the policies and procedures
- Develops a process (detailed in personal policies) for terminating employee/employer relationship

3. Develops and maintains community/professional relationships
    - Maintains good relations with all licensing authorities and community agencies (health, fire, subsidy office, school, and so on)

(continued)

- Represents and promotes the program in the community
- Keeps informed of current trends in ECE and is aware of and takes advantage of professional development opportunities
- Co-ordinates student and volunteer placements; liaises with college faculty
- Works collaboratively with organizations: schools, public health, library, community colleges, and universities
- Advocates for young children, their families, and staff
- Maintains a friendly and professional attitude with colleagues and community professionals

4. Has ultimate responsibility, provides reliable information necessary to make decisions within the program, and produces records necessary to aid preparing financial statements/reporting fulfilling criteria as detailed in Operating Criteria

- Prepares and manages budget, determines/monitors revenue sources, estimates expenditures for board of directors
- Applies knowledge of bookkeeping, accounting; skill in budgeting, cash flow, grant writing, and fund-raising
- Works with board to develop the annual budget; monitors the budget by reviewing the organization's financial status on a monthly basis
- Sets and collects parent fees; develops accounts receivable report
- Purchases supplies and equipment as required within budgetary limits
- Maintains adequate records of payroll, deposits, equipment, and supplies
- Prepares monthly reports on expenditures
- Monthly cash flow forecast; variances between actual and forecasts
- Determines expenditure priorities
- Follows preauthourized transactions
- Provides leadership in fundraising activities

5. Provides leadership creating a welcoming environment for all families and works in a collaborative partnerships with families

- Demonstrates respect for all families and recognizes the centrality of the family to the health and well-being of children
- Demonstrates respect for diversity, equity, and inclusion principles in work with young children, families, and communities
- Relates to families of diverse racial, cultural, ethnic, and socioeconomic backgrounds
- Respects differences in families' child-rearing values and practices
- Facilitates parental involvement and education
- Develops responsive relationships with parents of every child
- Responds to inquiries and/or requests for meetings from parent
- Contacts parents regarding illnesses and documents symptoms/communications

- Maintains confidentiality of family information and discussions
- Applies knowledge of family systems and different parenting styles
- Uses community resources to support family wellness
- Encourages and provides opportunities for families to participate in planning and decision making for their children
- Encourages parent feedback, conducts an annual parent questionnaire

6. Demonstrates leadership to create and maintain high quality ECEC programs by assuring compliance with relevant regulations and guidelines; implements opportunities for ongoing program planning as well as for continuous program improvement

   - Works in accordance with practices, detailed guidelines, and procedures available in policy, procedure manuals, and Public Health and consults ECE staff, board of directors in any new or unfamiliar situations
   - Be aware of policy changes; maintains an appropriate knowledge of legislation, quality practices, policies, and procedures that directly affect their professional practice
   - Contributes to the program complying with the Day Nurseries Act, City of Toronto Operating Criteria, other required legislation and adheres to all program policies
   - Contributes to development of , monitors and evaluates program policies
   - Follows employment standards and other HR related legislation
   - Establishes and implements healthy working conditions
   - Develops, implements, and evaluates ongoing communication strategies with team, board, and other stakeholders
   - Contributes to the evaluation of program and recommends modifications to improve effectiveness
   - Reviews team structure and mandate
   - Advises and supports the functioning of board of directors; participates in board meetings and work groups, and other functions
   - Prepares and presents reports to board of directors
   - Implements direction from board of directors and regulatory officials
   - Fulfils recordkeeping responsibilities, including:
     - Annual General Meeting and Board meeting minutes
     - Submits annual budget, audited financial statements, insurance renewal certificate, lease renewal to city
     - Wage subsidy and wage improvement utilization; Pay Equity report
     - Maintains legal, financial, children, and personal records
     - Maintains up-to-date records for each staff including (medical, employment contracts, police clearance, membership CECE, and so on)

(continued)

and conducts two behaviour guidance observations on each staff member annually.

- Completion of all required documentation such as attendance records, planning charts, child record counts, daily playground checklist, serious occurrence, flushing records etc.
- Enrollment management, procedures to wait list management
- Maintains fee records, invoices, receipts, tax receipts; city invoices
- Ensures that an annual playground report is completed annually
- Develops strategic business and annual operational plans

7. Fulfills health and safety responsibilities in collaboration with families, staff, and health professionals

- Responsible for the fire safety plan procedure and regulations under the Fire Code
- Ensures medication is labelled properly and administered according to policy
- Reviews menu plans ensuring that nutritional needs of children are being met
- Records and conducts monthly fire drills
- Ensures that all health and safety reports are completed
- Ensures that the daily playground checklist is completed and recorded daily
- Ensures that all playground checklists are completed
- Ensures the WHMIS binder up to date, adding data sheets for all products being used within the program
- Ensures that all chemical products are stored and locked appropriately at all times
- Ensures that all equipment is safe and/or repaired/discarded when necessary
- Trains all staff in health and safety procedures yearly
- Ensures that personal protective equipment is used as necessary
- Performs employee health and safety observations
- Understands supervisor roles and responsibilities of the Ontario Health and Safety Act

8. Actively demonstrates responsibility for own personal/professional growth and development to enhance practice and decision making.

- Demonstrates the ability to be a reflective leader and applies a repertoire of strategies
- Acquires an understanding of adult and career development, dispositions, and learning styles
- Participates in professional development activities to maintain a current knowledge of ECE theory, practices, and issues

- Keeps current on human resource legislation/issues, budget reporting, and so on
- Demonstrates understanding of emerging trends in child care sector and ability to relate to program administration
- Keeps current on curriculum issues
- Engages in ongoing professional learning, reflective practice, and critical thinking
- Accesses current evidenced-based research and transfers this knowledge into practice
- Participates in the performance appraisal process with board of directors
- Demonstrates capacity to problem-solve and make good choices
- Ability to evaluate ethical and moral dilemmas based on Code of Ethics
- Practices and promotes the ethical responsibilities in Code of Ethics
- Maintains confidentiality at all times

Stages of Director Development

As directors gain experience in their roles, they undergo a series of changes in how they view themselves and their jobs. They face similar problems and frustrations in each phase, but their ability to handle problems changes as they move toward maturity. Anthony (1998) applies a systems and human ecology theory to create developmental stages for directors and suggests possible professional development strategies for each stage, modelled on the work of Lillian Katz.

In the first stage, the director is working to understand her new role and administrative responsibilities. Attention is often at the microsystem level focused primarily of what goes on in each classroom. There is often limited understanding of the influence of the larger systems as discussed in Chapter 1. A strategy of trial and error is often employed. New early childhood directors must acquire additional competencies while they are establishing their authority and leadership. It is important to appear in control and become comfortable exercising authority. Success as an EC educator does not guarantee success as an administrative leader. New directors must establish credibility by being highly visible to staff and parents. New directors need to seek professional and emotional support from a variety of sources, including other directors, board members, and staff as well as their own personal support system. Some become part of a network that meets on a monthly basis. Through these experiences, they can acquire and apply knowledge from the wider sphere of EC professionals.

Among the developmental tasks at this stage are:

- mastering the essential organizational tasks of the job;
- learning to cope effectively with crises that arise;
- formulating a self-image as director;
- learning new skills while managing one's own level of stress;

- staying focused on what it takes to get the job done; and
- recognizing the importance of commitment to the job.

The director's professional development needs at this stage include ongoing feedback on performance; learning how, when, and whom to ask for support; acquiring a lot of new information on business practices, budgeting, **organizational structure**, policies and procedures, and human resources management; and, finally, learning techniques for managing stress and promoting health.

In the second stage, the director is managing organizational tasks well, is more comfortable in a leadership role, and has more realistic expectations of herself. She is consolidating gains, extending her knowledge and competence, strengthening her leadership, raising staff expectations, and strengthening relationships with staff. She looks for sources of support among associates in similar fields and other directors in similar positions. This reliance on professional contacts lessens the burden on personal relations. During this stage, the focus is on:

- managing specific areas in depth (e.g., staff development, family involvement, budgeting);
- developing broader areas of expertise;
- learning effective time-management skills, such as delegation and how to say no; and
- seeking support from outside the program.

Some strategies to help a director develop in these areas include visiting other programs, taking courses linked to administration, attending workshops and conferences on specific topics, and reading publications, such as *Child Care Information Exchange.*

By the time a director has reached stage 3, she is confident and secure in her role. Focus shifts from the classroom microsystem to their program's interactions with families and communities as exemplified in Brofenbrenneur's mesosystem. With increasing experience, these leaders gain an even wider perspective. They appreciate how government funding for social services, employment, and the education system, which are part of the exosystem, impacts children, families, and the program. They become more proactive, recognizing and respecting the strengths of staff members, she now promotes leadership and responsibility. Problem solving is viewed as an ongoing task. The areas requiring further development are:

- balancing the needs of people and operational tasks;
- identifying one's own strengths and limitations; and
- developing an effective, forward-looking vision for the program.

Strategies the director might use to achieve these goals include acquiring information to strengthen her awareness of how differences in personality types and communication styles can affect working relationships with both staff and parents, learning about the policies and procedures of other programs, and putting more effort into evaluating the program's effectiveness.

With sufficient experience, and a capacity for reflective practice, administrators reach the final and most influential stage. This stage is marked by an understanding of the complex, overarching system—Brofenbrenneur's macrosystem. She now has vision, and the ability to translate that vision into a reality that embodies ideals and can transmit those ideals to her practice. The director is mature and has dealt with a variety of problems and challenges. She possesses the characteristics of a mature professional: possessing self-knowledge, self-confidence, an in-depth understanding of problems and issues associated with her work including the impact of social policies, and the skills necessary to do an effective job. Seasoned directors know and evaluate themselves. They recognize and respect the strengths of their staff members. She may be looking for new challenges. The focus will be on:

- mentoring others, such as staff or new directors, and sharing professional expertise;
- taking on a leadership role in advocacy and becoming active in professional organizations such as those listed in the appendix; and
- finding new challenges and refocusing her energy.

The professional development focus is on sharing and giving rather than just taking in information, finding new projects and challenges through professional linkages, conducting workshops and writing, and expanding the existing program.

Growth through these stages is ongoing and frequently uneven. During their careers, directors may move back and forth from one phase to another when they work in new roles or unfamiliar settings. In some cases, directors may not move beyond the first two stages. Every director's approach to the job differs based on the background and previous experience. Careful attention to professional development and support can enhance success, increase job satisfaction, and prevent burnout.

CANADIAN INITIATIVE TO BUILD THE SKILLS OF EC LEADERS

Recognizing the need for opportunities for seasoned directors to have leadership development to address social policy, the Canadian Child Care Federation and the Muttart Foundation created an initiative in both Alberta and Saskatchewan. The focus is to facilitate the development of provincial and eventually, national leadership. The Early Learning Leader Caucus Project involves the development of two regional caucuses, which provide opportunities for early learning stakeholders to come together to first, address some the common leadership issues that directors face on a daily basis, and just as importantly to build on their individual and their respective communities' capacity to participate at both a policy and system level—regionally, provincially, and nationally. The project recognizes that in order to build coherent and realistic public policies for ECE, those working in the sector need to not only demonstrate the skills necessary to run a quality EC program, as well as to communicate to elected and government officials about what is needed at the policy level. Additionally, directors require the skill and capacity to interpret and communicate to the EC sector and the public what impact those government policies might have. The Early Learning Leader Caucus Project utilizes a mentoring approach to facilitate new leaders who will have the abilities and skills to meet these ambitious and essential objectives.

Leadership Attributes of an Effective Director

As previously stated, most leaders of EC programs come to their positions with little experience or education to prepare them for the awesome task of trying to create and maintain a quality EC program, combined with less-than-adequate facilities and resources. However, whatever the external factors, one has the power to shape the environment. Leadership toward that end has the potential to contribute to social change. A leader affects everyone involved in the EC program and influences the character of the facility. The leader has a major impact on the organizational climate—the attitudes, beliefs, and values of the individuals involved in the work setting. A strong leader helps others improve their job performance and inspires them to meet new challenges. An effective director is a person who combines skills and knowledge, with compassion. Not everyone excels in all of these ways at once. The following attributes are all characteristic of leadership.

Communicating a Vision

When a director has a vision for the program, it gives the work meaning. A vision inspires one to act. When a director believes she is building an organization that will make a difference, she exudes an enthusiasm that energizes everyone in the program—children, parents, staff, board members/owner, and community. The raw material for the vision is the collective views of the families; the vision is defined and articulated by the governing body, using information supplied by the director. Creating a vision expresses the organization's deepest values about children, family, work, and community. Organizations do not in themselves have values; the values that guide organizations come primarily from their leaders. A visionary director gives voice and unleashes the passions of her staff. They appreciate that the collaborative relationships with families are at the heart of the program. They realize their potential as advocates for social change.

Next, the director must translate the vision into achievable goals and motivate people to achieve these goals. By clearly communicating an organizational goal, such as "encouraging cooperative behaviour" or "expanding the program to include a family resource centre," the director can focus on the resources and efforts of the program toward achieving that goal. (Leadership and the program vision are discussed further in Chapter 4, "Planning and Evaluating the Program Goals," as well as in the resource The Visionary Director (2010)).

Determine whether the Program Is Meeting Its Goals

A director needs to keep her finger on the pulse of the program and continually assess the performance of the organization. The progress of the organization toward accomplishing its goals can be monitored using both informal and formal methods as discussed in Chapter 4.

As noted earlier, in addition to being aware of what goes on inside the centre, the director must keep up with changes in the EC field. The director needs to follow relevant trends in research, technology, government funding, business, and society in general. She can then better assess whether the program's goals and policies, such as the programs offered and hours of operation, are meeting the needs of current and potential users of the service.

Select Priorities

With many competing demands, it is essential for a director to focus her attention on areas where additional effort will have the most impact. Once the day starts and the myriad of telephone calls, visitors, and unexpected small crises compete for the attention of the director, it may seem impossible to stick to an agenda. The director must select those tasks that will provide maximum benefit to the program. She must learn to use a variety of time-management strategies, such as grouping, delegating, and planning a timeline. Voice mail, e-mail, and other electronic communication approaches are used to keep both in touch and in control of one's time.

An effective director will determine how well the program is functioning by:

- observing the program daily on an ongoing basis;
- arranging, planning, and conducting regular staff meetings, which update and educate;
- conducting parent interviews that will assist in determining whether the program is meeting its goals for the children;
- using anonymous parent and employee surveys on a regular basis; and
- obtaining feedback from the children themselves.

Encourage Participative Management and Leadership

A key leadership strategy is to develop an effective team. As noted earlier in building leadership, a director must recognize that she cannot accomplish everything by herself. Developing an effective team takes time and effort, but when educators participate in making decisions that affect them, they experience greater job satisfaction and higher morale. Team members can be given greater responsibilities and provided with opportunities to develop more skills. Involving people in making decisions gives them a greater stake in carrying them out.

A director doesn't work to make people love her but rather to make people love working with her. Employees' willingness to work hard will ebb and flow, in part depending on their current attitude toward their work and the director. Staff must be motivated to achieve the goals of the program. In part, this is achieved by involving staff in setting the program goals (Jorde Bloom 2000). To build commitment to the goal setting process, a director should involve staff members to shape goals they personally care about. Then they will have an investment in the accomplishment of these objectives. A sign of an effective director is to value both the individual and collective voice of the staff.

It is necessary to construct a stimulating and secure working environment for staff. To achieve this responsive environment, the director will have high expectations, respect the employees' autonomy (give them full responsibility for carrying out tasks), arrange opportunities for professional growth, provide feedback on performance, recognize achievements, encourage collaboration, foster creativity, and be there as a resource when needed. By delegating certain managerial responsibilities, the director can focus on specific tasks that only she is responsible to carry out. Participative management is based on the belief that when more people participate, a synergistic effect increases the possibility of better decisions. (These topics are elaborated on in Chapter 5, "Human Resources Management.")

Be an Effective Decision Maker

The skilled director recognizes that both logic and emotion are part of making decisions. She knows when to offer support, when to delegate to those who have the expertise to act on their own, and when to shoulder the responsibility. At times it is necessary to reverse a decision or insist on implementation in the face of opposition. To build credibility, it is important to be decisive. If a director takes forever to make routine decisions, fails to follow through on decisions previously made, or is inconsistent in decisions made about similar issues, then staff will doubt the director's ability and judgment. It is important to solicit staff input before making decisions. Occasionally, a director must admit that she is wrong and reverse a poor decision. Decisions must be made in a timely fashion, and they must be announced clearly and without apology.

Finally, a director must keep her work life in perspective. A fully committed effort at work does not preclude a life outside of work. A successful director understands the relationship between health and professional performance. She exercises regularly, eats well, and has a sense of humour; she is a model for her staff. It is useful to become involved in networking groups where directors can share with other directors the joys and frustrations of their jobs.

What Staff Expect of a Director

Establishing credibility as a director of an organization is not a one-time event; credibility must be built continuously—and occasionally rebuilt. Meeting mutual expectations and establishing trust is how a director achieves credibility. When a director strives to meet staff expectations, she can legitimately have certain expectations of the staff:

Staff expect a director to make good decisions. Many of the decisions a director makes involve financial, organizational, and tactical factors that few staff are aware of. Staff must trust that the director is balancing all these factors and making decisions that are in the best interests of the program. It is critical to keep staff in the loop about issues facing the program—both good and bad. However, there are times when the director has information that must be kept confidential.

Staff expect directors to listen. It is demotivating to believe that others do not respect your judgment. Employees need to believe the director values their opinions and takes their input seriously. Time needs to be created to discuss issues in a rational way.

Staff expect directors to have expertise. Staff respect directors who are knowledgeable and understand what is needed to deliver a quality EC program. They need to know that if they have a problem, they can turn to the director and get the support and guidance they need. Directors need to keep current with child development research and other aspects of knowledge listed in the director competencies outlined above. There is a link between this and the following point.

Staff expect directors to know what is going on. A concern occasionally expressed by staff is that the director is out of touch with what is happening on the floor. Directors must understand and care about the day-to-day issues that staff face. It is important to visit playrooms and be aware of issues faced by staff.

Staff expect directors to be fair. Staff must be convinced that they are treated fairly when it comes to scheduling, compensation, supervision, attention, and opportunities for advancement.

As with all positions participating in a performance appraisal process and evaluating one's own performance on an ongoing basis is a key aspect of being an effective director.

Evaluating Director's Effectiveness

There is usually an abundance of opinion about the director's performance—from the governing body, employees, parents, community members, and the director herself. The process used to evaluate a director's performance should provide a mutually supportive and professionally enhancing experience for all involved.

Performance appraisals are conducted annually. However, with a director who is new to the position or organization, it is appropriate to schedule more frequent sessions—perhaps twice during the first year. More frequent appraisals can also be useful in situations where the board and the director want to enhance their communication. The next step is to determine which criteria will be used to assess performance. Ideally, the director and board of directors will determine together which criteria will be used. Having a detailed job description provides a solid place to start. See detailed job description provided earlier in the chapter. Generally, a committee of the governing body is responsible for evaluating the director.

Enough time should be set aside for the process; a couple of meetings are usually required. Input about the director's performance can be sought from the following groups: parents, staff, **colleagues** of the director, funders, and other board members. After the feedback is compiled, a written report is prepared by the committee and reviewed with the director. The evaluation process is a valuable strategy for improving services to children and families.

FIVE TRENDS IMPACTING LEADERS

1. Emphasis on quality and accountability. There are greater demands for accountability that require directors to implement quality assurance strategies for the program, demonstrated children's learning, and performance appraisal systems that monitor, document staff performance and reporting on the overall quality of the setting.

2. Heightened competition for qualified early childhood staff. Attraction and retention issues continue to challenge early childhood programs. Retaining knowledgeable staff who are nurturing, knowledgeable, motivated, and committed to early childhood as a career is a challenge.

3. Pressure of integrating early childhood education into broader social service systems.
   In order to serve children and families in a more comprehensive manner, many early childhood programs are forging stronger linkages with education, health, and social service delivery agencies.

4. Greater competition for financial resources. There is strong competition for adequate levels of funding requiring expertise of the director and the governing body. The levels of funding provided by government and the ability of parents to pay do not cover the costs of effective early learning and care environments.

5. Serving children and families with more diverse needs. There are more children and families with diverse linguistic, cultural, ethnic, and religious backgrounds as well as children with special needs. Leaders need to resource opportunities for staff to continually develop their knowledge and skills to meet the needs as well as secure technical support and consultants.

Ways in Which Programs Are Organized

In Canada, early childhood programs may be operated by **non-profit** organizations, commercial or independent operators, or public organizations such as municipalities, and school boards who offer kindergarten and increasingly manage child care programs. It is essential for the administrative leaders to understand the functioning of these various structures.

The term **"auspice"** refers to the legal status and ownership of programs. The issue of auspice has often been a contentious one in Canada. One side of the discussion holds that child care is a **public good** and that privately operated centres should not profit from caring for children and that early childhood programs should be a fully funded public service (like education) or a community-based non-profit service supported by government funding, as it is in Quebec. The adherents of this view further believe that private businesses should not profit from government funding. They also question the ability of commercial ventures to provide both high quality care and turn a profit. Supporters of commercial child care often argue that caring for children is the responsibility of individual families. Their position is that, even if governments assist individual families to pay for care, governments should not determine where parents choose to send their young children. This is founded on the belief that the family, not the state, has primary responsibility on decision making for their child. They further argue that commercial programs are cost-efficient and focused on customer service. Different provinces and territories have adopted different ideological and legislative stances with respect to auspice and the funding implications of auspice.

Most programs are non-profit and sponsored by social service agencies, parent-run organizations, municipalities, colleges and universities, or churches. Some non-profit programs are stand-alone organizations operated, according to legal bylaws, by a voluntary board of directors that may include parents, community representatives, and individuals with specific expertise. A non-profit program might be operated by an agency such as the YMCA, Canada's largest not for profit organization. In a non-profit program, any budget surpluses must be invested back into the program or returned to the sponsoring agency.

Volunteers are more likely to work in various roles in a non-profit program, and training institutions in some parts of Canada are more likely to use non-profits for student placement experiences. Parents are often unaware of the legal status of the program they select for their children and tend to choose a setting based on cost or location.

Commercial programs, also referred to as "proprietary" or "**for-profit**" programs, are privately owned businesses. The director is responsible to the owner, who determines the organizational structure. About 25% of Canada's EC programs are commercial businesses, ranging from small owner-operated programs to larger chains. Most proprietary programs are found in Newfoundland and Alberta, while Saskatchewan has no commercial child care programs. These Canadian figures stand in sharp contrast to those for the United States, where about 60% of all child care programs are commercial operations. Presumably, government incentives for non-profit programs, or the lack of them, are reflected in these numbers.

Some programs are run as a public service under the auspices of a municipal government. This is almost exclusively in Ontario. Chapter 2 elaborated on the roles of municipalities.

Some Canadian companies have created EC programs to support the child care needs of their employees. They recognize that parents/employees with young children will need to deal with child-related issues while at work. These programs are quite expensive to operate and are very small in number. To support their workers' child care needs, some employers join with other employers to operate a program run by a consortium of employers.

Each province and territory has legislation that governs for-profit and non-profit corporations. Commercial programs distribute their profits to owners or shareholders, while non-profits are required to reinvest surpluses back into the organization. Non-profit organizations must have a board of directors that makes key decisions and manages the organization. In for-profits, owners may make decisions with little consultation with staff and or families. These differences may influence to some extent the primary goals of the organization. Non-profit programs will aim for a balanced budget, while for-profit programs will wish to turn some profit. Lyon and Canning (1999) note that these goals may influence the priorities of the organization (such as staff qualifications), and this in turn affects the quality of service offered.

The establishment of a non-profit program involves filing articles of incorporation. A non-profit corporation is a legal entity. The corporation protects individuals from certain liabilities by creating a decision-making board of directors. Corporations remain legal entities until dissolved by the board of directors or a court. Several documents, such as the bylaws of the organization, are required to incorporate. Board members are prohibited from any personal gain by virtue of their involvement with the organization. If the non-profit qualifies for charitable status, they are more likely to receive charitable donations from individuals and corporations.

Decision making tends to be more complex in non-profit programs, where there are more players and procedures. One challenge is that volunteer board members often do not have sufficient time to invest in thoroughly understanding all the educational, political, demographic, legal, and financial issues involved in operating an early childhood development program. Consequently, they may delegate some of the decision making to the director and follow her recommendations. Non-profits with boards of directors made up of diverse individuals may be more aware of broader changes in the community and more skilled at finding new sources of revenue.

In general, it is much easier and less expensive to set up a for-profit organization. It is too simplistic to believe that individuals who operate for-profit programs are driven solely by a desire for economic gain. Most early childhood entrepreneurs believe strongly in the importance of early childhood development and see their business venture as making a difference for children and families. Many of these small owner-operators struggle to break even. In fact, because the development of child care programs has occurred haphazardly over time, local for-profit operators may have stepped in when governments or other non-profits were unable to provide a service in a community.

Governing, Operational, and Advisory Boards

A governing body is responsible for the EC program responding to the needs of the community it serves and operating effectively. **Governance** refers to general and legal oversight of the operation. It relates to consistent management, cohesive policies, processes, and decision rights for a given area of responsibility. It does not implement the day-to-day operations, which remain the responsibility of the director and staff.

There are three types of boards: governance, operational, and **advisory**. A **governance board** makes and enforces policy and makes decisions that are binding upon the program. Governing boards are usually in place when the EC program is part of a larger organization. The governance board has direct accountability for the legal corporation and hires the director as its management representative to whom it delegates day-to-day operational authority for the program. The scope of authority for each level of management must be clear and cover all operational aspects. The director must have a clear understanding of what decisions she can make herself and what needs the approval of the entire governing board. For example, staffing and facility issues will fall under the scope of the director unless there is a fiscal impact that goes beyond the approved budget discussed in more detail in Chapter 9 "Financial Matters."

An operational board typically takes on some of the tasks that may normally be undertaken by senior staff, such as overseeing financial statements, meeting with bookkeepers, attending meetings with government officials at licensing time, or representing the organization at community meetings. The difference between governance and operational boards is typically related to the availability of staff infrastructure in the EC organization such as having access to accounting, HR departments, or both.

Advisory boards serve as a resource for the program by reviewing matters brought to them. Members are selected based on their areas of expertise. However, an advisory board/committee has no power to enforce; instead, it suggests policies and procedures or provides information to those who administer the program. They can recommend courses of action or strategies for improved practice. Management may follow, modify, or in extreme cases, ignore recommendations. Advisory boards do not need consensus and may give management a number of approaches from which to choose.

Both governance boards and operational boards may set up parent advisory committees. A parent advisory committee may meet several times a year. Its members act as consultants to the director of the program; they offer advice, resources, and raise any concerns about issues that may affect the program's quality. (Chapter 8, "Building the Partnership with Families," elaborates on parent involvement on boards.)

Skills and Knowledge of Governing Body

The size of a board of directors can range from as few as 3 members to 10 or more. The bylaws of an organization prescribe the minimum and maximum board sizes. The board should be small enough to act as a deliberative body. Small boards can be cohesive. Large boards provide an opportunity to diversify member representation, expertise, and responsibility. Early childhood organizations with a small staff can lack critical expertise and may rely on the community connections and support that can be provided by a board. In order for a larger board to function well, it needs an effective chairperson working collaboratively with the administrative director, as well as effective procedures and decision making.

Most early childhood programs include some parents on the board. Participation gives parents the opportunity to influence policies that govern the program and staff. Some boards have a chartered public accountant serve as treasurer or chair of the finance committee. A faculty member from a local college or university can bring expertise in curriculum and advice on how to meet the developmental needs of children to the board. The board should include someone with knowledge of health issues, such as a public health nurse or paediatrician. For a new organization, a director from another early childhood program in the community can bring firsthand knowledge of the issues faced by the program, such as setting appropriate fees and developing schedules. A board member with expertise in human resource issues is essential. This is not an exhaustive list. At various times, members with particular skills—from fundraising and public relations to facilities construction—may be required.

Defining Governing Bodies Responsibility

In *Maximizing Child Care Services: The Role of Owners and Boards,* Ferguson and McCormick Ferguson provide a framework for getting the best out of early childhood programs. Governing bodies play a key role in the provision of quality. In an early childhood program, the role of the governing body can be defined under six headings:

- *Direction.* Sets the direction for the provision of quality services, defining what the service intends to achieve and the client base.
- *Guardianship.* Hires, monitors, and evaluates the director and ensures that the resources necessary for the provision of a quality service are available so that the director can carry out her responsibilities in an efficient and effective manner.
- *Public Relations.* Ensures that the program is promoted and represents the organization to the public. Speak out on the organization's behalf and contribute to public discussions on policy and societal trends that affect early childhood services.

- *Advocacy.* Advocates to government, the general public, and the business community regarding the inherent value of early childhood programs.

- *Legal Conduct.* Ensures that all legal requirements of the organization—including employment and tax laws, licensing regulations, and business and incorporation laws—are being met.

- *Ethical conduct.* Upholds prudent and ethical best practices—to ensure that all actions of the organization and its representatives are carried out in an ethical manner.

These areas of responsibility are interrelated. More specifically, the governing body's responsibilities include:

- Create and review the **mission statement**, bylaws, and policies that govern the program, and review them annually. Develop all long-range and strategic plans.

- Ensure that the program meets the needs of the children, families, and community.

- Ensure that the program meets all legal requirements.

- Develop the annual budget; monitor the budget by reviewing the organization's financial status on at least a quarterly basis. Ensure that financial controls are in place to protect revenue.

- Meet regularly, and maintain accurate records of board meetings and operations.

- Actively participate with the administrative staff in overall planning process and assist with implementation of program goals. Ensure the director has the support needed to carry out the goals of the organization.

- Define qualifications, authority, and responsibilities of the director. Hire the director; facilitate an annual evaluation of the director's performance.

- Ensure that fair hiring and HR policies are established and implemented. Serve as a final appeal in disputes as specified in policies.

- Annually negotiate staff salaries, benefits, and working conditions.

- Survey families and employees to regularly evaluate the quality and effectiveness of the program. Recognize achievements and identify areas that can be approved.

- Serve as a link to the larger community (families, the public, government, media, . . .), promoting the program and advocating on its behalf.

There are purposeful practical and legal reasons why the governing body and staff should share some of the program responsibilities. These responsibilities may be augmented through the program contracting services to accountants and/or HR specialists. Following is a brief description of the generally accepted roles and responsibilities of each player.

Committees

The work of the governing body is often carried out by committees, although some small boards operate without them and large boards may have delegated responsibilities to staff if the infrastructure permits. Committee responsibilities are spelled out in the organization's bylaws. Some of the typical standing committees are executive, finance, human resource, program, and property. On occasion, ad hoc committees may be appointed by the board to perform specific short-term tasks and then report to the board. The chairperson may appoint members to each committee on the basis of their interests and expertise.

The *executive committee* is generally composed of the board's officers—the chairperson or president, treasurer, and secretary—with the administrative director serving as an

ex officio member. This committee advises on actions to be taken and changes to be made. It conducts board business between meetings and, in an emergency, can act for the full board. The president or chairperson is the designated leader of the organization and often speaks for the program at public meetings. The chairperson and the director need to develop a close working relationship and have regular contact between board meetings. The treasurer chairs the finance committee and works closely with the director to develop and monitor the budget. The secretary keeps minutes of all board meetings and the annual general meeting. Other duties involve updating bylaws and handling all correspondence specific to the board of directors.

The director assists the chairperson, helps volunteer committee members to implement action, and provides ongoing feedback on the impact of decisions on the day-to-day operations. The director functions as a resource person, assists in the recruiting of board members, ensures the development of an agenda, and takes responsibility for implementing assigned tasks. Administrative services such as mailing, copying, cheque writing, and so on are usually carried out by the director or her staff. As well as the director, other staff may be invited to attend board meetings, but none have a vote. Minutes of board meetings are often posted so that staff and families can monitor board proceedings.

Financial oversight of the program is usually assigned to a *finance committee*, which is chaired by the treasurer and includes the director as a member. This committee reviews the organization's revenue and expenditures, balance sheet, investments, and other matters related to the program's financial situation. They follow preauthorized transactions as detailed in standards such as the City of Toronto Operating Criteria.

It is responsible for submitting the annual operating budget to the board of directors for approval, comparing income and expenses to the approved operating budget, and arranging for the annual audit. Because they help prepare the budget and appropriate the funds, finance committee members must have a good understanding of the overall operation and the program philosophy. More on this is discussed in Chapter 9.

The *human resource (HR) committee* administers the organization's most valuable resource—its employees. The cost of salaries, payroll deductions, and benefits exceeds 60% of an EC program's total operating budget. The percentage is higher in high quality programs that offers better salaries and working conditions. Since staff are the means by which services are delivered, their skill level, job satisfaction, and commitment to the program, children and families served, all contribute to that effectiveness. It is the board's responsibility to establish the human resource policies that govern the employment of program staff. Human resource policies must reflect the legal requirements concerning employment—such as employment standards or health and safety requirements—and the specific policies of the program—such as vacation and sick-day accrual, employee performance evaluations, and **grievance procedures**. (HR policies are elaborated on in Chapter 5.) The board may also be responsible for approving and revising job descriptions and setting salary levels. In essence, the board of directors provides the framework within which the staff, through the director, is managed. The director implements the HR policies. The HR committee is responsible for hiring the director, preparing her employment contract, evaluating her performance, and, if necessary, firing her.

The responsibility for finding and maintaining a facility rests with the *property committee*. The busiest time for the property committee is prior to the launch of a program, when the committee must decide whether to purchase, construct, or lease a facility, and make decisions about renovations. They must also ensure that the program meets all zoning restrictions and bylaws. Once the program is established, the program director usually takes on the responsibility for the physical environment issues; however, the committee may continue to ensure that the building and grounds are clean, safe, and attractive, and that program equipment is maintained.

Enhancing or replacing major equipment may also come to the committee for approval within the context of budget expenditures.

As along with the program and strategies for family involvement, the *program committee's* responsibilities may include the professional development program for the staff. This committee recommends policies to the board on enrolment and grouping of children; the hours and days of operation; the learning program; and health, safety, and nutrition.

Other standing or ad hoc committees may include a fundraising, nominating, and/or grievance committee. The *fundraising committee* is charged with soliciting donations of cash, equipment, or services (such as printing or computer consulting). It may take on special-event planning, such as raffles, and other forms of community fundraising. The *nominating committee* screens potential new board members, and prepares a slate for election by the board of directors. It may be responsible for orientation of new board members. A *grievance committee* may be formed to act as a mediator for parent or staff complaints. This committee must be careful not to undermine the authority of the director and cause even greater problems.

The board of directors sets the overall direction of the program and is held legally accountable for its actions and decision making.

Working Effectively with a Governing Body

Since the board of directors and the director share responsibility for the operation of the program, effective communication between them is essential. The governing body is responsible for the overall operation of the program. Its members are elected at an **annual general meeting (AGM)**. Some boards are composed primarily of parents, while others include representatives from the community. In practice, board involvement runs the gamut from high-level governance to ongoing involvement with some day-to-day operations. Some directors cite boards that get involved in the day-to-day running of the program as their biggest concern, as they may undermine the authority of the director. Ideally, a board should function somewhere between these two extremes by carrying out clearly defined functions related to the organization's human resources, finances, facility, and program. Transparent, clear communication and decision making is essential to have productive EC environments.

Many boards meet on a monthly basis. In addition, a designate of the board must keep in close contact with the director. The director serves as the liaison between the governing body and the parents and staff. She both uses the board's knowledge to improve the program and helps the board to understand the rationale for decisions made based on her specialized knowledge of early childhood and the needs of families. Individual board members may have expertise in financial management, fundraising, human resource issues, health, property, or lobbying for children and family rights. Many board members are new to community work and need a comprehensive orientation to their responsibilities and this responsibility usually falls to the director.

Summary

The expanded EC field must move beyond a reliance solely on individual leaders toward a creation of a community of leaders. There is a need to foster leadership and encourage all stakeholders to see their individual roles in the leadership process, regardless of their position. An effective leader brings skills, knowledge, and commitment to the job. Directors fill a variety of roles, but all must balance the management and operation of the program with leadership and the support of and communication with the people who are the essence of a quality environment.

A smooth running governing body operates with the support of committees whose functions relate to the major components of the program's operation (finance, human resources). The principle responsibilities of a governing body include strategic planning, acquiring financial resources, and advocating for the program. Good communication between the governing body and director is essential for a well-run organization. The board creates policies and the director implements them. The board of directors of an early childhood program needs to develop policies and procedures that will serve as the guidelines for achieving program goals. The effective operation of the program depends upon the leader's ability to interpret and carry out a mission by fostering leadership, collaboration, and motivating all toward a collective, shared vision.

Key Terms and Concepts

Advisory board,   p. 97

Annual General Meeting (AGM),   p. 101

Auspice,   p. 95

Board of directors,   p. 69

Budget,   p. 72

Cash flow,   p. 79

Colleague,   p. 95

Corporation,   p. 72

Decision making,   p. 97

Director,   p. 71

Ex officio member,   p. 100

For-profit,   p. 96

Governance board,   p. 97

Governing body,   p. 79

Grievance procedure,   p. 100

Leadership,   p. 73

Management,   p. 73

Mentoring,   p. 72

Mission statement,   p. 99

Non-profit,   p. 95

Occupational Standards,   p. 75

Operations,   p. 76

Organizational structure,   p. 90

Policies,   p. 79

Procedures,   p. 79

Staff development,   p. 76

Stakeholders,   p. 81

Activities

1. Arrange a visit with the director of an early childhood setting. Discuss how much time is spent on various aspects of the job, such as communicating with the parents, staff, children, owner/board of directors, community stakeholders, and funders; keeping financial records; responding to emergencies; and so on.

2. Arrange with a director to attend a board of directors or advisory committee meeting. What topics were discussed? How were decisions made? What are your perceptions of the functions of these bodies?

3. For each statement that follows, indicate whether the primary responsibility rests with both the board of directors and the director (B) or only the early childhood development director and staff (S). If you feel that both are responsible, list them in order of level of shared responsibility:

   a) drafts the centre's annual budget for approval _____

   b) establishes HR policies _____

   c) plans fundraising events _____

   d) approves legal contracts and agreements _____

   e) analyzes unusual budget line-items (revenues and expenses) _____

   f) recommends new service directions for the program _____

   g) is legally responsible for the affairs of the centre _____

   h) writes grant proposals/applications to public/private sources _____

   i) prepares reports for funding agencies _____

   j) maintains the centre's financial records _____
   (Answers on next page.)

4. Identify a list of advantage and disadvantages of having parents on the governing board.

5. Identify the characteristics of a director that you respect.

Recommended Reading

Carter, M. and D. Curtis. *The Visionary Director: A Handbook for Dreaming, Organizing, and Improvising in Your Center, 2d ed.* St. Paul, MI: Redleaf Press, 2010.

Culkin, M., ed. *Managing Quality in Young Children's Programs: The Leader's Role.* New York: Teachers College Press, 2000.

Child Care Human Resources Sector Council. *Occupational Standards for Child Care Administrators.* Ottawa: Child Care Human Resources Sector Council, 2006.

Doherty, G. "Standards for Quality Child Care Programs"; "Standards of Practice for Administrators/Directors." In *Partners in Quality: Tools for Administrators in Child Care Settings.* Ottawa: Canadian Child Care Federation, 2000.

Goffin, S. and V. Washington. *Ready or Not: Leadership Choices in Early Care and Education.* Columbia University, New York: Teacher's College Press, 2007.

Jorde Bloom, P. *Circle of Influence: Implementing Shared Decision-Making and Participative Management.* Lake Forest, IL: New Horizons, 2000.

Jorde Bloom, P. *Leadership in Action: How Effective Directors Get Things Done.* Lake Forest, IL: New Horizons, 2003.

Marotz, L. and A. Lawson. *Motivational Leadership in Early Childhood Education.* Clifton Park, NY: Thompson, Delmar 2007.

NAEYC, NAEYC Code of Ethical Conduct for Early Childhood Program Administrators, July 2006.

Nolan, M. *Mentor Coaching and Leadership in Early Care and Education.* Clifton Park, NY: Delmar, 2007.

Sciarra, D.J. and A.G. Dorsey. *Leaders and Supervisors in Child Care Programs.* Albany, NY: Delmar, 2002.

Weblinks

www.childcareexchange.com
Child Care Information Exchange

This is a publication for directors of early childhood programs. The website has a comprehensive list of resources on program development, organizational management, planning and evaluation, and more. Additionally, ECEs can subscribe to ExchangeEveryDay, an electronic newsletter containing news stories, success stories, solutions, and trend reports.

http://cecl.nl.edu
The Centre for Early Childhood Leadership at National-Louis University

This site is dedicated to enhancing the management skills, professional orientation, and leadership capacity for early childhood administrators. The activities of the centre encompass four areas: training, technical assistance, research, and public awareness.

www.boardsource.org
National Centre for Non-Profit Boards

This site provides many hard-to-find resources, including books and videos on topics such as board ethics, bylaws, board basics, and strategic planning. Most helpful are comprehensive question-and-answer features, sample job descriptions for each member of the executive, and questions one should ask when considering joining a non-profit board of directors.

Answers to question 3 based on commonly applied organizational wisdom:
a) S, b) B, c) B/S, d) B, e) S, f) S/B, g) B, h) S/B, i) S, j) S.

Planning and Evaluating the Program Goals

Objectives

- **Describe a vision of an early childhood program.**
- **Define program philosophy.**
- **Examine the purpose and implications of a philosophy statement.**
- **Identify the steps in developing a philosophy statement and program goals.**
- **Policies and procedures reflect the goals and values of program.**
- **Identify roles in determining and implementing the program philosophy and goals.**
- **Using the vision to inform practice.**
- **Evaluating programs for indicators of quality.**
- **Describe the characteristics of effective program evaluation tools.**
- **Identify tools for evaluating program quality.**

Building a quality early childhood program requires creativity, energy, and resources. The director is charged with knowing the goals of the program, supporting involvement of families, staff, and stakeholders in implementing, assessing, and evaluating the program against the vision. When the performance falls short, she must take action to address the problem. Ongoing quality depends on staff development, mentoring, and support. Monitoring for quality involves appraising program performance, how the program functions as a whole, as well as the staff performance. It involves looking at the satisfaction with the program from the perspective of the children, staff, and parents as well as the impact of concrete elements of the environment. Leadership in the design and review of the program vision is crucial; it is the director who will lead efforts to put this vision into practice.

With increased public investments in early childhood, there are higher rates of accountability for programs such as government and public websites for families. In determining the level of quality, directors, families, and staff need to be involved in regular program evaluation that measures progress toward the program's goals and objectives. Among the areas that should be included: program quality, quality of children's experience on a daily basis, staff well-being, children's development and learning, family and community involvement, and overall satisfaction.

What Is a Vision in Early Childhood Programs?

Quality in early childhood settings rests on the goals, values, assumptions, and principles that guide the program. A vision of quality extends beyond a concern for good care and education, health, and safety to encompass children's total well-being and development. The program is thought of as the total experience of the children in the setting, not just those activities that might be termed "educational." The vision includes the program's relationship with each child and family. It acknowledges that children and families live and grow within different cultures and that all cultural beliefs and values deserve respect.

The report *With our best future in Mind* presents a vision for establishing a strong foundation in the early years. Ontario has implemented a full day kindergarten where in partnership with parents, young children will access quality programs that will help lay the foundation for a healthy and productive life.

OUR BEST FUTURE IS ONE WHERE CHILDREN ARE

- Healthy and secure;
- Emotionally and socially competent;
- Eager, confident, and successful learners;
- Respectful of the diversity of their peers.

Pascal, C., With our best future in Mind: Implementing Early Learning in Ontario, Ontario, 2009.

A vision imparts a realistic, credible, attractive future for the organization and provides direction for what the program strives to become. It is who we are, what we do, how and why we do it, and who we do it for. A vision for early childhood programs is formed using a combination of information and knowledge (relevant professional guidelines such as the Canadian Child Care Federation's quality statement) and a concern for the well-being of the **stakeholders** of the program who will, in turn, benefit from the implementation of the vision. The vision can inspire stakeholders to focus on goals and as well as energize them to work proactively to achieve them. It provides a dynamic concept for the future that motivates an organization to make changes, incorporate new ideas, and take new directions. It is through the process of working to achieve a vision that a program can achieve excellence. The vision first needs to be articulated, then owned by those who form it, and, finally, a strategic plan to achieve the vision needs to be outlined and followed. The philosophy is a statement of the values underlying the vision.

Defining a Program Philosophy

Today, some envision early childhood programs as the neighbourhoods of the twenty-first century, poised to transform the cultural ills of society through mutually respectful and empowering relationships among those who inhabit these neighbourhoods. Whereas, others may have a more limited vision of a place where children are cared for in a safe, loving environment. Every program needs its own vision of what it intends to be. This then becomes reflected in the daily activities, such as children's play, interactions between children and staff, interchanges between families and staff, and the way staff feel about themselves and others as they go about their work in the program. Everything about the program should be considered in light of this vision of quality: how the program looks, how it sounds, and what it expects from all involved.

The philosophy is a statement of beliefs reflecting the program's value system, based on theory and guided by research. A well thought-out educational philosophy articulates intentionality and demonstrates that the program knows what it is doing and why it is doing it? The statement defines the nature and purpose of the organization to families and the public at large. A **mission statement** may be used instead of "**philosophy.**" The philosophy of an early childhood setting determines the characteristics of the program; it has a direct impact on the development of the curriculum, the qualifications of the staff hired, the extent of family involvement, and interaction with the community.

After determining the vision and mission statement, the next step in planning is to set program goals for serving the children and families attending the program. After determining the needs of children and families, key stakeholders (parents, staff, board of directors/owner, community representatives) work to define the **philosophy** and decide how to shape the program to reflect it. Once program goals are chosen, decisions regarding the policies, human resources, physical facilities and equipment, family involvement, and so on should be consistent with the goals. The director's role is to act as the catalyst to facilitate the program goals. She must determine the process by which goals will be met, operationalize the strategies necessary to meet the goals, and evaluate the progress the program is making in fulfilling them.

Some envision EC programs as the neighbourhoods of the 21st century.

> ## DEVELOPING A MISSION STATEMENT
>
> A **mission statement** outlines the beliefs and goals that the stakeholders consider central to educating and nurturing young children and helps parents, the director, governing body, educators, support staff, and the community to accurately realize these goals. It is critical that this important declaration be established in a thoughtful, systematic manner.

In determining the program's priorities, consider the following statements:

- To ensure children the best start, to be prepared for school and academic success
- To enhance the self-concept and social skills as children learn to get along in the world
- To provide children with opportunities for play, adventure, exploration, and investigation
- To create a community where adults and children experience a sense of connection and new possibilities for making the world a better place
- To provide a service for parents while they work

The philosophy/mission statement is a dynamic, living document that reflects current research and responds to the changing needs of the community. Since the program philosophy is a culmination of beliefs and goals for early childhood development, it should be re-evaluated on an ongoing basis, incorporating new understandings by decision makers.

A philosophy is about goal orientation. It also serves as a yardstick to measure the performance of the setting in meeting its goals. Program goals for children and families are statements of what really matters in a program—reference points for assessing whether the policies and practices are achieving what they were intended to achieve. The hallmark of any successful organization is a shared vision among stakeholders of what they are trying to accomplish and why. Agreed-upon goals and ways to attain them provide the foundation for rational planning and action.

Who Determines the Philosophy?

Developing a vision for an organization occurs through a collaborative process that includes families, staff, and stakeholders. It takes into account standards and guidelines developed by relevant professional organizations such as the Standards of Practice developed by the College of ECEs provided in Chapter 6.

In the case of a new program, the individuals who are creating it discuss and formulate the program philosophy. Stakeholders often have very specific ideas about the program philosophy. Sometimes, the process is delayed until a director is hired, so that he or she can be involved in the development of the statement, since the director will be responsible for the implementation of this collective understanding as well as for meeting the goals articulated in the philosophy. In an established program, it is important to hire a director who can operate within the adopted philosophical framework.

Regardless of the initial inspiration for a program's purpose, in order for the philosophy to evolve, the involvement of others must be cultivated. It is critical to communicate the vision during the hiring process. Staff members must feel comfortable with the program's philosophy. Frustrations over incompatible philosophies can create unworkable situations for staff. The opportunity to participate in program decision making is a leading factor in the morale of staff. Involving staff in the revision of an existing philosophy statement gives them a critical stake in it.

Many early childhood directors lack experience in establishing and upholding a vision. Resources exist that can aid in the development of this skill. *The Visionary Director: A Handbook for Dreaming, Organizing, and Improvising in Your Center, second edition,* provides many specific examples to help directors develop and/or revise a philosophy statement (Carter and Curtis 2010). *Circle of Influence: Implementing Shared Decision Making and Participative Management* offers a balance of theory and practical tools for promoting change and increasing program effectiveness (Jorde Bloom 2000).

When a director meets with prospective families, she should discuss the philosophy statement with them to ensure that they understand the program beliefs and that they are consistent with their goals and traditions. It is not enough to make grand statements about the philosophy—parents want to see this vision in action. They want to see the ways in which parents and staff work together to provide the best experiences for their child.

Having a clear, jargon-free statement of intent based on a vision greatly benefits families. Early childhood programs are relationship based, and for some families, their supportive relationships with the staff help to fill the gap left by the absence of extended families. Encouraging the involvement of families builds their confidence in, awareness of, and desire to participate in their child's education. Families who feel a shared ownership of the vision feel more motivated to contribute. This can lead to real involvement in the program and a genuine parent–staff partnership. This inclusive approach has a positive influence on children's learning and development outcomes. (The creation of a **family-centred** program is explored further in Chapter 8, "Building the Partnership with Families.")

In addition, the philosophy statement provides ground for understanding between the program and colleges and universities that prepare future educators. When using a community program for field placement, post-secondary institutions need to be aware of the program's philosophy and be prepared to support it. During student orientation, the director and co-operating staff must provide multiple opportunities for the student to discuss the philosophy and its application.

Standard

Program Philosophy, Goals, and Objectives

A statement of the program philosophy and a statement of goals and objectives serve as the basis for decision making, daily practice, and program evaluation.

1. A written statement of philosophy clearly articulates the principles and values followed in an early childhood program.

2. There is a written statement of program goals and objectives, such as the ages of the children to be served and the types of services to be provided.

3. The statement of program philosophy is discussed with and given to and read by potential staff, family child care practitioners, assistants, and alternates (casual or temporary staff) before they begin to work in the program and copies of the statements are provided upon employment.

4. The statement of program philosophy is discussed with and given to parents/guardians before the child is enrolled.

(continued)

5. The statement of program philosophy is readily accessible at all times to families/guardians and people working in the program.

6. The statement of philosophy and the statement of program goals and objectives are reviewed on an annual basis.

Source: Gillian Doherty, in Canadian Child Care Federation (CCCF), *Partners in Quality: Tools for Practitioners in Child Care Settings* (Ottawa: CCCF, 2000).

Steps in Developing the Program Philosophy

A number of provinces (New Brunswick, Alberta, British Columbia, Manitoba, and Ontario) have developed curriculum frameworks for early learning, many of which are intended to complement, rather than replace, specific curriculum and pedagogical approaches such as emergent curriculum, High Scope, or Montessori.

These provincial frameworks provide a starting point for program decision makers determining their vision for the program. This can occur when a new setting is being developed or when an existing statement is being updated. Steps in developing a statement include:

Be Knowledgeable About Theories of Child Development
Key stakeholders preparing a philosophy statement must have a clear understanding of the various theories of child development and learning. Some theorists emphasize one area of development over another; some espouse a holistic approach.

Most of the curriculum models currently in practice follow the whole child approach. An example of a comprehensive, inclusive approach to early childhood education is the Reggio Emilia model, which involves an entire community in the development of a system of early childhood services. A resource that summarizes various theories is *Introduction to Early Childhood Education, sixth edition* (Essa 2011). Stakeholders should research various theories and choose an approach that can be integrated with the key values and beliefs of the stakeholders.

Consult with Stakeholders at Each Stage
Identify everyone involved in the EC program who will need to be consulted. This includes the board of directors/owner of the program, parents and children, staff and director, community representatives, and others who have a vested interest in the program. Invite representative **stakeholders** to form a work group. Ask participants to identify their values and what is important to them. Input can be solicited through a variety of formats, including questionnaires, discussions at meetings, or interviews. Use open-ended questions that facilitate the participants' exploration of their beliefs about quality early childhood experiences. (See box on next page.)

Identify Key Considerations
Jorde Bloom, in *Circle of Influence: Implementing Shared Decision Making and Participative Management* (2000), identifies 50 decisions that may need to be made in defining the philosophy. Some examples of these decisions include:

- deciding the curricular approach,
- determining educational objectives for each age group,
- setting the expectations for family involvement,
- identifying the criteria for hiring staff,
- determining the guidelines for staff performance appraisals, and
- determining the types of relationships with community agencies.

Identify Priorities   Once input from all the stakeholders has been gathered, identify the key areas of agreement, then assess how strongly each stakeholder feels about specific concepts. State explicitly any key values that should be maintained, for example, "We want to ensure that staff have an early childhood educational background." A number of methods can be used to build consensus among stakeholders, such as asking respondents to rank concepts from most to least important. Common threads of agreement will emerge as the priorities of individual stakeholders are revealed. These key points can then be used to draft the philosophy statement.

SHARED BELIEFS

Every experience in a child's early life has an impact on his/her development now and in the future. Parents and families are the primary and most powerful influence on children's early learning and development. Young children and their families live in communities that shape early experiences. Early learning programs need reciprocal partnerships with parents, families, and communities. These partnerships can be built by:

- acknowledging children's individual and diverse development and natural disposition to learn;

- being inclusive, supporting meaningful engagement and equitable outcomes for *all* children;

- recognizing that families, early childhood professionals, and healthy communities are key to quality, effective early childhood programs; and

- using the evidence of research, knowledge of professionals, the wisdom of practice, and the context of communities.

Source: Ontario's Best Start Expert Panel on Early Learning, Statement of Shared Beliefs, *Early Learning for Every Child Today: A Framework for Ontario's Early Childhood Settings* (Ontario: Ministry of Children and Youth, 2006).

Drafting the Philosophy Statement   The statement must be refined to reflect the feedback gathered. Once the draft has been circulated, all stakeholders should be given time to reflect on its implications and a chance to express their views and concerns. The final statement needs to be acceptable to all participants.

Operationalize the Statement   Once the development process has been completed, the next step is to operationalize the beliefs and values contained in the philosophy statement—in other words, use them to guide practice. Remember, a philosophy statement is a living document, and it should be reviewed on a regular basis.

Developing a Personal Philosophy

Critical to working effectively with young children and families in an appropriate way is a belief system that directs the interactions between people. The concept of formulating a **personal philosophy**, or mission statement, may seem intimidating; however, it should not be. Organizations have a mission statement outlining both what the program believes and hopes to accomplish. Based on the organization's beliefs about its purpose, the mission statement represents a commitment by the organization, and it determines the way an organization conducts business. Similarly, a personal philosophy—one's own beliefs and goals—determines an individual's actions. It commits the individual to certain intentions and implies a plan of action.

Sample

Philosophy Statements

Millbrook Children's Centre—A Learning Community for Children and Adults
Where children are valued for their ability to do meaningful work, their wonder and curiosity, their perspectives and ability to play.

Where families are valued for their bonds and traditions, their ability to play, their commitment to work, home, and community, and their dreams for their children.

Where staff are valued for their vision, their delight in children, their skill, heart, and knowledge, their commitment to families, and their ability to play.

We cherish what we can learn from each other.

Olivia Child Development Centre
Our program, in partnership with families, staff and community, provides high quality early childhood experiences which enhance the lives of young children in an integrated, educational environment. We

- value the child within the context of its family and community;
- recognise the integrative nature of children's play as it affects learning in curriculum areas;
- acknowledge and support children's individual learning styles;
- value the arts as symbol systems through which children make sense of themselves and their world;
- provide opportunities for discovery learning through self-selected activities, and encouraging the development of children's abilities to explore, investigate, imagine & problem solve;
- value daily routines as opportunities for learning and social development, ensuring these times are engaging and stimulating;
- respect the needs and rights of children to make choices & decisions by empowering them to take responsibility for routines and the care of their environment and materials;
- recognise the need for children to practice skills and consolidate their learning by providing opportunities for repetition of experiences and extension of their ideas;
- establish an enriched environment that stimulates the imagination, promotes creativity and enhances aesthetic development;
- value and support staff in their work with children, families and in their own professional development.

Many individuals are not very aware of how their beliefs influence their day-to-day life and work. Some early childhood educators believe deeply in the value of strong social relations and networks among the families in their program. Others may think the program's primary purpose should be providing programs for the children and passing on information to families.

Educators should seek employment in a program whose philosophy is largely compatible with their own personal and professional beliefs. Accepting a job in a program whose philosophy conflicts with personal goals and values can lead to dissatisfaction, friction, and turmoil.

Staff do not always fully agree with the policies and practices of their program. The greater the diversity in staff backgrounds, the wider the range of beliefs and values. It is acceptable for staff to be different and to believe in dissimilar things. It is also important that the program have a clear, articulated point of view, as well as goals that the staff understand and accept. For example, they must follow program guidelines for managing behaviour, even when this means that they may have to adapt their own practices.

A guideline is developed during the process of writing (down) of a personal philosophy. This statement grows and is adapted as one's knowledge and experience deepen. For example, a student's philosophy statement will evolve as she or he completes additional course work. After graduation, an individual should take out her or his personal philosophy periodically to reflect on whether or not it reflects current knowledge, understanding and experience. Increasingly, graduates report on opportunities to discuss their philosophy during job interviews. Evaluating one's day-to-day practice in light of one's statement of philosophy serves to keep ideals and realities aligned.

An individual's beliefs grow more comprehensive with experience and knowledge. This experience affects the development of one's philosophy. Examples of philosophical statements include common ideas and beliefs about children such as "All children have the right to inclusive education," "I believe children learn through play," and "Parental input and involvement are a critical component of the family-centred environment."

Shimoni and Baxter (2008) encourage educators to examine their own beliefs in order to understand the values held by families. They believe that through such **reflection**, educators can increase their understanding of differences in values and beliefs between themselves and parents. Educators must develop strategies that demonstrate respect and empathy to each family.

REFLECTION

- What do you think are the qualities of a good parent?

- Being as honest as possible, define your attitude toward working with families. Do you judge them harshly or leniently? In what situations do you find yourself passing judgement, perhaps even unintentionally, on families and their parenting choices?

- What is your belief regarding how discipline and guidance should be implemented within a family? How does your belief affect your interactions with parents whose beliefs differ from yours? Why do you think some parents spank their children?

- How does your attitude toward parents change based on ethnicity, income, sexual preference or marital status?

Using the Vision to Inform Practice

Directors must demonstrate a capacity to organize ideas and ideals in addition to time, talent, and tasks. This aspect of leadership is exercised through participation in the development of the program vision. The vision is the means by which directors capture the imaginations and engage the loyalty and support of staff, families, and stakeholders. It is the philosophy that provides direction for and gives meaning to decisions, the search for new practices, and the policies to improve effectiveness of the service. The vision can boost morale and self-esteem and act as a buffer against stress during times of change. (The director's leadership role was elaborated on in Chapter 3.)

Policies and procedures are critical to the delivery of quality EC programs and must reflect the philosophy of the program. Although most programs would state that they have a philosophy, it is not uncommon to find little attention is devoted to it. Often the documented statement outlines the program's intent to serve children, treat them respectfully, and meet their developmental needs. Directors hired into programs are seldom asked how they would like to see this statement brought to life. Philosophy statements are usually posted in EC settings and in parent handbooks, in the organization's website or program literature. To be useful, the statement needs to be reviewed often and used as a guide for decisions being made about the program. A well-constructed statement aids in hiring competent staff, enables the program to develop policies and procedures that are consistent, to develop alliances with other organizations that share the program's values and vision, and to guide major decisions. Figure 4–1 Turing the Vision into Action outlines the steps involved.

The philosophy statement needs to be reviewed often and used as a guide for decision making.

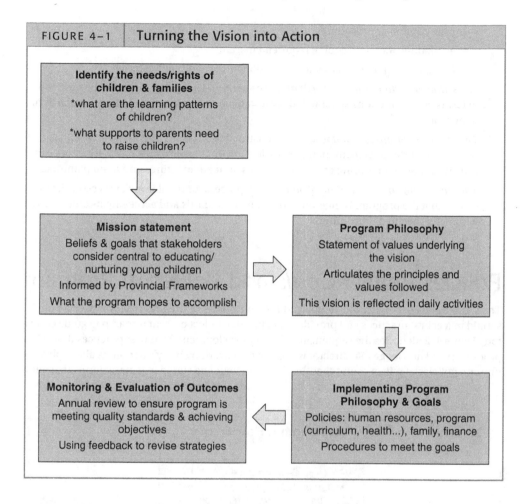

FIGURE 4–1 | Turning the Vision into Action

Identify the needs/rights of children & families
*what are the learning patterns of children?
*what supports to parents need to raise children?

Mission statement
Beliefs & goals that stakeholders consider central to educating/ nurturing young children
Informed by Provincial Frameworks
What the program hopes to accomplish

Program Philosophy
Statement of values underlying the vision
Articulates the principles and values followed
This vision is reflected in daily activities

Implementing Program Philosophy & Goals
Policies: human resources, program (curriculum, health...), family, finance
Procedures to meet the goals

Monitoring & Evaluation of Outcomes
Annual review to ensure program is meeting quality standards & achieving objectives
Using feedback to revise strategies

One of the characteristics of successful teams is that they have a set of achievable goals that are understood and accepted by all. Many staff teams have not had the opportunity to be involved in the development of the goals and policies that inform their practice. Some staff teams do not even consider this to be part of their responsibility. Given that the director or board of directors/owner may have imposed these goals and policies, not all staff may agree with, accept, or value them.

Because goals and policies are based on values, they can engender conflict. Individual beliefs, values, and perspectives that have a strong emotional component dominate the field of early childhood. Understanding that not all people are likely to accept or agree with the goals and policies of a program is important. Providing opportunities for discussion, the sharing of perspectives, and regular review of goals and objectives is necessary to minimize conflict. In situations such as these, directors need to facilitate open problem solving to resolve this issue.

Rood (1998) identifies four steps that a director can use to facilitate staff involvement:

1. *The definition of organizational and individual goals and/or objectives.* First, the director provides:

   • a clarification of the service and its purpose,

   • an outline for future directions,

- a description of procedures,
- an identification of resource requirements, and
- an explication of the roles and responsibilities of each staff member.

2. *The setting of individual standards and expectations.* Delegated tasks will be outlined in terms of the functions specified in each staff job description, including standards of performance.

3. *The provision of support and feedback.* Constructive feedback and assistance will be provided to individual team members to develop their expertise. As well, directors can provide ongoing mentoring and opportunities for team meetings and team planning.

4. *The monitoring and evaluation of outcomes.* A process for regular review is essential to ensure that the program is meeting professional standards and achieving its objectives within the specified time frame.

Policies Reflect *Goals* and *Values* of Program

The written policies reflect the values and the philosophy of the organization. Good policies should reflect best practices and provide standards that reflect current research to guide educators. Figure 4–2 identifies the sequencing of policy development from best practices through to procedures. A knowledgeable director will guide the governing body's decisions about philosophy and policies to reflect sound theories. Policies should be stated in general terms that allow

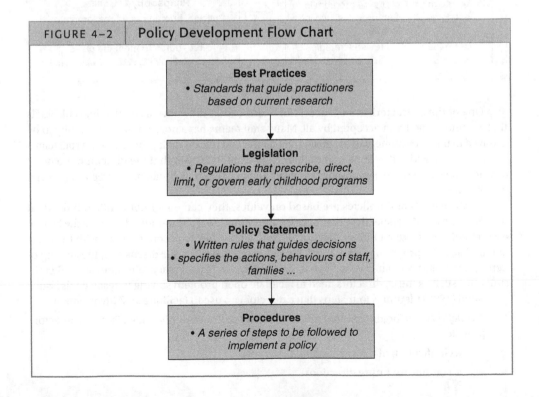

FIGURE 4–2	Policy Development Flow Chart

Best Practices
• *Standards that guide practitioners based on current research*

Legislation
• *Regulations that prescribe, direct, limit, or govern early childhood programs*

Policy Statement
• *Written rules that guides decisions*
• *specifies the actions, behaviours of staff, families ...*

Procedures
• *A series of steps to be followed to implement a policy*

the flexibility necessary for dealing with specific situations. Once established, policies must be followed consistently. They must be stated in writing and available to board members, staff, and parents. Policy and procedure manuals *communicate standards of performance*. A policy is a written rule that specifies the behaviours or actions permissible in the program and what the organization expects of employees. They also define what the employees can expect from the program.

Policies also reflect legislation, the regulations that prescribe, direct, limit, or govern early childhood programs. Policies:

- reflect the efforts of the organization to *anticipate situations*
- identify the *approach* for dealing with issues as they arise
- *guide thinking and action* by providing a *framework for making decisions*
- answer the *what* and *why* of daily operations
- explain *how goals and objectives will be achieved* in general terms
- are set by governing body—board of directors/owners

Policies and procedures are necessary to promote better understanding of expectations for both staff and parents. They can provide clarification and standardization of the program's governing rules as well as promote consistency and continuity in decision making. They determine the blueprint for achieving the established goals of the program.

Characteristics of Effective Policies

- **Congruent**. Policies are consistent and do not contradict one another.
- **Clear**. Policies must be stated/written clearly so that *everyone affected understands their meaning*.
- **Sensitive to tone**. For example, family-friendly policies convey respect for families. They should be *non-judgmental and they assume good intentions* on the part of families. Policies should not be written in a negative, legalistic tone.
- **Communicated**. Parents and staff must be made aware of policies. Directors review key policies at intake or hiring. Legislation may require a signed statement or contract agreeing to policies in areas such as behaviour guidance. Ensure that students and supply staff are aware of policies.
- **Stable/Responsive**. Policies should be stable, yet flexible. They respond to fundamental changes in goals and characteristics of the program. They should not change so frequently that they contribute to uncertainty, resulting in the staff and families not knowing what is expected.
- **Current**. Policies must *reflect current research*. Leaders must keep up to date through further education, literature, and standards developed by professional groups.

There are two types of policies that are needed for programs: general policies that address the legal and structural rules of the organization. Examples of the type of content these policies include are confidentiality, communication with families, or reporting of child abuse. There is more focus on program policies in Chapter 7 "Managing Safe and Healthy Learning Environments" and Chapter 8 "Building the Partnership with Families."

The second type is employment status policies that cover employees' rights and responsibilities. They include hiring practices, probation, and professional development. They must reflect legislation such as child care legislation, employment standards; directives, statutes, or standards that prescribe, direct, limit, or govern early childhood programs. This area is elaborated in Chapter 5 "Human Resource Management."

Programs must also develop procedures and rules for implementing each policy. Procedures specify how to handle certain tasks. The purpose of a procedure is to guide an implementation plan that is clear and uniform. There are two types of procedures: those that relate to policies and those that relate to program operation. For example, in developing a procedure for emergency evacuation, it will specify the steps to take in leaving the building with the children such as taking the attendance list and parent phone numbers.

The more carefully that policies and procedures are written, the more staff and families will connect them to the philosophy and vision of the program. In turn, they will more directly address the situations they are meant to govern, and ultimately, they will be more effective. Creating these effective operating systems establishes a comfortable work environment for the staff and enables them to meet expectations.

Evaluating the Quality of a Program

Evaluating and planning go hand in hand. In between is the everyday work of implementing plans. Too often many directors act without planning or evaluating their program. Directors need to build in time to discuss the areas they would like feedback on with staff. They need to know more about what are the program's strengths and what are the areas they want to improve. Taking the initiative to evaluate the program involves the team in a powerful process because they become invested in the results. The team becomes involved in knowing and doing something about improving the program rather than waiting defensively for outside evaluators to tell them what is wrong. Each year the program should evaluate the program using measures such as the surveys, and standard assessment tools described later in the chapter.

Although measures for assessing the quality of children's environments were developed originally for use in research and as self-assessment tools for directors and educators, these tools have also moved into the arena of public policy. They are now being used to make decisions about the program and inform families about the quality of settings. In fact the results of these measures are being posted on websites, some on a room-by-room basis where parents or potential users of the program can see how the room is functioning against various criteria. The City of Toronto Children's Services website is an example of this growing transparency of program quality.

The program goals, and the program itself, are designed to carry out the vision for the operation. Directors are accountable for the programs they administer, and the evaluation of how well the program is meeting its goals and objectives has become one of the director's most significant responsibilities. Directors may have a global impression that things are going either well or not so well with the program, but they often lack specific information. Information gleaned from an evaluation of the program can help directors turn those vague feelings into pinpointing what aspects of the program can be improved. The shift in a director's perspective from general intuitive understanding to pinpointing the specific concrete aspects for program improvement is made possible with information gleaned from program evaluation. Directors can in turn work with the staff and governing body and secure resources to address these concerns.

How does a program define quality? What methods are used to identify what is working in the program and what needs improvement? How is this information communicated to key stakeholders (families, staff, funders, and others)? To facilitate this communication and help all concerned to work together to improve program quality, a good evaluation process is essential.

The primary purpose of program evaluation is to improve the quality of the experience provided to children and families. All programs should undergo regular evaluation in order for the staff to engage in continuous reflection and improvement. Opportunities for staff to share reflections with team members, the director, and others provide incentive for reflection.

Quality early childhood settings use ongoing observations and appropriate assessments to gather information on children's learning and development; similarly, they use valid program evaluations to measure the quality of the program. Engagement in these activities benefits children by informing decisions about pedagogy and curriculum.

Observing children's behaviour and responses to the curriculum provided offers an overall sense of whether all children are meaningfully engaged. Monitoring early childhood development through the use of a developmental continuum can help educators understand how well their setting is meeting the needs of children and families as identified in the program philosophy or mission statement. Reflection on the presence or absence of children's challenging behaviours, strategies of guidance used, should be an ongoing component of staff or team meetings, providing stakeholders with an overall sense of program effectiveness. In order to conduct valid program evaluation, adequate supports are needed so that the program evaluation does not drain resources from the actual delivery of the service. These supports can be composed of consultation about the design of the evaluation and assistance in gathering and interpreting the data. Two agencies that provide these supports are the Alberta Resource centre for Quality Enhancement and the Affiliated Services for Children and Youth (ASCY) in Hamilton, Ontario, that provide a myriad of supports to EC programs, including monitoring quality through:

- frequent on-site observations,
- collecting parent and/or caregiver feedback each year, and
- developing action plans to address areas of need and to plan for improvement and providing consultation through early childhood consultants.

Some are concerned that the overall quality of early childhood programs is declining and that the universality of programs may impact high quality even further. Major barriers to program quality include: financial instability and insufficient government funding, inadequate levels of staff education and too few professional development opportunities, directors who are inadequately prepared for their jobs, and a lack of infrastructure support to programs. As well, major challenges with attraction, recruitment, and retention of staff are factors in many provinces and territories. Quality is directly related to the development and fulfillment of program goals. When quality is lacking, programs are constrained from attaining goals for services for children and families. Therefore, directors often have the sole responsibility to advocate, collaborate, and strive to secure resources to improve quality.

Since the goals for the program are closely tied to the philosophy of the organization, they evolve slowly. Nevertheless, each year, directors must carry out strategies for evaluating the program. The annual evaluation and planning processes should complement each other, with the evaluation providing the information to guide strategic planning. As well, the data collected from various evaluations can document how close to its goals the program has come. The evaluation process is essentially a self-renewal process. It is a means for developing teamwork and building collective action to bring about an understanding of the changes necessary to achieve program objectives and acceptance of responsibility for implementing those changes. The planning process can be used to set goals in areas needing improvement.

For example, the philosophy statement may state that the program serves children and families from a range of cultures, socio-economic groups, and children of varying abilities. This is an important shared value of the stakeholders. However, it may be found that this is not the case. A goal may be set to diversify the population served. Some of the barriers to achieving this goal may include a homogeneous staff, an environment that only reflects one culture, and materials that are available only in English. To meet the goal of increasing the diversity of the population served, the program could set specific objectives, such as:

- hiring qualified staff from representative backgrounds of the population served for the next available positions,

- providing professional development opportunities on a regular basis for staff to learn more about culturally relevant programming, and

- targeting suitable professional development events.

In addition, as one of the steps needed to achieve these objectives, the program will need to determine who holds the responsible and when the actions should occur. To get broader feedback on the functioning of the program in meeting diversity, the director could ask representatives of the community to review human resources, enrolment, health, and nutrition policies and procedures.

An ongoing evaluation process is an integral means for creating, designing, improving, and maintaining effective early childhood programs. When staff have an active role in evaluating the program and generating solutions, they feel a greater responsibility for implementing change and are more responsive to incorporating new practices. An example of a tool designed to improve the collaboration of an EC program with schools and other community agencies is from the City of Toronto Operating Criteria Working Together component. This tool is intended to assist directors in assessing their program's standing in working collaboratively with schools to aid in developing partnerships for child care and kindergarten. Its intent is to increase awareness of the EC program in contributing their expertise to the early year's team to achieve common goals and to identify obstacles and solutions in working toward inclusive access for young children and families. An ultimate goal is to develop a continuum of seamless supports from early childhood programs through to kindergarten programs.

Characteristics of Effective Program Quality Measures

The benefits that result from well-developed systems of high quality are recognized for the contributions they make to children's learning and development. The development of standards of quality and the use of tools to assess quality have contributed our understanding how these dimensions affect children. In the following section, some considerations when selecting tools will be overviewed. When evaluating quality, it is important to select a variety of appropriate measures that reflect various components of quality:

- First, staff need to use program tools that are consistent with the values and curriculum models being implemented in the program, such as the Preschool Program Quality Assessment which is used to measure the High Scope approach. Activities and curriculum reflect active dynamic learning philosophy. These program tools focus on key experiences that address social-emotional, physical, and cognitive development.

- Program assessment tools should define quality along a continuum. By using a continuum to rate quality, the assessment tools help programs identify where they are on the path to achieving quality and the successive steps they must take to continue their

FIGURE 4–3	**Quality Standard** EC Programs Working with Schools/Community Agencies				
Section 9 Working Together	**1 Does Not Meet Expectations**	**2 Needs Improvement**	**3 Meets Expectations**	**4 Exceeds Expectations**	**Score**
2. Talking to staff at neighbour-hood schools & family support programs	• Child care supervisor & staff do not speak to principal or teachers at neighbour-hood elemen-tary schools • Child care supervisor or staff do not speak to staff at Family Support Programs in neighbour-hood	• Child care supervisor & staff some-times talk to school staff • Child care supervisor & staff some-times talk to Family support program staff	• Child care supervisor & staff talk to the principal(s) &/or teachers at the school on a regular basis • Child care supervisor & staff talk to family support program staff on a regular basis	• **Early Years Management Team has been formed & hold documented meetings • **Early Years Staff Team has been formed & hold documented meetings	1 2 3 4 N/A

Comments
** Early Years Management Team: May include some or all of the following, child care supervisor, school Principal, family support coordinator, parent, Children's Services consultant, school board early years advisor
**Early Years Staff Team: The frontline staff working with young children and their families in kindergarten, child care and parenting/family support programs comprise the Early Years staff team. Other staff may include: school administrator, ESL teacher, child care consultant, resource educators, special education and support services through school boards, teacher, librarian, literacy co-coordinator, school boards' early years advisors.
Source: City of Toronto Operating Criteria Working Together Guidelines. Reproduced with permission.

progress. See Figure 4–3 which uses this continuum approach which aids programs to see what step they are currently at.

- Program evaluations are most helpful when they provide users with examples. To aid individuals to use the evaluation instrument fairly and objectively, it should be explicit about the practices and behaviours that define poor, acceptable, and excellent levels of quality. Instruments designed in this manner produce a higher level of agreement, or interrater reliability. (This means that instrument outcomes are similar despite having different evaluators.)

- Program evaluations are most informative when they are comprehensive. Tools should look at the process elements as well as the structural elements of quality (described in Chapter 1). Most instruments do a detailed job of looking at structural elements, such as the safety of the physical features or the diversity of the materials and equipment provided. However, many tools fail to pay equal attention to the most vital aspect of

Sample

Program Evaluation Tool

Human Resources	1 Does not meet criteria.	2 Needs improvement.	3 Meets criteria.	4 Exceeds criteria in some areas.	5 Exceeds criteria in all areas.
Program Staff Criteria: There must be at least one trained staff on duty at all times. Infant ratios (one staff member for every three infants) must be maintained at all times.	*Requires Immediate Attention*		Trained staff on duty at all times and the staff:child ratios always maintained.	More than one trained staff on duty at all times.	All staff on duty at all times are trained.
	Trained staff are not always on duty.	Trained staff are on duty except at day beginning or end.			

Source: Excerpted from Children's Services Division, *Operating Criteria for Child Care Centres Providing Subsidized Care in Toronto*, rev. ed. (Toronto: Community Services, Children's Services Division, City of Toronto, 2009). Used by permission.

quality—the nature of the interactions between practitioners and children. These interpersonal characteristics and or qualities are crucial to promoting child development. Additionally, complete program assessments will consider how practitioners interact with families and colleagues, opportunities for family involvement, the amount of support directors provide to staff, and how management secures adequate resources.

- An effective program quality evaluation tool can also serve as a staff development tool by helping staff and directors decide what areas they want to emphasize in professional development. An assessment of a program's quality should highlight its strengths and identify areas for improvement. For example, the program evaluation tool below identifies those steps needs immediate action.

- Effective tools can enable directors to observe individual staff and provide them with constructive feedback. Following the observation, the director and staff member can review and discuss the ratings, acknowledge areas of strength, and identify specific strategies for professional growth.

Tools for Evaluating the Organization

The choice of evaluation method will depend upon how the results are to be used. The key is to use a variety of methods that involve key stakeholders in the process. As well as standardized instruments, questionnaires, interviews, observations, and records and documents are all possible sources of data. Global assessment tools evaluate multiple factors in early childhood settings.

EARLY CHILDHOOD PROGRAM EVALUATION TOOLS

- Early Childhood Environment Rating Scale (ECERS)
- Family Day Care Rating Scale (FDCRS)
- Infant/Toddler Environment Rating Scale (ITERS)
- School-Age Environment Rating Scale (SAERS)
- Preschool Program Quality Assessment Instrument (PQA)
- Early Childhood Work Environment Survey
- SpeciaLink Inclusion Practices Profile
- Program Administration Scale

A widely used global evaluation tool is the Early Childhood Environment Rating Scale (ECERS). Its original purpose was for self-assessment. The tool is also used in research and for shaping public policy: to measure quality, methods for quantifying quality, and as a tactical approach in increasing quality in large numbers of programs. Developed by Harms and Clifford (1998/2004), the ECERS approaches the early childhood program from an ecological perspective. It has 43 items in 7 separate subscales: personal care routines, space and furnishings for children, language and reasoning, activities, interactions, program structure, and parents and staff. These items are rated on a scale of 1 (inadequate) to 7 (excellent). The scales offer descriptions of essential elements of quality. The scores for each playroom may be compiled to get a quality score for the program. Versions of the scale have been developed for specific types of early childhood programs serving infants, preschoolers, school-age, and home child care environments (Harms and Clifford 1998/2004; Harms et al. 1990; Harms et al. 1995).

The Preschool Program Quality Assessment Instrument (PQA) is a rating instrument designed to evaluate the quality of early childhood programs and identify staff professional development needs. The tool, developed by a diverse team of researchers, training consultants, and practitioners, was validated in a variety of early childhood settings following the High/Scope Educational Research Foundation philosophy as well as settings using other curriculum approaches. There are seven domains such as adult-child interaction, learning environment, staff qualifications, and development and program management. It uses a five-point rating scale (High/Scope Educational Research Foundation 2002).

There is a growing consensus among early childhood educators, directors, consultants, parents, and therapists about the factors that are important to provide and sustain effective inclusion. EC programs that are effective in including children with special needs require a mix of supports and resources within the program such as staff who are given time to plan and participate in individual program plans (IPPs) with community specialists. The SpeciaLink Inclusion Practices Profile is a tool for use with the SpeciaLink Inclusion Principles Scale to assess sustainable and evolving inclusion quality. These scales were combined in 2009. As more children with special needs attend community-based programs, this is a critical aspect of the program to evaluate. This tool is used for assessing inclusion quality in early childhood settings. It provides a picture of inclusion quality. The tool is similar in design to the ECERS-R formats. Some of the elements include: the role of the director and board of directors, supports available to staff, staff training, and preparing for transition to school. The creators recommend the tool be used along with ECERS as the terminology, procedures, and description are compatible. The areas assessed include physical environment, equipment and materials, the director and governance committees, staff support and training, therapies available to the program, individual program plans, families, involvement of typical children, and transitions to school.

Sample

SpeciaLink Early Childhood Inclusion Quality Scale

Note frequency and intensity of play that involves children with special needs and typically developing children.

Inadequate 1	Minimal 3	Good 5	Excellent 7
1.1 Typically developing children rarely interact with children with special needs. 1.2 Staff take no active role in encouraging inclusion.	3.1 Typically developing children sometimes interact with children with special needs, but mainly in a helping role. 3.2 Staff make ineffective comments or gestures to promote social inclusion.	5.1 Children with special needs are often included in group play, usually as "babies" or in other diminished status. 5.2 Staff suggest appropriate roles or dramatic situations that are inclusionary.	7.1 Children with special needs are included as valued participants in group social play. 7.2 Staff systematically use techniques of scripting, cooperative learning, and valued object sharing to promote social inclusion. 7.3 Staff receive specific training in promotion of inclusive social play.

Source: Sharon Hope Irwin, "SpeciaLink Early Childhood Inclusion **Quality Scale**," S.H. Irwin, (Wreck Cove, NS: Breton Books, 2009).

The Early Childhood Work Environment Survey developed by Jorde Bloom (2000) can be used to assess organizational climate and working conditions. Early childhood directors play a pivotal role in creating work environments that promote high performance and personal fulfillment. Assessing staff attitudes about organizational practices is one way directors can better understand the collective perceptions of the team and help improve overall morale and job satisfaction. When staff are dissatisfied with their work, the results are turnover, stress, and burnout—and even departure from the profession. In such a situation, it is impossible to maintain a quality program. This tool measures staff perceptions about relations with co-workers, supervisory support, decision-making influence, and other factors. The areas surveyed by this tool include:

Collegiality: the extent to which staff are friendly, supportive, and trust one another.

Professional growth: opportunities for professional development.

Director support: perceived amount of support given to individual staff members.

Clarity: the extent to which policies, procedures, and responsibilities are defined and communicated.

Reward system: examines the salaries and benefits, working conditions.

Decision making: the extent to which staff are involved in program decisions.

Goal consensus: the degree to which staff agree on the goals and objectives of the program.

Task orientation: the emphasis placed on good planning, efficiency, and getting the job done.

Physical setting: the extent to which the environment facilitates work and meets adult needs.

Innovativeness: the extent to which an organization adapts to change and encourages staff to find creative ways to solve problems.

This instrument measures staff's perceptions about a wide range of organizational practices. It can be administered annually to check the pulse of organizational functioning.

The families' satisfaction with the program is apparent when a setting gets referrals from friends of those families who are already enrolled. If dissatisfied, a family may take their child out of the program. Monitoring admissions and dropouts along with the reasons why can help the director understand the families' evaluation of the setting. A number of strategies can be used to solicit families' viewpoints and suggestions about the program's communication network, the meeting of mutual goals for children, and the ambiance of the environment. Most importantly, the daily interchanges with parents provide critical and ongoing informal feedback. In addition, a more formal approach should be taken. There is a myriad of questionnaires and rating scales available. Each program should determine which tool best suits its needs. See an example in *Partnerships: Families and Communities in Canadian Early Childhood Education, fourth edition* (Wilson 2010).

Program Administration Scale (PAS), developed by Talen and Bloom (2005), is based upon the belief that overall administrative practices are crucial for providing high quality outcomes for children and families. That without quality systems in place at the organizational level, quality interactions and learning environments cannot be sustained. It assesses quality in 10 areas: human resources development, personnel cost and allocation, centre operations, child assessment, fiscal management, program planning and evaluation, family partnerships, marketing and public relations, technology, and staff qualifications.

The tool was designed for early childhood program administrators, researchers, monitoring personnel, and quality enhancement facilitators, It was constructed to complement the widely used environment rating scales designed by Harms, Clifford, and Cryer. Both the PAS and the environment rating scales measure quality on a seven-point scale, and both generate a profile to guide program improvement efforts. If used together, these instruments provide a focused look at best practices at the classroom level and a broad view of program quality from an organizational perspective.

Summary

Each early childhood setting has its own characteristics that are articulated in its program philosophy and goals. One of the director's main tasks is to provide leadership in the development and implementation of the program philosophy and the evaluation of the program. A philosophy is a distillation of the ideas, beliefs, and values held by an individual, a group, or an organization. It has a direct bearing on curriculum development, staff hiring, the degree of family involvement, budget allocations, and the use of community resources. All key stakeholders—families, staff, the community, and other decision makers (board of directors or owner)—should be involved in the development of the philosophy statement. Everyone in the EC program should be informed of the philosophy statement. As well, each practitioner should continue to develop and reflect on her or his personal philosophy.

An inclusive vision for quality benefits all the stakeholders. An inclusive process encourages supportive relationships, open communication, and confidence in the program and is of benefit to both staff and management as well as families. The quality of a program is based on relationships: child–child, child–parent, staff–child, staff–parent, staff (staff, and so on). By creating a vision for quality that is owned by the stakeholders, a commitment to the pursuit of excellence is made, and a culture of self-reflection and continuous improvement is created. Forming a vision for quality is an important starting point for implementing quality processes in an early childhood program.

Programs need to evaluate the process and structural features of quality regularly and systematically. Reliable and valid measures of quality can be used to assess the effectiveness of interventions aimed at improving quality and as useful tools to develop program standards for the profession. As well, policy makers require tools to determine if EC programs are providing the quality of programs young children need and deserve and to assure public accountability for investments in programs. Only in this way can educators, researchers, and policy makers declare that the services delivered are of sufficient quality to promote the development of young children, encourage the involvement of families, and create supportive working environments for EC educators.

Key Terms and Concepts

Clarity,   p. 125

Collegiality,   p. 125

Family-centred,   p. 109

Goal consensus,   p. 125

Innovativeness,   p. 125

Mission statement,   p. 107

Personal philosophy,   p. 111

Philosophy,   p. 107

Reflection,   p. 113

Stakeholders,   p. 106

Task orientation,   p. 125

Activities

1.   Request the philosophy statement from your field placement and determine the statement's implications for planning the program for children. Is the statement compatible with or contrary to your beliefs? Discuss your observations with your co-operating staff.

2. Collect three philosophy statements from a community early childhood programs. Compare these statements. Identify how each statement complies with your present understanding of quality. What do you feel that might be missing? Draft an ideal personal philosophy statement.

3. Design a brochure, web page, or short video that explains the benefits of parent–staff partnerships for the children, families, and educators.

4. Brainstorm what you could do if your personal beliefs came into conflict with those of your co-operating teacher at your field placement. What are the pros and cons of each option?

5. Use one of the tools reviewed in the chapter to assess the functioning of a playroom. Discuss your findings with the room staff.

Recommended Reading

Carter, M. and D. Curtis. *The Visionary Director: A Handbook for Dreaming, Organizing, and Improvising in Your Center, 2d ed.* St. Paul, MI: Redleaf Press, 2010.

Jorde Bloom, P., M. Sheerer, and J. Britz. *Blueprint for Action: Achieving Center-Based Change through Staff Development, 2d ed.* Lake Forest, IL: New Horizons, 2002.

Jorde Bloom, P. *Circle of Influence: Implementing Shared Decision-Making and Participative Management.* Lake Forest, IL: New Horizons, 2000.

Weblinks

www.eccdc.org
Early Childhood Community Development Centre
The Child Care Resource Link for Owners and Boards on this site provides a listing of resources to help decision makers maximize their operations. The web page is organized around six key areas of responsibility: direction, guardianship, public relations, advocacy, legal conduct, and ethical conduct. Included are bibliographies and lists of contacts, links, and articles.

www.specialinkcanada.org
SpeciaLink: The National Centre for Child Care Inclusion
A resource and research helpline, SpeciaLink, provides personalized responses to specific questions; referrals to other organizations; and sources of help, information, and technical assistance. It also provides the SpeciaLink Newsletters, fact sheets, books, and videos, as well as a speakers bureau. It maintains an alert network of key mainstream child care advocates across the country, who can quickly identify and respond to opportunities and threats to mainstream quality and funding.

Human Resources Management

chapter 5

Objectives

- **Understand the director's role in creating a supportive and professional work environment.**

- **Identify regulations and quality standards relating to human resources.**

- **Review effective human resource management policies and procedures, programs, and practices.**

- **Create a supportive work environment and build an effective team to maximize staff retention, engagement, and organizational resiliency.**

- **Outline strategies for performance management, personal and professional growth, and career advancement.**

This chapter examines an EC program's roles and responsibilities in relation to people management, team building, and organizational development. With the support of a board of directors/owner, the director is responsible for creating an environment responsive to the needs of adults as well as those of children. Directors and supervisors are responsible for establishing and maintaining quality standards for their agencies. Effective leaders create organizational cultures and work environments that support quality and ongoing learning. The director leads the team, supports each team member to reach full potential, continuously demonstrates professionalism and commitment to the principles of healthy child development, building relationships with parents and other services in the community. The director supports each team member's understanding of the vision, mission, and values of the organization; its policies and procedures; its practices and protocols; and its program philosophy.

Supporting Knowledgeable and Responsive Early Childhood Educators

Early childhood educators have tremendously complex and challenging responsibilities that occur at the most impressionable ages of children's development—the early years. There is no room for mistakes. Many studies place ECEs at the fulcrum of quality. At this fulcrum, they balance many things simultaneously. First, they must balance the child's development; they must weigh the needs of a group of children while supporting the needs of individual learners. They need to balance different learning styles using a variety of teaching methods. Finally, they need to balance their role in the classroom with their role as advocates in the policy world.

Research identifies the most critical factor affecting children's early learning—after parents—is the quality of the professionals delivering programs. Children benefit most when their teachers have high levels of formal education and specialized early childhood professional preparation. Those with professional preparation, knowledge and skills in child development, and early childhood education are more likely to engage in warm, positive interactions with children, offer richer language experiences, and create high quality learning environments.

The work environment of early childhood settings influences adults' responsiveness to children, families, and communities. Staff require supportive supervision and opportunities to participate in ongoing professional environment to ensure that their knowledge and skills reflect the profession's growing knowledge base. Early childhood settings that are offered within this infrastructure of support, with working conditions that facilitate an early learning environment and reasonable levels of compensation, are assessed to be of better quality and are associated with better outcomes for children (Beach et al. 2004; Goelman et al. 2000). EC educators require a working environment that provides time for program planning, observation and documentation, opportunities for **professional development**, and ongoing conversations with families.

The document *Occupational Standards for Early Childhood Educators* (Child Care Human Resource Sector Council 2010) serves as the baseline document detailing EC knowledge and skills. It outlines skills, abilities, and core knowledge in nine areas. Occupational Standards describe what a person in a particular occupation needs to know and be able to do to be considered "capable." The Occupational Standards for Early Childhood Educators were developed for the EC sector, by frontline ECEs who perform the tasks and responsibilities of the job on a daily basis. Occupational standards can be used for:

- developing job descriptions
- conducting performance appraisals
- informing and assessing Early Childhood Educator professional program curricula
- identifying ongoing professional development needs
- informing certification/registration measures

In addition, both the Ontario Best Start Expert Panel on Early Learning (2007) and the Expert Panel on Quality and Human Resources note that directors provide leadership in creating a workplace that values the practice of knowledgeable, responsive, and reflective educators who consistently:

- integrate theoretical frameworks, research findings, and their own daily experiences to guide their interactions with young children and their families;
- develop responsive relationships with individual children and the group;

- respect family and ethnocultural diversity and appreciate the multitude of strengths of each child;
- communicate with family members and other professionals about what they are doing and why they are doing it;
- actively participate in play, guiding children's planning, decision making, and communication, and extending children's explorations;
- ensure that the environment and daily practices protect children's health, nutrition, safety, and well-being;
- identify concerns early and seek resources and/or provide appropriate interventions; and
- work with others in the community to support children's well-being.

To enable the use of these abilities requires knowledgeable leaders who are better able to **mentor** staff, promote best practices, communicate effectively with parents, and link families to other services.

HR Management: The Director's Responsibilities

In creating a strong and effective staff team, the director must:

- make thoughtful decisions about hiring, training, and supporting staff members;
- foster strong professional relationships focusing on individual strengths, areas for development, career aspirations, and interests; and
- provide leadership through effective communications, mentoring, and modeling professional behaviours; opportunities for continuous development; constructive feedback; and direction to continuously renew, revitalize, and strengthen the team.

A director of the EC program may be a member of a multi-site, multi-service organization, part of a municipality, report directly to a board of directors or an owner. Therefore, the governance body may vary, but the role of the program director must be clear. The director must ensure that program policies are followed. The operations of the organization must develop the operational policies based on the governing policies set out by the board of directors. Consequently, along with the program's governance body (board of directors or owner), the director may have the following human resource management responsibilities:

- create a professional work environment that meets the needs of the children and families;
- develop and implement effective human resource management policies that define roles and responsibilities, meet or exceed employment standards established by the provincial/territorial government, comply with a **collective agreement** where applicable, and fit with the program's philosophy and mission statement;
- demonstrate effective leadership needed to create a learning community and a supportive workplace, including strategies to maintain stable, knowledgeable staff and providing opportunities for ongoing program planning and career development as well as for continuous program improvement;
- provide leadership in recruiting, selecting, orienting, supervising, and motivating staff to high levels of performance;

- Develop and implement procedures and protocols to effectively and consistently manage performance, such as conducting regular performance reviews; and

- provide access to personal and professional development opportunities for team members.

Building a Talented, Creative Staff Team

Before designing a job description for a new position or recruiting candidates to fill a vacancy, review the program's mission statement and goals as outlined in Chapter 4 and carefully consider the program philosophy. Some questions to ask at this step are:

- How well is the program fulfilling its mission and accomplishing its goals?

- How does the organization measure its success and determine its need for development?

- How committed are the staff to the mission and goals of the program?

- How do staff become engaged in the workplace and remain committed to helping the organization reach its goals?

- How does the staff integrate the program philosophy in daily activities?

- Do the children and families become connected to the program, and what factors contribute to them staying involved?

A top-notch team is created by putting together the right combination of people with complementary and compatible skills, interests, and values. Directors face the ongoing challenge of finding career-committed professionals to work effectively with young children and families. Professional experience, education credentials, and personal characteristics are important elements.

Recruitment and retention is a known challenge facing the EC sector. Although there are many contributing factors, a lack of leadership and HR management skills within the sector contributes to recruitment and retention challenges. Research shows that improving human resource management (HRM) skills and practices of administrators is a strategy to improve job satisfaction of employees, which can reduce turnover by up to 20%. The Child Care Human Resource Sector Counsel has developed a HR Tool Kit focused on developing management tools specifically designed for EC employers.

These resources can enable employers to more effectively recruit, manage, and retain staff, as well this project addresses the overall recruitment and retention challenges in the sector. It will also contribute to skills development by:

- providing employers with training/information workshops on the importance of effective human resources management and also how to use the HR toolkit created

- promoting human resources management tools and best practices by providing workshops to capacity building organizations, such as professional EC associations.

A strong team works well together; they share a common philosophy; they support each other; and their skills and knowledge are compatible and complementary. A strong team provides a richer program for the children and families, and also provides opportunities for staff to share their expertise and skills with one another.

For children, the quality of the program is determined by the attitudes, knowledge, and skills of the people who nurture and provide a rich array of learning experiences. To maximize program quality, directors need to create work environments that encourage employees to make a long-term commitment to the program and want to contribute to the program's success.

Given the importance of well-qualified staff, an employer must attract and keep knowledgeable, skilled professionals. A well-planned and implemented recruitment strategy is a key first step.

Whether the goal is to build an entire staff team for a new program, fill a vacant position, or replace someone who is on a leave, the overall approach to finding the most suitable candidate/s will be the same. A staff member's role will be defined by the specific job responsibilities, the objectives of the program, and the community in which the program is located.

An organization must have a clear vision, code of conduct, and policies and procedures guiding the organization. The program director must ensure that the program is staffed accordingly. Some questions to ask are:

- Describe a person who would complement and strengthen the staff team.

- What level and type of education does the candidate need to possess?

- How much and what kind of experience is necessary?

- What personal characteristics and attributes do we need to build a strong team?

- Which desirable characteristics are "must-have," which are behaviours that "can-be-taught," and which are "could-be-developed-on-the-job"?

- Which skills and knowledge can be developed on the job with careful supervision, mentoring, and professional development?

- What supports must the program have to provide the professional development and what resources are needed to develop the required skills?

Answering these questions will help programs focus the search process to maximize program quality.

Human Resources Policies and Procedures

Every organization needs a set of written rules of professional behaviour as well as guidelines that are consistent with the culture of the organization. Effective **HR policies** balance the staffs' need to feel secure, confident, and challenged in their daily work with the director's need for effective program management.

The program's **human resources (HR) policies** (historically referred to as **personnel policies**) reflect the philosophy of the overall program, convey the program's values, and express the management principles. Policies must comply with, and ideally exceed, federal and provincial/territorial employment legislation, provincial/territorial child care legislation, municipal regulations, and occupational standards for quality.

The HR Policies and Procedures Manual is an important written document outlining details about the employment relationship, including hiring practices, termination procedures, and conditions of employment; management expectations; and operating procedures related to the staff team. It is a living document that is reviewed and updated on a regular basis. There is a need for clarity and consistency of HR information.

This manual includes details about organizational structure; roles, responsibilities, and accountability (reporting and supervision procedures); evaluation and disciplinary procedures; health and safety matters; and a description of the process to amend policies. HR policies are communicated to new employees at the time of hiring/orientation and made available for reference to all employees.

Developing and Amending HR Policies

Policies and procedures need to be reviewed periodically to reflect changes. As the program changes, the director determines if revised and/or additional policies are required. It is good practice to discuss these changes with the staff discuss possible content with them and ask for feedback. Generally, the board of directors/owner, directly or through an HR committee, develops HR policies; the director is responsible for implementing them. These roles are discussed in Chapter 3.

When organizations develop HR policies and procedures, they must comply with or exceed applicable laws, such as the provincial/territorial employment standards or labour legislation, which includes regulations on leaves, minimum wages, and hours of work. In a unionized work environment, policies must also conform to union requirements, which are outlined in a negotiated collective agreement.

The personnel policies should include a statement that outlines the procedure for amending the policies. On an ongoing basis, operators, staff, and director review the HR policies to determine any changes that are necessary. The decision makers then follow the amendment procedures. Once a change is adopted, the director needs to inform the staff of the changes.

Recruitment, Hiring, Orientation, and Termination
Designing Job Descriptions

Role clarity reduces uncertainty, minimizes conflict, and decreases workplace stress. A well-written job description can motivate employees and volunteers and serves as the foundation for an effective **performance appraisal** process. The job description encompasses all aspects of the position. The requirements for employment and the duties listed should reflect the philosophy and vision of the program. The description is written to clarify expectations yet retain the personal freedom of educators to carry out the performance of their roles according to their own unique style. Well-written job descriptions provide a framework within which an individual can function creatively while performing the tasks required.

Job descriptions are tools to provide guidance to applicants about the job's specific duties. When recruiting, it is important that job descriptions are complete and up-to-date. EC settings are dynamic rather than static, meaning that they must grow and develop to meet changing community needs. Job

Job descriptions are tools to provide guidance about the educator's specific duties.

descriptions must reflect any changes as result of this growth. Job descriptions should include the following key elements:

- *Job title:* a simple description of the nature of the job.
- *Accountability:* who the employee reports to (supervisor's full title), frequency of performance reviews, and length of **probationary period**, if applicable. It gives the employee a clear understanding of who will evaluate her work.
- *Job summary:* a brief description highlighting the general characteristics of the position. This summary is often used in recruitment activities.
- *Job requirements:* education, experience, skills, and personal qualities. Minimal qualifications are determined by licensing standards and union contracts; however, to achieve quality, a program would exceed these basic requirements.
- *Roles and responsibilities:* a more detailed statement of what duties the employee is expected to fulfill. This section outlines the tasks for which the employee will be held accountable.
- *Minimum performance standards:* EC is an intensely physical occupation and requires that educators are able to lift small children. Also, the staff must have good communication skills and be able to communicate clearly and intelligibly with children, families, and other professionals.
- *Salary and benefits schedule:* the range of compensation for the position and the **benefits**.
- *Work schedule:* hours of work, work schedule, vacation entitlement, and other work arrangements available such as job sharing.

Job descriptions are prepared prior to hiring a new employee. Job descriptions may be altered while someone is already in the position. In this case, the employee must be given ample notice for any changes. Job descriptions are usually included as part of the staff handbook.

The job description becomes the standards against which employee competence is measured. Thus it is also a management tool that defines program expectations and employee responsibilities, and supports program goals. On a regular basis (minimum annually), the director meets with each staff member to review her existing job description and assess her individual and team strengths and the need for further development.

It serves as an agreement between the employer and employee. It carries the weight of a legal document when used to support hiring, disciplinary, and termination activities. The legal weight of a job description means it must be complete and include all required duties. Attention to details can help directors avoid staff problems and potential legal problems later. As a legal document, it enables the program to meet legislative requirements for non-discriminatory employment practices.

Identifying Potential Candidates

Successful leaders think about recruitment as a continuous process. Continuous recruitment means establishing systems that help fill vacancies as they occur by generating a pool of applicants. There is no one-size-fits-all approach. Continuous recruitment strategies must be individualized for the program.

Given the relatively small pool of qualified personnel, EC programs will likely find themselves competing against other employers for staff. Directors will need to recognize the challenge of recruiting suitable applicants. This challenge, along with strategies to expand recruitment, are being researched by a number of provinces and the Child Care Human Resources Sector Council.

Directors must consider unique features of the program or work environment that will attract the desired candidate, and highlight these features in creating a posting for the job. Post the job internally to ensure that current staff have the opportunity to apply. They should not hear about a position from outside. Staff may know of a suitable candidate to recommend. Often desirable candidates can be drawn from those who have completed student placements with the program or are currently working as replacement staff.

Networking is an important strategy. Most communities have a support group of other EC supervisors to share resources information and access emotional support for successes and challenges.

Advertise the position in diverse communities. Keep in mind the many possible combinations of education, experience, and personal attributes that could characterize qualified applicants, and target recruitment strategies accordingly. Programs must establish and follow the same procedures for recruiting, interviewing, and filling vacancies each time the need arises.

Finally, consider the cost-effectiveness (in terms of both time and money) of potential recruitment strategies. Frequently recommended strategies include:

- actively encourage applications from current staff;

- generate word of mouth among colleagues;

- notify parents of recruitment needs;

- participate in job fairs and career days;

- use networks of non-profit organizations and other professional associations;

- notify career-counselling offices at local college and universities that deliver programs in early childhood education;

- notify faculties of human development, psychology, social work, education, and other disciplines within colleges and universities;

- advertise in professional and community newsletters; and

- post on websites for early childhood organizations, non-profits, or practitioners (e.g., the site for Child and Family Canada, Monster.ca, or Charity Village).

Hiring for Diversity   Directors should actively recruit educators who reflect gender, ethnic, cultural, and linguistic diversity. A diverse staff is more likely to help family members from all backgrounds feel welcome in the setting. Staff must be able to meet the children's diverse developmental, cultural, linguistic, and educational needs. They need to have an understanding of socio-cultural and economic issues pertaining to the communities in which the children live. This knowledge can be useful in supporting families on the continuing of development of the child's home language and in the acquisition of English and/or French. Staff who speak more than one language and are knowledgeable about more than one culture are an invaluable resource in a diverse community.

A second consideration in recruitment is gender. Our society continues to warm up to the idea of men working with very young children. Expectations are changing. However, we still have a long way to go, even within our own sector. Children have the right to be nurtured and educated in a gender balanced environment. Parents often want their children to have positive male role models.

Compared to the number of similarly qualified women, there are relatively few qualified men available to fill the positions. Finding qualified men will start with the expectation that men should be involved in the care and education of young children. Recognition will need to be given to the fact that men may have to be invited into our sector.

Canada has less than 4% male staff, whereas the European Economic Union is targeting 20% male staff in EC by 2015. This situation stems in part from societal beliefs that women have a natural, instinctive ability to nurture children and men do not. Male staff can fill a special role for young children, particularly those who grow up in single-parent homes without a male role model. Yet, men leave the early childhood field at a greater rate than women. Some male educators have reported that they were subject to subtle prejudicial attitudes from parents, female co-workers, and directors. Misconceptions about men who work in early childhood settings include the following stereotypes: men may get romantically involved with co-workers or parents, or male practitioners are more likely than females to abuse children. There is a need for staff to examine individual attitudes and help increase parental awareness of the value of male staff members.

Marc Battle, instructor at Red River College in Winnipeg, noted that it is important that the field know that men leave because of the hostile work environment. That sometimes there are those subtle prejudicial attitudes, but overwhelmingly men are tired of having their own play histories as children demonized—"no superheroes in day care," "no guns in day care," that programs often have outrageously small block areas and very large dress up areas, "use quiet inside voices" and the complete elimination of anything that even smells of a risk of very active play. And often male ECEs are told by their equally trained female colleagues, "Don't you know better?" when male colleagues create opportunities that resemble the kind of play that they, as children, engaged in.

Like female staff, male colleagues report poor compensation and working conditions as a pivotal factor affecting recruitment and retention. These economic factors often prevent men from entering or staying in the early childhood field.

Strategies to encourage and support male educators:

There is a need to increase the number of males working in EC programs.

Here are some considerations for bringing more men into the field and encouraging them to stay:

- Babysitting is one way that boys discover they like working with young children. In school-age programs, encourage boys to learn skills required to care for children. Support older boys who would like to read to and mentor young children.

- Directors should do everything they can to ensure that at least two male staff are employed at any time and that they are connected with other men in the sector through support groups, etc. Visit the website www.menteach.org listed at the end of this chapter. Research tells us that these types of supports significantly increase the length of employment of men in the field.

Incorporate positive images of men: Display images of men interacting young children; select picture books with positive male characters; help male staff to be visible at the program. When making men more visible and showing pictures of men engaging in work, males insist that any images should portray men doing men things—we know women like pictures of men holding babies, but guys want to see pictures of men building forts with kids or kicking a ball.

Increase the number of male staff working in the program: Invite men perhaps from the extended family, community members, or high schools to volunteer in the program. Actively recruit male educators for field experiences as well as targeting advertisements toward men placed in the "general" section of the newspaper. This is where young men without professional qualifications may be looking for a job. For example, *"Looking for a few good men with the courage to work in early childhood settings. ABC Child Care believes gender balance is good for young children."* (An ad like this in Winnipeg drew 30 responses.)

- Be recruiters for the profession. When directors find men who feel comfortable working with young children, they should encourage them to pursue a career in early childhood.

- Examine possible gender bias in interactions and in the environment. Use gender neutral language; include a variety of props and apparel for dramatic play; have open discussions about gender bias.

- Don't add to the fear and discrimination already present by having restrictive policies for men. Staff are staff. Assign tasks based on criteria other than gender. Men can and should change diapers. Women can and should lift boxes. Encourage females to lead sports activities.

To build an effective team, directors and staff need to help male staff feel comfortable, connected, and valued. Consider what it is like to be in a minority. Imagine what it would be like to be the only woman working with dozens of men. Each staff member should support male co-workers to stay connected.

These considerations are compelling. Review documentation such as policy manuals, philosophy statements, parent handbooks, or other documents outlining program beliefs and guidelines. Consider adding statements like: "The presence of men is essential to the lives of young children" and "Preference will be given to candidates from the same cultural and linguistic backgrounds as the families served."

Screening and Interviewing Potential Candidates

The process begins by selecting the team to screen applicants for interviews. Research shows that EC educators want to be involved in decisions that directly affect them and one of those decisions is the selection of colleagues. Co-worker relations are paramount in creating a nurturing

EC environment. How compatible educators are and how they interact with one another greatly influence the quality of the program. Involving staff in helping to determine which applicant is the best fit for the program is both complicated and time-consuming. However, in building goal consensus, nurturing collegiality and encouraging greater commitment to a shared vision is an important characteristic of programs with successful staff retention.

The interview process provides an opportunity for the director, program staff, and applicant to ask questions, provide information, and get to know each other. A good match will increase the possibility of success and improve the likelihood of the staff person remaining at the centre. Staff changes are unsettling to children, families, and other staff. When a program hires someone who doesn't work out, it wastes the time and energy it took for recruiting, interviewing, hiring, and orienting the person—and the disheartening requirement to begin the process over again.

Many programs use a standard five-step process for hiring: screening, interviewing, observing, selecting, and negotiating. The first step involves the initial screening of resumés against the identified requirements. The screening step of the process is to determine who will be interviewed. Things that should be looked for include:

- Appearance of the application;
- Missing information in the candidate's summary of professional experiences;
- Career progression;
- Match with the program's fit criteria—do they meet the requirements of the job?

The director and representatives of the hiring team determine the applicants to be interviewed. The second step involves the preliminary interviews, which narrow the field by determining how well the candidates' qualifications fit the program's needs.

In the third step, potential candidates may be invited to participate individually in the playroom for a minimum of two hours, providing the opportunity for the director and/or staff to observe their skills in interacting with children, perhaps parents and other staff.

The fourth step involves the interviewing team selecting a candidate for the position following a thorough assessment of the candidate's resumé, the results of the interview, an assessment of the observation, discussion of the program's needs, and information gathered during the reference checks.

The fifth step involves the offer of employment. Usually the director prepares the offer, presents it to the candidate, and completes the negotiations.

As noted earlier, involving staff in the hiring process contributes to building a strong team. Staff may be included in the process by reviewing resumés or applications, asking questions and/or taking notes during the interview, and observing a candidate's style of interaction in the playroom. A staff member who participates in selecting a candidate is likely to be more supportive in facilitating the new member's integration into the staff team.

AREAS TO COVER WHEN INTERVIEWING A CANDIDATE

- education, skill, and experience related to the position
- knowledge and understanding of child development
- personal philosophy of early childhood
- demonstrated ability to plan a learning program
- strategies used for guiding and supporting children's behaviour

- evidence of problem-solving strategies and conflict resolution style
- methods used for involving families in the program
- commitment to ongoing personal and professional development
- attitude, talents, attributes, and characteristics
- interpersonal and communication skills
- compensation expectations and availability (possible start date) and any terms and conditions

Conducting an Interview   Open-ended questions and proposing or providing scenarios contribute to learning how a candidate thinks and responds. For example, "What does a family need in order to raise a responsible, happy child?" As well as providing information about the candidate's skills and knowledge, this type of question allows the team to explore how well his or her philosophical beliefs match those of the program. Decide on the questions before the interview, ask each candidate the same questions, and thoroughly document all responses. Some examples include:

- Explain why you want to do this kind of work, and tell us what attracts you to this position.
- Describe an approach you have used in the past to calm a child, redirect inappropriate behaviour, introduce a new activity, etc. Describe the situation, your strategy, and the results of your action.
- Describe your greatest strength in working with young children and families.
- What professional development opportunities have you pursued in the past year?
- Describe your personal philosophy.
- How might employers/colleagues describe you? If they had to name one quality that gets in the way of your success, what would it be?
- What new skills would you like to learn? How do you learn best?
- Describe your ideal work environment: the people, the relationships, the program, the setting.
- Describe how you have managed in a situation when you were faced with people with values that are different from your own.
- Describe a stressful situation you were recently in, and describe how you managed the stress.

The interviewing team must be aware of human rights legislation and know which questions are legal and illegal to ask. It is good practice to have a human resources consultant to review the list of questions to ensure that you are not violating these laws. Among the types of questions you cannot directly or indirectly inquire about include: marital status, pregnancy, union affiliations, family information, etc. All applicants are asked the same questions, and their answers must be well documented.

Time invested in planning a thoughtful and thorough hiring process contributes to both the interviewing team and candidate having many opportunities to exchange information and make well-informed decisions about the job match. Remember, while a candidate is being interviewed, he or she is also interviewing the program. Effective hiring procedures result in greater compatibility between the employee and the program, a higher level of job satisfaction, and, ultimately, a higher quality program.

Checking References

Prior to making a job offer to a candidate, it is important to check references. It is important to invest time to conduct a thorough background check on the candidates being considered. To gather information about a candidate's previous work performance can be through a telephone check, a written check, or both. The goal is to get a view of the applicant's skills and knowledge from another point of view. References generally include professional references from people who have supervised or worked with the candidate, criminal references from the local law enforcement authority, and health checks from a recognized health professional. Before contacting previous employers or other reference, be sure to get the candidate's written permission.

Professional References   The director should tell the person giving the reference what position the candidate is applying for and give a brief overview of the important qualifications for the job. Ask the referee to describe how the candidate's characteristics or experience demonstrate that he or she will be able to fulfill the job requirements. Ask about the referee's general experience with the candidate. Ask them to describe the areas in which the candidate needs to grow or requires support or professional development.

Criminal Reference Checks   Most provinces have established background-check requirements for both candidates seeking employment and volunteers. The director must make a criminal and abuse registry check on each applicant who is a serious contender for the position. Checks are performed using the applicant's name, date of birth, and more recently fingerprints. One must be very cautious when hiring individuals who will work directly with young children. An individual must be free of any history of substantiated child abuse or neglect. Those in the decision-making role need to develop policies for how to handle a **criminal reference check** that comes back showing a conviction. Criminal reference checks do infringe on the rights of individuals who have records. In the field of early childhood, however, the rights of adults with criminal records are subordinate to the rights of the children, who need to trust and depend on the staff members.

Health Checks   All staff must possess the physical and mental health to perform the tasks required. All jurisdictions have health requirements that include: a physical assessment stating that the individual is free from communicable diseases, a negative tuberculin test or follow-up on a positive one, and an immunization record. The successful candidate provides these records prior to commencing employment.

Extending an Offer/Signing a Contract

Once the hiring team selects a candidate, an offer is presented stating the terms of employment and a compensation package. Once the offer is accepted, an employment **contract** is put together. A contract is a binding legal agreement between an individual and the board of directors/owner specifying the services the staff member will provide and the remuneration to be paid for those services. Other details documented in a written contract include the date of hiring; probationary period; performance appraisal process; pay for the period covered by the contract; benefits; conditions for termination; and, in some cases, the termination date.

New Employee Orientation

When done right, employee orientation programs are the foundation of the program's professional development strategy. Too often it is haphazard with a cursory overview of centre policies and procedures, with a quick tour of the facilities. Too many new educators are thrust into the job with little guidance.

Integrating new staff members takes commitment, determination, and patience. A well-planned, individualized orientation program sets the stage for open communication and is an opportunity to model good practice. An effective process introduces new staff members to general aspects of the program, such as philosophy, objectives, curriculum, program, and strategies for family involvement. A detailed orientation process is necessary when new employees start their jobs.

A good orientation program covers the essential technical aspects of the job and program operations. The employee reviews essential elements of the position and completes all paperwork required by licensing body. The orientation should also introduce the employee with information about the history and mission of the organization, its culture, policies and procedures, operations, and administration including but not limited to acquainting employee;

- *Overview of the program:* culture, values, and vision and their place in it;
- *Organizational structure:* board of directors, staff reporting.
- *Terms of employment:* job descriptions, hiring procedures, compensation, discipline, termination, conflict resolutions/problem solving, resignation/termination.
- *Performance-appraisal:* process and probationary period.
- *Benefits for employees:* holidays, sick days, health benefits, insurance, **staff development**.
- *Expectations of employees:* behaviour guidance, reporting requirements, health and safety, family/staff/child relations, attendance.
- *Policies, procedures, and protocols:* confidentiality, documentation, and record keeping.

The formal orientation process takes place over several months, including time for on-the-job orientation when the new staff member can review program policies and procedures, the staff manual, and learn the specific responsibilities of the position. Compiling accessible written resources can contribute to the new employee making the transition to informed decision making and finding their own answers.

Current staff play an important role in integrating new staff by serving as mentors. Mentors can help provide the orientation. More important, mentors can introduce the new staff member to the team and families. Mentors can be safe havens for new employees with questions that they may not feel comfortable asking the director.

The period spent orienting the new employee, introducing her/him to the children and families, and familiarizing him/her with the overall operation is time well spent. Strategies to assist parents in welcoming a new member of the staff may include a profile in a newsletter and/or on a bulletin board and a welcoming introduction at a parent meeting. Such measures will help to build a successful long-term relationship with staff members, and they will feel respected and valued as a member of the team. Orientation helps new educators function optimally in their jobs. Because each educator brings different skills, knowledge, and abilities to the job, their orientation needs to be individualized.

Managing Performance
Goal Setting and Performance Appraisals

EC educators have many job functions. They are responsible for the early learning and care of young children, planning curriculum, collaborating with other educators, assessing children's development, maintaining health and safety guidelines, communicating with families, and so on. See Job description of Registered Early Childhood Educator in the next page. New staff, even those who are experienced, should be expected to perform all of these functions at once. Leaders along with staff need to assess their skill level in various areas and assess what supports are needed to continue to grow professionally.

Directors have the overall responsibility for performance management, although sometimes board members/owners are involved. Some directors view performance management as one of the most difficult, time-consuming, and emotionally challenging tasks they face. Yet, when staff performance is consistently managed and performance regularly reviewed, it can become the springboard for professional growth, program improvement, and staff motivation. Many programs use the job description as the basis for the performance management process. New practitioners or new hires may have performance reviews weekly for the first two months and once a month for the next two months; then, if the person is performing as expected, perhaps quarterly thereafter.

The annual or semi-annual review provides an opportunity to both reflect on staff performance and ensure that the job description is updated to represent increased responsibilities. Directors can use the review process to identify strengths and needs, design opportunities for addressing and reinforcing those areas, and develop the unique potential of each staff member.

Every performance management meeting should include a brief review of the staff member's functioning since the last meeting, a review of the goals set at the previous meetings, and plans for the next period. All performance meetings should be documented, and the documentation summary of the discussions should be initialled by both the employee and their supervisor. This documentation provides a foundation for personal and professional development but can also provide the basis for providing recognition, offering a promotion or salary increase, or for a decision to terminate employment.

In a supportive climate, a performance appraisal process is motivating, builds competence, and increases commitment to the organization. All staff members need to know that they are valued and respected for their work. It is a challenge for directors to create an atmosphere that encourages all staff to enhance their knowledge, skills, and participate in self-assessment—and one that values creation of a quality program. A director plays a vital role by providing ongoing support and giving staff open, honest, and regular feedback. While it is up to the individual to make the decision to change her or his behaviour, this feedback on performance provides direction for change. It makes individuals aware of what they do well and can help them improve their performance. Such feedback need not be directive. The best evaluation model is one where director and staff work together to identify challenges, generate solutions, and explore alternatives.

Such an appraisal model concentrates on the staff member's performance, rather than on her or his character. It is specific rather than global and focuses on the future rather than the past. Regular, open communication will have a more enduring impact on an individual's self-esteem and overall performance than any specific resources that are provided to the individual. Both Caruso and Fawcett (1999) and Sciarra and Dorsey (2002) provide a comprehensive look at supervision practices from a perspective that acknowledges the stages of employee development.

Sample

Job Description—Registered Early Childhood Educator

Job Summary
Under the direction of the director and in co-operation with colleagues, plans, implements, monitors, and evaluates the program in accordance with provincial regulations, Toronto Operating Criteria and program philosophy.

Qualifications

- Early Childhood Education Diploma from a recognized Community College or A.E.C.E.O. equivalency.
- Current registration with the College of Early Childhood Educators.
- Maintains a current CPR and First Aid Certificate.
- Experience working with children from infancy to 5 years of age.
- Experience working with diverse families.
- Experience working with children with special needs.
- Demonstrates leadership, flexibility, creativity, and innovation.
- Self-motivated, excellent communication and interpersonal skills, good organizational skills, patience, self-control, tact, sound judgment, discretion, sensitivity, and a positive outlook.
- Clear police check.
- Verification of medical suitability of the successful candidate.

Summary

- Planning, directing, and implementing quality programming using Emergent Curriculum principles to enhance the physical, social, emotional, and cognitive well being of the children.
- Implementing and designing learning plans for all children, both individually and for the group.
- Maintaining ongoing communications with families, staff, and the community.
- Providing ongoing supervision of playroom, playground, group, and routine activities.
- Demonstrating a professional approach and contributes to team cohesion.
- Demonstrating appropriate instructional techniques to Early Childhood Education students, and directing, monitoring, and evaluating their progress.

Job Responsibilities

1. *To create environments that are carefully planned to meet individual needs and facilitate the children's progress in all areas of development*:
   - Demonstrates commitment to children's learning by providing age-, individual-, and developmentally-appropriate activities to enhance cognitive, physical, emotional, and social development.

(continued)

- Uses a variety of teaching techniques, including modelling, observing, questioning, demonstrating, and reinforcing.
- Provides a daily balance of quiet/active, indoor/outdoor, and individual/group activities.
- Creates and maintains meaningful learning environments for children.
- Implements a schedule that incorporates child-directed activities, care routines, and transition times.
- Develops, implements, and evaluates programs to promote and enhance creativity in all areas: arts and crafts, drama, sensory domain, cognition (literacy, numeracy, . . .), emotional awareness, music appreciation, science and nature, and fine- and gross-motor activities.
- Uses a variety of teaching/instruction strategies to support learning during play and small group activities, including observing, questioning, coaching, modelling, demonstrating, and scaffolding.
- Provides social experiences that foster co-operation, respect for others, and self-sufficiency.
- Plans and implements opportunities that facilitate understanding of a variety of cultures and value systems.
- Provides experiences and play materials that actively promote anti-racist and non-sexist attitudes.
- Plans and carries out activities that encourage problem solving.
- Maintains files on each child consisting of samples of the child's work.
- Observes children's progress and behaviour to ensure that the program meets individual and group needs.
- Respects the rights of each child and sensitivity to the individual needs and diversity of children.
- Participates in team meetings in order to discuss the implementation of the overall program, share information, and discuss progress of individual children.
- In collaboration with team and families, recommends the referral of children to community agencies.
- Incorporates intervention programs, such as speech therapy, to meet the individual needs of children.
- Participates in educational assessment conferences with community agencies.

2. *Ensures the health, welfare, and safety of the children are a priority*:
   - Observes and assesses the development of individual children.
   - Provides an emotionally supportive environment and shows sensitivity to the individual needs of children in all aspects of their development.
   - Participates with other staff to ensure the safety of children. Scans the learning environment and anticipates when support or intervention is required.

- Monitors safety of all areas used by children, including washrooms and playground.
- Checks learning materials and equipment used in activities to ensure safe functioning.
- Reports unusual situations, such as allergies, accidents, parental requests and concerns, or behavioural irregularities.
- Provides/arranges for first aid in case of emergencies, fulfills recoding-keeping responsibilities as required, and prepares accident reports and/or Serious Occurrence reports.
- Administers medication as authorized by physician, and maintains records of all medication administered.
- Conducts a daily health check of children.
- Accommodates for children's allergies; is aware of signs and symptoms; prevents risk of cross contamination, develops an allergy response plan with the family; can administer an EpiPen in the event of an anaphylactic reaction.
- Contacts parents regarding illnesses and documents symptoms/communication.
- Ensures that children have adequate nourishment and any special dietary requirements (culture, allergies, . . .) are met.
- Uses positive, fair, and consistent methods of behaviour guidance in accordance with the program's policies.
- Consistently helps children regulate emotions and behaviour, and focus attention.
- Supports children's logical thinking and problem-solving skills by demonstrating respect and concern for others while at the same time establishing responsible limits.

3. Contributes to a welcoming environment for all families and forms collaborative partnerships with families:
   - Demonstrates respect for all families and recognizes the centrality of the family to the health and well-being of children.
   - Develops responsive relationships with parents of every child.
   - Demonstrates respect for diversity, equity, and inclusion principles in work with young children, families, and communities.
   - Respects differences in families' child-rearing values and practices.
   - Responds to inquiries and/or requests for meetings from parents regarding their child's progress and behaviour.
   - Encourages and provides opportunities for families to participate in all aspects of planning and decision making for their children.
   - Implements a variety of communication strategies with families (e.g., bulletin boards, family newsletter, family literacy program, special events, and social networking).

(continued)

- Shares information with families on a regular basis, plans and attends parent interviews and parent evenings, and acts as a resource to families.

4. Contributes to the program exceeding the standards set by legislation, program policies, and the expectations of the board of directors:

- Keeps aware of policy changes and maintains an appropriate knowledge of legislation, quality practices, policies, and procedures which directly affect their professional practice.

- Contributes to the program complying with the Day Nurseries Act, City of Toronto Operating Criteria, other required legislation and adheres to all program policies.

- Contributes to the evaluation of program and recommends modifications to improve effectiveness.

- Interacts and collaborates with colleagues and other professionals in ways that demonstrate respect, trust, integrity, and accountability.

- Participates as a resource and/or mentor through sharing professional experiences, resources, and role modelling best practice.

- Models skills and provides feedback to ECE students that support their theoretical training.

- Actively participates in staff meetings and other functions.

- After discussion/consultation with supervisor, other duties may be assigned on a temporary basis.

  - Fulfils record-keeping responsibilities, including:

    - Completes and posts weekly program/curriculum chart (indoor and playground).

    - Records ongoing observations, gathers children's work samples, completes children's daily charts.

    - Completes all required documentation such as attendance records, planning charts, child record counts, daily playground checklist, Serious Occurrence, and flushing records.

    - Completes student evaluation forms and reviewing student activity plans and documentation panels to support ECE student's learning within a timely basis.

5. Actively demonstrates responsibility for own personal/professional growth and development to enhance practice and decision making.

- Participates in professional development activities to maintain a current knowledge of ECE theory, practices, and issues.

- Engages in ongoing professional learning, reflective practice, and critical thinking.

- Accesses current evidenced-based research and transfers this knowledge into practice.

- Participates in the performance appraisal process.

- Demonstrates capacity to problem-solve and make good choices.

- Practices and promotes the ethical responsibilities in Code of Ethics.
- Maintains confidentiality at all times.
- Complies with any continuing competence measures required by the College of Early Childhood Educators.

Source: This job description was compiled from materials from Occupational Standards for Early Childhood Practitioners (2010); Standards of Practice from College of Early Childhood Educators.

Supporting Staff Development—The Director's Role

The relationship between the director and staff is a critical element in improving performance. The quality of the director's skills combined with the degree of trust between the director and the staff determines the success of the performance appraisal process.

Early feedback that clarifies the expectations of the program can be especially helpful to new staff. Performance reviews give the employer feedback on the results of the selection process, can acknowledge superior performance, and provide a basis for career planning and professional development. The performance management system used must fit the professional skills, maturity, and experience of the staff. A comprehensive approach to assessing

Study *Understanding Quality in Context* found higher quality where directors held high expectations and confidence in their staff.

staff performance will use a variety of formats to meet the needs of individual practitioners at each stage of their development. (The stages of professional growth are discussed in Chapter 6, "Promoting Professionalism.")

The need for ongoing professional development is universal, whatever an individual's profession. EC professionals must continually enrich their knowledge and increase their sense of professionalism over the course of their careers in order to implement current research-based practice. Professional development is more than taking a course or attending a workshop. To be a reflective theory-based professional requires considering on one's vision for children and families, professional philosophy, ethical values, and professional plan.

Directors who have higher expectations hire educators with certain skills, knowledge, and performance in classroom practices and child outcomes. In the study *Understanding Quality in Context: Child Care Centres, Communities, Markets and Public Policy (2010)* found higher quality in EC programs where directors had high expectations and a high degree of confidence in their staff. The strategies associated with higher expectations for staff included:

- Establishing personal relationships with the staff;
- Supporting them through compensation;
- Supporting professional development and growth;
- Motivating educators to pursue professional growth and development;
- Setting up a staffing structure that enabled educators to be responsive to children; and
- Providing sufficient supplies and materials.

In order for directors to put these supports in place for their staff, they often had access to additional financial resources to finance professional development costs. These directors created an environment that enhances the professional life of the staff and contributes to the development of relationships within the program. Such an enabling environment flows from the program philosophy and values. Such activities not only rejuvenate individual staff members, their benefits often have a ripple effect when new ideas and resources are shared with other staff members.

Directors need to ensure that resources—time and money—are available for staff development. Staff opportunities for continuous growth not only bolster morale, they also enhance the program's ability to foster children's healthy growth and development. Some programs provide funds for staff to take relevant courses through colleges or universities and/or give staff members time to complete their field placements and/or daytime courses. Increasingly, e-learning programs are providing new opportunities for professional growth and development. Examples of online opportunities include attaining credentials, collaboration, policy discussions, and access to guidelines for appropriate practice.

To keep staff well-informed, there needs to be a resource area in the staff room stocked with videos, professional magazines, journals, and books. Investing in a professional library is a cost-effective way of enhancing program quality. Noteworthy resources should be circulated among staff, students, and families.

There are some professional resource centres that provide professional development opportunities, such as Child Care Connections Nova Scotia, West Coast Child Care Resource Centre in Vancouver, Affiliated Services for Children and Youth in Hamilton, the Early Childhood Development Centre in Niagara, and Alberta Resource Centre for Quality Enhancement in Edmonton. Local colleges and universities can be another important source of support, particularly for staff who are completing course work or continuing their education.

Creating a Great Place to Work

In *Improving the Quality of Work Life*, Jorde Bloom et al. (2010) identifies a number of factors affecting the quality of the work environment and, ultimately, the quality of the setting. These factors include the amount of support received from the director, opportunities for professional development, clarity of job expectations, an equitable reward system, and a responsive and physical **work environment**. In order to have a dynamic workforce, staff must feel welcomed, respected and adequately resourced as illustrated in Figure 5-1.

The general layout and design of space can help or hinder staff in carrying out their jobs and powerfully influence moods and attitudes. Staff must have the proper equipment, materials, and resources to do their work effectively. (This aspect of early childhood settings is discussed in detail in Chapter 7, "Managing Safe and Healthy Learning Environments.")

The director must be attuned to potential health hazards in the workplace. The Canadian Pædiatric Society (2008) cites the following health hazards for early childhood educators: increased risk of illness, toxic substances in art supplies and cleaning agents, back problems from heavy lifting and frequent bending, physical strain from using furniture in an environment designed for children, poor lighting, high noise levels, and stress. Another major health hazard comes from the common tendency among some educators to ignore their own health needs,

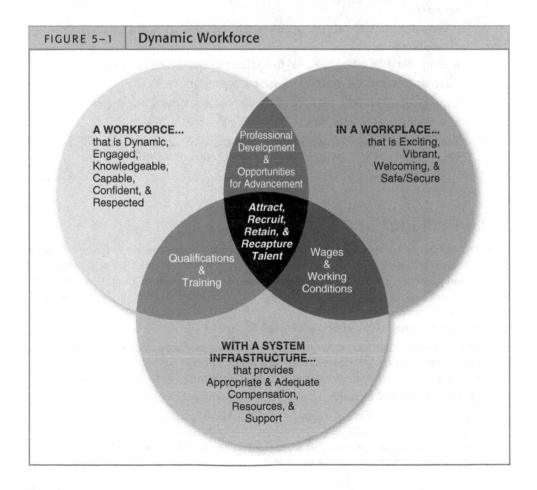

FIGURE 5–1   Dynamic Workforce

A WORKFORCE...
that is Dynamic,
Engaged,
Knowledgeable,
Capable,
Confident, &
Respected

Professional
Development
&
Opportunities
for Advancement

IN A WORKPLACE...
that is Exciting,
Vibrant,
Welcoming, &
Safe/Secure

*Attract,
Recruit,
Retain, &
Recapture
Talent*

Qualifications
&
Training

Wages
&
Working
Conditions

WITH A SYSTEM
INFRASTRUCTURE...
that provides
Appropriate & Adequate
Compensation,
Resources, &
Support

because they feel responsible for meeting children's needs first and/or they lack extended health benefits and time off, or there are no available replacement staff.

Managing for Wellness   Directors provide leadership and manage in a manner that promotes and enriches both organizational health and individual well-being. Staff have the right to a safe, healthy work environment. There should be a space where staff can relax. Leaders can reduce stress by coaching staff to tackle challenges collaboratively and by being available to discuss concerns. As workforce diversity increases, managers need to remain aware of ways to support employee's health and wellness and work–life balance. A survey of employers revealed that eldercare resource and referral has nearly doubled and paid leave for adoptive parents is up by 30%. Two-thirds of the companies surveyed offer the option of working part-time; 50% offer a compressed workweek; 45% flex-time; and 40% job-sharing (Child Care Information Exchange 2001).

IN THE STAFF RESOURCE AREA

- Reference materials on early childhood, parenting skills, and community resources.
- Information available about upcoming conferences and workshops on a variety of topics.
- A computer with Internet access to facilitate use of online resources.
- Journals and publications of professional organizations.
- Catalogues and brochures from distributors of equipment and materials.
- Newsletters and information on current legislation.
- Textbooks and audiovisual resources concerned with various aspects of child development, administration, child guidance, curriculum, etc.

Documentation and Record Keeping

Employee Records   HR management involves maintaining up-to-date **employee records** on each individual staff in accordance with provincial/territorial regulations and the program's policies and procedures. Employee records must be current and confidential. They should be kept in a secure place, and access should be restricted to the individual employee and the director/immediate supervisor.

Items often contained in an employee record include:

- *Personal information,* including employee's name, address, and telephone number; social insurance number; names, addresses, and telephone numbers of those persons to be contacted in the case of an emergency; physician's name; and telephone number.
- *Application material,* including transcripts, references, and resumé.
- *Health records that meet licensing requirements,* including a physical assessment stating that the individual is free from communicable diseases; a negative tuberculin test or follow-up on a positive one; and an immunization record. These should be updated in accordance with local regulations or at least every two years. Any on-the-job injuries

should be documented, along with the treatment given. Records of frequent absences due to illness should also be included.

- *Employment record,* including start date, leaves, salary levels, history of salary increases, vacation accruals, benefits documents, and termination.

- *Professional development history,* including transcripts from any courses completed after hiring, certificates documenting participation in professional development activities, etc.

- *Performance appraisal records,* including goals set and plans for the next period.

- *Record of any disciplinary action taken,* documented as per HR policies. These records should not be kept after they have fulfilled the purpose for which they were intended.

Employment records can be computerized and must be kept confidential by restricting access through the use of password protection. Individuals have a legal right to privacy, and directors must keep abreast of the privacy laws pertaining to record keeping, security, and confidentiality. As of 2004, Canada's *Personal Information Protection and Electronic Documents Act* came into effect. The Manitoba Child Care Association (MCCA) has developed resources to aid EC programs in developing a privacy policy. Employment records must be stored in accordance with regulations even after employment is terminated. Emergency information for each employee should be easily accessible and always current. It should include information on any allergies or conditions that may be critical in an emergency.

Conflict Resolution and Problem Solving

Ideally, the director has created a working environment that promotes self-discipline. However, from time to time, situations arise that need to be addressed. These tend to cluster around a few issues: concerns about co-workers who make the job difficult or are perceived to negatively impact the program quality, problems with staff or volunteers who behave unprofessionally, or a staff concern that the director does not manage people effectively.

Solving these problems is challenging. Rarely does one quick, easy answer suffice. Often the problem is complex and multi-faceted. The more complex the problem, the more time-consuming and difficult it can be to find a solution. In most cases, the director will have to provide leadership and make tough decisions.

Requesting an individual meeting with the person involved to discuss the concern is the first step. However, the best way to handle problems is prevention. The director can minimize conflicts by creating a supportive work environment that facilitates the establishment of positive working relationships among co-workers and by building strong and effective teams based on an atmosphere of mutual trust, respect, and honesty. In Saifer's *Practical Solutions to Practically Every Problem: The Early Childhood Teacher's Manual, Revised Edition* (2005), there are very helpful suggestions to aid staff in preventing problems and resolving concerns.

Regular contact with each employee, ongoing performance appraisals, and immediate feedback can prevent or quickly resolve any conflict or solve problems. Dealing with situations early can mean easier and quicker resolution. An astute director will recognize signs of dissatisfaction and immediately identify its cause.

The first step for a staff member to address an issue or resolve a situation should be to speak directly to the person involved. Many situations can be solved this way. If that fails, the next step is to involve the director. Everyone involved has the right to see that conflict resolutions reach a logical conclusion. The conflict resolution policy should be discussed with staff and acted upon, so that individuals appreciate its validity. The director needs to establish herself as a person who will listen to concerns, take complaints seriously, address issues quickly and consistently, solve problems competently, and resolve conflicts fairly.

At the heart of every conflict resolution procedure is the fundamental question of the rights and responsibilities of employment. A **conflict resolution** procedure is a written statement informing employees that they have the right to express complaints and that the employer will review and respond to their complaints. A common area of concern is the interpretation of HR policies. No matter how clearly policies are written, there are always situations that do not fit the existing policies and will require a judgment call. Second, there may be an employee–supervisor conflict. A conflict resolution procedure will include an explanation of how an employee can appeal to a higher level in the organization regarding a decision or action made by a supervisor or director. For example, if an employee is not satisfied with a director's decision, the employee may appeal to the board of directors/owner by following a policy and the procedures set out by the board of directors.

When an employee is not performing as expected, the concern needs to be discussed immediately. If necessary, the director may need to take disciplinary action as outlined in Steps in **Corrective Action** following. Should an employee fail to meet the minimum performance standards, fail to comply with the policies and procedures of the program, or violate any program rules, the issue should be discussed with the employee and followed up in writing. If the employee fails to correct her or his actions or change his or her behaviour, or continues to break the rules, she or he should be given a written warning including the consequences of continued behaviour or unsatisfactory performance. For example, if an employee is repeatedly late for work without explanation—the memo or letter may include the following "*As part of your employment agreement you agreed to arrive on time. However, you have been consistently late without notice, including arriving for your scheduled shift 15 minutes late on the 15th of July, 25 minutes late on the 28th of July, and 40 minutes late on the 30th of July. As we discussed during our meeting of August 1, for the safety of the children and the integrity of the program and out of respect for your team members, you are expected to arrive ready to work at the time indicated on the shift schedule posted on the staff bulletin board. As per our HR policies, if you are unable to work the scheduled shift, you must notify the director at least one week in advance. Continued failure to arrive on time will result in your termination of employment.*"

Steps in Corrective Action   While constant conflict is likely a sign of deeper problems, occasional conflict is a part of life and occurs in the best organizations. Following are a series of steps to make taken:

1. Corrective Discussion

2. Adverse Report

3. Verbal Warning

4. Written Warning

5. Termination

Corrective discussion. An "in-the-moment" or scheduled informal discussion related to an observed need for improvement in a particular area of practice. The discussion should include the supervisor's account of the behaviour in question or observed lapse in practice, followed by an opportunity for the staff member to respond to the concern, and then both staff and supervisor collaboratively identify strategies to correct the behaviour.

Adverse report. It follows the corrective discussion. This step serves as the first written account related to a supervisor's ongoing dissatisfaction with a particular area of practice. Adverse reports should be issued during a face-to-face meeting and include an opportunity for a staff member to respond to the claim. In a unionized environment, a staff member may request the presence of his or her union steward during their meeting. The union steward also receives a copy of the adverse report (including the staff member's response) for his or her records. Adverse reports may be kept in a staff member's file for up to one year. In a non-unionized environment, a third person as a witness to the discussion may be helpful.

Verbal warning. Usually issued as a third warning related to an ongoing lapse in practice. A verbal warning serves as the second form of written documentation and may be kept on file for up to one year. A verbal warning is typically presented to the staff during a face-to-face meeting. In a unionized environment, a staff member can reserve the right to respond (in writing) to the verbal warning and/or grieve the notice of dissatisfaction. Also union representation is typically present at this meeting as well to act as a "voice" for the staff member.

Written warning. Usually serves as the third written form of dissatisfaction related to a particular lapse in practice. A written warning is typically presented to the staff member during a face-to-face meeting. In a unionized environment, a staff member can reserve the right to respond (in writing) to the written warning and/or grieve the notice of dissatisfaction.

Termination. This final step includes letter of termination; it may also include details related to a termination agreement between the employee and the employer, such as severance pay and letter of employment.

Termination of Employment

Employment can be terminated by the employee (quitting) or employer (firing) or employment agreement (contract ends, program closes). Termination of employment for any reason is disruptive and unsettling for the children, families, and staff.

When employment is terminated, the physical, emotional, and mental well-being of children must be considered. Since a relationship is established between the children, their family, and the staff, any termination of employment should be communicated to everyone involved.

If an employee leaves a program, he or she should have the opportunity to say goodbye to the children and the families as well as the staff team. The length of a typical notice period should be documented in the HR policy and procedures manual.

The notice period is either a working notice or pay in lieu of notice. Programs may opt to pay the employees if they are being terminated due to poor performance and their continued presence may cause stress or tension with the rest of the staff team, parents, or children. The notice period may be waived in the case of a significant breach of contract or illegal act.

If the employer decides to terminate the employment based on a performance issue, inappropriate behaviours, unacceptable situation, or legal matter, the employer will determine how the news is communicated to the staff, children, and families. Any communication should be immediate, clear, and concise. The program will need to ensure that it is protecting employer/employee confidentiality and the employee's right to privacy. Swift communication from the director conveys decisive management, minimizes rumours from spreading, and demonstrates a commitment to quality.

A decision to terminate someone's employment is never easy. However, when a staff member is not performing at an expected level and support and professional opportunities have not been successful, the decision to terminate is inevitable. Termination must be for a just cause and due process must be followed. Conditions for termination should be clearly defined in the HR Policy and Procedures Manual.

The policy should be clear, and the director must implement the policy consistently. Evidence of any performance concern needs to be documented (time sheets, staff schedules, meetings held to discuss the issue, etc). After documentation, careful reflection, attempts to resolve the issue, and assessment of the consequences for the program, the staff, and the children, the director may need to follow through and terminate the employment.

The director must inform the board of directors/owner of the intent to terminate the employee if the policy/procedure requires notification. The director may need to consult with an attorney to ensure the interests of the organization are protected.

A thoughtful director will not underestimate the impact of a termination on the staff, the children, and their families. Sciarra and Dorsey (2002) outline strategies to heal a staff after a dismissal.

Setting the Stage for Effective Communication

Early childhood educator cites a work environment where his or her opinions are valued and where he or she can work co-operatively with others as a source of job satisfaction. Effective communication is a key element in a supportive work environment. Staff meetings are one of the most critical forums for ensuring effective communication. Meetings are essential for the smooth functioning of any organization; yet, few people speak favourably about having to attend. Some staff too often view meetings as a burden and waste of time.

The relationship between a supervisor and staff is built on dialogue. A supervisor speaks with every action, policy, project, failure, and achievement. When a supervisor speaks or fails to speak—how he/she acts or fails to act, she reveals what she thinks and how she regards her staff. Those who respond to her leadership, although verbally silent, nevertheless reply in kind whether they produce or fail to do so, whether they develop symptoms of emotional distress, or whether they stay or go.

In early childhood programs, meetings are the primary vehicle for decision making and problem solving. Most programs have a series of meetings at various levels to gather individuals together to talk about the program and/or to share concerns or discuss mutual interests.

Quality programs have regular team meetings. Team meetings should be held as often as is productive. It is essential to plan each meeting carefully and involve staff in the creation of an agenda. Circulate the agenda to the staff ahead of time so that they can make a meaningful contribution to the meeting. Determine, in advance, what is to be accomplished (solve problems, receive reports, plan strategies, give direction to staff, provide an opportunity to develop skills, clarify issues, or share information).

There are no ideal meeting times that meet the needs of every setting. The time and frequency of meetings will vary depending on the amount of business to be carried out. It may be better to schedule weekly or biweekly meetings that are brief and productive than to make meetings longer and less frequent. Meetings should start and end on schedule. Good time management will allow more to be accomplished.

Productive meetings not only contribute to a sense of accomplishment, they can also serve to promote co-operation and feelings of **collegiality**. Follow up the meeting with brief, timely notes on topics discussed, decisions made, and action items to be completed. These notes provide clarification, are helpful for future reference, and inform those who were absent. They are also a tool used to assess the effectiveness of staff meetings (Jorde Bloom 2002, *Making the Most of Meetings—A Practical Guide*).

If staff are expected to attend meetings outside of regular work hours, it should be made clear in advance that their attendance is required and it should be clarified whether there will be any reimbursement or comp time for attending meetings.

Leave Policies

A program's leave policy is intended to fulfill the employees' need for time off in a way that maintains program quality, effective program management, and consistent staffing. Leaves may be with or without pay.

Paid leaves include vacation time, sick days, and personal leave. Unpaid leaves include parental leave, bereavement leave, disability leave, and leave for jury duty. Minimum leave policies are based on provincial/territorial employment legislation and collective agreements.

Leaves can be confusing because they involve workplace policies; provincial and territorial labour standards; and sometimes federal employment insurance benefits programs such as maternity leave, parental leave, and compassionate leave. They may also include benefits from your insurance program such as a short-term or long-term disability benefit.

Leaves, program closures, or staff holidays will vary depending on the community, religion, and culture of the staff and families using the program. Each of these policies needs to be clearly documented in the HR policies and procedures manual and all employee and parent handbooks. Documentation should include details such as eligibility requirements, what is paid/unpaid, what can be accumulated, what happens to unused days, and what is the process for applying for time off (notice period, start dates, return dates, approval process, appeal process).

Programs may choose to offer leaves above the minimum requirements, for example offering three weeks vacation instead of the two weeks required by law. In addition to statutory holidays, program closures or staff holidays may vary depending on the religions and cultures of the staff and families served as well as the community. Any additional provisions, the program closure, and holiday policies should be clearly documented and included in the HR Policies and Procedures Manual and any employee and parent handbooks.

In designing leave policies, the program should consider legislative requirements (ratios, employment legislation); program quality; staffing continuity; team effectiveness; costs for replacements (recruiting, hiring, orienting, managing replacement staff); and return-to-work plans following long periods of absence such as maternity, parental, or disability leave.

The Role of Unions

As early childhood educators experience fighting for improved compensation and working conditions, questions usually arise about representation of the field by unions, federations, or professional associations. The key question emerging is that of who should represent the interests of early childhood educators?

Employees in a unionized environment come together to negotiate wages, benefits, and working conditions as a group, rather than negotiating as an individual. A **union** is an organization of employees formed for the purposes that include regulation of relations between member-employees and their employer. It can be a local, provincial, national, or international union. It can also be an independent employee association. A collective agreement is a written contract of employment, covering a group of employees (bargaining unit), who are represented by a certified union. The agreement contains provisions outlining the terms and conditions of employment. It covers the rights, privileges, and duties of the employer, the union, and the employees. Collective agreements must have a minimum term of one year, but can be terminated earlier under certain conditions. Once an agreement expires, the union and the employer must engage in a process to renegotiate the agreement which in turn must be ratified by a vote by employees.

While compensation and working conditions are the items most frequently associated with collective agreements, such agreements also cover other issues such as personnel policies, hiring procedures, performance appraisals and promotion systems, grievance, provision for professional development, breaks, and input into program decision making. Most collective agreements also provide protection against harassment and unjust discipline and dismissal.

Hadley (2001) found that Canadian women in unionized workplaces have more opportunities to progress in their career because of the benefits of job security, wage protection, and care for their own child on-site or financial support for an early childhood experience in a community setting. As well, there are positive impacts on income levels, benefits offered, and pension plans. In fact, the study found women were sticking with traditionally female jobs because of the compensation levels achieved by unions.

Non-salary benefits frequently contribute as much to job satisfaction as salary benefits do. They are critical in helping staff provide better services. For example, input into a program's decision-making process can be an attractive guarantee in a contract. Members of Services Employees International Union (SEIU) Local 299 in Moose Jaw, Saskatchewan, negotiated a provision guaranteeing that their employer would meet with them once a month to hear concerns on matters affecting the quality of the program. Examples of other innovative contract provisions include a staff room "for the use and enjoyment of employees" and reimbursement for the cost of dry cleaning or shampoo occasioned by an outbreak of lice at the program.

Several studies have indicated that unionization strongly influences staff satisfaction and program quality. Staff also recognize the union or professional association as a long-term political ally that can assist early childhood practitioners in advocating for better funding and expanded services. The strength and unity of representation can be used to influence government funding for quality early childhood programs.

For staff employed by large commercial child care chains, unions have been quick to identify child care organizations that operate with large profit margins and are then able to negotiate increases in staff wages without raising parent fees.

Only a small percentage of the early childhood workforce is unionized. According to *You Bet I Care!*, unionization is most prevalent in Quebec (19.2%), Ontario (18%), and Saskatchewan (15.5%). No staff reported being in a union in Newfoundland, Prince Edward Island, or the Territories. The staff in unionized programs earned an average of over three dollars per hour more than did their colleagues in non-unionized programs (Doherty et al. 2000a).

The diverse and isolated nature of the early childhood delivery system, coupled with a high turnover rate, has historically worked against the development of successful organizing campaigns. However, with initiatives with expansions of ECE working in schools in kindergarten programs, provides an opportunity for unions to add significant numbers to their membership. For example, in Ontario by 2016 there will be 20 000 new ECEs working in schools. There are legitimate concerns that with so many unionized ECEs working for large public sector school board will this divide the profession into haves and have-nots, making it even more difficult for community EC programs to attract and retain qualified staff.

Summary

To competent, career-oriented educators, their job is more than a means to earn money. Their work is an important part of their lives. Their profession gives them a sense of accomplishment; helps them feel valued, trusted, and respected; and makes them feel safe and secure. Early childhood education is physically and emotionally demanding. The director is responsible for ensuring policies, practices, work environment, and organizational values are responsive to staff needs and contribute to their job satisfaction.

Children need environments where they feel secure and free from anxiety. Minimal staff turnover and stable staff–child groupings build security for the children and allow for consistent application of the program philosophy. High staff turnover adversely affects both the children and staff morale, which in turn decreases program quality.

Numerous surveys such as *Who Cares?* (Whitebrook et al. 1990), *You Bet I Care!* (Doherty et al. 2000a), and *Working for Change: Canada's Child Care Workforce* (Beach et al. 2004) show that educators stay in the field longest when they have professional education, compensation commensurate with their education, and good working conditions.

Employees in early childhood environments have the same legal rights as other workers. Both federal and provincial laws protect workers with respect to minimum wage, overtime pay, and a variety of working conditions. Directors, owners, and board of directors must be aware of these laws and ensure their HR policies and procedures reflect and surpass legislation.

Over the past decade, considerable energy has been devoted to the improvement of compensation and working conditions in early childhood settings. Many educators are underpaid, and some continue to feel they are undervalued by society. However, while recognizing this general inequity, educators can feel that their own program's policies are equitable and just. It is essential for directors to have systems in place to ensure that pay, job security, opportunities for professional development, and opportunities for career advancement are fairly administered and clearly communicated to all staff. Unionization uses multiple strategies to improve both educators' compensation and working conditions. It represents a bottom-up approach because it relies on the collective voices and votes of individual ECEs.

The factors that impact the effectiveness of early childhood programs are multi-faceted and complex. Numerous studies support the contention that educators have a significant impact on a program's quality. It is critical to develop and follow thoughtful, systematic procedures when seeking new staff members. A well-planned and carefully executed orientation program provides a sound base for new staff.

Once the staff are hired, the director manages the program and implements HR policies fairly and consistently. Directors have key roles and responsibilities in facilitating each staff member's growth as a professional. This requires fair and effective opportunities for professional development, supervision, and performance appraisal. It is essential to establish a relationship with each employee based on trust and mutual respect. Some HR practices and records are required by various regulatory agencies. HR policies serve to make working conditions better for staff, which aids job satisfaction and, in turn, program quality.

Key Terms and Concepts

Benefits, p. 134	HR policies, p. 132
Collective agreement, p. 130	Mentor, p. 130
Collegiality, p. 154	Performance appraisal, p. 133
Conflict resolution, p. 152	Probationary period, p. 134
Contract, p. 140	Professional development, p. 129
Corrective Action, p. 152	Staff development, p. 141
Criminal reference check, p. 140	Union, p. 155
Employee records, p. 150	Work environment, p. 149

Activities

1. Collect job applications from three different employers. Note the different kinds of information requested.

2. Arrange meetings with several directors to discuss compensation, benefits, and their orientation procedures.

3. On a scale of 1 to 5 (1 = weak, 5 = strong), rate yourself on the following traits:

   - team player
   - participator
   - flexibility
   - problem-solving skills
   - creativity
   - energy
   - communication skills
   - resourcefulness

4. Contact the director of your field placement and request permission to attend a staff meeting. Assess how staff are involved in decision making. What went well at the meeting? What could have been handled differently? To gain a deeper understanding, arrange to share your observations with the director.

Recommended Reading

Caruso, J. and M. Fawcett. *Supervision in Early Childhood Education: A Developmental Perspective.* 2d ed. New York: Teachers College Press, Columbia University, 1999.

Child Care Human Resource Sector Council. *Occupational Standards for Early Childhood Educators.* Ottawa: CCHRSC, 2010.

Child Care Human Resources Sector Council. A Portrait of Canada's Early Childhood and Care Workforce, Child Care Human Resources Sector Council, 2009.

Child Care Human Resources Sector Council. Recruiment and Retention Challenges and Strategies: Understanding Workforce Shortages in ECEC, Child Care Human Resources Sector Council, 2009.

Jorde Bloom, P., M. Sheerer, and J. Britz. *Blueprint for Action: Achieving Center-Based Change through Staff Development.* 2d ed. Lake Forest, IL: New Horizons, 2005.

Jorde Bloom. *Making the Most of Meetings: A Practical Guide.* Lake Forest, IL: New Horizons, 2002.

Jorde Bloom, P., A. Hentschel, and J. Bella. *Creating a Healthy Organizational Climate.* Lake Forest New Horizons, 2010.

Nolan, M. *Mentor Coaching and Leadership in Early Care and Education.* Clifton Park, NY: Delmar, 2007.

Sciarra, D.J. and A.G. Dorsey. *Leaders and Supervisors in Child Care Programs.* Albany: Delmar, 2002.

Weblinks

www.ccsc-cssge.ca
Child Care Human Resources Sector Council (CCHRSC)
The CCHRSC is a pan-Canadian, non-profit organization that addresses pressing human resources issues in the child care sector. Its projects develop research, strategies, and tools to meet the needs of the child care workforce and achieve related goals. Priorities include increasing the respect for and recognition of the child care sector, improving work conditions, and stimulating research. Its website includes resources on topics related to unionization, recruitment and retention, and training and development.

www.ccw.org
Centre for the Child Care Workforce
This non-profit research, education, and advocacy organization is committed to improving child care by upgrading compensation and working conditions and by reducing turnover of child care centre staff and family child care providers. The site lists research papers, publications, and information about training events.

www.hrsdc.gc.ca
Human Resources and Skills Development Canada
This government website provides information for individuals and employers. For HR management, follow the links to Business. You will find information and resources on hiring, labour standards, occupational health and safety, and work–life balance. It also provides details about maternity, parental, adoption, and compassionate care leave benefits. You can also access all provincial labour legislation by following the appropriate path.

www.monster.ca and www.workopolis.com
Online Employment Sites
These two are Canada's largest online recruitment sites, listing jobs in all sectors including early childhood education.

www.charityvillage.com
Charity Village, Online Employment in the Non-Profit Sector
This employment website is dedicated to the non-profit sector, providing news, information, and resources for executives and staff. Charity Village lists thousands of jobs in the Career Centre and many HR management resources in the Resource Centre.

www.menteach.org
Men Teach
This website offers one place to find and exchange information and resources about men teaching. It has information for practitioners, directors, and students. The site provides the latest research findings and data about men working with children.

www.hrcouncil.ca/policies
Human Resource Sector Council
This site provides advice to smaller non-profit organizations who are developing and updating HR policies and procedures.

Promoting Professionalism

chapter 6

Objectives

- **Develop an understanding of professionalism.**
- **Recognize the obligations of the early childhood profession.**
- **Understand professional preparation requirements and career opportunities.**
- **Introduce professional terminology.**
- **Understand a code of ethics as a part of professionalism and consider its implications.**
- **Outline the role of reflective thinking as a method to improve practice.**
- **Identify the role of unions and professional groups.**

The Evolving Field of Early Childhood Education

For some time, early childhood was simplistically viewed as child care, whereas it is now recognized as a key period of children's development. Early childhood educators are professionally prepared to work with young children ages from birth to eight years. The role of ECEs is to understand the nature of young children, their developmental needs, and the environments in which they reside. Professional ECEs maintain a continuous involvement in ongoing learning in order to be current in their knowledge of development and research-based appropriate practice. Among the challenges that face this field are adequate sustained funding, commensurate compensation, and recognition for additional levels of education. Professional and advocacy organizations are working to support and strengthen the early childhood profession and to advocate for resources.

What Characteristics Contribute to a Competent Early Childhood Professional

What does it take to be an effective ECE? Effectiveness depends on a combination of knowledge, skills, and personal characteristics. Children benefit most when their teachers have high levels of formal education and specialized early childhood professional preparation. Those with specific preparation, knowledge, and skills in child development and early childhood education are more likely to engage in warm, positive interactions with children, offer richer language experiences, and create more high quality learning environments. Opportunities for staff to receive coaching, mentoring, supportive supervision and to participate in ongoing **professional development** help ensure that their knowledge and skills reflect the profession's ever-growing knowledge base.

Providing high quality early childhood education for a group of young children requires knowledge of children's unique learning patterns, developmental levels and needs, as well as personal attributes such as patience, energy, and commitment. Other essential qualities identified by experts in early childhood include shared values, beliefs, **ethics**, a commitment to children, an ability to work with families as partners in their child's development, and practice based on well-founded pedagogy. An early childhood professional is one who demonstrates up-to-date knowledge and strategies, reflective practice, and continual learning about evolving theoretical foundations of early education and care.

Personal Attributes

While aspiring practitioners can increase their knowledge and develop their skills, their personal characteristics are more likely to be fixed. The competent early childhood educator must have suitable personal characteristics for working with young children—passion, perseverance, patience, a nurturing disposition, openness to new ideas, a tolerance for ambiguity, flexible thinking, and maturity.

Being an ECE is not always easy. There are many challenges. One must want to make a difference in children's lives, as this passion can sustain and motivate through financial and physical challenges. Educators need to be secure within themselves so that they can function with principles rather than

Educators must be lifelong learners and seek out knowledge on current research.

prescriptions, use authority appropriately, and acknowledge mistakes. Also needed is an ability to put one's own needs on hold while meeting the needs of others. This must be balanced with taking care of one's own physical, emotional, and spiritual wellness, as described by Pimento and Kernsted (2010).

A key attribute of an effective ECE is a love of learning. To inspire children with a love of learning, practitioners must be lifelong learners and seek out knowledge on current research.

There must be an appreciation for diversity. Staff must demonstrate the ability to have respectful interactions with families whose backgrounds differ from their own. These qualities are revealed through neither resumé nor interview, but rather by observing educators' work with children and families. Clear, consistent evidence of an educator's personal integration and inner sense of security is vital for her or his success with children and families.

We know intuitively that these are important qualities. Although attempts have been made to clearly and systematically determine what qualities make a competent practitioner, it is difficult to demonstrate concretely the impact of these qualities on the quality of children's experience. Individual staff members can be evaluated by observing their interactions with children, families, and staff and monitoring their implementation of curriculum.

However, desirable personal attributes alone are not enough to guide professional practice. Even the most dedicated practitioners sometimes encounter challenging situations. Practices such as mentoring or obtaining peer support provide opportunities for ongoing professional growth and stability.

CHARACTERISTICS OF AN EFFECTIVE ECE

Authentic	Knowing who you are and what you stand for
Available	Open to responsive interaction with children, families, and co-workers
Respectful	Appreciates that one's life is enhanced through exposure to people of different backgrounds
Passionate	Desire to make a difference and a belief that it is possible
Creative	Able to work in less than ideal environments or with limited resources
Fair	Demonstrates intercultural competence; responds to each child and family equitably
Flexible	Anticipates and values the need for change. Pragmatic perseverance; Willingness to fight for one's beliefs
Individualizes	Adapts program to individual child's needs and interests
Knowledgeable	Knows current teaching strategies and matches them to children's interests, needs, and developmental levels
Love of learning	Educators who are lifelong learners send children the message that learning is valued
Pragmatic	Able to compromise in a win/win manner, while making progress toward their goals
Willingness to take risks	Unafraid to shake up the status quo to achieve goals for children
Professional	Conscientious about carrying out responsibilities; uses strategies to keep personal pressures from interfering
Reflective	Reflects upon performance and acts on constructive feedback

Source: Adapted from Laura Colker, *Twelve Characteristics of Effective Early Childhood Educators* (NAEYC, Washington, 2008).

Early Childhood Education as a Profession

Early childhood educators understand that what they do is important. Many realize that the level of professionalism in the field of early childhood influences the quality of environments. The term "professional" tends to imply an individual who is dedicated, knowledgeable, specialized, educated, well-paid, and ethical individual. Early childhood educators seek recognition of their professional role. Increased recognition of educational qualifications, enhanced compensation, and improved working conditions usually accompany professional status, and these are clearly warranted and appropriate goals for which to strive. These are crucial conditions to ensure that the profession attracts and retains knowledgeable and experienced educators.

Professionalism is a dynamic process whereby an occupation can be observed to change certain characteristics in the direction of a profession. It is a complex and intriguing issue to explore. As a concept, professionalism has been studied from a variety of perspectives and is thought to be the answer to many of the dilemmas within the field of early childhood education. Yet, the field of early childhood faces many barriers to being recognized as a profession—from both society and practitioners themselves. As well, it suffers from a lack of conceptual clarity and standardized terminology. Another dilemma is whether to be exclusive (keep out persons with no professional education) or inclusive (ensuring individuals from diverse backgrounds have access to the field).

Professionalism is a fluid experience. It is ongoing and never ending. Education, knowledge, and experience inform practice, ever reshaped by the unfolding incoming flow of new knowledge and experience. Through ongoing reflective practice, what is known is re-examined, reconfigured, and refined. From this perspective, professionalism is envisioned as a constant state of becoming.

Elements of Professionalism

Professionalism refers to a combination of competencies in a particular field of knowledge and identification with a group of colleagues that can collectively define and support best practices. Early childhood educators in Canada are in the process of identifying themselves as professionals, within the criteria recognized generally by the public. In fact, in Ontario, ECEs are officially recognized as professionals through legislation as well as through an established professional College of Early Childhood Educators. Whitebook et al. (2001) identify the following benchmarks in professionalization:

- Defining a distinct and exclusive body of knowledge and practice
- Establishing training and certification processes
- Increasing political influence
- Increasing the economic well-being of its members
  Additional benchmarks include:
  - Considering how much formal, specialized education is required to enter the profession as well as whether there are formal expectations for continued professional development.
  - The need for a **code of ethics** and process for accountability. If there was unethical behaviour, how would it be dealt with by a professional body?

FIGURE 6–1 | College of Early Childhood Education—Regulatory Body

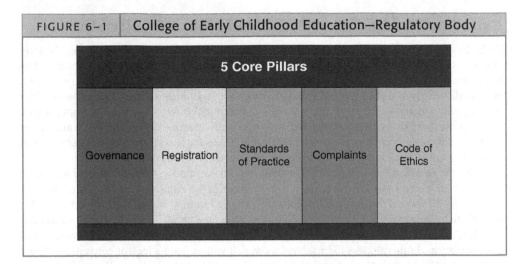

5 Core Pillars

Governance | Registration | Standards of Practice | Complaints | Code of Ethics

COLLEGE OF EARLY CHILDHOOD EDUCATORS

The College of Early Childhood Educators is the first self-regulatory body for the field in Canada. The Ontario provincial government, through the *Early Childhood Educators Act, 2007*, gave the profession of early childhood education the privilege and responsibility of regulating itself in the public interest. The College, by law, is authorized to set qualifications and requirements for those who wish to work as ECEs and register those who meet them. This provides the public with confidence that individuals practicing the profession of early childhood education are qualified and do so competently and ethically.

The college is developed on five core pillars as depicted in Figure 6–1: governance, registration, standards of practice, complaints leading to discipline of members, and a code of ethics as illustrated in the above figure. These areas are fleshed out further in this chapter. Members of the College are held accountable to practice in accordance with the Act, regulations, and by-laws. The by-laws will prescribe a set of professional and ethical standards, which the College developed in consultation with its members and stakeholders. The Code of Ethics and Standards of Practice was developed for members to guide practice.

To use the title of Early Childhood Educator or Registered Early Childhood Educator (RECE) and to practice the profession, one must be a member of the college. The College maintains a public register of its members so that at any time an employer, parent, or member of the general public can look up a person working as an early childhood educator to confirm he or she is registered with the College. Applicants must satisfy educational and training requirements and provide documentation of the education. If a member has a term, condition, or limitation placed on his or her certificate of registration, that information is available on the public register.

In the event that the competence or professional conduct of a member of the College is called into question, the College has a fair legal process by which it investigates the complaint and, if necessary, refers the matter for a disciplinary hearing. This provides the public with confidence that individuals practicing the profession of early childhood education are qualified and do so competently and ethically.

All of these roles of the College exist to protect the public interest. The existence of a self-regulatory body for ECEs ensures accountability in the profession and provides for safe, ethical, and professional practice of early childhood educators across Ontario.

The Need for Specialized Education

Numerous research studies and policy documents report consistent and significant associations between higher education levels and quality programs and better outcomes for children. Adults who have post-secondary education in early childhood development tend to be more responsive to children and provide them with stimulating activities that are appropriate to their developmental level. Early childhood educators who have an ECE or related credentials are more likely to be responsive and emotionally available and provide a stimulating environment that promotes language and cognitive development and skill acquisition. They more likely use the kinds of questioning, listening, and reflecting strategies that facilitate children's expressive and receptive language development. Knowledgeable professionals understand children's emotional, social, and cognitive development and are able to recognize and use "teachable moments" (Doherty 2000a).

Educators of young children need to purposefully use multiple approaches that include strategies that range from structured to unstructured and adult-directed to child-directed. Children bring different backgrounds, interests, experiences, learning styles, needs, and capacities to learning environments. Educators' consideration of these differences when selecting and implementing pedagogical approaches helps each child succeed. Pedagogical approaches also differ in their effectiveness for teaching different elements of curriculum and learning. For a program to address the complexity inherent in any early childhood setting, a variety of instructional approaches must be employed.

In a high quality early childhood environment, qualified staff will use specialized skills to meet the needs of the group as a whole while remaining focused on the needs of each individual child and family. The kind of specialized knowledge gained through professional preparation includes a foundation in theory and research. This foundation supports the development of appropriate individualized, concrete, and experiential programs for young children. The value of such programs is seen in the children's developmental outcomes, such as increased social interaction with adults, development of pro-social behaviours, and improved language and cognitive development.

A profession bases its work on a specialized body of knowledge and expertise that is applied to situations in the workplace. Some feel that the public does not understand the role of an early childhood educator and therefore does not appreciate the need for specialized professional education. Parents with children in an early childhood setting tend to have more of an appreciation for those who work in the sector, even if they do not have an entirely accurate view of the work involved. There is an ongoing need to increase under-standing of what is involved in early childhood education and the specialized knowledge required. Part of the issue around respect has to do with the fact that those working in the sector feel that early childhood education itself is not well understood. The fact is that child care programs benefit the economy by enabling parents to remain in the workforce, as well as help young children develop to their full potential. It is necessary to lay to rest the assumption that working with children is something that anyone can do. This assumption is the root cause of the unsatisfactory compensation that characterizes the early education field in Canada.

One of the primary attributes of professionalism is having mastery over a formal body of knowledge not accessible to the public. Specialized knowledge in early childhood development is derived from developmental psychology and other fields. A great deal of knowledge exists about how to care for and educate young children from birth through age 8. Developmentally appropriate practice bases decisions about best practices for young children on child development research and current knowledge of learning. This offers a body of specialized knowledge to practitioners. This knowledge gives the professionals the competence to carry out their work.

There are a number of related professions that share some common or overlapping knowl-edge bases. Some examples of these would include elementary teachers, pediatric nurses, child and youth workers, and pediatricians. There are also areas of unique knowledge such as the in-depth understanding of early development, the value of play in learning, and the practice of group care for young children.

Professional judgment involves assessing events, weighing alternatives, and estimating the potential consequences of decisions and actions based on that knowledge. Consequently, the choice of courses of action is based on specific expertise acquired through professional preparation and ongoing professional development. Educators must continually challenge and evaluate professional judgments and practices to ensure that they are based on the best available information. As the body of knowledge changes, so do the concepts of best practice. Professional development activities such as discussions with co-workers and/or mentors, attending work-shops, and reading professional journals enable individuals to gain new knowledge and keep skills and abilities current.

Both the Canadian Child Care Federation and the Child Care Human Resources Sector Council consulted widely with the field to determine what practitioners need to know upon graduating and used this in the development of **occupational standards** for both ECEs and directors.

Standards of Practice

Standards of Practice provide a framework of principles that describes the knowledge, skills, and values inherent in a profession. These standards articulate the goals and aspirations of the profession. These standards convey a collective vision of professionalism that guides the daily practices of members of the Ontario College of ECE, currently the only province to have adopted them. Professional standards are the profession's own benchmarks of quality beyond the requirements of legislation, and they contribute to the quality of early childhood settings. Professional organizations adopt standards of practice to ensure that members apply uniform procedures and principles in response to typical situations using their best professional judgment.

Principles for the Standards of Practice

STANDARD I: Caring and Nurturing Relationships That Support Learning

A. ECEs recognize that families are of primary importance in children's development and that children are best understood in the context of their families.

B. ECEs make reasonable efforts to familiarize themselves with available information[i] regarding the relevant family circumstances of children under the member's professional supervision (including, but not limited to, relevant information concerning the child's health, legal custody and/or guardianship[ii]).

C. ECEs strive to establish and maintain ongoing and open communication regarding the development and learning of a child under the member's professional supervision with the child's parents and/or legal guardians.[iii]

D. ECEs are attuned to the needs of children and families and advocate with families on behalf of children. They provide nurturing learning environments where children thrive and families are welcome.

E. ECEs establish professional and caring relationships with children and families. They engage both children and their families by being sensitive and respectful of diversity, equity and inclusion. ECEs are receptive listeners and offer encouragement and support by responding appropriately to the ideas, concerns and needs of children and families.

F. ECEs ensure that in their relationship with the child's family, the needs and best interests of the child are paramount.

STANDARD II: Developmentally Appropriate Care and Education

A. **Knowledge and Application of Theory and Practice**

   1. ECEs demonstrate a thorough knowledge of child development theories. They use this knowledge to plan, implement and assess developmentally appropriate learning strategies.

   2. ECEs recognize children's unique characteristics, and access the resources necessary to adapt the early learning environment to suit the child. ECEs recognize that child development milestones and behaviours vary and they acknowledge and respect those differences.

B. Consideration of Children's Needs

   1. ECEs provide care and education to individuals, small groups and large groups. They make ongoing decisions concerning children's need for support and assistance.

   2. ECEs foster children's independence and inter-dependence. They provide opportunities for children to develop the skills needed to regulate their behaviour and to make decisions.

(continued)

C.   **Support of Learning Styles**

1.   ECEs recognize that children have different learning styles. They focus on the whole child and plan caring and creative learning opportunities that reflect individual learning styles. ECEs, through these learning opportunities, foster the development of a child's sense of self.

STANDARD III: Safe, Healthy and Supportive Learning Environments

A.   **Safe**

1.   Early Childhood Educators maintain safe and healthy learning environments.

B.   **Healthy**

1.   ECEs obtain and familiarize themselves with information concerning any relevant medical conditions, exceptionalities, allergies, food restrictions, medication requirements and emergency contact information relating to children under their professional supervision. This information is obtained and reviewed in a timely manner, when a child comes under the member's professional supervision or as soon after that time as the information becomes available.

2.   ECEs provide opportunities for young children to experience nature, and to understand their relationship to their natural environment and to the world.

3.   ECEs promote a healthy lifestyle including but not limited to nutrition and physical activity.

C.   **Supportive**

1.   ECEs support children in culturally, linguistically and developmentally sensitive ways and provide caring, stimulating and respectful opportunities for learning and care that are welcoming to children and their families, within an inclusive, well-planned and structured environment.

STANDARD IV: Professional Knowledge and Competence

A.   **Knowledge**

1.   ECEs are current in their professional knowledge about the continuum of child development and the pedagogy related to early learning, curriculum, program planning, parenting and family dynamics. They apply this knowledge in their practice with individual children, and in small or large group settings. ECEs know and demonstrate how to address the child's physical, cognitive, language and emotional/social development and well-being in an integrated and holistic way.

2.   ECEs know, understand and abide by the legislation, policies and procedures that are relevant to their professional practice and to the care and learning of children under their professional supervision.

3.   If there is a conflict between the College's Code of Ethics and the Standards of Practice and a member's work environment and/or the

policies and procedures of his or her employer, ECEs have an obligation to comply with the College's Code of Ethics and the Standards of Practice.

B. **Practice**

1. ECEs plan and develop play-based curricula and programs along a continuum of early childhood development. They plan and prepare a child-centred program that provides learning opportunities for all the developmental domains. ECEs provide individualized assistance and opportunities for children to develop a sense of belonging to a group and provide safe and secure supervision of children based on age and stage of development.

2. ECEs assess, obtain information about and familiarize themselves with the levels of development of the children under their professional supervision for the purpose of planning and developing curriculum and programs which are appropriate to and meet the needs of the children.

3. ECEs observe and monitor the learning environment and anticipate when support or intervention is required.

4. ECEs observe, assess, evaluate, document and report on children's progress along all domains of child development. As they work with children, families and other adults, ECEs set goals, make decisions, resolve challenges, decide on developmentally responsive activities and experiences, provide behaviour guidance and work collaboratively in the best interest of the children under their professional supervision.

5. ECEs ensure that their decisions and actions in their professional practice are appropriately supported by a credible body of professional knowledge in the field of early childhood education. ECEs are able to explain the foundations of their practice and their decision-making processes and to communicate to parents and other professionals the benefits of play for child development.

C. **Professionalism with Colleagues and Other Professionals**

1. ECEs work collaboratively with colleagues in their workplaces in order to provide safe, secure, healthy and inviting environments for children and families. By supporting, encouraging and working collaboratively with their co-workers, ECEs enhance the culture of their workplaces. They build effective relationships with colleagues and other professionals by using clear verbal and written communication, and positive interpersonal skills.

2. ECEs build a climate of trust, honesty and respect in the workplace. They respect the privacy of colleagues and handle information with an appropriate level of confidentiality. ECEs support experienced colleagues, those who are new to the profession and those students aspiring to the profession.

3. ECEs who are responsible for supervising students, volunteers and/or other staff (collectively referred to as "supervisees") provide guidelines, parameters and direction to supervisees that respect their rights. ECEs ensure a level of supervision which is appropriate in light of the supervisee's education, training, experience and the activities being performed.

(continued)

4. ECEs, working collaboratively with community resource persons and members of other professions, access the resources and expertise available in their communities. They strive to facilitate community partnerships for the benefit of children and families.

D. **Professionalism with the College**

1. ECEs have a duty to co-operate fully with all the College's policies and procedures and conduct themselves in a manner which demonstrates respect for both the College and other individuals involved. This duty applies where, among other things, an investigation of a complaint or mandatory report regarding a member is underway, a matter has been referred to the Discipline Committee or the Fitness to Practise Committee for a hearing or there are other assessments, reviews, investigations or proceedings before the College which involve a member.

E. **Professionalism as an Individual**

1. ECEs strive for excellence in their professional practice and critical thinking. Early Childhood Educators access current evidence-based research and are able to transfer this knowledge into practice. They are aware of the need to enhance their own learning in order to support both children and families. Early Childhood Educators demonstrate their commitment to ongoing professional development by engaging in continued learning.

2. ECEs recognize that they are role models for children, families, members of their profession, supervisees and other colleagues and avoid conduct which could reasonably be perceived as reflecting negatively on the profession of early childhood education.

STANDARD V: Professional Boundaries, Dual Relationships and Conflicts of Interest

A. ECEs are in a position of power and responsibility toward children under their professional supervision. This necessitates that care be taken to ensure that these children are protected from the abuse of such power during, after, or referable to the provision of professional services.

1. ECEs do not abuse physically, sexually, verbally, psychologically or emotionally a child who is under the member's professional supervision.

2. ECEs do not use information about a child or family obtained in the course of a professional relationship, and do not use their professional position of authority, to coerce, improperly influence, harass, abuse or exploit a child who is under the member's professional supervision, or the child's family.

3. ECEs do not solicit or use information from a child who is under the member's professional supervision or the child's family to acquire, either directly or indirectly, advantage or material benefits.

B. ECEs establish and maintain clear and appropriate boundaries in professional relationships (including relationships with children under the member's professional supervision and/or their families and/or supervisees[i]) and do not violate those boundaries. Boundary violations include sexual misconduct and other misuse and abuse of the member's power. Non-sexual boundary violations may include emotional, physical, social and financial violations. Members are responsible for ensuring that appropriate boundaries are maintained in all aspects of professional relationships.

C. ECEs do not engage in professional relationships that constitute a conflict of interest or in situations in which members ought reasonably to have known that the child under their supervision would be at risk in any way.[ii] ECEs do not provide a professional service while the member is in a conflict of interest.

1. ECEs evaluate professional relationships and other situations involving children under the member's professional supervision and the families or guardians of those children for potential conflicts of interest and seek consultation to assist in identifying and dealing with such potential conflicts of interest.

2. ECEs avoid conflicts of interest and/or dual relationships with children under the member's professional supervision and/or their families or with colleagues or supervisees that could impair the member's professional judgment or increase the risk of exploitation or harm to children under the member's professional supervision.[iii]

3. If a conflict of interest situation does arise, ECEs declare the conflict of interest and take appropriate steps to address the conflict.[iv]

STANDARD VI: Confidentiality and Consent to the Release of Information Regarding Children and Their Families

A. ECEs respect the privacy of children under their professional supervision and the families of those children by holding in strict confidence all information about them and by complying with any applicable privacy and other legislation. ECEs disclose such information only when required or allowed by law to do so or when the necessary consent has been obtained for the disclosure of the information.

1. ECEs provide parents and/or legal guardians, on request, with access to records maintained by the member in respect to their child or such parts of those records as are relevant, unless there is reasonable cause for refusing to do so.

2. ECEs comply with any applicable privacy and other legislation. ECEs obtain consent to the collection, use or disclosure of information concerning children under their professional supervision, or their families, including personal information unless otherwise permitted or required by law.

3. ECEs employed by an organization maintain a thorough understanding of the organization's policies and practices relating to the management of information.[i]

B ECEs who are responsible for complying with privacy legislation establish clear policies and practices relating to the management of client information

(continued)

and make information about these policies and practices readily available in accordance with any applicable privacy or other legislation.[ii]

C.   When ECEs are employed by an agency or organization, College standards of confidentiality may conflict with the organization's policies and procedures concerning confidentiality. Where there is a conflict, College standards take precedence.

D.   ECEs shall not disclose information concerning or received from children under their professional supervision, or the families of those children, except in accordance with the following requirements:

  1.   When in a review, investigation or proceeding under the Act in which the professional conduct, competency or capacity of a College member is an issue, the member may disclose such information concerning or received from a child under the member's professional supervision or the child's family as is reasonably required by the member or the College for the purposes of the review, investigation or proceeding, without the consent of the individuals to whom the information relates. ECEs do not divulge more information than is reasonably required.

  2.   When disclosure is required or allowed by law or by order of a court, ECEs do not divulge more information than is required or allowed.

  3.   ECEs have individuals (or, in the case of children, their parents or guardians) sign completed consent forms prior to the disclosure of information relating to them, where consent is required. In urgent circumstances, a verbal consent by the individual (or, in the case of a child, the child's parent or guardian) to the disclosure of information may constitute proper authorization. The member should document that this consent was obtained.

  4.   When consent to the disclosure of information is required, Early Childhood Educators make reasonable efforts to inform the person whose consent is being sought of the parameters of information to be disclosed and to advise that person of the possible consequences of such disclosure.

E.   ECEs inform the parents or guardians of children under the member's professional supervision early in their relationship about the limits of confidentiality of information. For example, ECEs explain the need for sharing pertinent information with supervisors, co-workers, administrative staff and volunteers.

F.   ECEs obtain consent from the parents or guardians of the children under their professional supervision before electronically recording, photographing, audio or video taping or permitting third party observation of the children's activities. ECEs comply with the requirements regarding use or disclosure of information for research or educational purposes set out in any applicable privacy and other legislation.

G.   Early Childhood Educators may use public information and/or non-identifying information for research, educational and publication purposes.

STANDARDS OF PRACTICE: Endnotes

STANDARD I: Caring and Nurturing Relationships That Support Learning

i.   See: Standard III. B(1): Early Childhood Educators obtain and familiarize themselves with information concerning any relevant medical conditions, exceptionalities, allergies, food restrictions, medication requirements and emergency contact information relating to children under their professional supervision. Such information is obtained and reviewed in a timely manner, when a child comes under the member's professional supervision or as soon after that time as the information becomes available.

ii. Throughout the Standards of Practice contained in this document, the term "parent" includes parents and/or legal guardians, except where otherwise indicated.

iii. See Standard VI. Confidentiality and Consent to Release of Information Regarding Children and their Families, subparagraphs A(1) and D(3) regarding access to records maintained by a member in respect of a child by the child's parents and/or legal guardian.

STANDARD V: Professional Boundaries, Dual Relationships and Conflicts of Interest

i.   See: Standard IV. C(3): "Supervisees" include students, volunteers and/or other staff supervised by the member.

ii. "Conflict of Interest" is defined as a situation in which a member has a personal, financial or other professional interest or obligation which gives rise to a reasonable apprehension that the interest or obligation may influence the member in the exercise of his or her professional responsibilities. Actual influence is not required in order for a conflict of interest situation to exist. It is sufficient if there is a reasonable apprehension that there may be such influence.

   One of the hallmarks of a conflict of interest situation is that a reasonable person, informed of all of the circumstances, would have a reasonable apprehension (in the sense of reasonable expectation or concern) that the interest might influence the member. The influence need not be actual but may simply be perceived. However, a mere possibility or suspicion of influence is not sufficient to give rise to a conflict of interest. The interest must be significant enough to give rise to a "reasonable apprehension" that the personal, financial or other professional interest may influence the member in the performance of his or her professional responsibilities.

iii. "Dual Relationship" is defined as a situation in which an Early Childhood Educator, in addition to his or her professional relationship, has one or more other relationships with a child under the member's professional supervision, the child's family, a colleague or a supervisee, regardless of whether this occurs prior to, during, or following the provision of professional services. A dual relationship does not necessarily constitute a conflict of interest; however, where dual relationships exist, there is a strong potential for conflict of interest and there may be an actual or perceived conflict of interest. Relationships beyond the professional one include, but are not limited to, those in which the College

(continued)

member has a personal, familial or business relationship with a child under the member's professional supervision, the child's family, a colleague or a supervisee. Members embark on an evaluation of whether a dual relationship might impair professional judgment or increase the risk of exploitation or harm to a child under the member's professional supervision.

iv. It may be extremely difficult or impossible for members working in certain small communities or remote locations, or in certain ethnic or religious communities to entirely avoid dual relationships or situations which may give rise to a conflict of interest. In those circumstances, members should declare the conflict of interest, take appropriate steps to address it, attempt to eliminate the conflict if possible and take steps to reduce or eliminate any resulting risk of harm or exploitation to children under the member's professional supervision.

STANDARD VI: Confidentiality and Consent to the Release of Information Regarding Children and their Families

i. The member must maintain a thorough understanding of the organization's information management policies and practices, including those regarding:

1. When, how and the purposes for which the organization routinely collects, uses, modifies, discloses, retains or disposes of information;

2. The administrative, technical and physical safeguards and practices that the organization maintains with respect to the information;

3. How an individual may obtain access to or request correction of a record of information about the individual; and

4. How to make a complaint about the organization's compliance with its policies and practices.

ii. Privacy legislation currently includes the federal *Personal Information Protection and Electronic Documents Act, the federal Privacy Act, the Personal Health Information Act, 2004, the provincial Freedom of Information and Protection of Privacy Act and the Municipal Freedom of Information and Protection of Privacy Act.*

Source: Used with permission of Ontario College of Early Childhood Educators (Toronto: CECE, 2010).

Practicing professionals are committed to performing consistently at high standards, without permitting personal matters to affect their work or relations with children, colleagues, or employers. Regardless of the environment, young children deserve to be cared for and educated by adults who possess the appropriate knowledge and skills. The process of professionalizing creates greater consensus among practitioners on the meaning of critical terms and concepts. Greater consensus supports work toward shared goals.

Entry to Practice

A major characteristic of a profession is that all practicing professionals have a designated level of knowledge, experience, and qualifications prior to entering the occupation. Provincial and territorial governments outline requirements for entry to the field. In Ontario, the provincial government passed the Early Childhood Educator's Act 2009, which requires that all persons who wish to use the title "early childhood educator" or "registered early childhood educator," as well as any individuals who works within the *scope of practice* of an early childhood educator, are required be a member of the College of Early Childhood Educators. The college has established professional standards of practice, qualifications, and ongoing professional development for early childhood educators.

No province or territory requires all practitioners in early childhood programs to have related post-secondary credentials. Since in most parts of the country it is not mandatory to undergo an accrediting process by a professional organization, some practitioners choose to forgo this option. These attitudes limit the professionalization of the field. While some provincial early childhood organizations have a certification process in place, this process may be viewed as duplicating the role of the licensing authority, may appear to be optional, or has varying levels of commitment from the field. In Newfoundland and Labrador, it is mandatory to become certified in order to work in a licensed child care setting. Certification is carried out by the Association of Early Childhood Educators, Newfoundland and Labrador (AECENL), funded through the provincial government. Credentialing is the process of identifying qualifications required to do a particular job. The Child Care Human Resource Sector Council publishes an *Online Guide to Credentialing in Canada's ECEC Sector*: This site enables individuals to search, compare, and browse the requirements to work in Early Childhood Education and Care (ECEC) across Canada.

Code of Ethics and Accountability

A strong foundation in professional ethics is an essential part of the professional repertoire of every ECE. Professional ethics involves reflection on professional responsibility that is carried out collectively and systematically by the membership of a profession. Early childhood educators work with one of society's most vulnerable groups—young children. The quality of interactions between young children and their teachers has an enduring impact on children's lives. The intimacy of the relationship and the potential to cause harm demands a commitment on the part of early childhood professionals to adhere to the standards of ethical practice. A number of provinces have developed a code of ethics or are using one developed by the Canadian Child Care Federation. In Ontario, all ECEs are bound by the one described below as they are required by legislation to be a member of the College of ECE.

Standard

Ontario College of Early Childhood Educators
CODE OF ETHICS

Members ("Early Childhood Educators" or "members") of the College of Early Childhood Educators are committed to the Code of Ethics. The Code of Ethics reflects a core set of beliefs and values of care, respect, trust and integrity. These beliefs and values are fundamental to members of the profession and guide their conduct.

A. Responsibilities to Children
Early Childhood Educators make the well-being and learning of all children who are under their professional supervision their foremost responsibility. They value

(continued)

the rights of the child, respecting the uniqueness, dignity and potential of each child, and strive to create learning environments in which children experience a sense of belonging.

Early Childhood Educators are caring, empathetic, fair and act with integrity. Early Childhood Educators foster the joy of learning through play-based pedagogy.

B.   Responsibilities to Families

Early Childhood Educators value the centrality of the family to the health and well-being of children. They recognize and respect the uniqueness and diversity of families.

Early Childhood Educators strive to establish and maintain reciprocal relationships with family members of children under their professional supervision. These relationships are based on trust, openness and respect for confidentiality. Early Childhood Educators collaborate with families by exchanging knowledge and sharing practices and resources.

C.   Responsibilities to Colleagues and to the Profession

Early Childhood Educators interact with colleagues and other professionals in ways that demonstrate respect, trust and integrity. Through their conduct, Early Childhood Educators strive to enhance the status of the profession in their workplaces and in the wider community.

Early Childhood Educators value lifelong learning and commit themselves to engaging in continuous professional learning to enhance their practice. They support experienced colleagues, those who are new to the profession and students aspiring to the profession.

D.   Responsibilities to the Community and to Society

Early Childhood Educators value and engage in collaboration with community agencies, schools and other professionals.

Early Childhood Educators recognize that they contribute to community and society by advocating for and promoting an appreciation of the profession, children and early learning.

Source: Ontario College of Early Childhood Educators (Toronto: CECE, 2010).

To claim to be a professional is to declare publicly that one adheres to goals and values that go beyond immediate interests. Ethics is the study of right and wrong, duty and obligation. It involves using knowledge and skills to make responsible professional decisions—a fundamental skill of a competent early childhood educator. **Professional ethics** concern the kinds of actions that are right and wrong in the workplace. Personal attributes, values, and morals form the necessary foundation for an individual's professional practice. They need to be complemented with professional values and standards of ethical behaviour that apply to all members of the profession.

In order to attain true professional status, educators must adhere to a common code of ethics such as the one noted above, developed by the College of ECE in Ontario. One of the hallmarks of professionalism is its recognition of and adherence to a code of ethical conduct. Such a code embodies guidelines for behaviour and facilitates decision making when an educator faces an **ethical dilemma**—when he or she must determine appropriate conduct in the face of conflicting professional values and responsibilities. Clearly stated standards in a code of ethics provide a common ground for educators who strive to do the right thing for children, families, and colleagues.

A code of ethics differs from the policies, regulations, and legal obligations that govern the field of early childhood. A code provides guidance for individuals, not the regulation of programs. Members of the profession create its code of ethics, whereas they are rarely the ones to write regulations and licensing requirements. Regulations and laws are necessary to govern the field and provide basic protections for children and families; nevertheless, a professional code represents a higher standard of performance.

A code of professional ethics provides common principles for dealing with dilemmas—principles based on a belief in the value of childhood as a unique stage of life, knowledge of child development, a valuing of family and cultural ties, and a desire to help individuals reach their potential through supportive relationships. Such a code is created through discussions with colleagues who reflect on challenges that occur regularly within the profession.

The process of developing a code of professional ethics may begin with the standard predicaments that educators face in the course of their day-to-day work. All early childhood educators are faced daily with dilemmas. Many of these situations do not have easy solutions but can be resolved using defined professional ethics to guide decision making. Ethics may be defined as the way associates in a group specify their responsibility to their clients, one another, and the community in which they work. Statements found in a code of ethics guide educators in collectively expressing their commitment to children, families, colleagues, and community. This statement represents what is right rather than what might be expedient. What is best is not always easy to determine, and a code of ethics is an essential tool to guide staff in their daily decision making.

Ethics and the Early Childhood Educator provides a thoughtful framework for exploration of ethical challenges facing early childhood educators (Feeney and Freeman 2005). The authors provide examples of issues and the educator's obligations to children, families, colleagues, and community. For example, an ECE may be forced to choose between the needs of a parent and the needs of a child. Often, programs need to make the decision that a mildly ill child would be better cared for at home than if he or she remained at the program.

It is important for the public to have confidence that the profession will meet its obligations and serve the public good. The protection of vulnerable children demands that all individuals working with children conform to the highest standards of ethical conduct. Professionals not only agree to operate according to a high standard of behaviour, they also agree to monitor the conduct of others in the field. Penalties (fines or suspension/termination of one's right to practice) may be levied against members of the profession who are incompetent or fail to act in accordance with standards of ethical practice.

The code of ethics developed by the Ontario College of Early Childhood Educators, in consultation with educators and stakeholders, is included earlier in this chapter. The principles found in the code were developed for use by adults who work with children and families in a variety of early childhood settings. They are intended to guide practitioners and protect the children with whom they work. Professionalism creates additional ethical obligations to colleagues and the profession.

A final component of professional ethics is **altruism**—when work is service-oriented and client-focused. Ideally, members are expected to perform their services with unselfish dedication and an emphasis on social goals. From its beginning, the practice of early childhood has been grounded on the principle of improving the lives of young children and families. On this criterion, early childhood educators rank highly, since their concern is with children and families. Given that the field is dealing with human lives, educators must be accountable—and must therefore care about what they do and how they do it.

Professional Preparation Programs

Entry to practice for most professions depends on a prescribed level of pre-service education. Such professional education ensures that early childhood practitioners learn the knowledge and techniques necessary for informed and effective performance before they begin work.

In working toward commencing a career in early childhood, a foundation step is the professional preparation that an individual undertakes when making decisions about their own career aspirations and professional development. These education programs should recognize the diversity of settings, populations, and roles within the field of early childhood that an educator may undertake.

Professional preparation programs are often driven by the various requirements of service providers as well as those defined by regulatory structures. Early childhood educators enter the field through various paths. Some individuals complete their professional education programs prior to assuming a professional role. For many others, professional education programs follow their decision to work with young children. Professional qualifications are included in the minimal requirements set by each province and territory in Canada. Formal professional development opportunities bearing academic credit are available through colleges and universities with some institutions working together to provide career pathways. These pathways are called **articulation agreements**. The length of the program offered by colleges and universities ranges from one year certificate programs to graduate work at a masters and doctoral level. Articulated credentials, such as two-year diplomas to degree programs, can provide a means by which individuals can achieve a higher credential and open up additional career opportunities with potentially better remuneration or move into a new role which has fresh challenges. Educational ladders between ECE credentials improve the quality of the early childhood workforce and programs for children.

Effective educational ladders are based on the ability to build on the foundation of a previous level, such as by obtaining a degree through building on, rather than duplicating, coursework and supervised work experience completed for an ECE certificate or diploma. Articulated courses and credentials require a consensus about the coursework and/or experiences that will be recognized as credit towards an ECE diploma, certificate or degree. Clear pathways from one training institution or education level to another are also required, as is the development of sequential curricula.

If Canada follows international trends, provinces will begin to require degrees for program supervisors, such as the leadership degree offered by a number of Ontario colleges. Ultimately, it is likely that this will become a requirement for early childhood educators who are responsible for a group of children, similar to kindergarten teachers. The majority of Canadian ECE practitioners do not have this level of training at present.

Ongoing professional preparation opportunities are increasingly structured to support individuals who are working in the field to obtain their ECE credential. Some examples of this include the apprenticeship program in Ontario, the distance education modular approach in Quebec, and the alternating classroom/work placement approach offered at Red River College in Manitoba and Holland College in Prince Edward Island.

While professional preparation alone does not guarantee high ECE quality programs, the quality of the program improves when the staff has this education in early childhood development. Beach et al. (2004) in *Working for Change: Canada's Child Care Workforce* found that 60% of early childhood educators and assistants had a post-secondary credential compared with 53% across all occupations.

Competent educators need a theoretical grounding in order to develop a conceptual framework in which to observe and respond appropriately to children. Field placement experiences are a critical component that enables the application of theory to practice. Colleges and universities operate best practice lab schools where students learn firsthand how to provide high quality inclusive programs. In these experiences, a student has the opportunity to practice and develop skills with the guidance of a knowledgeable cooperating staff. Field placements provide the opportunity to learn to interact effectively with young children and families, as well as to work as part of a team.

More specialized knowledge and skills may be added around the core curriculum, as required. For example, many educators learn about the areas of employee rights on the job and working with children who require extra supports.

An essential skill and knowledge area is the educator's appreciation of the diversity of families. Demonstrating respect for diversity, equity, and inclusion are prerequisites for children's optimal development and learning. Educators must take into account the differences each child and family brings to an early childhood setting, including appearance, age, culture, ethnicity, race, language, gender, sexual orientation, religion, family makeup and environment, socio-economic status, and developmental abilities. In order to provide a sense of belonging for children and families, educators must engage in dialogue about the principles and shared beliefs that relate to inclusion, equity, and diversity. They must recognize each child is a citizen with rights and unique views about how they wish to participate in the world.

Most college and university programs are infused with the philosophy of diversity, enabling students to graduate with an understanding of the breadth of human culture, an appreciation of issues such as bilingualism and home language retention, and an ability to respond proactively to bias and prejudice. In order to keep pace with changes in the families served, educators must be prepared to participate in lifelong learning.

Legislation and Self-Governance

Professional bodies have the authority to regulate their members and their practice through self-governance. The recognition of these groups is usually embedded in legislation. As noted earlier, Ontario established a College of Early Childhood Educators. This college provides public accountability and, ultimately, a more respected status for its members. As part of the process, a clear definition of an early childhood educator's role is defined in the Scope of Practice as:

The practice of ECE is the planning and delivery of inclusive play-based learning and care programs for children in order to promote the well-being and holistic development of children, and includes:

- delivery of programs to pre-school children and school-aged children, including children with special needs;

- assessment of the programs and of the progress of children in the programs;

- communication with the parents or persons with legal custody of the children in the programs in order to improve the development of the children; and

- such other services or activities as may be prescribed by regulation.

Source: *Scope of Practice defined by legislation in the Ontario ECE Act 2007*

Accreditation is a process of self-regulation and an additional way that the public and other professionals can recognize early childhood programs that exceed required standards. While "licensing" implies meeting minimum standards, "accreditation" means performing to model standards. With accreditation, a representative body recognized by the service community, establishes quality standards. An example of this is the Alberta Association for the Accreditation of Early Learning and Care Service, which evaluates ECE agencies. Alberta also set up the Resource Centre for Quality Enhancement to provide support to EC programs to meet increased standards, including consultation, resources, and access to professional development.

Accreditation is founded on the beliefs that for change to be real and lasting, it must be initiated by the early childhood organization, and that program improvement results from a collaborative problem-solving approach involving the director, staff, and families in a systematic review of the program's strengths and weaknesses. In some models, excellence in settings is verified by visits and assessment by the body granting accreditation. A study of programs accredited by the National Association for the Education of Young Children (NAEYC) confirmed the positive impact of accreditation and also indicated that the process facilitated improvements to the program, which led to even higher quality In some areas there is a growing trend to offer a higher rate of government funding to accredited programs.

Some of the benefits of accreditation include:

- improvements in staff development, communication, and morale;
- measurable program improvements; and
- increased confidence on the part of families that they have made a good decision in choosing an accredited program for their children.

As the profession evolves, educators are becoming more knowledgeable about theories of development and learning and more skilful in applying these in their daily work with children and families. Professionals must continually strive to do their best for young children and families through informed, ethical practice. Furthermore, we must be willing to share this perspective with others. (Chapter 10, "Advocating for Canada's Children," provides a variety of strategies for public education.)

As early childhood education comes of age, there is a growing awareness of the importance of specialized expertise and education. As educators work together on common goals, they invest part of themselves in the process, and this investment contributes to our shared professionalism. This enhanced sense of collective purpose is what makes educators willing to become involved in voluntary efforts toward the improvement of early childhood programs.

In the words of one educator, "It is in this subtle area of private endeavour that a profession, in its totality, achieves greatness. Sometimes it is called professional spirit. It is the result of the association of men and women of a superior type, with a common ideal of service above gain, excellence above quality, self-expression beyond motive, and loyalty to a professional code beyond human advantage." (Pat Dickenson, personal communication). This is the commitment needed to realize quality early childhood experiences for every Canadian child.

Stages of Professional Growth

There is no one method of improving the performance and facilitating the growth of ECEs. Directors need to assess the developmental characteristics of each staff to select the most effective approach—this takes into account the individual's knowledge, level of skill, and experience. Individuals vary greatly in the length of time they spend in each stage:

- Stage I—Novice
- Stage II—Emerging Practitioner
- Stage III—Experienced Professional
- Stage IV—Maturity

The typical behaviour of an early childhood educator is described at each of these stages along with the specialized training and professional development appropriate to each level.

In the initial years of working, the novice practitioner moves through a number of developmental stages. An experienced colleague serving as mentor can identify the stage of development and provide appropriate strategies to stimulate reflective thinking and professional growth.

STAGES OF DEVELOPMENT—EARLY CHILDHOOD EDUCATORS

Developmental stages		Professional development needs
I.	Novice	On-site support and feedback
II.	Emerging	Mentorship, access to specialists
III.	Experienced	Further education, membership in professional organizations
IV.	Maturity	Leadership in professional organizations

Stage I—Novice

While each educator is unique in her knowledge, skills, and motivation, making the transition from student to beginning teacher can be daunting. From a director's point of view, it is important to get new staff oriented and productive as soon as possible. Novice educators can be both exhilarated and terrified at having responsibility for a group of vigorous young children. Novice educators need support, encouragement, reassurance, comfort, and guidance. Mentoring can be particularly helpful for new graduates feeling the responsibility of a classroom. One aspect of the job that may make a novice practitioner feel most competent includes the structural elements such as arranging the environment and establishing the daily routine. Being concerned with structure is a logical entry point to the curriculum and one where the novice can experience immediate success in activities such as labelling materials

On-site support from a mentor is an effective professional development strategy.

to support the children's independence. Staff in this primary stage should not be supervising students who are on field practicum.

Mentors can provide encouragement, insight into the reasons behind children's behaviour, and instruction in specific skills. The mentor-coach can introduce new employees to policies and procedures, helping them to understand the structure and culture of the organization. On-site support and mentoring from experienced staff are the most appropriate strategies to support the novice staff in the first stage of development.

Stage II—Emerging

As they pass the novice stage, educators may realize the areas that they need more experience and knowledge in, as well as those in which their skill sets need strengthening. In this second stage, educators are comfortable with the structural elements of the program and focus on their teaching strategies. They may practice a particular strategy for a period of time until it becomes a natural part of their interactions with children. Educators interpret what is happening in their classroom and may then try alternative approaches. During this phase, emerging practitioners may move their attention to situations that deviate from the norm. They learn by observing, modelling, and doing and thrive in a supportive environment that encourages problem solving. They learn to structure physical environments and activities in a way that reduces the need for external controls. At this stage, practitioners benefit from focused feedback and collaborative problem solving new curriculum approaches.

As they develop further and master fundamentals, emerging educators are ready to develop more advanced skills. To stay motivated and avoid burnout, they require exposure to new ideas. In the later stages of this phase, individuals are ready for performance appraisal systems that facilitate introspection and personal goal setting. Possible methods include video analysis, pairing with a mentor—most often a lead teacher—along with regular opportunities to review issues that have arisen in the course of daily practice.

Stage III—Experienced

At level three, the educator has a good understanding of the curriculum. Sometimes an educator may see his or her teaching strategies as the only way to implement the program. Some practitioners in this stage reach a professional plateau. He or she needs to realize that a philosophical framework is flexible and can be carried out in a variety of ways. It is desirable that in dissimilar settings with diverse populations of children that the curriculum should be implemented differently. The educator may be comfortable with the established program and routines, and after several years of implementing the same curriculum to children at the same age level, she or he may no longer feel challenged. The practitioner may search for stimulation, asking, "What's new in the field? Are there any new strategies I haven't considered before?"

Working with educators at this stage can be challenging for the mentor-coach. It is important for experienced practitioners to become interested in learning about new developments in the field, as well as to have opportunities for meeting with colleagues from other programs. Professional development opportunities can be particularly beneficial at this stage as well as active involvement in a self-assessment process. Some may look inward to re-examine core values, beliefs, and options. Helpful strategies include reflective journal writing, identifying patterns, and developing professional portfolios.

Stage IV—Mature

Mature educators perceive themselves as committed professionals. They understand the rationale, purposes, and philosophy of the curriculum well enough to adapt it to a variety of situations. They may choose to focus on other aspects of the program such as family literacy. This final stage is reached by individuals at different points in their careers and represents a coming to terms with themselves and their profession. They have developed a philosophy of education and recognize the critical nature of early learning. Mature educators acknowledge the need for continual professional growth and self-renewal. They are committed to improving the early childhood profession and see sharing information as an essential part of this goal. They are often searching for the meaning of social, economic, historical, and political influences on society. Mature educators need opportunities to interact with others searching for similar insights and participate in events where their questions can be addressed.

These four stages of professional development can be viewed as ever-widening circles, as the early childhood practitioner matures and develops. All practitioners benefit from opportunities to expand their knowledge and skills throughout their careers.

Continuing Competence and Professional Development

The purpose of **continuing competence** is to ensure that professionals are aware of new knowledge in their own and other disciplines. In some professions, the individual must fulfill a specified number of professional development hours each year in order to maintain registration in the professional body. For example, a certified social worker is required to fulfill 75 hours of professional development over a five-year period. Government regulations can also influence staff participation in professional development. Regulations in Prince Edward Island, Manitoba, and Newfoundland and Labrador require that individual educators in licensed settings are required to document a specified number of hours of professional development. For example, in Newfoundland, in order to renew certification, practitioners must validate professional development every three years. British Columbia grants a licence to practice to individual caregivers. Renewal of this licence requires the individual to have participated in at least 12 hours of professional development within the previous five years (Beach et al. 2004).

An additional process used to improve performance is early childhood educator self-reflection. Professionals consider their assumptions about how children learn. They then step back and think about the curriculum they have planned and how it can be improved. This process is termed "**reflection**." It can be defined as a process that facilitates the development of future action by the contemplation of past and current behaviour. It is like a conversation in one's mind. **Reflective practice** is a style of teaching that is based on questioning what one is doing and why; on thinking how theory is translated into practice and how practice informs theory, is to enter into a way of working where professional development takes place day after day in the classroom. Reflection is a characteristic of professionals that helps them gain better perspective on, insight into, and understanding of their work. It is critical to the developing of professional judgment.

Among the strategies used by professionals to keep current with emerging research findings and trends in their field and throughout their career include: internships, field work, membership in professional organizations, self-study, in-service workshops, professional literature, and conferences. Educators may use a variety of methods for self-study and informal professional development depending upon their individual learning style. Examples include reading professional journals and books, viewing professional multi-media presentations, taking on-line courses, participating in staff meetings and in-house workshops; receiving reflective supervision and mentoring by more experienced educators; discussing situations with peers; and using professional websites.

Often professional development serves to provide specialized knowledge and skills, beyond the general entry level, which can facilitate various career paths. Various roles within the field require that educators acquire additional specific skills and knowledge. Professional groups and post-secondary institutions offer an array of professional development opportunities in order for practitioners to meet the diverse needs of children and families in a variety of settings. As well, the profession must further develop a framework for professional development that conceptualizes the coming together of regulation, education, and compensation. Perhaps the College of Early Childhood Education will create an infrastructure to bring together these strands.

By designing and completing a professional development plan, ECEs can ready themselves for each step on a professional development ladder/lattice. Most important is the empowerment that comes from taking charge of one's personal and professional development and becoming the best qualified educator one can be.

Ladders, Lattices, and Career Paths of Early Childhood Professionals

Many Roles Exist Within the Field of Early Childhood in a Variety of Settings   Professionals in the field provide direct service to young children and families from birth through age eight, as well as those who administer ECE programs and those who provide professional development. Positions vary in the specific knowledge and levels of education that are required. Among the possible roles within the field are early childhood educator, director, family resource staff, family child care provider, resource teacher working in an integrated setting, kindergarten teachers, and others. Figure 6–2 identifies education linked with various roles within the field.

Career mobility or professional advancement can progress in two directions—upward moving to higher levels of responsibility, also, horizontal or lateral, with an educator becoming increasingly adapt and knowledgeable at the same level. These movements represent increases in knowledge, responsibility, authority, and compensation, sometimes within a setting. An individual's professional goals may involve both upward and lateral features. One may envision their career growth plan as a path, journey, or ladder. Whatever plan is envisioned requires time and financial resources to further education.

An early childhood career lattice incorporates multiple, interlocking **career ladders** providing for the diverse roles and settings within the profession. In a lattice, each rung of the frame represents a level with predetermined criteria for advancement to a new step or opportunity for an educator to take on a new role. By clearly setting the standards and recognition for movement, a **career lattice** can aid individuals in making career decisions based on professional goals. In essence, the individual is helped to take control of her or his own professional development.

Lateral moves recognize and reward experience and knowledge by providing new and meaningful challenges for people who have been in the field for a number of years. Vertical moves enable early childhood educators to gain more qualifications and experiences in order to achieve greater responsibility and compensation.

FIGURE 6–2		Sample Career Ladder	
Level	**Role**	**Description & Responsibility**	**To Qualify**
Level 1	Early Childhood Assistant	Adults who work under the supervision of an ECE/lead teacher* Work independently only for short periods with children in an ECE's absence.	1. 18 years or older 2. Standard First Aid + child specific CPR 3. Criminal Reference Check 4. TB test, immunization, and health assessment
	Family/Home Child Care Provider	Responsible for a group of children; provides care and learning opportunities that meet the needs of small groups of children in partnership with parents and in collaboration with agency staff.	1. 18 years or older 2. Standard First Aid + child specific CPR 3. Criminal Reference Check 4. TB test, immunization, and health assessment 5. Meet minimum provincial standards
Level 2	Early Childhood Educator	Responsible for a group of children; plans and implements learning opportunities and care that meet the needs of all children in partnership with parents and other community professionals. Responsible for implementation of the provincial curriculum.	ECE Diploma or ECE Degree; equivalency certificate.
	Family Resource Program	Provide information and programs to support children, families, and caregivers to enhance strengths; guided by the provincial curriculum.	Degree or diploma in ECE, Human Services or related field and Certificate in Family Supports.
Level 3	Pedagogue or Assistant Supervisor	Provide pedagogical leadership; plan, implement, and evaluate curriculum; assesses children's progress; supervise, coordinate and/or mentor staff and students; work with families and community professionals; collaborate with Kindergarten teacher in education system.	Leadership experience mentoring/supervising staff/students, facilitating professional development and pedagogy. Option 1: Degree in ECE/Child, Youth, and Family Studies Option 2: Related degree + ECE diploma or College Graduate Certificate Program (Infant/Toddler or School Age)
	Resource Educator	Facilitate inclusion through consultation, role modeling, providing resources, training, and support special needs	Option 1: Degree in ECE/Child, Youth, and Family Studies Option 2: Related degree + ECE diploma or College Graduate Certificate Program (Resource Teacher)
	Resource Consultant	In addition to above, provide case management, service coordination, community education, and liaison and family-centered services.	Option 3: Three year Resource Teacher diploma In addition to above, an adult education credential

(continued)

Level	Role	Description & Responsibility	To Qualify
	Resource Centre/OEYC Supervisor/ Manager	Provide information to support children, families, and caregivers to enhance strengths, build capacity, and further community development. Program is guided by the provincial curriculum.	Option 1: Degree in ECE/Child, Youth, and Family Studies Option 2: ECE diploma + Family Support Worker or BSW or SS diploma
	Home Child Care Coordinator/ Visitor	Recruit and support providers; monitor and ensure program standards are maintained; match families with providers; provide in-service training. Build capacity and further community development.	Experience mentoring or supervising adults, facilitating professional development and pedagogy. Option 1: Degree in ECE/Child, Youth, and Family Studies Option 2: Related degree + ECE diploma + College Graduate Certificate Applied degree
	JK/SK Teacher in a fully integrated program	Plan, implement, and evaluate provincial curriculum and kindergarten program; provide pedagogical leadership; assess and report children's progress; work with families and community professionals; collaborate with pedagogue in Ministry of Education or ELCC program; work with parents.	Option 1: Minimum of university degree + ECE diploma + Teaching Certificate Option 2: ECE-related degree and Teaching Certificate Option 3: Joint credential (under development)
Level 4	Centre Supervisor/ Program Director	Administer, supervise, and evaluate an ECE program. Provide pedagogical and human resources leadership (affirm values, set goals, articulate vision) and carry out management functions (orchestrate tasks, set up systems to carry out mission).	Option 1: Degree in ECE/Child, Youth, and Family Studies + College Graduate Certificate Program (ECE Administration) Option 2: Related degree + ECE diploma + College Graduate Certificate Program* (Management) Option 3: Leadership/Management ECE Degree (in development) *Other generic management training + pedagogy
Level 5	Manager/ Executive Director	Responsible for multi-program operation.	Above plus 2 or more years in Administration

In addition, a career lattice model can serve as a supportive framework to motivate early childhood educators to achieve higher levels of performance, career advancement, and fulfillment. In the field of early childhood education, each level of the lattice is tied to qualifications, experiences, and to increased responsibility and compensation. There are several entry points, and it is possible to move to new positions vertically to higher levels or laterally to different position within a level. For example, an individual may begin working in an early childhood setting while enrolled in an early childhood education program. She or he would begin at a pre-level but then move vertically up the lattice when the credential is successfully completed. Sometime later, this same individual may change assignments within the same program to work with another age group. This move would constitute a horizontal or lateral movement. The lattice framework recognizes that continued professional growth can lead to movement around the lattice, into diverse roles and positions facilitating growth and professionalism within the early childhood education field. A diagonal move might constitute both a move to a higher level, such as becoming a Lead ECE, or a move from one setting to another, such as a move to an integrated ECE/school setting. Figure 6–3 identifies roles working directly with children as well as roles that are not working directly. Additionally there are roles requiring increasing levels of education.

Whitebrook and Bellm found that involvement as a mentor reduced by almost a third the incidence of leaving the field among experienced early childhood educators. Orientation programs that include high quality mentoring, common planning time, ongoing professional development, an external network, and a performance appraisal process are critical to improving **staff retention**. Many of these strategies were reviewed in Chapter 6. This information suggests that more attention needs to be given to strategies that support professional advancement within the field.

Methods of Enhancing Professionalism

At a national level, the Canadian Child Care Federation has facilitated work toward creating a supportive infrastructure for professionalizing the field. This organization has stimulated consensus building on defining a specialized body of knowledge; it also researched training and certification processes. The Child Care Advocacy Association of Canada, the Child Care Human Resources Sector Council, CCCF, and others are working collaboratively for increasing economic well-being through relationships with governments

Competent educators seek out opportunities to improve their skills and knowledge. Self-assessment is an indispensable route to professionalism. It helps one to be accountable to others; even more important, it makes one accountable to oneself. This process of validating accomplishments and identifying where work is still needed can lead the practitioner to feel more confident about her or his role. Directors and peers can assist by providing feedback on strengths and support in the areas needing improvement.

Certification and accreditation were mentioned in Chapter 1 as means of improving quality in early childhood settings. Both methods incorporate self-assessment as part of the process. These programs can improve standards of practice and promote the professional image of early childhood education. **Certification** is the awarding of a credential that identifies persons who possess the competencies needed to be a knowledgeable early childhood practitioner. Voluntary certification recognizes the educational qualifications of practitioners in a variety of early childhood settings. Individual employment policies may require that staff be certified. The qualifications required for certification stipulate that certified practitioners possess specified levels of professional competence or, in the case of British Columbia, Alberta and Newfoundland and Labrador, a level of educational qualification.

There are no national certification standards for early childhood educators equivalent to those for kindergarten and primary school teachers. The roots of this discrepancy are probably as much economic as academic. Early childhood educators are generally paid less than school teachers, and some decision makers fear that raising educational requirements would further increase the pressures for higher pay, thus increasing the cost of services.

Professional organizations in three provinces offer voluntary certification: Alberta, Nova Scotia, and Ontario. The process of certification varies among the different provincial organizations. Among the methods used to assess candidates are peer evaluation, self-assessment,

FIGURE 6–3	Career Tree

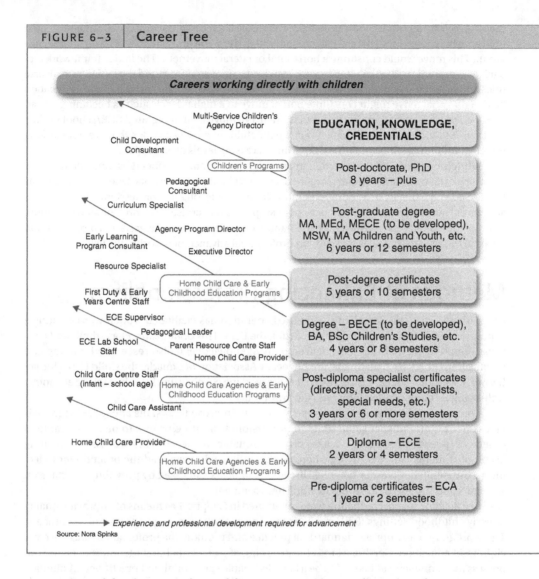

Careers working directly with children

Careers	EDUCATION, KNOWLEDGE, CREDENTIALS
Multi-Service Children's Agency Director	
Child Development Consultant	
Children's Programs	Post-doctorate, PhD 8 years – plus
Pedagogical Consultant	
Curriculum Specialist	
Agency Program Director	Post-graduate degree MA, MEd, MECE (to be developed), MSW, MA Children and Youth, etc. 6 years or 12 semesters
Early Learning Program Consultant	
Executive Director	
Resource Specialist	
First Duty & Early Years Centre Staff	Home Child Care & Early Childhood Education Programs	Post-degree certificates 5 years or 10 semesters
ECE Supervisor	
Pedagogical Leader	Degree – BECE (to be developed), BA, BSc Children's Studies, etc. 4 years or 8 semesters
ECE Lab School Staff	Parent Resource Centre Staff
Home Child Care Provider	
Child Care Centre Staff (infant – school age)	Home Child Care Agencies & Early Childhood Education Programs	Post-diploma specialist certificates (directors, resource specialists, special needs, etc.) 3 years or 6 or more semesters
Child Care Assistant	
Home Child Care Provider	Diploma – ECE 2 years or 4 semesters
Home Child Care Agencies & Early Childhood Education Programs	Pre-diploma certificates – ECA 1 year or 2 semesters

⟶ Experience and professional development required for advancement

Source: Nora Spinks

a set exam, and development of a portfolio. However, only a small number of practitioners in each of these provinces are certified. The certification process needs to be better promoted, recognized, and valued by the early childhood field as a step toward becoming a profession. Newfoundland and Labrador's regulations require certification of the staff of all licensed child care services.

Another route is **Recognition of Prior Learning**, which allows experiential learning to be identified, evaluated, and equated with an amount of post-secondary credit. There is growing interest in PLAR as a mechanism for granting advanced standing to candidates with related work experience. This process is not a replacement for academic credit, but a mechanism for recognizing prior learning. Among the assessment measures used are the presentation of a portfolio, transcripts from other institutions, challenge examinations, and performance evaluations. Early childhood educators with the appropriate background will find that assessment of their experience will enable them to complete a diploma or degree.

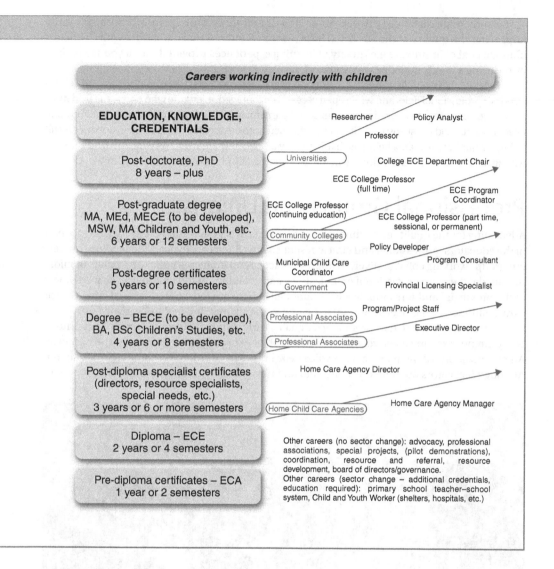

What Are the Possible Consequences with Professionalizing?

Historically there was a concern that increased professionalism would cause a rift between early childhood educators and families. A few parents don't equate education of early childhood staff with positive child–staff interactions. Some may associate education and professionalizing with institutional, uncaring settings for their child. Another concern is that professionalism by setting strict standards for entry and advancement could inevitably exclude some individuals. Raising the level of professionalism will necessitate increasing compensation levels, which will mean increasing the cost of services. In most provinces, this would entail substantially increasing government funding and/or parent fees.

Some of the aforementioned barriers are interrelated. Traditional routes to professionalism have tended to establish exclusionary, hierarchical systems of credentials; result in increased costs; and create distance between professionals and those they serve without necessarily improving the quality of the service. These results would not be compatible with the field's ultimate goal of improving the quality of learning experiences provided for all young children by ensuring a highly qualified workforce.

To avoid these pitfalls, the **early childhood profession** has faced these challenges. Early childhood is a professional field, and while open access is encouraged, everyone who enters the field must make a commitment to upgrade credentials and participate in ongoing professional development. Leaders in the field must ensure that meeting the increased costs of professionalizing does not result in higher quality programs being available to only a select few children. As well, the field must be willing to exclude those individuals who behave unethically or incompetently in their work.

Professional Groups and Unions

Advocating for the quality early childhood services that every child should have access to is part of the educators' professional and ethical responsibility. Effective advocacy depends on numerous groups working collaboratively to improve practice and influence policy and public opinion. In Canada, there are professional organizations and coalitions at the national level, with others at the provincial and territorial levels. Additionally, there are local networks that advocate for early childhood issues. It is important to belong to an organization and to be involved.

Join an organization that is working for quality early childhood in your province or territory. Every member's name adds weight to the efforts of these organizations' efforts to affect change. An organization will help make each voice heard through coordinated campaigns for action. Although legislators are unlikely to listen to an individual's recommendations, they are more

Only a small percentage of the field is unionized.

likely to be persuaded by broad-based support. Organizations provide members with information about issues and options as well as a common sense of interest and purpose.

In addition, membership can facilitate contacts that may be personally and professionally meaningful, provide access to research data or information about legislation and funding, and assist with the development of skills. Through contacts at meetings, individuals may learn of employment opportunities, and directors may meet potential staff members. Professional organizations provide forums for expressing ideas, opportunities to discuss concerns with other professionals, and a place to speak before a group.

In addition, there is a need for early childhood educators to establish and reinforce ties with healthcare professionals, educators, and other groups concerned with families, children, and issues related to poverty.

Unions have long served as political allies of the field, advocating for better funding and expanded services for children and families. Employees in unionized settings come together to negotiate wages, benefits, and working conditions with their employer as a group, rather than negotiating as an individual. The rights and responsibilities are laid out in a collective agreement. A **collective agreement** is a process in which a union and a employer focus on issues such as wages, working conditions, grievance procedures, as well as benefits such as health, dental, disability insurance, and pensions. Collective bargaining can be an effective way for sectors to improve wages and working conditions. As well, unions may offer additional supports such as professional development, leadership training, and equity initiatives. You Bet I Care! also found that collective bargaining led to improved benefits in one-third of the programs (Doherty 2000a).

Unions across Canada advocate for public policy for universal child care, have bargained for improved family and child care benefits for their members, and have worked to improve the wages and working conditions of its members. In fact, in Quebec, the Confédération des Syndicats Nationaux negotiated an agreement for their members that will bring their salaries to $39 000 in 2011.

With the growing number of ECEs, projected to be 25 000 by 2016 in Ontario alone, working in the education system in full-day kindergartens, there has been significant activity to unionize these positions. The education sector has a long history of unionization. Teachers have acquired a sense of empowerment, attained greater recognition, and improved their economic status. These are all important goals for the ECE profession. Unions have collaborated with groups such as the Ontario Coalition for Better Child Care to raise awareness and advocate for public policy and funding.

The Canadian Union of Postal Workers (CUPW) has programs which support members whose children have special needs. The organization established a fund to pay for additional staff, add safety items to child care programs, and purchase equipment and toys to enable programs to meet the needs of a more diverse age group. As well, CUPW offers a 35% to 45% to enable children of employees to attend child care programs. CUPW supports 11 projects across Canada, including a family resource centre that offers training and supports to caregivers, a toy lending library, and community referrals. As well, it runs a summer camp program and short-term emergency care service.

CUPW worked with SpeciaLink to develop a program to support families of children with special needs. The union became more aware of the high levels of stress and exhaustion, the limited child care services, the greater transportation needs, and the great deal of time needed to attend medical appointments confronted by these families. The union developed an education program for their members to assist them in becoming effective advocates for improved services. This one example illustrates the many ways unions work in partnership with the early childhood community to support families in their search for quality environments and to pressure governments to provide both the leadership and funding to achieve these goals.

Summary

Characteristics of a professional include a commitment to quality practice and lifelong learning. Early childhood practitioners share the responsibility of identifying ways to continually improve their practice with children and families. This chapter outlines the stages in an individual's growth as a professional and strategies to facilitate growth at each developmental stage. By directors' understanding the developmental levels of staff, they are better able to provide individualized strategies such as opportunities for coaching, mentoring, questioning, problem solving, and clarifying expectations. Engagement in ongoing professional development can move an individual to the next level of competence and can provide entry into a higher position, moving through and across the career lattice. Professionals in early childhood programs believe in and support a code of ethics as well as the importance of being accountable for their actions. Unions and professional organizations make significant contributions to the growth of the field of early childhood.

Key Terms and Concepts

Accreditation,   p. 179

Altruism,   p. 177

Articulation agreements,   p. 178

Career ladder,   p. 184

Career lattice,   p. 184

Certification,   p. 187

Code of ethics,   p. 163

Continuing competence,   p. 183

Early childhood profession,   p. 190

Ethical dilemma,   p. 176

Ethics,   p. 161

Occupational standards,   p. 166

Recognition of Prior Learning,   p. 188

Professional development,   p. 161

Professional ethics,   p. 176

Professional judgment,   p. 166

Professionalism,   p. 163

Reflection,   p. 183

Reflective practice,   p. 183

Staff retention,   p. 187

Activities

1. Identify professional and/or advocacy groups in your area, and which organizations you want to learn more about. Contact them and arrange to attend a meeting and/or subscribe to their newsletter.

2. Invite a guest speaker from a union to talk with the class. In small groups, identify how unionization aids in the retention of staff.

3. Why is it important for a profession to have a code of ethics? Divide into small groups to brainstorm answers to this questions. Reflect on the following points: ECE professionals are doing a job that is essential to society; professionals can monitor their own behaviour.

4. Brainstorm a list of essential qualities that you think all ECEs should hold. Compare with lists developed by other groups, how are they similar/different from each others?

Recommended Reading

Feeney, S., and N.K. Freeman. *Ethics and the Early Childhood Educator: Using the NAEYC 2005 Code ed.* Washington, DC: National Association for the Education of Young Children, 2005.

Jorde Bloom, P. *From the Inside Out: The Power of Reflection and Self-Awareness.* New Horizons, 2007.

Tertell, E., S. Klein, and J. Jewett, eds. *When Teachers Reflect: Journeys Toward Effective, Inclusive Practice.* Washington, DC: National Association for the Education of Young Children, 1998.

Child Care Human Resources Sector Council. *Occupational Standards for Early Childhood Educators.* Ottawa: Child Care Human Resources Sector Council, 2010.

Weblinks

www.ccsc-cssge.ca
Child Care Human Resources Sector Council

This group identifies and works to improve workforce skills and learning challenges faced by the field. They have completed a labour market study and have developed occupational standards for directors and ECEs.

www.cccns.org
Child Care Connection NS

CCCNS offers a variety of resources to assist ECE practitioners in their work, including mini journal, professional development opportunities, an annual conference, and advocacy activities.

www.arcqe.ca
Alberta Resource Centre for Quality Enhancement

ARCQE is an agency dedicated to providing technical assistance to the early learning and care service sector through provision of supporting quality and building capacity to those it serves. As a provincial organization, ARCQE is unique in designing support and resources specific to the needs of the Alberta child care community. This is accomplished by research and best practice, mentorship and coaching, professional development and training, and resource development.

www.mentoringpairsforchildcare.org
Mentoring Pairs for Child Care

Mentoring Pairs for Child Care (MPCC) is a credit recognized program designed to enhance child care quality by matching less experienced supervisors (mentees) with more experienced child care supervisors (mentors). Each mentoring pair then works their way through a process of group learning, one-on-one conferencing, networking, and guided communication. The Child Care Human Resources Sector Council's Occupational Standards for Child Care Administrators provides the framework for the program, enabling both mentors and mentees to deepen their understanding of the requirements for excellence as supervisors.

www.naeyc.org
National Association for the Education of Young Children

NAEYC has online resources for improving professional practice and links to resources for self-study courses. For example, there are conversations demonstrating a process for using the NAEYC Code to address ethical dilemmas. They explore strategies for furthering recognition of the code and its use by all who provide services to young children and their families.

Managing Safe and Healthy Learning Environments

Objectives

- **Outline considerations of quality safe/healthy EC environments.**

- **Identify key players in providing safe, healthy learning environments.**

- **Discuss regulations, quality standards, and principles of health policies and practices.**

- **Identify considerations in providing a nutrition program.**

- **Introduce universal design principles and outline benefits of "greening" of EC environment.**

- **Provide guidelines for purchasing equipment that is safe, healthy, and promotes children's learning.**

- **Overview maintenance of safe environments for children.**

Providing Safe, Healthy Environments

Good programs exist in all sorts of spaces, from environments specifically designed for young children to shared classrooms to storefronts. Criteria for evaluating environments fall into three categories—safe, healthy, and conducive to optimal learning. In addition, the environment should be welcoming and accessible for children, families, and staff. Directors are ultimately responsible for their program's health, safety, and **nutrition** programs. The EC program promotes the nutrition and health of children, and protects children and staff from illnesses and injury. They work closely with families, staff, and health professionals to create safe, healthy learning environments. The program's design and **maintenance** of its physical environment supports children's learning and allows for optimal use.

Although the space does not determine the program, the environment regulates the experience. The physical facilities, the arrangement of space, and the equipment available can make quality easier or more difficult to achieve. Facilities can be made physically and psychologically more comfortable by applying an understanding of how children develop as well as structuring

194

the environment to facilitate interactions. Well-organized, equipped, and maintained environments support program quality by facilitating the learning, comfort, health, and safety of all who use the program.

Directors must meet and ideally exceed provincial regulations that provide a baseline for acceptable care of children. A licence gives a program permission to operate; it does not guarantee quality. Good program policies should reflect best practices and quality standards that reflect current research to guide educators' promotion of the well-being of children and families. Yet, regulations are powerful tools for establishing basic standards for health and safety provisions in a physical setting. Since directors often have full responsibility for the planning, implementation, and monitoring of the key areas of health, safety, and promoting children's learning, it is necessary to be informed about the elements involved and the importance of these components to the children, families, and staff in the program.

Operating a Healthy and Safe Program

A coherent approach to health and safety in group settings for young children is always a work in progress. New information and research comes forward from health professionals, and changes in public perceptions which transform the attitudes and opinions of families and ECEs. Directors must develop health practices and procedures for children and staff in keeping with current information. The right balance of challenge, safety, and clear health policies is critical. The key is to create a safe and healthy environment where families and children feel secure. To benefit from education and maintain quality of life, children need to be as healthy as possible. Children depend on adults, who are also as healthy as possible, to make healthy choices for them and to teach them to make such choices for themselves. Educators need to ask themselves how they can promote children's optimal health and development, improve sanitation and reduce the spread of disease, eliminate injuries, and be prepared for emergencies.

While some degree of risk taking is desirable for learning, a quality program prevents hazardous practices and environments likely to result in adverse consequences for children and staff. Establishing safe programs includes hiring qualified and nurturing staff members; providing ongoing development for staff (e.g., understanding the duties and responsibilities of employers and staff regarding hazardous workplace materials); frequently assessing the environment for potential hazards (through inspections by health and safety representatives); purchasing non-toxic art and play materials; maintaining fresh air, ventilation, and heating in classrooms; monitoring the use of chemicals, including pesticides; and reducing the risk of harm or accident.

The benefits of incorporating healthy and safe practices are numerous for staff, children, and families. For example, appropriate hand washing reduces the frequency of respiratory illnesses and diarrhoea. This means fewer sick children at the program, fewer absences for children, and a reduction in staff illness that can lower the program costs by requiring less replacement staff.

In addition to establishing safe practices, the director recognizes that children will get sick, injured, or have difficulties because of their immature immune systems. For example, infants and toddlers frequently handle and mouth objects. A young child's breathing zone is closer to the ground, where heavier pollutants can be more concentrated.

Health-focused programs also need to increase the amount of physical activity children engage in daily to provide an optimal balance between activity and rest and reduce the occurrence of childhood obesity. Cumulatively these practices can contribute to child and staff health as well as reduce parents' absence from work to care for an ill child, reduce visits to health care professionals, and reduce health care costs.

Early Childhood Program Policies and Practices

Early childhood environments must promote wellness and protect the health and safety of children and adults. Caring adults can build awareness and teach the decision-making skills to children needed to identify healthy diet and activity options. When children understand and appreciate the importance of good nutrition and an active lifestyle, they have a kind of protection or immunity against the challenging environments. Most experts agree that the widespread availability and promotion of unhealthy food options combined with reduced opportunities for physical activity has created a set of conditions that threatens children's health. EC programs can give children protection against this threat by making modifications to program practices and teaching methods using innovative and newly available tools by:

- increasing the daily amount of movement and physical activity for all children;
- helping children develop a healthy body image and learn about nutrition; and
- involving families to encourage that newly established good habits are continued at home.

As well, thoughtfully considered health **policies** and **procedures** are critical to optimal EC programs. The director works with staff to develop policies, procedures, and practices and implement them to safeguard everyone's health and safety.

Well-written policies reflect provincial/territorial child care regulations, the expertise of the staff and parents, along with the most current evidence-based information available. Regulations, as previously noted in Chapter 2, are minimal requirements based on legislation. Quality programs build on this regulatory foundation by using quality standards to create fuller, inclusive policies. Program policy and procedure manuals are living documents that evolve as program staff become informed by new knowledge and past experience. Regular review of policies with staff assures their familiarity with the information and that enforcement will be more consistent. When educators are more aware of their responsibilities, they become more conscious of their actions. Policies must be practical and they must be used. They must not sit on a shelf or just be practiced during a licensing visit.

The category of health and safety policy covers the evaluation of children before admission, care and exclusion of ill children, health services such as screening and immunization, management of injuries and emergencies, provisions for rest/sleep, staff training in health and safety, and the surveillance of environmental problems.

Program Policy and Procedure Manual

As stated good policies should reflect best practices and provide standards that reflect current research to guide educators' promotion of the well-being of children and families. Policies and procedures are necessary to promote better understanding of expectations for both staff and parents. They can provide clarification and standardization of the program's governing rules as well as promote consistency and continuity in decision making. They determine the blueprint for achieving the established goals of the program.

Policy manuals are legal documents outlining the program's philosophy, goals and objectives, and how the staff intends to meet regulations, the most current information available as well as drawing upon what the staff has learned from managing previous health and safety issues. High quality programs build on the foundation of regulations to develop broader, fuller, inclusive policies that reflect their knowledge and skills. Many policies are official statements of the program's adherence to provincial regulations, such as the mandated reporting of child abuse.

Policy manuals are living documents. The field's knowledge of children's well-being including nutrition, health, hygiene, safety evolves more quickly than legislators can make or change regulations. Comprehensive policy manuals incorporate the unexpected. For example, what steps to take if an unauthorized person arrives to pick up a child. An effective manual adapts to the changing needs of a distinct EC setting. Policy manuals should be provided for the parents' and staff's reference and made available on the program's website.

Programs need to develop procedures and rules for implementing each policy. Procedures specify how to handle certain tasks. The purpose of a procedure is to guide an implementation plan that is clear and uniform. There are two types of procedures: those that relate to policies and those that relate to program operation. For example, in developing a procedure for emergency evacuation, it will specify the steps to take in leaving the building with the children such as taking the attendance list and parent phone numbers.

The more carefully that policies and procedures are written, the more staff and families will connect them to the philosophy and vision of the program. Creating these effective operating systems establishes a comfortable work environment for the staff and enables them to meet expectations.

Families need to have a clear understanding of program policies, expectations, and the rationale for them. When changes occur, parents need to be kept up-to-date. Providing parents with access to a policy handbook serves to reduce the potential for conflict. A handbook helps parents better understand the rationale for policies concerning food or transitional objects from home or why they need to inform the program if they will be arriving late for pickup.

The policy handbook serves as a valuable orientation for families who are new to the program, as well as a reference for currently enrolled families, and helps them understand their responsibilities and what to expect. Content may include a description of health and safety precautions to be taken by the family and staff, including the program policy on administration of medication during the program and the procedures used by the staff if a child becomes ill while at the program; immunization records and completion of emergency information and health history forms; information about meals and snacks and any adjustments to the posted menus; procedures for accommodating special diets or restrictions; a description of the legal obligations of the staff to report any evidence of suspected child abuse; and staff responsibilities to do with parental custody and access.

Both *Caring for Our Children: National Health and Safety Standards—Guidelines for Early Care and Education Programs,* 3rd ed. (2011) and *Well Beings: A Guide to Promote the Physical Health, Safety and Emotional Well-Being of Children in Child Care Centres and Family Day Care Homes* (2008) are valuable resources for developing informed content that reflects current medical research for policies. Also, Chapter 4 "Planning and Evaluating the Program Goals," Chapter 5 "Human Resources Management," and Chapter 8 "Building Partnerships with Families" provide more detail on handbooks and policy development.

HEALTH AND WELLNESS POLICY AREAS

- daily admission and exclusion procedures
- children's health records
- confidentiality and access of records
- administering medication

(continued)

- behaviour management
- care of an ill child
- notification of parents in the event of illness/injury
- medication
- emergency plan
- staff health records
- staff illness
- training in first aid
- occupational health and safety policy for staff
- management of infectious disease
- reporting of suspected child abuse and neglect
- sanitation policies and practices (hand washing, diapering/toileting routines)
- nutrition for children and staff
- food handling and mealtime maintenance of the facility and equipment
- smoking and prohibited substances

Each province and territory's licensing requirements identifies the types of policies and records that EC programs are required to maintain. Some examples of the types of information that would be collected include:

- information to be collected and maintained in individual files;
- lines of communication, who has access to the information, and confidentiality;
- management plans and reporting requirements for children and staff with illness; and
- medication policy of what is permitted, storage, administration, and record keeping.

Directors are aware of licensing requirements and regulations in their province/territory that affect plans for the environment, both inside and on playgrounds. Directors have responsibilities to staff as well as to the children. For example, there will likely be regulations regarding staff professional development, the amount of space required for each child, the number of toilets/change tables, space for mildly ill children, and areas for adults. Licensing authorities carefully review program records during renewal visits. All provinces/territories regulate physical space and some provide checklists of requirements and procedures. As previously noted, regulations refer to minimal requirements—not what is needed to provide a program that promotes each child's optimal development. There needs to be more information available regarding quality considerations, good design, and resources for health and nutrition.

Wallach and Afthinos found that licensing regulations for outdoor areas lag behind those for indoor environments. In addition to checking provincial/territorial regulations, directors will also work within municipal guidelines. Building codes may specify the kinds of changes that can be made to space. Public health departments have requirements for the preparation and storage of food and cleaning supplies. The fire department has specific concerns such as fire walls and doors. Provincial health and safety legislation establishes rules and responsibilities for government, employers, and staff and sets minimum health and safety standards for the workplace.

Regulations relate to the following areas:

- requirements of health, fire, and zoning authorities;
- group sizes and room capacities: square metres per child, both indoors and outdoors;
- health and safety regulations;
- occupational health and safety standards for employees;
- playground requirements; and
- regulations regarding physical environment. (The licensing bodies listed in the appendix will be a resource to up-to-date information.)

Quality Standards

With compulsory provincial regulations representing minimal standards forming a baseline, quality standards can, in effect, raise the excellence of the service. A representative body, recognized by both service providers and the EC community, may establish quality standards that are above the licensing requirements of the provincial/territorial government. EC programs can apply on a voluntary basis for evaluation against these standards and, if found to meet or surpass them, are granted accreditation status such as in Alberta. Additionally, staff can independently use tools to evaluate the quality of their programs against higher standards as identified in Chapter 4. Increasingly some governments are tying funding levels to achievement of standards which exceed licensing requirements.

Healthy Environments

Healthy children enjoy daily activities and have the energy and enthusiasm they need to grow and develop. Families feel increased confidence when an educator practices healthy habits and provides a healthful environment. In these environments, children are sick less often and usually less severely.

Young children in EC settings are highly vulnerable because of:

- close contact among children and adults, through feeding, diapering, toileting, and sharing objects, particularly moist sensory materials and items used in water play;
- children's underdeveloped immune systems;
- features of children's small body structures, such as the distance between the nose and throat and the middle ear;
- bumps and scrapes on the skin that can afford infectious agents entry into the body; and
- children's lack of understanding of how to protect themselves from infectious agents.

The incidence of infectious disease can be substantially reduced with good practices and education of practitioners in personal hygiene and environment sanitation. Pimento and Kernsted detail excellent practices in *Healthy Foundations in Child Care* (2010).

A key consideration in any EC facility is environmental control, including lighting, heating, cooling, and acoustics. Attention to these aspects can positively affect both child and adult behaviour as well as save money through energy saving practices.

Pediatric experts from government environmental health agencies and the American Academy of Pediatrics wrote the *Handbook of Pediatric Environmental Health,* 2nd ed. (2003), which presents concise summaries of the evidence that has been published in the scientific literature about environmental hazards to children, and provides guidance to physicians on how to diagnose, treat, and prevent childhood diseases linked to environmental exposures. There is a chapter dedicated to early childhood settings.

Building a Health Care Partnership with Families

Early childhood practices play an important role in children's health. Families appreciate knowing that the program is interested in their child's well-being. Developing enlightened policies around health lets parents know that the program takes their child's well-being seriously. Programs should think through policies and practices regarding health and introduce them to parents at the pre-enrolment interview. Staff serve as liaisons in maintaining children's complete and up-to-date health records and aiding parents in identifying health resources. Parents are required to provide a medical history for the child and an emergency contact form, which should be updated at least annually.

Young children often get sick. Preschoolers, on average, get between six and eight upper respiratory infections per year. This makes life difficult for the child—who doesn't feel well—and the parents—who must find substitute care or take time off work. To make this situation easier on everyone, programs must:

Set clear guidelines when creating or reviewing health care policies.

Talk to a health care professional and the provincial licenser to ensure that the program is up-to-date regarding health regulations.

Take into account the staffing and environment when setting program policies about children's illness and the administration of medication. For example, how ill is too ill to come to the program? What kind of attention can be provided for a child who is mildly ill without risking the health and safety of other children and educators?

Communicate policies to families. It is necessary to put health policies in writing for families and post them on the program's website. When families know policies and the reasons behind them from the start, they can make plans and adhere to them.

Keep accurate records. The Canadian Pædiatric Society's *Well Beings* (2008) provides samples of forms to aid in keeping complete health records for every child, including immunization history; medications the child is taking; any known **allergies**; and up-to-date information on the child's doctor, parents' or guardians' work phone numbers, and a contact to call in the event parents can't be reached. Update emergency information regularly with parents to keep it current.

Share observations. Since educators see the children every day, they are in a good position to observe any health concern that may be present. Let parents know if the child complains of any aches or pains or if a change in the child's behaviour has been observed—for example, a usually active child who seems listless, or a good eater who does not seem to be hungry.

Encourage families to exchange information. If a child is absent, ask the family for a reason. This way, educators can alert other families when a child in the group has a contagious illness, such as strep throat, that requires medical attention. Ask families to bring in a copy of the pharmacists' prescription information sheet or articles they have found helpful.

Additional strategies for communication with families are looked at in the next chapter. Healthy settings depend on:

- thoughtful, strictly followed sanitary routines, including careful diapering/toileting procedures, regular handwashing, and proper food handling that are regularly monitored and evaluated;

- development of a checklist of sanitation practices and sign off with date and time by the staff member who is fulfilling the requirement;

- policies regarding staff and child illness and contagious conditions that minimize the likelihood of infection;

- careful attention to stress and adaptation of the environment and routines to reduce stress;

- ensuring that staff follow universal precautions to prevent transmission of blood-borne diseases;

- good ventilation and lots of fresh air;

- environment kept at an appropriate temperature (18°C–20°C) and free of drafts;

- adequate humidity (30%–70%);

- smoke-free environment;

- clean air and water free from toxins and allergens;

- setting free of vermin; and

- pets that are free of disease and kept in clean cages.

The Canadian Pædiatric Society's *Well Beings* (2008) is an excellent reference on developing comprehensive health and safety policies. Included are sample health forms, detailed guidelines for admission and exclusion, and monitoring forms for health and sanitation. This resource was developed by the Canadian Pædiatric Society in consultation with early childhood specialists.

Protecting Staff Members' Health

Educators are exposed to infectious illnesses while working with young children. Staff are obliged to have their immunizations up to date as contact with children puts them at risk for contracting a variety of infectious diseases. A staff member's illness can become a health hazard to children and co-workers, necessitate the costly replacement of the staff with a substitute, and cause a lack of consistency for the children.

Directors need to advocate with boards of directors/owners for proactive employee health policies. Policies to protect the staff's health include:

- pre-employment health assessment, tuberculin test, and updated immunizations;

- practicing good handwashing;

- professional development opportunities to learn techniques that reduce the physical hazards of work, methods for handling potentially hazardous products, and ways to deal with bodily fluids safely;

- exclusion criteria for staff with infectious disease; and

- adequate paid sick leave.

Staff health records should include results of pre-employment physicals, updates at regular intervals, records of work injuries, and emergency instructions including information on the staff member's special health needs, such as allergies, physician, and contact instructions.

Role of EC Programs in Improving Health of Young Children

We've all seen the alarming statistics on the "obesity epidemic" among children and witnessed firsthand the declining physical fitness of children. But can EC programs play a prevention role? A recent study, Children's Activity and Movement in Preschools Study, suggests that there is much that programs can do! The study of five- to five-year-olds in NIEER (January 2010) found that:

- Children were engaged in moderate to vigorous physical activity during only 3.4% of the preschool day.
- Four- and five-year-olds were less physically active than three-year-olds.
- Males were more active than females.
- Children in higher quality EC settings were more likely to engage in physical activity than children in programs of lower quality.

While conventional wisdom holds that preschoolers expend lots of energy, this study found this is not always so. Clearly, some EC programs are currently part of the problem, not the solution. There is significant need for EC programs to design their spaces and their activities to stimulate more vigorous physical activity. Although spending more time indoors, children were more likely to engage in physical activity when outdoors. The five most common outdoor activities involved open space, fixed equipment, ball and object use, socio-dramatic props, and wheel toys. The first three conditions are associated with high levels of moderate to vigorous physical activity. While indoors, the five most common scenarios were nap time, large group, indoor transition, snack, and manipulative. All of these conditions are largely sedentary in nature and resulted in very little physical activity. However, teacher-arranged physical activity and music exercises, while observed rarely in EC environments in the study, were related to very high levels of physical activity. Therefore, the researchers called for more teacher involvement in promoting preschoolers' physical activity. In view of the high levels of sedentary activity observed, the researchers call for careful attention in designing outdoor spaces for preschoolers. Designs should include sufficient open spaces and specific outdoor play materials associated with increased levels of physical activity.

In "Making a Difference in Early Childhood Obesity," Huber addresses educators' concerns with obesity reduction initiatives. One concern EC teachers may have is whether efforts to increase activity and teach nutrition will require replacing existing curriculums and lesson plans. Advocates of obesity prevention programs recognize that this kind of change isn't practical or necessary. Instead, the emphasis is on modifying what educators already do. EC programs are more likely to affect a child's decision-making process when educators recognize that teaching young children how to make healthy choices isn't a separate subject, like math or reading. It's a way of thinking that can be a part of every subject and needs to be integrated into the whole program.

"Globesity," a lead story in Newsweek (March 22, 2010), referred to recent statistics that more than 1 billion adults worldwide are obese or overweight. Among the multitude of solutions proposed was to adopt a more European approach. Sweden and Norway forbid advertising of any kind to children under 12 on commercial TV shows. The French removed more than 22 000 food and drink vending machines from schools and replaced them with water fountains. Denmark banned transfatty acids in 2003 and put a tax on saturated fat.

Early Childhood Nutrition Programs

ECEs have the opportunity to improve children's food choices since they interact with them daily. Family members and educators can influence children's food preferences by providing healthy food choices, offering multiple opportunities to prepare and eat new foods, and serving as positive role models through their own food choices. To be successful, this type of effort requires a deep commitment from educators, program directors, and families. For example, family-style meals are encouraged because they give staff an opportunity to eat with children in an atmosphere that allows them to model healthy eating and talk about healthy food choices.

The director's role in planning the nutrition program is wide ranging. Ensuring adequate nutrition and food policies and practices is important for healthy development due to the effects of hunger and malnutrition on the young child. Adequate nutrition is essential for growth and development as well as maintenance of the body. Brain research data indicate that including or not including certain foods can affect brain development, from both physical and emotional perspectives. Dietitians of Canada provide many useful resources on their website www.dietitians.ca.

The program's nutrition objectives may include planning the food services, providing and serving nutritious meals and snacks, supporting parents to meet children's nutritional needs, identifying children's nutritional issues, and implementing nutrition education for children through daily activities. There is increased parental awareness of the need to transform the food culture back into one that is healthful, responsible, and sustainable using locally grown food which is packed with more nutrients than food that has traveled long distances. Some parents are putting pressure on programs to accommodate these values.

There are often children attending with special health care needs, food allergies, or special nutrition needs. Parents want a peace of mind that comes with customized menu plans for their child with allergy or dietary restrictions. The program, in consultation with a health care provider and the child's family, should provide an individualized plan. Programs need to accommodate using substitute items like gluten-free bread, dairy-free soy yogurt, and alternative and vegetarian meals. Children with special dietary needs want to enjoy the same variety of delicious, nutritious food as their friends.

The director oversees the menu planning. In an all-day program, this may involve breakfast, lunch, and two snacks daily. The content on the plate that a child sees before them is the result of a complex process, involving political and technical processes. Nutritionists may work out menus that take into account the seasons, and guarantee a balanced supply of all the elements that children need for growth. Menus need adapting to different medical, religious, and ethnic requirements, and to the choices of the children themselves.

Foods may be either prepared at an EC facility that complies with health standards or catered another facility and transported to the program using appropriate sanitary containers and maintaining safe temperatures. Increasingly EC programs are using catering companies to provide their nutritional requirements. Sometimes this occurs when programs do not have complete kitchens. There are some caterers that specialize in preparing food for young children and

Many children are susceptible to food allergies and intolerances because their immune systems are immature.

have nutritionists oversee menus. A drawback to having food prepared offsite is that they are not under the control of the program and there is less opportunity for children to have educational opportunities in the kitchen. Some larger programs have a cook and/or assistant to carry out this function. Employees should have appropriate qualifications and experience planning meals for young children and special diets. Programs should access a nutritionist who is familiar with the unique nutritional needs and preferences of young children and can give advice on menu plans. Currently, no province or territory specifies any credentials for food service personnel, although in some regions, the public health department requires the completion of a food handler course. Programs are beginning to recognize the unique professional development needs of cooks. A useful document is *Best Practices for Child Care Cooks* (George Brown College 2000).

As part of a program's conditions for licence, public health inspectors will review the food preparation, equipment, and storage and serving facilities annually. In a smaller program or in a family child care home where the provider does all the cooking, meals must be ones that can be easily prepared. Regardless of how the food is provided at the program, the early childhood educators are responsible for ensuring that the children have access to adequate nutrition each day. Generally, food consumed at the program constitutes a large portion of the child's daily intake, so meals must include the daily requirements as outlined in the revised *Eating Well with Canada's Food Guide* (Canada 2011).

Both families and educators have an impact on children's nutritional habits. In some programs, financial constraints or limited kitchen facilities mean that parents must bring some or all of the food. However, new food hygiene requirements make it more difficult to bring in birthday cakes or other food made at home by the parents. Programs need a refrigerator in which to store food and some appliance with which to heat food (stove, microwave, or hot plate). Parents of infants often supply meals along with formula or breast milk. All food must

Cooks need opportunities for professional development.

Source: Photo courtesy of Glenn Brown

be properly stored and labelled. Breastfeeding is necessary for optimal brain development. Quality programs support the continuation of breastfeeding by providing a comfortable space for a mother to be with her infant.

Although children decide on how much or whether to eat, adults are responsible for the foods offered. Some strategies programs employed to promote their partnership with families include:

Post weekly menus in an easily seen location so that parents know what food is served each day. This can aid parents in supplementing whatever the child had to eat at the program.

Provide parents with information about appropriate food choices. Share information through websites, newsletters, bulletin boards, or handouts. If the child brings food from home for lunches or celebrations, suggest nutritious foods.

Keep parents informed about their child's food intake. Some programs have educators complete daily charts indicating how much the child ate. This written approach is particularly helpful with infant and toddler groups.

Develop a partnership with parents to plan food choices. The diets of very young children need to be carefully considered to respond to religious and cultural restrictions, avoid food allergies, digestive upsets, and poor nutrition.

A large number of young children are susceptible to food allergies and intolerances because their immune systems are immature. Ensure that parents inform staff of all food allergies and sensitivities. Common allergens include nuts, chocolate, dairy products, wheat, seafood, and eggs. When menus include these foods, be sure that there is a substitute, preferably something similar in appearance that can be served to the child with the food allergy. Some programs have become nut free due to the severity of nut allergies for some children. To ensure that no allergens are served, staff should double-check all food before giving it to the child.

Be aware of families' food practices. Many families are practicing vegetarians, and programs should accommodate these values.

Provide parents with recipes for foods the child particularly likes. Many children talk about a popular menu item, and the parent may want to prepare it at home.

Consider the child's ethnic background and incorporate foods using familiar ingredients. Some families may participate in new food experiences with the children.

Be sensitive to the family's financial resources. Some families do not have an adequate budget to buy a consistent amount of food throughout the month. Programs should have enough food available to provide extra servings to hungry children.

Early childhood programs should include nutritional education for young children. Nutrition should be an integral part of the total curriculum, which should include opportunities to learn about food, good diets, and the preparation, storage, and origins of food. Children need opportunities to develop socially acceptable eating behaviours.

Programs are increasingly building their ability to respond to children with food allergies. In Ontario, the revised regulations require EC programs to develop a written anaphylaxis policy that includes the following:

- strategy to reduce the risk of exposure to anaphylactic causation agents;
- communication plan for the provision of information on life-threatening allergies;
- individual plan for each child with an anaphylactic allergy that includes emergency procedures; and
- staff development plan from a parent or physician in case of an anaphylactic reaction.

STRATEGIES FOR RESPONDING TO FOOD ALLERGIES

Develop written policies. Have parents provide a doctor's statement outlining the specifics of the condition and what to do if the child is exposed. Post a list of children and their reactive foods in the food preparation and serving areas. Provide adequate training to administer emergency allergy medication. Have families provide additional medication to bring along on field trips.

Establish written procedures. Each person's role (staff and parent) is outlined. Staff should receive training from medical professionals on how to administer emergency medications.

Plan menus that consider allergies and intolerances. Children with allergies should eat food similar to other children to reduce feelings of difference or isolation. Allergy-specific cookbooks are useful for special diets such as wheat-free diets or diets for children who are lactose intolerant. Cooks must have professional development in planning special diets and label reading.

Ensure snack and mealtimes are safe. Staff must provide close supervision so the child does not have contact with offending foods or drinks or touch utensils that may contain traces of the allergens.

Plan and monitor food experiences thoroughly. Avoid using offending ingredients. Review recipes and labels for contents. Ensure food containers such as egg cartons or yogurt cups are cleaned thoroughly.

Communicate with families, children, and other staff (including replacement staff). Successful management of food intolerances and allergies requires a cooperative, team approach.

Source: Marna Holland, "'That Food Makes Me Sick!' Managing Food Allergies and Intolerances in Early Childhood Settings," *Young Children* (NAEYC, Washington, DC, March 2004), 42–46.

Considerations of Quality Safe, Healthy, Learning Environments

The director's responsibilities regarding the environment include the effective use of space—indoor and outdoor environments, playrooms, administrative space, storage, and areas such as the kitchen. Some areas are used mostly by children, some only by adults, and some are shared. The selection, variety, and maintenance of learning materials and equipment are vital parts of planning. The purchase of equipment is generally based on philosophical, developmental, practical and financial considerations. The director, collaborating with staff, acquires, arranges, distributes, maintains, evaluates, and remodels the space. *Partners in Quality: Tools for Practitioners in Child Care Settings* (CCCF 2000b) identifies standards of excellence for program environments (a sample appears below).

Quality Standards

ENVIRONMENTS IN EARLY CHILDHOOD PROGRAMS

The director should ensure a safe, healthy, well-organized environment and a planned curriculum that meets the needs of the children and their families by:

- defining and explaining program goals and objectives to staff and families;
- ensuring that policies, procedures, and practices are developed, implemented, and reviewed annually regarding such issues as:
    - safeguarding children's health, safety, and nutrition;
    - maintaining updated medical and developmental progress records on all children;
    - implementing positive and instructive behaviour guidance policies and procedures;
    - providing appropriate supervision of children both indoors and outdoors;
    - handling sick or injured children and emergencies;
    - obtaining parental consent where applicable;
    - release of children at the end of the program period; and
    - reporting protection concerns and complying with court orders.

(continued)

- planning and ensuring that required professional development is provided in areas such as protocols and procedures for reporting protection concerns and complying with court orders and emergency evacuations;

- developing and implementing plans for responding to allegations of misconduct by educators, volunteers, support staff, or others working within the EC setting;

- ensuring physical environments that are safe, clean, and organized to provide for quiet and active activities and that have materials and equipment that are appropriate in size and function and to provide access to safe outdoor play space;

- providing leadership and support in the development of the children's daily program so that activities and materials are developmentally appropriate and balance activity and restful times;

- using and promoting the use of a variety of observational techniques to assist in:
  - identification of children's skills, interests, and needs
  - evaluation of activities provided for children

- ensuring that educators have an adequate level of human and other resources to enable them to provide quality care and education;

- implementing a variety of communication techniques for providing families with information about the service and their children;

- developing a variety of user-friendly approaches that encourage and support children and parents to express their needs and preferences and to have meaningful input into policy and program development; and

- encouraging inclusion of children with special needs, and children and their families from all cultural and ethnic backgrounds.

Source: Gillian Doherty, in Canadian Child Care Federation (CCCF), *Partners in Quality: Tools for Practitioners in Child Care Settings*, 2000.

Advances in policy development and EC professional practice have led to the expectation that it is appropriate and advantageous to include children with disabilities (special needs) in community-based EC programs. As more efforts are made to provide opportunities for young children with special needs to participate in inclusive programs, steps need to be taken to ensure that children and their parents benefit from programs and address each child's unique needs. Many early learning programs have consciously adopted a set of principles that reflect a strong commitment to include all children in the community, to ensure their full participation in the program, and to support their parents as full partners.

The SpeciaLink Early Childhood Inclusion Quality Scale (2009), developed by Dr. Sharon Hope Irwin is a tool for assessing inclusion quality in early childhood centres and for helping centre move toward higher quality inclusion. The scale provides a picture of sustainable and evolving inclusion quality—an emerging issue as more children with special needs attend community-based centres. See the SpeciaLink Inclusion Practices Profile along with the SpeciaLink Inclusion Principles Scale to assess sustainable and evolving quality to support the inclusion of children with special needs as introduced in Chapter 4. These resources incorporate universal design principles. To ensure the environment meets the needs of all children, it is important to consider **universal design principles** so that hallways are wide enough to accommodate wheelchairs and counters are at a reachable height.

Principles Guiding Universal Design of EC Environments

How can universal design help EC professionals to further assure that all children have opportunities to learn? Universal design principles guide professions in designing programs in which all children and families have full and equitable access to learning and social opportunities. These principles were first introduced in the field of architecture to address considerations for designing physical spaces for all people, including individuals with physical and cognitive disabilities. It was recognized that this design framework would serve everyone. People who use wheelchairs benefit from curb cuts and ramps and so do bicycle riders and parents pushing strollers. The following points comprise a framework for universal design of EC programs:

Physical environment enables all children to have access to and equitable opportunities for full participation in all program activities. This includes structures, permanent and movable equipment and furnishings, storage, and materials. How will children be seated to accommodate different motor abilities and activity levels so that everyone can move about or attend as needed? Consider varied seating options so that a child may sit on a mat or chair, lie on the floor, or use specialized seating. Expand the meeting area so that all children can be present and focus their attention on activities.

Health and safety components promote wellness and minimize risks and hazards for all children. All children, regardless of health status or conditions, have ongoing access to learning without interruptions due to illness or injury. Do the planned activities accommodate children with different energy levels and health conditions? Consider safe floor covering for passage for any child, for example, a child in a hurry, who has visual impairments, or uses a wheeled stand.

The socio-emotional environment offers all children equitable access to and full membership in the group, and it supports their socio-emotional development. How can the educator support children in interacting with, learning from, and helping one another? Set up a learning environment with books, print materials, and other artifacts in French, English, Aboriginal, and other home languages that respect and promote language and literacy learning, and that reflect diversity in unbiased ways. Planning for small group as well as large group times. Support children's interactions and play through emotional availability.

The learning environment gives all children equitable access to learning opportunities through information and activities in multiple formats and multiple means for engagement, expression, and learning. This includes the curriculum, practices, materials, and activities. What kinds of support and encouragement will be needed to engage all children in learning? The educator may employ multiple formats, including print, verbal, video, and/or concrete objects, repeating key words in the child's home language, and using simple sentences with gestures.

Individual assessment and program evaluation practices provide multiple approaches to finding out what the child knows and can do in order to equitably assess individual learning, development, and educational progress. What are some different ways children can demonstrate their engagement and learning? Educators should be aware of the multiple ways that children can evidence their learning, such as by pointing to, using words from their home language, and/ or using complete sentences in English.

Family engagement practices support the equitable access and engagement of all families in the full range of experiences. This includes ongoing communication, learning opportunities, and program involvement activities. An educator can identify what opportunities for involvement she provides that accommodates varied work/family demands and/or time constraints. Programs can offer multiple opportunities for families, translate materials, and provide resources to families to support their child's learning at home.

Guidelines for Selecting and Maintaining Equipment

Selecting learning materials The type of curriculum used at the program influences the selection of learning materials and equipment. A program with a special focus on cognitive development may, for instance, purchase a variety of materials that offer children math and science experiences. Programs with a curriculum that uses learning centres can break down needs by the science, art, or block areas. Some programs are being influenced by the Reggio Emila approach, which emphasizes the use of natural products and real objects rather than plastic replicas. There are many excellent resources that explore this learning materials, including Greenman's *Caring Spaces, Learning Places: Children's Environments That Work* (2005).

Equipment is likely to be one of the EC program's largest non-staff expenditures. Therefore, it is important to make wise choices. Staff select and use materials, equipment, and furnishings to support the curriculum, meet program goals, and foster the achievement of desired outcomes for children. Equipment selection is based on many factors, including personal preferences and curriculum. Whether purchasing a shelf for the book centre or equipping an entire facility, the process of selecting learning materials and equipment requires research, planning, and organization to ensure that selections are safe, versatile, durable, appropriate, affordable, and increasingly sustainable. It is necessary to establish the budget before the selection process begins. A master plan should be created to purchase the basics first and add items as additional funds become available. (See Chapter 9, "Financial Matters," for a review of considerations in the budgeting process.) When purchasing outdoor equipment and furniture for a new facility, use a formula based on the cost per child as a guideline. The cost per child will be higher for younger children with higher staff:child ratios.

Full enjoyment of the new equipment will only result if staff preferences, curriculum, quality of construction, ease of maintenance, safety, and budget are all considered. Here are some questions to ask:

- *Durability:* How long will it hold up? Group use is at least 10 times as hard on equipment as home use.
- *Safety:* Sharp edges or corners? Parts to swallow? Toxic finishes? Will the item be pulled or tipped over? Will it wear or break in a manner that will make it dangerous?
- *Health:* Does it allow for easy cleaning and disinfecting?
- *Size and scale:* Is it the right size and scale for projected and unanticipated use by all the adults and children—including those with special needs?
- Is it consistent with the program goals? Will it offer developmentally appropriate experiences and autonomy?
- Will it facilitate the educator task? Equipment should also be selected with a view to preventing injury due to repetitive strain.
- *Aesthetics:* Is the design attractive? Do the colour, size, and shape add to or detract from the overall aesthetic (e.g., will there be too much bright plastic equipment)?

Selection of all equipment should reflect criteria as well as the Canadian Standards Association (CSA) guidelines found in *Children's Play Spaces and Equipment* (2007). Whether adding a new piece to an existing playroom or creating a full equipment list for a new program, the process of selecting the right equipment and furniture requires careful planning. The first criterion is to buy something that will be enjoyed by both the children and staff, is meaningful for the curriculum, and is functional.

When possible, take design preferences into account. Staff may source through websites, catalogues, or attendance at conferences where they tour exhibits and find items that appeal to them and fit the program's requirements. A key strategy is to visit other programs and talk to staff about the furniture and equipment they prefer. Thorough research at this stage of the process will help ensure that the investment made will be a good one.

Always keep in mind the number and ages of children in the program. If mixed-age groups use the playroom, purchase equipment that fits more than one group, or choose equipment that fits the smaller children, so that the room will accommodate everyone. Provide for flexibility and versatility. Equipment that can be assembled in different ways will be more interesting to children and provide creative learning opportunities. Avoid thematic furniture pieces that tend to inhibit a child's imagination. Some equipment can be used both indoors and outside providing a wider variety of learning experiences for children.

In determining the suitability of equipment, children with special needs must be considered. A child who cannot walk independently, for example, may need a table or easel that can be

Programs need to stimulate more vigorous physical activity.

used by the child while sitting in a chair or wheelchair. When children who do not have special needs use these same materials, they may develop greater insights into the experience of children who do. Refer to Universal Design Principles provided earlier.

Another consideration is the back care of staff; back injuries are the most common type of injury for early childhood educators. These injuries are usually caused by inappropriate lifting and carrying and poor design and layout of the furniture. Adult chairs with shorter legs can be used to provide adequate back support for staff; to avoid back strain, sinks and counters should be built to suit an adult's height. The change table should have walk-up steps, particularly for toddlers. These types of adjustments can decrease the incidence of muscular skeletal injuries by reducing the amount of lifting required. Other strategies are identified in *Healthy Foundations in Child Care* (Pimento and Kernsted 2010).

Outdoor Space

The outdoors area provides a great place for sensory motor exploration, experiencing the environment, and interacting with children and adults. The OECD affirmed that the physical environment is an important element of quality. They expressed concern about the lack of adequate and available outdoor space in Canada. They felt that children did not spend adequate time outdoors and this area needed improvement. This is in contrast to Finland and Sweden where children spend much of their day outside, even in winter. As noted earlier, there is a need for EC programs to design their spaces and their activities to stimulate more vigorous physical activity, as a recent study found that children were engaged in moderate to vigorous physical activity during only 3.4% of the day.

Many of the principles for indoor environments can be applied to outdoor space. Outdoor areas are designed with a variety of natural and manufactured surfaces, have equipment to accommodate motor experiences, and activities such as dramatic play. There should be spaces where children can play alone or with a friend. The program makes adaptations so that children with disabilities can fully participate in outdoor curriculum.

Programs vary in their ability to provide outdoor play areas, particularly in urban settings. Make the best use of what is available, remembering that even small spaces can be sites for quality outdoor experiences. Experiences can change with the addition of "loose parts"—materials that can be stacked, sorted, separated, lined up, dumped, and so on. Natural materials include rocks, stones, leaves, sand, wood, and water. Changes in the seasons offer new sensory opportunities. Some key considerations include:

- *Sufficient square footage:* A space that is too small results in crowding and too few play experiences. As well, with active children, when crowding occurs, accidents are more likely.
- *Drainage:* Good drainage is essential. Decks and platforms should offer a flat surface that drains easily and can be used for water play or when the ground is wet.
- *Non-toxic landscape:* All vegetation should be checked to make sure that there are no poisonous plants.
- *Good layout and zoning:* Defined play areas, clear pathways, and challenging equipment placed on the perimeter are best. Location of areas such as swings and bike paths must be well thought out.
- *Provide shade:* Roofs, canopies, and umbrella mounts are good alternatives if there is not adequate shading from trees.
- Consider ways to *increase the adults' convenience and comfort,* for example, with the addition of pillows, hammocks, and accessible changing/toileting areas to increase outdoor time.

Ideally, outdoor spaces offer a variety of stimuli. All programs should find community parks and safe routes to go for walks.

Selecting and Maintaining Playground Equipment

Start by considering the goals of the outdoor program. What sorts of experiences are desired for the children? Once a director has clarified the objectives with staff, they must then evaluate how well different pieces of equipment will help accomplish these objectives. In comparing pieces of playground equipment, a primary consideration is the quantity and quality of activity made possible by each piece. Generally, the equipment selected should encourage children to engage in a wide range of social, motor, and imaginative play experiences. Equipment should provide opportunities for upper- and lower-body development. It should be appropriately scaled and equipped for the children who will use it—and it must be fun for the children.

The purchase of playground equipment is one of the biggest decisions made by programs. Not only does it involve committing a large amount of the program's resources, it also impacts on the children's outdoor experiences for a number of years. Directors should speak with other programs about their experiences with various products and vendors.

CONSIDERATIONS IN SELECTING EQUIPMENT

- appropriateness and opportunities for learning
- safety
- type of construction material
- installation
- maintenance
- warranty

Young children's physical safety is the prime concern in evaluating any piece of playground equipment. The most serious injuries that occur in early childhood settings happen on the playground. According to the Canadian Institute of Child Health (2000), the leading cause of injury that requires hospitalization is falls. As with indoor equipment, all equipment is required to meet the standards set by the Canadian Standards Association in 2007. These standards also indicate modifications that should be made to equipment to make it accessible to children with a wide range of special needs. Prior to using the playground, the first staff to arrive in the morning should carry out a safety check looking for items that need immediate attention, such as removing animal feces from the sandbox or picking up sharp items. Some provincial regulations require the completion of daily written checklists. Most playground injuries can be prevented with proper supervision. Directors should ensure that staff understand this, and that when overseeing children, they ensure that play equipment is being used safely. Assess how easy it will be for the staff to supervise the children. Can staff see every part of the equipment and playground? Can they quickly reach a child anywhere on the playground? Some things to look for: Are there any sharp edges, bars, or supports where children could easily hit their heads? Are there any aspects of the equipment that might tempt the children into dangerous behaviour? Are there any entrapment areas?

The safety of the area underneath the structure is a key consideration. Falls to the surface account for nearly 70% of all playground injuries. A perfectly safe piece of equipment can become hazardous if it is erected over the wrong surface. Installation can be as expensive as the purchase of the equipment itself. CSA standards specify the types of materials that can be used beneath a piece of equipment and how deep the materials must be. Paying the experts to install the equipment is clearly the safest, quickest, and easiest approach, although it can add 25% to 40% to the cost. Using a parent group will save money; however, this course of action may result in voiding the manufacturer's warranty, and the program may be liable for any accidents that occur. Some companies will perform a post-construction inspection to verify that everything was done appropriately, thus maintaining the warranty and the manufacturer's liability. Annually thereafter, it is the program's responsibility to have the playground re-certified.

Sample

Policy for Supervision of Children

The board of directors and staff are committed to providing a safe, healthy, quality child care program for all children by:

- ensuring that the minimum staff:child ratio as outlined in the Provincial Licensing Regulation is maintained at all times;
- appropriately enhancing the staff:child ratio to accommodate the needs of children who require additional support;
- for field trips and challenging activities, enhancing the adult:child ratio to one adult to four to six children by utilizing practicum students and volunteers;
- orienting and training all staff in supervision procedures/techniques; and
- ensuring that the children are supervised at all times.

Sample Procedures

- Daily written sign-in/out forms will be completed by the parent/legal guardian and authorized pickup persons verified by the director.
- Head counts will be done every five minutes and after any transition.
- If children are divided into small groups, each staff will have a list of the names of children in their group.
- Developmentally appropriate activities will be provided that meet/challenge the needs of all children.
- A minimum of two staff will be present at all times when a child who requires additional supports is attending the program.
- Enrolment and attendance tracking will be done on an ongoing basis to ensure staffing ratios meet the program policies for typical and enhanced ratios.

Source: Adapted from the Policies and Procedures for Child Care Programs, *Tough and Sensitive Issues, Part II*, developed by Westcoast Child Care INFORM, Vancouver, BC.

EC programs face the need to balance opportunities and the need for safety. In *What's the Risk of No Risk* by Deb Curtis (2010), it concludes: "Keeping children safe is paramount to the work we do every minute when we are with children." We must always stop or prevent situations that threaten children's well-being. But when we do intervene on behalf of children's safety, we can do it with the understanding that life has many challenges and risks, and children deserve experiences and tools to learn to negotiate on their own.

When children are involved in a situation we think is too risky or dangerous, rather than just stopping them, educators can offer alternatives that keep them safe while preserving opportunities for them to develop to their fullest potential. This work requires paying attention to the children's perspectives, by ensuring that children have opportunities where they feel exhilaration, while still being protected and supported by adults and their friends. Support children in learning that determination pays off, and they can become competent decision makers, able to assess risks, contribute to the well-being of others, and reap the rewards of their efforts.

Another key element of safety is maintenance. Accidents on playground equipment are often the result of poor maintenance. No matter what type of equipment is purchased, directors must establish and adhere to a strict schedule of inspection and maintenance. A safety audit is an essential first step. Ideally, checklists are designed that are relevant to each playground and building to help staff identify and correct potential safety hazards. *Well Beings* (2008), as well as others, will be a source for a generic list that can provide a good starting point for a program developing a custom one. Playground hazards come in many forms and are hard to spot without knowing what to check. A safety audit rates the seriousness of hazards from class A to C. A class A hazard can cause a major injury or death and needs to be corrected immediately. A class C hazard may cause minor injuries, such as scrapes or splinters, and may need to be dealt with in long-term planning and budgeting.

If a playground structure is well maintained, not vandalized, and not exposed frequently to extreme weather conditions, it should last from 10 to 20 years. Be sure to ask questions about what is included in the warranty and whether there are conditions that will void the warranty. As a final step, staff should visit programs using the equipment the program intends to purchase. In this way, they can evaluate the quality of the installation as well as the durability of the product. Most important, they can observe how children are using the equipment. Are the children taking full advantage of all its features? Do the children using it exhibit enjoyment? What is the injury record for that particular piece of equipment?

Selecting, Maintaining, and Storing Learning Materials

Learning materials should capture the child's interest and inspire further exploration through actions or questioning. They should engage the children's active involvement. They should place realistic demands on children's dexterity, skills, and cognition. They should be simple enough that children understand how to produce the desired effect, yet provide a challenge. Well-chosen learning materials can be used for years in many different ways. The very young child will use the learning material to discover textures and explore and manipulate various parts. An older child may use the same learning material for pretend play or to try on roles, imitate adult behaviours, refine motor skills, develop symbolic thought, or enhance language skills.

While learning materials constitute a small portion of the budget, they are critically important in shaping the experiences the children have while in the program. As well as assuring that learning materials do not represent a threat to the health and safety of children, purchasers want to ensure that they have sound educational value.

In a group setting, learning materials are used a great deal by children and they must be durable. How learning materials are put together is a factor in their durability and ongoing safety. As with other pieces of equipment, evaluate how much maintenance will be required to preserve the appearance and structural integrity of a learning material. Determine how materials can be cleaned and choose the appropriate solutions. The learning material will last longer and be healthier for children if bacteria and dirt can be easily washed off.

Inspect learning materials for potential hazards such as choking or poisoning. Look for small parts that could fit in a child's mouth or long cords that could ensnare a child. Toxicity or poisoning is an important safety issue. Ensure that there were no toxic paints or dyes used to produce the learning material. These considerations are much more thoroughly explored in *Healthy Foundations in Child Care* (Pimento and Kernsted 2010).

Going Green

Children are vulnerable in their early years, and, developmentally, they are susceptible to environmental hazards that may affect their potential for long, healthy lives. Children deserve healthy, safe places to grow and learn. When educators understand what is safe, environmentally friendly, and healthy when it comes to practices and products used in EC settings, there are many benefits in store. Such advantages include:

- Providing the healthiest environment available to growing children
- Increasing attendance and staff productivity

Poor indoor air quality can lead to absent employees, sick children, and lost efficiency. Many remedies for poor indoor air quality are simple, cost-effective, and have lasting benefits. In the article "The Toxic Paradox: Can We Really Protect Our Kids from Everything?" (New York Times Magazine, February 8, 2009), Orenstein talks about the anxieties parents face in trying to protect their children from a growing, changing number of environmental concerns. With greater awareness of how the environment impacts the health and well-being of the children and families, there is a move toward green EC settings. "Going Green" is a term often used in reference to environmentally responsible practices applied to many different contexts, such as transportation, building construction, and water conservation.

Some settings offer locally grown or organic food; use non-toxic cleaners and art supplies; recycle and reuse materials, compost, and garden; and move activities outdoors as much as possible—all in an effort to live and teach children to live in a sustainable way. These kinds of practice provide a learning environment whereby children learn to respect the earth and its resources. Each simple activity holds the potential to impel enduring and widespread change, including introducing a compose system for food waste, using natural cleaners and gardening in the classroom, and using windowsill planters.

One resource is Evergreen, a not-for-profit organization that envisions a sustainable society where individuals live in harmony with and contribute meaningfully to their local environment by creating innovative resources and by transforming educational values. They provide support to transform EC and school spaces to become more green. For more ideas, visit www.evergreen.ca.

The Go Green Rating Scale for Early Childhood Settings (Redleaf Press 2010) is a comprehensive, research-based tool to help measure the greenness of settings, provides a comprehensive set of green standards, evaluates practices, and takes steps toward environmental improvement that will contribute to children's potential for long, healthy lives. The handbook explains the science and research behind each item in the rating scale. The tool helps programs to:

- measure the setting's greenness
- evaluate practices
- take steps toward environmental improvement to prevent inadvertently exposing children to hazardous chemicals and conditions
- inform families about the benefits of green child care

  Categories evaluated in the rating scale include:

- air quality
- cleaning products
- chemicals found in soaps, lotions, and sunscreen

- pests and pesticides
- chemicals found in plastics
- lead and other contaminants, such as mercury, formaldehyde, and fire retardants
- stewardship and green living, including recycling and waste reduction

In *Go Green Rating Scale for Early Childhood Settings Handbook,* the author outlines some of the ways **greening** an EC program can save money, such as by a one degree decrease in thermostat setting during the winter will result in a 5% savings in heating costs; or replacing a standard toilet with a low-flow toilet can save over 16 000 gallons of water a year. Boise concludes that green practices such as conservation, reduced purchasing, and purchasing durable, functional items make good economic sense.

By helping make the world a safer, healthier place for young children, Going Green can also be used in the context of peace education, as there are strong relationships between education for peace and education for environmental sustainability. The Green Approach to peace education focuses on helping children care about the natural world in their own community. There are reasons to believe that once children learn to respect and care for plants and animals with which they are familiar they are more likely to develop a sense of caring and respect for other people as well. EC educators have been catalysts for social change many times in the past. They can be poised to instigate real social change through sustainable practice.

Managing, Securing, and Storing Equipment

Since considerable program resources are spent on equipment, it must be kept secure. Prior to the delivery of new equipment, a director should consider how equipment will be managed. Once received, all equipment should be checked and inventoried. A maintenance plan should be developed to minimize repairs and the need to replace parts.

Early childhood programs typically do not leave out items of high interest to burglars—cash, high-tech equipment, or medication. Few programs report incidents of vandalism, and those that do occur are usually minor. Some strategies to improve program security include:

- Keep expensive, portable equipment locked up when not in use. Desktop computers should be bolted down. Provide a secure place for staff to store their personal effects while at work.
- Ensure that all entrances and gates are secured with high quality locks. Some programs have their buildings linked to local security companies.
- Establish and enforce financial procedures that provide for strict control of funds at all times. Enforce policies and procedures that limit exposure. Require fees to be paid by cheque or credit card, keep payments in a locked box, and deposit them in the bank quickly.

Providing adequate storage at EC programs is always a challenge. Both short-term and long-term storage should be considered. Items needing short-range storage include learning materials used daily and materials that will be consumed quickly. Most EC programs have problems storing materials when they are not being used or organizing closets without having everything fall out. Good organization and labelling and adequate storage space help to create an environment that supports practitioners and support staff. Storage designed so that children can easily retrieve and replace materials will support their developing independence. The director's job is to supply the best storage system possible and establish routines that lead to easy accessibility of equipment for everyone. It is also the director's responsibility to ensure the staff's safety. Ideally, to be ergonomically correct, storage shelves should be at eye level. If storage is overhead, lighter objects should be placed highest and sturdy adult-sized stools or stepladders should be available to aid access. These routines make putting things away less burdensome for all.

Evaluating the Environment

As the children mature, or whenever the composition of the group changes, the arrangement of the space will need to be reassessed. There may be spaces that are not used or are underused, areas that are constantly messy and disorganized, and places where play is not as constructive as it could be. How the children and adults use the space needs to be observed. If an educator is constantly walking through play areas and disrupting the activities, there may be a need to look at the pathways. Look at space from a young child's point of view. What does the child see and feel? Periodically it can be helpful to have someone who works outside the room come in to observe. An outside observer can point out both areas that need attention and areas that are working well. (Some of the program evaluation tools described in Chapter 4 can be used to assess the physical environment.)

A familiar space offers a feeling of security. Change should be thoughtful. Involving the children makes alterations in space less stressful. It takes time to tell whether a change in the environment will have the desired results. For most changes, children, families, and staff will need a few weeks to adjust and determine whether the change was helpful or not.

Space for Adults

Working in EC programs is demanding both physically and psychologically. Programs need to provide a comfortable space for the staff, parents, and visitors. Staff rooms should facilitate interactions as well as be a relatively quiet place for reflection and breaks. Staff need access to a preparation-and-planning space with a desk or table and chairs; cabinets in which to store resources and materials; and a computer, photocopier, laminator, etc. Staff require a secure place to store personal belongings.

Space is required in which to hold meetings with parents and with students and faculty on field placement. The program needs to consider the environment where parents exchange informal information with staff on a daily basis. It should include a resource area with a bulletin board to encourage parents to browse materials. Often programs ensure that the children's environment is wonderful, yet neglect to make sure the environment also meets adult needs.

Summary

EC environments promote the wellness and protect the health and safety of children and adults. A comprehensive approach to high quality child health, safety, and nutrition services requires the cooperative involvement of directors, health professionals, families, and staff members. The health goals in an EC program are to provide health care, prevent health problems, and coordinate health plans with families and children's health care professionals. Programs should also develop policies that promote the health of early childhood educators.

Caring adults can build awareness and teach the decision-making skills to children needed to identify healthy diet and activity options. There is significant need for EC programs to design their spaces and their activities to stimulate more vigorous physical activity. A recent study found that children in EC settings were engaged in moderate to vigorous physical activity during only 3.4% of the day. Children in higher quality EC settings were more likely to engage in physical activity than children in programs of lower quality. Universal design principles guide professions in designing programs in which all children and families have full and equitable access to learning and social opportunities.

In order to protect their children from a growing, changing number of environmental concerns, there is a move toward green EC settings. Some settings offer locally grown or organic food; use non-toxic cleaners and art supplies; recycle and reuse materials, compost, and garden; and move activities outdoors as much as possible—all in an effort to live and teach children to live in a sustainable way. This kind of practice provides a learning environment whereby children learn to respect the earth and its resources.

EC programs face the need to balance opportunities and the need for safety. When children are involved in a situation we think is too risky or dangerous, rather than just stopping them, educators can offer alternatives that keep them safe while preserving opportunities for them to develop to their fullest potential.

Family members and educators can influence children's food preferences by providing healthy food choices, offering multiple opportunities to prepare and eat new foods, and serving as positive role models through their own food choices. EC programs are more likely to affect a child's decision-making process when educators recognize that teaching young children how to make healthy choices isn't a separate subject, like math or reading. It's a way of thinking that can be a part of every subject and needs to be integrated into the whole program.

Menu planning and supervision of nutritional staff are an important part of a director's responsibilities. Nutrition at the program is highly important for young children, since program meals often provide up to 80% of the young child's nutritional requirements. Staff members need to know the nutritional requirements of young children, how to provide a nutritious diet, and how to create an appropriate meal and snack environment by sitting with children and modelling appropriate nutritional habits.

Good policies should reflect best practices and provide standards that reflect current research to guide educators' promotion of the well-being of children and families. Policies and procedures are necessary to promote better understanding of expectations for both staff and parents. They can provide clarification and standardization of the program's governing rules as well as promote consistency and continuity in decision-making. They determine the blueprint for achieving the established goals of the program.

Key Terms and Concepts

Allergies,   p. 200

Greening,   p. 217

Maintenance,   p. 194

Nutrition,   p. 194

Policies,   p. 196

Procedures,   p. 196

Universal design principles,   p. 208

Activities

1. Develop a health care policy. Your policy could address:
    *   practices you will put in place to protect children's health (diet, exercise, hygienic practices, fresh air, etc.)
    *   immunization schedule that assures all staff are up-to-date
    *   policies and practices concerning what to do when a child becomes ill
    *   responsibilities of parents and program regarding children who are ill (e.g., reporting child's exposure to contagious disease/keeping child at home)
    *   health information parents must provide to the program (immunizations documentation, child's health record)
    *   procedures for reporting workplace injuries
    *   opportunities for professional development to reduce the potential hazards of work (proper lifting techniques, safe handling of potentially hazardous products, procedures for cleaning up of bodily fluids)

2. Identify what provincial regulations require in the area you are developing. Research quality standards to determine which one(s) apply.

3. Observe two meals in an early childhood program. Evaluate the meals according to the following factors, rating each *excellent, good, fair,* or *poor:*
    *   attractiveness of location
    *   cleanliness of setting
    *   comfort of seating
    *   use of developmentally appropriate utensils
    *   appearance of food
    *   encouragement of child's independence
    *   food served considers ethnicity of children
    *   educator interaction with children
    *   general atmosphere

4. Investigate the services for mildly ill children available in your community. For each service, outline the benefits and drawbacks, costs to the families, who operates the service, and the population using the service.

5. Develop a plan for a field trip. Consider the following:
    *   age group for which the activity is developmentally suitable
    *   adult:child ratio required
    *   length of time the group will be away from the program
    *   form of transportation
    *   what staff will need to bring with them (e.g., food, beverages, diapers, first aid kit, emergency contacts, cellphone).

6. Using a safety checklist, go through your home, including each room and any outdoor areas, and assess its suitability to be a family child care home. If applicable, be sure to include both front yard and backyard, garage, shed, carport, and basement space. Note changes

that could be made to your home to make it a safer place for a family with young children (your own family, if applicable) or for children in care. Examples include replacing/repairing loose tiles or installing a light fixture in a stairwell or a padlock on a shed.

Recommended Reading

American Academy of Pediatrics & American Public Health Association. *Caring for Our Children: National Health and Safety Standards: Guidelines for Early Care and Education Programs,* 3rd ed. Washington, DC: American Academy of Pediatrics & American Public Health Association, 2011.

Boise. *Go Green Rating Scale for Early Childhood Settings Handbook*. Redleaf Press, 2010.

Canadian Pædiatric Society. *Well Beings: A Guide to Promote the Physical Health, Safety and Emotional Well-Being of Children in Child Care Centres and Family Day Care Homes*. Toronto: Creative Premises Ltd., 2008.

Greenman, J. *Caring Spaces, Learning Places: Children's Environments That Work*. City: Exchange Press, Inc., 2005.

Pimento, B. and D. Kernsted. *Healthy Foundations in Child Care,* 4th ed. Toronto: Nelson, 2010.

Canadian Standards Association, Children's Playspaces and Equipment, 2007.

Weblinks

www.healthyenvironmentforkids.ca
Canadian Partnership for Children's Health and Environment

This website provides a variety of resources, such as guides to less toxic products, information on the impact of the environment on children's health, and a section with answers to frequently asked questions about children's environmental health in Canada.

www.ccohs.ca/oshanswers/information/govt.html
Canadian Centre for Occupational Health and Safety

This site provides resources on many issues such as injuries, work-related diseases, and ergonomics (the study of the relationship between people and their working environment, especially as it affects safety), as well as research on health and safety and lists of government contacts—including regional offices for occupational health and safety.

www.dietitians.ca
Dietitians of Canada

The Healthy Start for Life Environment Scan available in the Resource Centre of this site is designed to promote the development of healthy eating and activity patterns for toddlers and preschoolers. Parents and practitioners will find a plethora of resources at this site to aid with fussy eaters and to stimulate increased physical activity.

http://nrckids.org
National Resource Centre for Health and Safety in Child Care and Education

The NRC's primary mission is to promote health and safety in out-of-home child care settings throughout the nation through an extensive website. Information is directed to practitioners, researchers, parents, and legislator on a wide range of health care topics, standards, and guidelines.

Building Partnerships with Families

Objectives

- **Heighten appreciation of the role of the early childhood educator in supporting families.**

- **Demonstrate understanding of the complexity of families and the stressors facing them.**

- **Build an understanding of the importance of family-centred practice.**

- **Increase awareness of the importance of program philosophy reflecting diversity of families.**

- **Identify policies and strategies for building partnerships with families.**

- **Discuss the purpose and identify the content of a family handbook.**

- **Distinguish between family engagement and family involvement.**

Young children are integrally connected to their families, and educators share with families the responsibility for young children. In order for families to feel truly comfortable and connected in early childhood programs, educators must recognize the importance of children's families and establish positive relationships with them based upon mutual trust and respect.

Young children with different abilities, challenges, resources, and cultural backgrounds together with their families attend early childhood settings. The children bring unique life experiences and orientations. They and their families benefit most when they are fully included and when they feel that they belong. Children grow up with a strong sense of self in environments that promote the attitudes, beliefs, and values of equity and democracy and support children's full participation.

A vital goal in EC practice is sustaining strong, healthy families. Although supporting and strengthening families has always been a part of the early childhood educator's role, now the field has a robust research base providing evidence about family strengthening strategies. Educators also benefit from ongoing professional development focused on families in order to effectively implement good practice.

Families are the first and most powerful influence on children's early learning and development. Raising healthy children is complex. Families live in, and belong to, multiple communities that may support or thwart their ability to augment young children's optimal development.

To establish and maintain collaborative relationships with each child's family, the director and staff must have considerable skills. Program directors can set the stage with program practices that respect all families, provide leadership in developing a vision and philosophy that guide the setting's curriculum and pedagogy.

Some educators believe that working with families is the most challenging part of their job. With significant numbers of young children being away from home for many hours a day, an important role for EC educators is as a facilitator of the transition between the two environments. Ongoing collaboration between families and program staff results in greater consistency for the children and is a key strategy for bridging the gaps between home and program. The younger the child, the more vital this consistency is. When educators work closely with families, fostering their sense of belonging and gaining their confidence, EC educators strengthen each family's capacity to support their child.

Responding to a Variety of Family Structures

The structures of families in EC programs vary widely from the traditional family of two married parents who live together with their biological offspring. Today's families include lone-parent families, teen parents, blended families, grandparents raising grandchildren, foster families, and same-sex parents. The Vanier Institute of the Family defines family as "a group of two or more people, children, siblings, foster parents, grandparents, uncles, aunts, cousins, friends, and any others who consider themselves a family."

Within each family, there are many variations. Educational level, socio-economic status, occupation, temperament, and personal experiences all influence values and beliefs. So do all the other cultures families belong to—race, language, ethnicity, religion, gender, workplace, age, sexual orientation, political orientation, time, and place. Each family has a unique culture of its own.

More than 250 000 immigrants relocated to Canada in 2008 (Vanier, 2010). In 2001, over 19.6% of the Canadian population was born in another country. These high levels of immigration have resulted in growing racial and ethnic diversity. Many children attending early learning programs have recently immigrated. Immigrant families often experience isolation and loneliness when they come to Canada. Researchers note that EC programs should be a crucial aspect of immigrant families' integration and inclusion in new societies. Many newcomers' home language is neither English nor French. To work effectively with all types of families, many staff must increase their understanding of ethnic, cultural, and socio-economic backgrounds different from their own.

The structure and lifestyle of a family are known to influence its ability to participate in, and its feelings of comfort about, program-related activities. Fewer children are being raised in families where parents are married. There has been a three-fold increase over the last 20 years in common-law parents. As well, rising rates of separation and out-of-union births mean more

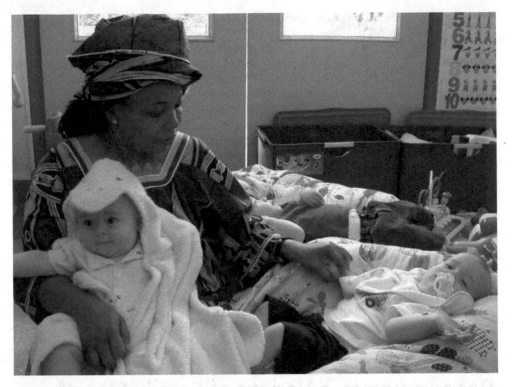

EC programs are a crucial aspect of immigrant families' integration and inclusion in new societies.

children are experiencing life in lone-parent families. There are increased numbers of mid-life Canadians becoming parents for the first time. Therefore, EC educators must develop an understanding of the families of the children they are working with in order to plan and provide flexible family-involvement opportunities.

A fuller understanding of individual families helps educators become more culturally competent and culturally responsive. This knowledge assists them in creating strategies for involving all the families of the children in the program.

Understanding the Changing Roles of Families

The family is and always will be the most important factor in a child's life. Family is where children experience the emotional and physical nurturance vital to their well-being most closely/ intimately and deeply. **Parents** share this task of child rearing with EC educators. For some time, mothers in the workforce have been the norm. In 1967, fewer than 20% of mothers with young children were in the paid labour force. In 2009, the percentage has climbed steadily reaching 73%. For women today, motherhood does not signal a withdrawal from paid employment. The consequences of this change are numerous, with implications for the women themselves, their families, and their employers.

The tug-of-war between work and home has become more challenging. A study conducted by the Conference Board of Canada (Bachmann and MacBride-King, 1999) found that new and greater demands at work, and aging parents add to the challenges faced by working parents. Work lives have become more demanding, and technology has brought with it the need for 24 × 7 support and availability. Half of the Canadians surveyed said they were experiencing high or moderate levels of stress. Among the reasons cited for this pervasive stress were fear of unemployment, low or frozen wages, heavy debt loads, or working fewer hours than needed. These developments have created a "time famine," where parents face the challenges of balancing work and family demands. At home, the time for quality family time as well as household work has diminished. Roles, responsibilities, and expectations around the sharing of domestic labour have changed, although women continue to carry the majority of the load. Parents have a shrinking amount of time to spend with the family. A child's early years were identified as the most demanding period in the lives of parents. Lack of family support plays a role, too. Increasing mobility means that family members often do not have anyone around to help out when children, parents, or elderly relatives are ill. The experience of juggling multiple and often conflicting work and family demands is commonplace. In the study *Ask the Children,* Galinsky found that children worry when their parents are tired and stressed. She identifies techniques that early childhood educators can use to help parents reduce stress:

- help parents learn techniques for managing stress. Parents need to find ways to "turn off work," including activities such as meditating before leaving work, listening to music, or changing clothing;

- share with parents techniques for creating a homecoming ritual to smooth the transition from work to home; and

- encourage parents to set realistic expectations about what they can accomplish at home. Being successful at two or three things is more effective than trying to achieve too many.

There is a new imperative for employers and governments to consider how best to support employees in their work and family roles. While some businesses recognize that their employees lead increasingly stressful lives, progress to implement family-friendly policies in the work place has been slow. Similarly, public supports for families such as child care and access to flexible hours vary widely across Canada, resulting in tremendous inequities as noted in Chapters 1 and 2. Flexible work arrangements afford employees greater control over their work and family lives, often resulting in reduced work-family conflict, improved moral, higher employee retention, increased productivity, and lower absenteeism.

REDUCING STRESS FOR FAMILIES—BACKUP CHILD CARE

Balancing work and a family is a juggling act. When regular child care arrangements fall apart, this often means a parent has to miss work to stay home with their young child because few people can rely on relatives or neighbours to step in. This situation is stressful for employees, and disruptive for employers.

In 2002, Canadian Imperial Bank of Commerce (CIBC) was the first company in Canada to offer employer-paid backup child care dedicated to its employees, offering care to 1500 families rather than full-time child care to 40 families. To serve a larger number of staff is one reason why CIBC was attracted to this type of service, and why they invited ChildrenFirst to present the options available, as

(continued)

well as the costs and benefits of such a service. CIBC commissioned ChildrenFirst to create a purpose-built child care program in their Toronto office tower.

The CIBC Children's Centre offers backup child care to a maximum of 40 children. There are no full-time spaces, and children cannot attend if they are sick. Because the program is highly regulated, parents must register their children before they can participate in the program. Once registered, parents can register to use the service up to a limit of 20 days per child per year with exceptions under extenuating circumstances.

The company found it more equitable to provide backup support for more employees than to run a regular EC program that would only serve a few families. Although 1500 employees are registered to use the centre, it is all 12 000 employees who benefit from the service. The message is that "everyone benefits when your colleague is able to show up for work."

The company estimates that since it opened, the program has saved the company about $1.5 million in productivity costs. These are the direct savings from the parent being at work when the service is used. This is a good return on the company's investment.

Backup child care is one component in a healthy workplace/work-life balance strategy. It provides an opportunity to communicate the importance of work-life balance for everyone. It enables human resources staff to talk about how these programs can contribute to the health and well-being of employees. CIBC has played a leadership role by offering the first employer paid backup child care in Canada. Their positive experience serves as a pilot and a model for others to follow.

What Is a Strengthening Families Approach?

A key aspect of EC practice is strong, healthy families and EC professionals who are well prepared to support them. Supporting and strengthening families has always been a part of the EC professional's role. **Family-centred practice** describes respectful collaboration between families and EC practitioners. The underpinnings of a family-centred practice reflect respectful collaboration between families and early childhood educators based on the following premises:

- family is central to the child's life;
- each family has its own strengths, competencies, resources, and ways of coping;
- every family is respected and accepted on its own terms, without judgments or preconceptions; and
- each family's race, culture, ethnicity, religion, language, and socio-economic status are respected.

When educators and parents recognize each other's expertise and acknowledge that differences in opinions and approaches are natural, they can use their combined strengths to develop trust, set goals, make plans, and solve problems. The child, the family, and the program all benefit. The following premises are included in a framework to strengthen families:

- **Provide quality EC programs** through evidence-based practice. Incorporate practices such as promoting play to foster social skills and learning; understand cultural contexts to ensure that learning is meaningful, relevant, and respectful; and ensure that quality early learning experiences strengthen and promote children's healthy development.

- **Acknowledge the importance of the family** in child development, and amplify the family's involvement with their child's early learning and development. Respect families as decision makers for their children and themselves.

- **Develop reciprocal relationships with families.** Engage in an ongoing exchange of information. When EC professionals develop strong, positive relationships with families, they can respond more effectively to signs of family stress by providing support and, when necessary, linking families to community resources. Educators can work with families and other professionals to support children's learning and developmental needs. Communication about sensitive issues is much easier when a healthy relationship is in place.

- **Build on the children's and families' strengths.** Regularly review children's developmental progress with parents. For children, foster development of their resilience, social and emotional health, appropriate peer relationships, positive self-esteem, and strong coping skills and strengths.

- **Help families to understand and respond to a range of behaviours.** EC professionals strengthen families by providing information about appropriate expectations and age appropriate guidance techniques that help children learn acceptable behaviours as well as developing consistent approaches between the home and early childhood setting.

- **Stay informed about professional responsibilities** and actively participate in ongoing professional development. Educators need ongoing professional development in order to understand complex families. This helps professionals develop strategies and apply them effectively.

This **"strengthening family"** perspective is radically different from the once-traditional model, in which professionals considered themselves experts who determined and implemented interventions for children without family input or participation. Family-centred practice is not defined by a particular set of methods or procedures; rather, it requires a perspective-taking and willingness to embrace values that are respectful of and lead to collaboration with families.

The first step is to establish the families and children as the focus of the service. The needs of all family members must be recognized. Focus on the family as the constant in the child's life and acknowledge the influential role of the family in the child's development.

Second, support and respect family decision making by regarding family members as essential members of the partnership and primary decision makers about their child's education and care.

Lastly, provide flexible, responsive, and comprehensive services designed to strengthen child and family functioning. This principle incorporates the need to respect family culture and diversity and helps families mobilize their informal resources, including friends and neighbourhoods. All families can benefit from information related to community resources. Some will need to access these services for their child and family. EC settings that incorporate family resource centres and work closely with community services promote caring communities for children and their families.

A key feature of a family-centred collaboration is that it is a continually evolving relationship. It creates an environment in which children and parents are free to ask questions. There is an ongoing process of evaluation and rethinking approaches. The relationship changes and grows.

Establishing Collaborative Partnerships with Families

Families must feel welcome—that the EC program is their own. Some parents fear that their child rearing practices will be criticized. Others may feel inhibited due to their own experiences with school. A strengthening families approach communicates feelings of acceptance and respect to families.

Young children need their families and teachers to work together. In a collaborative relationship, parties are mutually respectful; each person has ongoing input. A full partnership between a family and an EC setting means the family has significant influence over its child's experience at the program. This partnership with families means that parents, as a group, can have significant influence on the program's operations that determine the experience the children have in the program, including curriculum issues, allocation of resources, and family policies (such as drop-off/pickup procedures).

Research shows that **family involvement** in EC settings benefits children and multiplies children's opportunities for learning. When parents are involved in the program, their children's achievement improves. Children make friends more easily and are more successful learners. Parents who are involved in EC settings tend to be more supportive of children's learning, and their children tend to have positive outcomes in primary grades (Cleveland et al. 2007). Early childhood settings can reinforce the interrelationship of care and learning and the benefits of direct family participation in children's early learning and development. But the greatest benefit to children of a successful home-school partnership is that children are more motivated to succeed. Allred, Briem, and Black found that parents who feel ownership of their child's goals are more likely to consider these goals as top priorities in the family routine.

Building relationships isn't always easy. Families may have very different expectations and styles from those of the educator. Some parents may bring negative attitudes and feelings about school and teachers. Many parents need affirmation and reassurance to build trust and deal with their feelings of uncertainty, inadequacy, and sometimes even intimidation. Communicating effectively and working together successfully requires effort, yet the rewards can be great. The web of family and community is the child's anchor for early development.

Family engagement, rather than involvement, takes a strengths-based perspective. It recognizes that all families are involved in their children's learning and well-being in some way. This approach emphasizes concepts that are continuous, reciprocal, and strength-based. While EC programs encourage family participation in decision making related to the child's education, families in addition to participating in the decision making also act as advocates for their child. Consistent two-way communication is facilitated through multiple forms and is responsive to the language spoken by the family. EC programs place an emphasis on creating and sustaining learning activities at home and in the community that enhance each child's early learning. Families create a home environment that values learning. EC programs and families collaborate in establishing goals for children. Finally, EC programs create an ongoing and comprehensive system for promoting family engagement by ensuring that program leadership and ECEs are dedicated and knowledgeable, and receive the supports they need to fully engage families. Figure 8–1 illustrates both program resources and family resources which contribute to high levels of family engagement.

Engaging Culturally Diverse Families

Each family has a unique culture of its own. Culture is a way of describing race, language, ethnicity, religion, gender, workplace, age, sexual orientation, political orientation, time, and place. Within each family, there are many variations, including educational level, socio-economic status, occupation, temperament, and personal experience which influence values and beliefs. Culture is a fundamental building block in creating a child's identity.

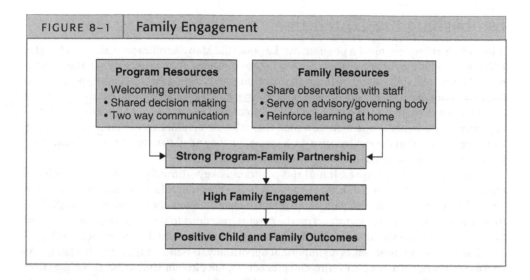

FIGURE 8–1 | Family Engagement

Different cultures have unique ways of viewing the world; preferred ways of social organization; and specific language patterns, learning styles, and concepts of acceptable behaviour. Demonstrating respect for diversity, equity, and inclusion are prerequisites for optimal development and learning. Preconceived notions about children's ethno-cultural backgrounds, gender, abilities, or socio-economic circumstances create barriers that reduce engagement and equitable outcomes.

Children attending early learning programs are recently immigrated and unlike many children who arrive at EC classrooms and find familiar environments and teachers who speak English, many culturally and linguistically diverse children may feel like they are moving "from one world to another." In some immigrant groups, children learn social relationships and appropriate interactions by observing and participating in large, extended family networks that are traditional. Different cultures will have different expectations for children's role in these networks, expectations that will contribute differently to children's emotional development and concept of self. When children observe family members speaking in two languages, they learn that there are multiple acceptable ways to express ideas and that both languages have value. When EC education settings reflect the values and practices of children's homes, they will then be able to reinforce the concepts that children learn at home.

It [would] be a perfect program if they can read not

only popular stories but also Somali stories at the circle time.

—Somali mother

Particular communities have important values and needs. For instance, Aboriginal communities may emphasize a connection to nature, elders, keeping their home language. Early childhood settings in Francophone communities may put an emphasis on language learning. In a community including immigrant and refugee families, early childhood settings should enrich the environment with artefacts reflecting culture, language, security, and transition. The setting may also incorporate peace and global issues.

Early childhood settings can be pro-active in identifying strategies that will respect families' diverse backgrounds and value this diversity as an asset that enriches the environment for everyone. Children benefit when they learn early to live together comfortably with others who look, act, and speak differently than themselves.

Establishing the Connection

A family's first impression of a program can be powerful. Many families who are searching for EC programs for the first time are unsure of how to make the right choice. While the director plays the key role, staff should be integrally involved in developing family-friendly policies and implementing these on a daily basis. Families expect a great deal from programs, and these expectations depend on the age of the child. Directors need to convey to families that they appreciate the parents' desire to make a good choice for their child. Every effort should be made to assure parents that they will receive the information they need to make the right decision for their family, even if it means choosing another program.

The parents' first impression of the program is key—how they feel about both the environment and their initial interactions with staff. A less tangible thing that helps a parent feel welcome is the manner in which staff members handle a telephone call. It is very difficult to perceive what has the most impact on the parents' reactions to the program; directors need to be alert to any number of subtle factors that may influence parental attitudes and feelings.

The enrolment interview is an important opportunity to build a rapport with a family. As well as reviewing the necessary forms and procedures, the director should ask about the child, how he or she likes to be comforted, and the child's preferred activities. Reassure the parents that they should always feel comfortable to ask a question or tell the staff how she or he can make things easier for the parents and child. Sometimes, families also need reassurance that no staff will never replace the parent in the child's heart. Seeing posted photographs of children and their families conveys a link between the program and the family home.

In order to assess the messages sent to parents, staff may reflect on these questions:

- Did the parents receive the information they needed when they contacted the program?
- Do the program materials recognize the uniqueness of each family and communicate a willingness to meet individual needs?
- Do staff communicate in a manner that conveys that families are important?
- Were the parents encouraged to bring their child on their first visit to the program?
- Was the visit scheduled at a time when playroom staff were available to speak with the parents?

Some programs encourage families to visit the program several times, with the child, before the child's start date. As well as making the child feel comfortable in the new setting, this enables the parent to see the staff in action and sense that loving attention given to each child.

Creating a community in EC programs is all about building relationships. When a new family joins the program, there is a unique opportunity to initiate a relationship that will last through the years that the child attends the program and beyond. The people in an EC program can become an extended family for the child and parents.

Communicating with Families

Respectful, ongoing communication is the foundation of a solid partnership. When families and EC staff communicate effectively, positive relationships develop, problems are more easily solved, and child outcomes improve. Too often, program communication is one way—without the chance to exchange ideas and share perceptions. The two-way sharing of information that characterizes effective communication between the home and EC setting is vital to improved child outcomes. Partnering requires give-and-take conversation, goal setting for the future, and follow-up. Contacts with families range from informal interactions during arrivals and departures to more structured **parent conferences**. Through these interactions, educators and families communicate information they feel is important or of mutual interest. Important interchanges occur most commonly each morning and at the end of the day. Pickup and drop-off times can be hurried and stressful. It is key that EC educators maximize the opportunities presented by this interchange and make it an important part of their daily routine. These informal contacts and exchanges are the single most productive aspect of family engagement.

During these transition times, a good practice in exchanging information with families is to provide information they can use or do something about—such as about the child's day at the program (or time at home), behaviour, or health concerns. This kind of discussion will often lead to decision making.

Staff should ensure that they connect with every parent on a daily basis. This can involve a chat or, simply, eye contact and a smile or wave. Directors need to ensure that staffing is sufficient to enable educators to feel confident that the children are well supervised while they are speaking with a parent. Often, parents arrive to pick up their children at the same time, which can be challenging for the staff. Rotating shifts can mean that the child's primary caregiver is not available for discussion at pickup time. Since these interactions are so vital, there need to be safeguards to ensure that such communication occurs regularly. If a staff member determines that no regular contact is occurring, some other mode of communication should be implemented.

SUCCESSFUL PROGRAMS

- Use a variety of formal and informal strategies (including conversations).

- Disseminate information to families in language that they can understand, including policies and procedures.

- Schedule opportunities for family participation, keeping in mind the varied schedules of working, studying, and stay-at-home parents.

- Communicate with families regarding positive child outcomes, behaviour, and achievement as well as concerns.

- Facilitate opportunities for families to communicate with other community professionals, such as resource teachers and elementary school staff.

- Provide ongoing staff development to prepare educators to respond respectfully and effectively to families who vary in culture, language, special learning, and developmental needs.

Multiple information vehicles should be employed that include new family orientation, small group meetings, documentation panels, and web pages. Telephone calls are both convenient and effective ways to communicate. Some parents have work situations that allow them to receive telephone calls freely and they may welcome the staff keeping in touch. Others may wish to be called only when there is a specific concern or in an emergency.

Using Internet-based Communication

The increase in the use of technology has opened up new possibilities for communicating with families using tools such as video-taping, e-mail, and the creation of classroom and/or program

Programs can use a variety of internet-based methods to facilitate communication with families.

web-pages. A variety of internet-based communication methods exist to facilitate the frequency of two-way contact between families and EC educators. Unlike one-way communication in which families are merely informed of their child's progress, two-way approaches invite parents to be engaged in their child's learning process and create an ongoing dialogue. Many of these internet-based methods such as e-mails and websites are used to enhance informal communications such as conversations held at drop-off and pickup, along with more formal parent-teacher conferences and notes sent home. Although technology should never replace direct contact with families, it can be extremely effective when families and teachers do not have opportunities for casual contact as in rural areas. Technology can enable staff to provide updates on the child's progress. Some parents may feel more secure with a program that enables them to link to video cameras in the playroom. Families may log on at a convenient time to observe their play. However, these approaches are not substitutes for face-to-face communication.

Create a Classroom Website   Many EC programs have created websites. In developing a classroom website, it is recommended that they are password protected, limiting access to the parents of the classroom. In addition to print resources, embed newsletters, announcements, family handbook, permission slips, and volunteer opportunities. If a significant number of the families whose home language is not English, find supports to post messages in their home language(s).

Post Photos on the Classroom Website   In order to aid families to see the process through which their child learns, creates photo essays—a series of photos with captions that capture the children engaged in a project. Sequenced photos give families a picture of their developmental progress. Post photos of the children's work—building or planting seeds. Change the photos regularly and ensure to display each child's work at least once a month. Do not use the children's names in the captions.

Create a Family Response Link on the Website   This strategy enables families to monitor and comment on their child's progress. Parents can complete a brief online form to provide comments and questions and e-mail them directly to the ECEs.

Send Individual E-mails to Families About Their Child's Activities and Accomplishments   Although educators need to reach out to families when a child is facing challenges at the program, e-mail can be too easily misinterpreted and impersonal for these sensitive types of communications. Educators can send e-mails to share short anecdotes about children's developing interests, and newly acquired skills. These types of spontaneous, positive communications can create two-way conversations where parents share anecdotes and/or questions.

Communicate Logistical Information Through Group E-mails   Group mails can be a good way to remind families about upcoming events, such as field trips and parent conferences and requests for signed permission forms.

Communicating Policies

Families need to have a clear understanding of program policies, expectations and the rationale for them. Policies that are ambiguous are a potential source of conflict between families and staff. Most programs provide families with information during the initial orientation and on a daily basis. During an orientation meeting, the director reviews the program's philosophy, purpose, and mandate, in addition to its policies and procedures. Families should understand their rights, know how the program functions, and have access to minutes of board meetings. For example, when parents enrol their child, they should be informed that the program cannot operate with stability unless all fees are paid on time. Second, a policy manual should be provided for the parents' reference. These can be made available on the program's website. When changes occur, parents should be kept up-to-date. Providing parents with a policy handbook serves to reduce the potential for conflict. A handbook can help parents better understand the rationale for policies concerning food or transitional objects from home or why they need to inform the program if they will be arriving late for pickup.

However, conflicts can still arise when a parent feels that she or he was not informed. On occasion, parents may be given information during transition times when they have other things on their minds. Transition times are often stressful times for families; it is rarely the best time to ask parents to remember details about program policies. Providing opportunities for families to have input into the development, evaluation, and revision of policies enhances the likelihood that families will comply with them.

Early childhood educators identify the caring for ill children as one of the most difficult issues they encounter. For parents, trying to continue to meet the demands of work or school, while managing the care of their ill child, is extremely stressful. When a parent receives a call from the EC program to pick up a child who is ill, in addition to worrying about the child, the parent is faced with rescheduling his or her work, and making a doctor's appointment. Few employees have a family responsibility benefit. Consequently, parents may have to use their own sick leave benefits, if eligible, or take time off work without pay. These factors help to explain why some parents bring their child to the program even when the child is not feeling well.

Early childhood educators are responsible for communicating a clear understanding of the program's exclusion policy to families. Staff:child ratios make it impossible to give the required individual attention to a child who is sick, and most children would prefer to be at home when they are ill. When considering an informed health policy, directors should refer to *Well Beings,* in which the Canadian Paediatric Society (2008) recommends exclusion criteria for EC programs.

Another potential point of conflict that policy should deal with is safety precautions, such as who is authorized to pick up the child. Families must feel confident that educators will not permit an unauthorized person to take their child from the program. However, occasionally a parent is unable to get to the program, and he or she may arrange for someone who is not listed as authorized to pick up their child without communicating this to the program. It is necessary to clearly communicate the program procedures and rationales to families.

Understanding the potential sources of conflict and developing strategies to prevent and overcome them will ultimately enhance the relationship between ECEs and families and benefit the children.

Family Handbook

A well-organized and effectively written family handbook communicates essential program information and is given to parents during the enrolment process. It outlines the obligations and responsibilities of families and staff. Caring for children is a cooperative effort shared by staff and parents, and the development of a parent handbook is an example of putting this commitment into action.

Information included in the handbook needs to be tailored to fit the program and the family population. The handbook should use language that is readily understandable. It should reflect the values upon which the program is based, conveying respect for families. Whenever possible, make the handbook available online and provide written information in the family's primary language. Arrange the information in a logical and attractive manner that makes information easy to locate. Policy manuals are living documents that evolve with changing needs. The director needs to consider when the information needs to be revised and how changes will be communicated to families. In writing, reviewing, and revising the policy manual, the director should draw on the expertise of families, staff, and professionals in the community.

The handbook serves as a valuable orientation for families who are new to the program, as well as a reference for currently enrolled families. Parents need to know to keep emergency information current. The list of suggested items that follows is not exhaustive, but provides a useful starting point for content:

- *Philosophy:* a statement of centre's philosophy and a description of the services of the program.
- *Policies:* information about program policies that directly affect families, such as the hours of operation, fees and arrangements for payment, and pre-admission requirements such as immunization records and completion of emergency information and health history forms.
- *Health and safety:* a description of health and safety precautions to be taken by the family and staff, including the program policy on administration of medication during the program and the procedures used by the staff if a child becomes ill while at the program.
- *Program:* an outline of the daily program along with an explanation of how it fits the program philosophy.
- *Food:* information about meals and snacks and any adjustments to the posted menus; procedures for accommodating special diets or restrictions.
- *Guidance:* an outline of the program's philosophy and policies regarding behaviour guidance.
- *Legal:* a description of the legal obligations of the staff to report any evidence of suspected child abuse; staff responsibilities to do with parental custody and access.
- *Family engagement:* participation and resources available to families; services available, such as parent conferences to discuss the individual child, group meetings, and referrals.
- *Items from home:* guidelines for the child's use of transitional objects; bringing toys and food from home.

The handbook is a convenient tool for acquainting families with the program and helping them to understand their responsibilities and what to expect. However, it must be supplemented with other written and verbal communications to keep parents informed of program events and the progress of their child. Parents should sign off that they have read and understood the handbook.

Sample

Policy for Custody and Access Arrangements

EC programs often serve families who are in conflict, separating or divorced. Consequently, early childhood facilities must have clear and consistent policies regarding the status of children when family arrangements are governed by custody and related court orders. The most common type of custody arrangements are:

- Informal arrangements—usually emerging from a situation of abandonment by one parent or an agreement within a family.
- Written agreements—developed by a family, court-appointed family advocate, or mediator determining custody or access arrangements.
- Court orders—including temporary, continuing, and permanent custody orders, supervision orders, interim orders, and restraining orders.

Guidelines

- Enrolment or registration forms should request information about the existence and details of a family's custody arrangement and separation agreement.
- It should be made clear to enrolling families that copies of written custody arrangements, either legal or informal, should be submitted to the centre to be placed in the child's file. Without the information in custody and court orders, centres will not be able to honor legal or informal arrangements.
- The policy should include reference to who has access to a child's files and information about the child's progress.
- Some centres develop policy

Policy Statement

If the parents/guardians have agreed to live separately, ABC Child Care Society will assume that the information from the enrolling parent/guardian will be followed. However, without a custody or court order on file at the centre, ABC Child Care Society cannot deny access to the non enrolling parent/guardian. If this arises, the policy on unauthorized persons will be implemented.

If custody has not been legally determined and conflict between the parents/guardians and/or other family members is evident, ABC Child Care Society may not be able to care for the child unless both parents/guardians and/or other family members sign a written agreement confirming details reauthorization for pick up and access to information about the child.

If a family has a custody or court order, a copy must be placed in the child's file and details about all arrangements contained in the legal documents will be followed at all times.

(continued)

Staff of ABC Child Care Society will call the police if assistance is required to enforce a custody or court order.

Verbal and written information about the child will be shared with the enrolling parents/guardians unless otherwise agreed upon. Permission to share information with others will reflect the policy on confidentiality.

Source: Adapted from the Policies and Procedures for Child Care Programs, *Tough and Sensitive Issues, Part I*, developed by Westcoast Child Care INFORM, Vancouver, BC. info@wstcoast.org

Family Participation

When parents participate, both families and programs reap benefits. Parents express greater confidence in programs when they have opportunities to contribute regularly. They feel more welcome and appreciated. In addition, when a parent is involved in a program event, it communicates to the child, "I care about what you do here." Participation is valuable to the program and meaningful to the parent.

Family members bring tremendous skills and knowledge that benefit the program. The concept of family participation in an EC program is multi-faceted, embracing a range of options and levels. Participation will vary according to each family's time and ability to contribute. Some families will invest a great deal of their time and energy in the program. Others need all their resources to cope with the stresses they face. Early childhood educators must be flexible, able to recognize each family's capabilities, and set expectations accordingly. Parents may sit on policy-making committees, participate in fundraising, volunteer in the playroom, or act as resources. Parents may be involved in operational aspects such as hiring or contributing to staff performance appraisals. One of the main rationales for involving families is that people feel a commitment to decisions in which they have a part in.

Effective decision-making boards can promote a true partnership between families and the early childhood program that provides support for the program, empowerment for the families, and increased mutual understanding. Parents can help to set policy by serving as members of an advisory committee or as family representatives on the board of directors or a board committee.

Programs that actively enlist parent participation and input communicate that families are valued as full partners in the care and education of their children. Studies have shown that programs where families are involved in decision making and advocacy bode well for child outcomes and have greater public support.

Parents as Members of Advisory Boards

Advisory boards give families influence in the programs their children attend. Many EC programs include parents as members of planning and advisory groups that work with the director and other staff, often as a sounding board for program issues. Advisory boards may meet several times a year. They offer advice and resources as well as raise concerns about current and future issues that affect the quality of the program for their children. They may suggest topics for parent meetings. In some programs, parents serve as playroom representatives who keep other families abreast of new activities in the program. As well, advisory board members may be available to respond to parents' questions and concerns. Parent representatives may attend staff or board of directors meetings.

Members of a Board of Directors

Participation on a **board of directors** gives parents an opportunity to influence the policies that affect the program and ultimately their child. When considering issues, board members need adequate information on which to base their decisions. Parents in these roles may need support to identify problems, generate solutions, understand regulations, and to communicate recommendations.

There are challenges to involving families on boards. Some parents may have a limited understanding of issues facing EC programs. Often they have many other demands on their time, and their awareness of the learning program, routines, and interactions is incomplete. As well, some parents may have trouble separating their personal agenda from their role as parent representatives. Occasionally, they may face a conflict of interest—if they vote to raise staff salaries, then their own program fees will increase. The director plays an important role in helping parents understand links between working conditions for the staff and the quality of service provided.

Occasionally, it is challenging for some educators to accept that they are accountable to people who have no formal education in early childhood. Practitioners who are comfortable with parental influence and control tend to be those who are experienced and knowledgeable in their field and confident in their ability to resolve different perspectives.

Sample

Family and Community Relations

Task: Form collaborative partnerships with families.

Early childhood educators (ECEs) form collaborative partnerships with children's families that honour the family's role as the child's primary caregiver; respect its child-rearing beliefs and values; and provide meaningful opportunities for families to determine their children's ELCC experiences. ECEs adapt their programs to the needs of diverse families, respecting each family's composition, language and culture. They help connect families with needed resources, furthering the child's healthy development and learning.

Sub-Tasks

- Build and maintain meaningful relationships with parents.
- Orient families to the program.
- Communicate with families.
- Collaborate with parents on the developmental progress of their children.
- Provide parent resources.

Task: Advocate for children and families.

ECEs advocate for children and their families by establishing ties between parents and various resources required and by advocating for support from governmental agencies and associations. They identify the needs of children and families through clear communication of accurate information.

(continued)

Sub-Tasks

- Make connections between families and resources.
- Provide an inclusive environment.

Task: Provide an inclusive environment

ECEs provide an inclusive environment for children and families through the integration and acceptance of unique and diverse familial and cultural realties, including cultural and religious diversities and a variety of family compositions. ECEs also ensure the acceptance and complete inclusion of children with special needs through program modification and the development of inclusion plans.

Sub-Tasks

- Implement inclusion policy.
- Meet with families to identify strengths and needs.

Source: *Occupational Standards for Early Childhood Practitioners* (Ottawa: Child Care Human Resource Sector Council, 2010.

Home Child Care and Families

A family child care provider invites families as well as their children into her home. As with group EC programs, the child's life is shared by the parents and family child care provider as partners. Parents want to know about their child's day, to smooth transitions, and provide consistency. The provider needs to know what occurred in the child's life and how the child felt and acted since leaving the previous day. Families are keen to hear the joys and achievements of the child's time in care as well as any concerns.

As trust develops, problems are more easily resolved. To achieve this openness, family child care providers:

- Appreciate each child and talk with the parent about observations.
- Support parents by trying to understand their situation and perspective.
- Share something with each parent every day.

Often new caregivers are eager to meet everyone's needs. It is important for caregivers to recognize that they cannot please all of the parents all of the time. They may over commit themselves, working too many hours or taking on too many children. It is necessary to set realistic expectations.

Family child care providers have to determine how to handle the unique needs of each individual family. Flexibility is desirable within a framework of policies and expectations and the plans for the day. Working families need consistent child care, and young children need consistent caregivers. The family child care provider should arrange for reliable substitutes who know the children and can stand in when the provider is ill, or on vacation.

The family child care provider should communicate her expectations and preferences to families in writing. Use of contracts, newsletters, daily notes, e-mail, or bulletin boards saves time, avoids misunderstandings, and allows the provider to focus conversations on less routine matters. Sometimes listening to a parent supportively, without making judgments or recommendations, makes a big difference. Time spent in this way may be time gained in the long run.

While caring for children, the family child care provider becomes very close to the families served. It is necessary to set a professional tone which includes respecting confidentiality, which is critical to building trusting relationships with families. Some providers develop friendships with families. This can be rewarding for all, but it is important that the caregiver not try to be a social worker or therapist for the parent. When families need special help, the family child care provider should refer them to an appropriate community service.

Resources for Families

All families, at one time or another, need or want more support than their network of family and friends can provide. Often families have adequate support networks and can access services without the assistance of the program. But for those families who do require help, the rapport established with staff through daily interactions can be crucial. Often these interchanges can be instrumental in aiding families to get the help they need. It is necessary to respect the parents' ability to make choices on their own. Up-to-date information and other resources can help families make good choices and decisions affecting their children and themselves. ECEs, particularly the director, must make themselves aware of the different resources available in their community.

There are services that can provide support for a wide range of family concerns. Educators need to keep current and be aware of subsidy waiting lists, costs, admission criteria, and so on. Families may benefit from knowing about food banks, where to get inexpensive children's clothing, or criteria for accessing bursaries for program costs. This is where the staff's well-developed networks with other professionals are critical; as program staff can smooth the way for families seeking service. Once the information has been researched, staff must discern what will be the most effective way to encourage families to utilize resources. For some, a display of resources from different organizations—in the parent resource centre or on a bulletin board—is all they need.

The old conception of professionals as good-willed experts dispensing knowledge and advice has given way to a collaborative approach in which families and professionals are partners. A key to this approach is to know when and how to call upon other professionals and resources in the community. The primary role of families is recognized and respected. Families know their child in ways no one else can. And there is acknowledgment, without blame, that families have limits to their knowledge, skills, and resources. For many families, parent education and support can provide additional knowledge and reassurance. It can be a powerful prevention tool. This support can directly combat many of the parental factors that can be harmful for children: isolation, stress, unrealistically high expectations, and a lack of knowledge about non-damaging discipline methods (Bennett 2008).

The journal *Zero to Three* polled 3000 families about their knowledge of child development. It found that there are major gaps between what families believe are effective parenting practices and what child development specialists know to be appropriate expectations for young children. The report *What Grown-Ups Understand about Child Development: A National Benchmark*

Survey (Yankelovich 2000a) suggests that these misunderstandings can have a serious impact on the mental health of young children. Some of the findings:

- More than 50% of the respondents thought using flash cards with young children would increase their intellectual ability. Child development specialists, on the other hand, stress that using flash cards does little to help children develop important concepts about their world.

- More than 60% of grandparents surveyed said that repeatedly picking up a three-month-old crying infant would spoil the baby. In contrast, child development experts encourage this type of empathic response to a baby's crying as a means of building trust and a secure attachment to caregivers.

- More than 60% of families of children under the age of seven think spanking is an appropriate regular form of discipline and 25% expect a three-year-old to sit still for an hour or more. Child development specialists know that such unrealistic expectations can result in abusive practices.

Families do not raise their children in a vacuum. Policies and programs have a direct impact on the ability of families to support their child's healthy growth and development. The results of this study underscore the importance of providing accurate information about child development and practices to families. (For more information, visit the *Zero to Three* website at www.zerotothree.org.)

Summary

Families are the first and most powerful influence on children's early learning and development. A crucial goal in EC practice is sustaining strong, healthy families. Quality EC settings must provide early experiences reflecting the diversity of the wider society in which children live. When the EC education setting reflects the values and practices of child's home, it reinforces the ideas that children learn in the home. Children grow up with a strong sense of self in environments that promote the attitudes, beliefs, and values of equity and democracy and support their full participation.

Today's rapidly changing world holds many social and economic challenges, and virtually all families with young children need some support. Supports given to families have the most impact in the first years of a child's life. EC programs must adapt to accommodate changes in society and provide much-needed support to families facing considerable challenges. The director sets the tone of the program and supports staff members in establishing effective relationships with families and gaining an appreciation of family structures. Directors review policies and procedures to reduce obstacles to engagement and ensure a strengthening family approach.

Beginning the journey toward increased cultural competence requires staff to rethink their assumptions and consider life's issues through the lenses of families who come from backgrounds different from their own. To work with families in a manner that supports and empowers them, EC practitioners need to clarify their own goals for family involvement, appreciate the parents' goals for their child, and work with families to foster these goals.

Staff need to work collaboratively with community organizations to support families. Parent participation in EC programs benefits the program, the child, and themselves. There are many ways parents can be involved in the program. At the same time, the program must be realistic about what parents can do and help individual families to participate in ways that are both meaningful and manageable for them. A collaborative approach that recognizes parents as partners is key.

Key Terms and Concepts

Advisory board,   p. 236

Board of directors,   p. 237

Family-centred practice,   p. 226

Family engagement,   p. 228

Family involvement,   p. 228

Parent,   p. 244

Parent conferences,   p. 231

Activities

1. Determine if there is a listing of social service agencies available for your community. Identify potential resources and support systems for families of young children.

2. Visit an EC program. What evidence of communication with parents do you see? Look at bulletin boards, pictures on display, and other written material. What kind of engagement do you notice between parents and staff? Check the program's website.

3. Interview several directors of early childhood programs about their goals for parent engagement. How do their goals differ?

4. In small groups, role play that a parent is inquiring about the program, with the possibility of enrolling his child. Give him a brief explanation of the program.

Recommended Reading

Ali, M., P. Corson, and E. Frankel. *Listening to Families: Reframing Services.* Toronto: Chestnut Publishing, 2009.

Canadian Child Care Federation. *Canadian Institute of Child Health Nourish, Nurture, Neurodevelopment Resource Kit.* Ottawa: Canadian Child Care Federation, 2001.

Newman, R. *Building Relationships with Parents and Families in School-Age Programs.* Nashville, TN: School-Age Notes, 2000.

Oates, J. *Supporting Parenting, Early Childhood in* Focus. Bernard Van Lear Foundation, 2010.

Shimoni, R. and J. Baxter. *Working with Families: Perspectives for Early Childhood Professionals.* 4th ed. Don Mills, ON: Pearson Addison-Wesley, 2008.

Wilson, L. *Partnerships: Families and Communities in Canadian Early Childhood Education.* 4th ed. Toronto: Nelson, 2010.

Westcoast Child Care Resource Centre. *Towards Partnership/Vers un Partariat: Multi-Language Resources for Families in Child Care/Ressources multilingues pour les familles ayant un enfant en garderie.* Ottawa: Westcoast Child Care Resource Centre, 2001.

Weblinks

www.parentsmatter.ca

Appreciating that to do the best possible job, the Parents Matter site provides resources for parents, links to useful sites and materials, directory of family resource programs and Making Choices—a parenting program inventory.

www.familiesandwork.org/
Families and Work Institute
Non-profit research organization that addresses the changing nature of work and family life, merging work-life issues, topics of vital importance to all sectors of society, and for fostering connections among workplaces, families, and communities.

www.zerotothree.org
Zero to Three
This organization promotes the health and development of infants and toddlers by translating research and knowledge—specifically information about the kinds of early experiences that help children thrive—into a range of practical tools and resources for use by parents and professionals who influence the lives of young children. Parenting resources provide science-based information and tools designed to help parents and caregivers nurture their young children's development.

Financial Matters

chapter 9

Objectives

- **Outline the items in an operating budget.**
- **Discuss the director's/operator's financial role.**
- **Identify types of budgets.**
- **Review major categories of expenses.**
- **Discuss sources of income.**
- **Describe the budget process.**
- **Appreciate the impact of full enrolment and fee collection on budget.**
- **Using a computer for administrative financial tasks.**
- **Review the family child care business budget.**
- **Discuss small-business practices and marketing in relation to the field.**

Although money does not guarantee high quality early childhood services, better quality programs cost more. The nature of a child's and family's experience in an early childhood program depends in large measure on whether the full costs of providing a quality experience can be sustained. The factors that promote quality have a price. Better quality programs spend more per child on staff compensation, including administrative salaries, and professional development than programs providing lower quality. Two major components of financial management are developing a system for managing resources and obtaining adequate funding. When families are primarily responsible for the costs of early childhood, the need to keep programs affordable constrains quality. (Chapter 10, on advocacy, proposes that when all Canadians have a stake in the quality of services provided to young children, more potential resources will be available.) The nature of a child's early childhood experience is determined by a program's ability to:

- Foster meaningful relationships between children and adults by promoting staff continuity for children and by enhancing staff–parent relationships, limiting the number of children per adult.

- Ensure that staff have the specialized educational background and knowledge of early childhood development needed to build relationships with young children and their families.

- Provide adequate compensation (salaries and benefits) and good working conditions to attract and retain qualified staff.

- Establish a safe and stimulating environment that enhances children's ability to learn.

The crisis facing many Canadian EC programs is rooted in the failure to recognize the conflict between three basic needs—the children's need for quality learning experiences, the staff's need for commensurate compensation, and the families' need for affordable programs. These needs are difficult to fulfill simultaneously. This chapter will explain some of the basic tools of financial management that any director should be able to use and that board members/ owners understand.

The Director's Role in Financial Planning

An important requirement of a director's job is to ensure that there are sufficient funds to establish and operate a quality program. Some EC administrators are responsible for all aspects of financial management, while others delegate or contract out all or parts of this task. Administrators need to be familiar with, and actively pursue every possible revenue source for the EC program and be able to estimate program expenses through continuous monitoring. They are responsible for forecasting, managing, and monitoring revenue and expenditures to maintain the viability of the service. This task is a key aspect of effective program implementation and sustainability.

Most early childhood directors come to the profession because they want to work with people. Few receive adequate preparation in financial management. The ability to understand, plan, and control an organization's finances is a central and critical skill. The study Understanding Quality in Context found that it was not only the level of revenue that matters to programs, it was how effectively directors manage their financial stress through effective management of revenue and related constraints. As most programs operate painfully close to running a deficit on a daily basis, directors must manage money effectively. If income and expenses are not carefully planned and controlled, a program can go out of business in a remarkably short period of time.

Some may view the budget process as time consuming and intimidating. Directors may see budgeting, recordkeeping, and financial calculations as tasks that can more easily be performed by a financial professional isolated from the program. Some directors without training or experience in financial management may believe that they can turn the financial aspect of the program over to someone else, while retaining control of the program's policy. Such a belief is totally wrong! All hopes, dreams, and aspirations for what the program will accomplish for children, families, and staff are expressed in the language of money. Every line in the budget is a policy decision that directly determines what a program will be. It is very difficult to influence program policy without controlling the budget process. At the same time, using expertise such as a payroll provider is the single biggest timesaver for directors.

Financial planning affects all major aspects of the program. Consequently, it should involve input from all those involved in the program—the owner/board of directors, staff,

Equally important to quality as the level of revenue is how effectively directors manage their financial stress.

and parents. This may be accomplished through parental representation on the board of directors or holding a meeting to discuss rationale for impeding fee increases. Advice from parents, financial experts, and staff can supplement the director's skills, strengthen the program, and contribute to team building. By considering everyone's ideas, a more accurate conception of budgeting priorities, appropriate expenditure level, and revenue sources can be derived.

In the area of financial planning, directors must produce a well-informed budget that takes into account the various sources of **revenue**, including parent fees, government grants, fundraising, and the projected range of expenditures. Directors must ensure that policies, procedures, and practices are in place to support the management of **cash flow**. Additionally, directors need the skills and attitudes that will enable them to work both independently and with others to carry out their financial responsibilities.

Developing a budget requires creative decision making, an ability to look at past business practices, and the vision to predict future expenses and income. A budget is written for a specific period of time, typically a year, and is a tool for helping EC directors predict program success, or in some cases, lack of success. *Some programs are destined to failure because their expenses outweigh their income.* A good budget will determine success or failure before an operator invests a great outlay of financial and emotional resources. Budget information can also help EC directors make educated decisions about the potential growth of the program. In the field of early childhood, staffing encompasses the greatest portion of the budget. Between paying staff wages, payroll taxes, and benefits, there is, typically, not a great deal of money left to pay for all of the other expenses.

Who Makes the Budget?

In a non-profit organization, the director, generally in cooperation with the finance committee, draws up the budget. The board of directors then reviews, suggests revisions, and ultimately approves it. In a commercial operation, the owner develops the budget with input from the director. A budget should reflect responsive planning that responds to input from the staff and parents. In the case of a new EC program, the group of people or individual responsible for getting the program started will develop a budget early in the planning stage to determine that the program will be viable.

Types of Budgets

When a centre is beginning **operations**, the director prepares two budgets: the **start-up budget** and the **operating budget**.

- *Start-up budget.* This budget consists of all the one-time expenses incurred in starting a program, including initial building expenses (the down payment on the purchase of the building, the cost of renovations, or rent deposit), the purchase of major equipment, the director's salary for a period of time prior to opening the program, the expenses of publicizing the program, and utility charges during this period. A capital funding grant may be needed, or the project may be able to be internally financed. The equipment and learning materials—for the activity and care areas, office, computers, and kitchen—are a major part of the start-up budget. All equipment may be purchased at the beginning if there are sufficient resources but not if cash flow is tight. Consider rental equipment such as a photocopier. Total start-up costs vary widely.
- *Operating budgets.* These budgets are used when programs become operational and annually thereafter. The period covered by a budget depends on circumstances, such as, if operating a 10-month program from September to June, then it makes sense to prepare a budget for a 10-month period. On the other hand, a year round program with little variation in enrolment usually prepares a budget from January until December. Before any financial transactions are made, the budget must be approved by the board of directors/owner and possibly third parties that are providing operating funds. Once approval has been given, the director must follow the approved financial plan. The budget for the following year is prepared well in advance of year end leaving adequate time for the approval process.

Step-by-Step Guide to Preparing a Budget

A **budget** is a statement of goals for one year, stated in financial terms. It is an important financial planning tool that can help an organization control expenditures and identify potential problems. A budget calendar should be established with milestones identified to meet each step. For programs receiving funds from government agencies, this timetable is generally predetermined.

SAMPLE BUDGET CALENDER OF EVENTS

JANUARY
- Assemble payroll information for T4/T4-A preparation

FEBRUARY
- Final date for T4/T4A submission is month end
- Review monthly cash flow assumptions and adjust monthly cash flow forecast if necessary (*)

MARCH
- Annual financial statement should be finalized and approved by the board (*)
- If eligible, prepare application for GST rebate (*)
- Complete and submit Employee Health Tax (EHT) annual return by March 15

APRIL
- Prepare cash flow forecast for summer period

MAY
- Prepare Worker's Compensation return if applicable

JUNE
- Final date for filing of Revenue Canada returns (T2/T3010-1/T1044) is June 30 (*)
- Annual General Meeting held before month end (*)
- Update/finalize summer period cash flow forecast
- Ministry of Education (EDU) grant utilization forms due (Direct Operating Grant (DOG)/Wage Enhancement Grant (WEG)) (*)(**)
- Provincial Annual Return and Special Notice filings due (***)

JULY
- Review summer cash flow forecast assumptions and adjust budget if necessary

AUGUST
- Enjoy well-deserved rest!

SEPTEMBER
- Assemble information for Toronto Children's Services budget (City of Toronto only)(**)
- Update monthly cash flow forecast for changes in enrolment/service levels (*)

OCTOBER
- Complete City of Toronto Children's Services budget by month end (**)

NOVEMBER
- Assemble information for next year's monthly cash flow forecast

DECEMBER
- Finalize and obtain board approval for next year's monthly cash flow forecast (*)
- Review staff salaries and fees charged (*)

NOTES:

*This schedule assumes a budgeting process based on a calendar year. If your budget is for a different period, for example from April to March, then you should adjust the items marked with an asterisk accordingly.

**Applies to childcare centres only.

***Filings in conjunction with T2 or T3010-1

Source: Reprinted with permission. Phil Cowperthwaite, "A Treasurer's Calendar of Events," developed by Cowperthwaite Mehta, Toronto, ON. www.187gerrard.com. Financial Management, Governance, July 13, 2010.

In planning a budget, there are two key considerations. First, the budget should be related to the overall planning of the EC program. Money must be allocated strategically to achieve program goals. Second, the key decision makers of the program need to be involved at each step of the budgeting process. These leaders must set long-term goals for the organization, decide upon program priorities, and, ultimately, assume financial responsibility. They must be involved in the forecasting as well as the monitoring of budgetary expenditures. The decision makers must also determine on an annual basis whether the program should:

a) run at a break-even level (neither make a profit nor incur a loss);

b) operate with a small surplus; or

c) operate at a deficit (assuming the program has a substantial financial reserve that should be reduced).

The following steps are part of the successful budgeting cycle:

1. Make a Wish List

This step involves reviewing what the program wants to accomplish in the coming year. The decision makers determine objectives for the upcoming year; the director's job is to provide the route. A question to ask is: What would we do if cost was not an issue? This process forces people to think systematically about the program's mission, programs, activities, and long-range goals. The program may have conducted a self-evaluation process or had feedback from an external consultant and/or licensing officer to identify goals such as improving the outdoor playground or increasing opportunities for staff development. In these examples, allocating money for professional development or construction of a new playground would be included on the wish list.

2. Project Expenditures

After a wish list has been finalized, each item on the list must be costed out. The task of estimating expenses can be daunting at first. To make the task more manageable, focus effort on key items, such as staffing. Items of less significance, such as office supplies, do not need to be estimated individually; estimate a reasonable figure for the category using last year's expenditures as a guide.

Include the foundational costs of keeping the program operating (staffing, food, materials). In addition, the costs of new items will have to be estimated. Costing is not always an easy process. One approach involves **incremental budgeting**, which relies on information contained in the budget for the prior year. To the figures in the previous year's budget, the director may add a percentage increment to cover inflation and other factors. A second technique requires that each line be newly calculated, regardless of how much was assigned to each line in previous years.

The previous year's figures can be immensely helpful in estimating the coming year's budget. It is important to review the current year's figures to see how accurate last year's projections were. It is better to estimate costs marginally on the high side. If new programs are added, this may increase administrative costs. Thus, it is unrealistic to try and accurately calculate how much would be spent directly on the new program.

It is critical to understand the relationships between revenues, fixed costs, and variable costs. **Fixed costs** are those that tend to stay constant at least in the short term. Fixed costs are incurred regardless of the size of the program. Rent/mortgage, property taxes, and the director's salary are examples of fixed costs. Some of these costs, such as the director's salary, are the same in a given facility whether the program serves 25 or a hundred children. **Variable costs** are those that increase as the number of children served increases. Staff salaries are the largest variable cost in an EC program. The greater number of children served, the more practitioners must be hired. The age of the children served is an example of factors affecting variable costs—the younger the children, the higher the ratio of adults to children and consequently, the greater the number of staff required. Other variable expenses include curriculum supplies, **maintenance**, food, and equipment. These expenses all increase and decrease as the number of children in the program changes. Programs with **fee subsidy** agreements are required to use guidelines for their budget submissions. These types of guidelines may not allow for some aspects of quality, such as enhanced ratios, or for program enrichments, such as a music teacher. Whatever the budget format, the following expense categories would be included.

Salaries　A competent director recognizes the complexities of cost-effectiveness in the provision of high quality programs. Although licensing regulations set minimum standards for staff:child ratios, the program may decide to hire all ECE staff to provide a better program. Quality EC programs often stipulate qualifications for their professional staff that exceed the requirements of the province or territory. The rate of pay is usually determined by the quality of the staff the program is seeking to attract, their professional qualifications, the local job market, and the type of program. Programs that want to recruit and retain capable staff must provide an attractive compensation package. The amount is determined by the number of staff, their rate of pay, and the hours they work. The director must be aware of the relation between compensation levels, employees' self-esteem, and staff stability. Some programs control costs by closely monitoring the number of children attending each day and by altering the number of staff accordingly.

The Salary Area Is the Largest Expense Budget Category　A program can expect to pay 70% to 90% of its operating budget to cover wages. A small percentage error (5%) in this category can throw off the whole budget. The salary category is the area that most time should be spent on. Estimating gross salaries starts with listing all the staff positions and estimating the gross salary for each position for the upcoming year. This line should include salaries for all full-time and part-time staff, including the director, professional staff (including assistants and substitutes), a cook, a maintenance person, and administrative personnel. Then review the program HR policies (discussed in Chapter 5) in regard to salary scales and benefits. Hiring policies that specify a certain education level or amount of previous experience will affect salary levels.

For staff paid on an hourly basis consider the board approved salary levels. Then, estimate the number of hours likely needed by staff in that position for the coming year. These rates must comply with minimum-wage laws and any other employment regulations. For hourly paid positions, include vacation pay costs. For settings operating a 10-month program, they provide vacation pay at the end of the school year.

Replacement staff are needed for absent staff (illness/vacations). Guidelines suggest budgeting for five weeks of replacement staff for each permanent position; for example, consider allocating 10% for replacement staff.

Benefits   There are two kinds of **benefits**: those that are mandatory required by law and those that are offered by the program and included in the employee contract. Mandatory benefits include taxes the program is required to pay to the government, such as the health tax, and required employer contributions to Employment Insurance, the Canada Pension Plan, and Workplace Safety and Insurance. In some jurisdictions, payments to Worker's Compensation are mandatory, and in other regions, they are optional. These costs should be estimated at approximately 9% of salaries.

Other benefits, which may include extended health coverage, dental coverage, professional development, planning time, and retirement or pension plans, may comprise about 4% of gross salary costs. *You Bet I Care!* found two-thirds of teaching staff received paid coffee breaks, but only one-third received paid lunch breaks. The 1998 study of *You Bet I Care!* found some improvement over the 1991 *Caring for a Living* survey in terms of the percentage of educators who received compensation for overtime, including attending parent meetings, paid planning time, and staff meetings after hours (Doherty et al. 2000a). The program incurs the costs involved in maintaining accurate records for each employee and filing reports with various government agencies.

Benefits that augment the individual's salary or provide a measure of longer-term security are particularly important in an occupation with low wages. Most of the staff are women, with many under the age of 40. Consequently, job-protected maternity leave and reduced child care fees for employees' children are valuable benefits. It is important to note that reduced child care fees is a taxable benefit. Disability insurance and a pension plan are important when the wage level makes saving very difficult. Having paid sick days and being permitted to carry them over from one year to another provides some protection should an individual experience a prolonged illness. These provisions, necessary to establish a humane environment, can add considerable additional costs to the budget. **Personnel policies** also affect expenses indirectly through the cost of replacement staff replacing regular staff off on sick leave, professional development days, or vacation.

Professional Fees and Contract Services

In this last category to do with personnel, include all services provided by individuals not on the payroll. These usually include an accountant, custodian, music or art teacher, a lawyer, curriculum specialists, and—unless the program pays benefits for them—replacement staff. This amount is determined by reviewing the program's HR policies. If the program uses consultants, they are usually paid on a per diem basis plus expenses.

Facilities

The largest cost in the physical plant category is the rent or mortgage payments for the facility. Also included in this category are utilities (heat, electricity, water, property tax, and insurance). Building insurance covers all the items associated with fire, weather, burglary, and liability insurance. Approximately 5% to 10% of the budget is used for rent or mortgage and 5% to 6% for utilities. In *You Bet I Care!*, 34.5% of non-profit centres and 3.4% of commercial programs reported subsidized or free rent (Doherty et al. 2000a). Similar numbers of programs reported subsidized or free utilities. Programs that do not have to pay the full costs of their facility can redirect these funds to other areas of the program, thereby enhancing quality. It is important to note the growing trend of many cash-strapped school boards that are no longer providing free rent to child care programs. The costs for **maintenance** and repairs to the facility and grounds are part of this budget item. Regular maintenance cuts costs in this area in the long term. It is impossible to predict these costs, so an appropriate amount must be allocated.

Supplies and Equipment   The large number of consumable supplies used in EC programs cost very little in relation to costs for staff, rent or food. Staff need to be aware of how supplies are used. All of the art materials, office supplies, cleaning supplies, and paper products used in the program should be identified, then the quantity of each item needed should be determined. Whenever possible, supplies should be ordered in volume from the least expensive source. At the same time, when buying items in bulk, consider the amount of storage space available, the shelf life of the item, and any additional costs of shipping or delivery. It is recommended that a program have an inventory level to carry it through two months of operation. Many programs buy co-operatively with other programs. As an example, this part of the budget covers all items that cost less than $5000 in City of Toronto budget guidelines.

Transportation   This category may include the lease or purchase of vehicles used to transport the children to the program, to school, and/or on field trips, insurance, fuel, maintenance, and licence fees. In rural areas, programs often contract with a company to provide transportation or rent a vehicle for specific occasions. Because of financial, safety, and liability concerns, many parents provide their child's transportation to the program. Costs for staff members to travel to professional development meetings or other programs may be included in this category.

Food   These costs are typically the second highest expenditure. They vary between 5% and 10% of total expenditures. Many programs provide a nutritious meal and two snacks per day, with food either prepared on the premises or catered. For programs preparing food in-house, costs range from $2.00 to $2.50 per child per day excluding staff time, whereas catered foods cost about $4.50 per child per day. Consideration should be given to providing sufficient food for the staff to eat with the children. This is also considered a taxable benefit for employees. Food expenses are small in comparison to salary expenses. Even if estimates are off by 20% in this category, it will result in a variance of only 2% in the total budget, whereas if a similar error occurred in the salary category, it would result in a variance of 18% in total costs.

Other Expenses   Other items include telephones (cellphones for field trips), advertising (usually higher during start-up when there are vacancies to fill), and annual audits, which are needed to assure board members and government agencies that funds have been properly handled.

3. Project Revenue

Four factors have a significant bearing on a program's financial solvency: primarily enrolment, fees, the number of staff, and salaries. Revenue comes to programs from several sources: parent fees, fee subsidies, government salary enhancements, operating grants, and special needs resourcing. GST rebates, fundraising, and interest usually are less than 1% of the budget. A program's resources, specifically what families are willing to pay for fees, strongly influence compensation levels for staff and the quality of program offered. Establishing fees for service requires a constant balancing act between what it costs to run the program and what price the market in the program's community will bear. Figure 9–1 illustrates the need to balance competitive wages with affordable fees. Providing services for infants-toddlers has much higher staffing requirements than for older children. Historically, directors have undercharged for this age group and subsidized the cost with older children in the program. However with many provincial governments providing full day kindergarten, and these children not attending child care full-time, this is no longer an option.

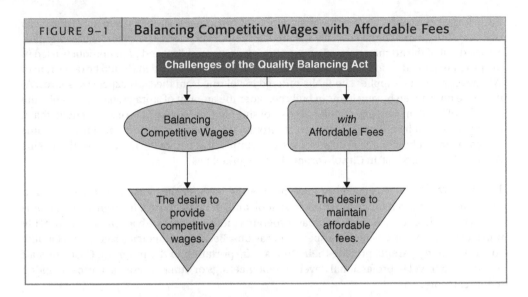

FIGURE 9–1 | Balancing Competitive Wages with Affordable Fees

It is important to understand the difference between restricted and unrestricted funds. Unrestricted funds, such as parent fees or monies derived from fundraising, have no particular limitations on how or when they are to be used. Restricted funds, such as parent fee subsidies and salary enhancement funding from governments, come with very specific requirements that dictate how and when the funds may be used. Be conservative about forecasting income. Some directors factor in under-enrolment of 2% to 10%.

Parent fee and subsidy revenue is calculated by multiplying the expected number of children in the program by the fees to be charged. This is best done on a group by group basis. Enrolment can fluctuate substantially over the year. Periodically throughout the year (at least quarterly) revise revenue estimates, taking into account changes in expected enrolment.

4. Compare

This step is also known as the "read 'em and weep" step. There may be often too much expense and not enough income. Decision makers must act responsibly and only plan to fund what the program can reasonably afford to pay for.

5. Set Priorities

It is time to scrutinize which programs and activities will be included in the budget. This step can be very challenging. Priority setting is linked to the philosophy—the organization's reason for being. Decision makers must determine what meets the needs of the children and families and what is best for the organization. The only way to address a significant imbalance is to trim down salary costs by reducing the number of staff or increase enrolment. During discussions of the budget, some may defend a special project that they feel must be included whereas others may reject any new activity.

6. Balancing the Budget

If the projected expenses exceed the projected income, the budget is not balanced. Decision makers will need to reduce expenditures or increase income. To reduce expenditures, review variable and irregular expenses to determine areas where money can be saved. In the area of payroll, it may be determined that there are times in the day when staffing could be reduced while maintaining required ratios, always taking into consideration collective agreements where applicable. Or, a director might review those areas in which the program is exceeding licensing standards. If the shortfall is small, the staff may revisit the materials and equipment requested.

An alternative strategy for balancing the budget is to increase income. Communicating with parents on the budget and keeping them informed of the financial situation will aid families' understanding of the costs of quality early childhood experience. Most programs hold meetings annually to discuss the budget and give parents the opportunity to ask questions and provide input on alternative sources of funding. Questions such as "How much must parent fees be raised in order to balance the budget?" "Could all the families afford this increase?" and "How will the program deal with a number of families withdrawing their children because they cannot pay the increased rates?" are considered.

7. Get Budget Approval

After all the initial groundwork is completed, the budget must be approved. In a small commercial program, this will involve the owner reviewing all the computations. In a larger operation, the approval step may involve submitting the budget to a corporate office, whereas in a non-profit community centre, the budget will be approved by the board of directors, possibly after approval from the finance committee. It is necessary to document decisions in minutes and keep financial statements. Given that so much time is spent developing the budget, some may assume that this step is just a formality. However, the decision makers need to be responsible and assure themselves, for example, that all the projected revenues will be forthcoming, particularly those additional funds that will have to be raised.

8. Monitor and Amend

Most budgets will need to be amended and modified over time to accommodate new information and changing conditions that occur over the year. It is necessary to create a mechanism for ongoing budget review. There needs to be an approach that allows some flexibility, yet requires approval for any significant changes.

The advantage of doing a monthly cash-flow analysis is that the director can predict well in advance cash problems anticipated throughout the year and act to prevent a surprise decrease in the bank balance. It is the responsibility of the decision makers to review the budget on a regular basis and make adjustments as necessary. Cowperthwaite and Mehta acknowledge that, while preparing an annual review of revenue and expenses is important, cash flow must also be monitored, because due to fluctuations in monthly revenue and expenses, a program could run out of money in August even though the budget suggests that the program will be viable until December. Programs can experience significant fluctuations in outlays for salaries and benefits due to months in which three pay periods occur. Also, the timing of some receipts, such as operating grants, may not coincide with biweekly pay periods.

Sufficiency of Revenue

Although sufficient funding does not guarantee high quality early care and education, at least some costs are clearly associated with delivering better quality services. Nearly all program inputs—including staff, supplies, equipment, food, and space—are constrained by revenue (and the availability of in-kind donations). Some recommend if enrolment drops, consider adding more supplies/food to make the centre "better" to attract more children to fix the revenue problem. Figure 9–2 illustrates variable affecting the financial strain on programs.

- *Primary revenue sources.* For day-to-day operating costs, EC programs typically rely on a primary funding source tied to child enrolment and/or attendance. Primary revenue sources among programs include the following.

- *Private-pay families.* Many programs are wholly or primarily reliant on fees from parents as their main revenue source. Not surprisingly, most of these programs serve middle- to high-income families. Some programs that primarily relied on parent-paid fees also serve a number of children whose fees were covered through subsidy.

- *Families whose fees are paid through fee subsidy or funded vouchers.* Government fee subsidies are usually paid directly to service providers by the government on behalf of eligible families. Funding from these sources is dependent on the continuing eligibility of families for the assistance and subject to certain limitations on payments that can reduce the amount of revenue collected per child, compared with revenue from private-pay families.

- *Additional funding sources.* Recurring annual operating grants are important to a program's viability since they can provide a certain degree of financial stability. Beyond these

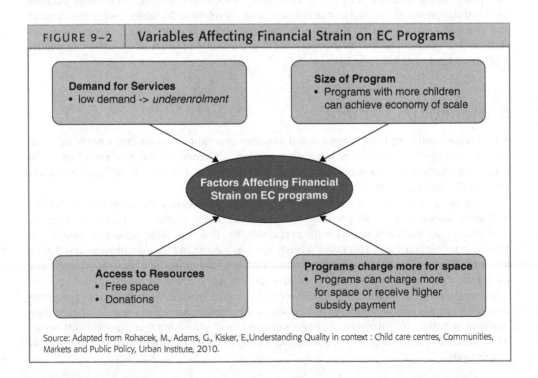

FIGURE 9–2 | Variables Affecting Financial Strain on EC Programs

Demand for Services
- low demand -> *underenrolment*

Size of Program
- Programs with more children can achieve economy of scale

Factors Affecting Financial Strain on EC programs

Access to Resources
- Free space
- Donations

Programs charge more for space
- Programs can charge more for space or receive higher subsidy payment

Source: Adapted from Rohacek, M., Adams, G., Kisker, E.,Understanding Quality in context : Child care centres, Communities, Markets and Public Policy, Urban Institute, 2010.

main funding sources, directors tap into various other financial resources, including special grants (such as to assist with meeting licensing requirements, accreditation, space expansions, special initiatives related to early literacy, and/or purchase of playground equipment); scholarships for staff; funding for wage supplements; and special fundraising activities.

• *Inkind resources.* Some centers supplemented their budget with in-kind inputs. Although they are not cash revenue, for some programs, in-kind inputs represent a substantial resource for which revenue would otherwise have to be allocated or generated. Free or reduced space costs are the most common in-kind assistance. Other types of in-kind inputs such as parent assistance with building maintenance, accounting, or other management services provided by organizations with which centers were affiliated, or donations of materials and equipment or free or subsidized utilities and janitorial/maintenance services.

A program's resources strongly influence staff compensation levels and the quality of program offered. A large U.S. study found that in-kind donations, such as subsidized rent, enable programs to allocate a larger portion of their revenue to staff compensation and programming (Rohacek et al. 2010). *You Bet I Care!* found that, on average, 49.2% of program revenue comes from parent fees, 30.5% from government fee subsidies, and 17.5% from other government grants such as operating or salary-enhancement grants. Forty-two percent of programs engage in their own fundraising, although nationally, this activity accounted for less than 2% of program revenue. Fifty-one percent of programs reported that they receive some type of in-kind donation. Non-profit programs reported receiving more than twice the amount of donations than did commercial centres. *You Bet I Care!* found considerable variation across provinces in the proportion of revenue coming from each source (Doherty et al. 2000a). Since parent fees and subsidies provide a significant portion of a program's revenue, consequently the director should ensure that this source gets more time and attention.

Income is related to the number of children enrolled in the program, whether the program is full-time or part-time, and the fees per child. Parent fee and subsidy revenue is calculated by multiplying the number of children in the program by the fees to be charged. It is recommended that this figure be calculated separately for each age group served. The calculation itself is not difficult; however, predicting the actual revenue can be challenging as enrolment fluctuates over the course of the year. It is challenging to operate a program at 100% enrolment. When children leave, others will not always take their place on the same day. A well-run program operates at between 95% and 98% enrolment. Careful attention to attendance records is key to ensuring that non-attendance is not non-enrolment. The previous year's budget and current year's financial statements can be helpful. Enrolment variations, such as a drop in enrolment during the summer months, should be expected. As well, factor into revenue estimates some allocation for uncollected fees.

Almost all of EC revenue is tuition collected on behalf of the enrolled child. While government or philanthropy may sometimes provide revenue, this funding is rarely provided as general operating support. Full enrolment is the cornerstone of EC finance, regardless of whether the program relies of public funds (subsidy) or parent fees, or a combination. Unless a program is over-enrolled (a practice that is generally prohibited in licensing regulations because it could result in attendance that exceeds ratio or group size limits), it is not possible to operate at 100% enrolment.

To have full enrolment, increasingly programs are considering a flexible approach. Lowe (2001a) notes the case of one program which was having trouble filling 32 full-time spaces. It decided to retain 24 full-time spaces and create eight flexible ones, accommodating up to 20 more part-time children. The director observed that this flexible approach served the families as well as the bottom line.

Monitoring enrolment and acting quickly to address any shortfall is the key to financial stability. Directors must carefully track attendance, in each classroom on a regular basis, and plan in advance which children will be "aging out" of the program or moving to a different playroom. Without careful monitoring and active outreach to fill vacant spots, it is easy for these natural transitions to cause funding gaps. In a small program, everyday that a spot is unfilled, it can make a big difference. Over time these losses add up and can lead to serious financial shortfalls.

Parent Fees   In some jurisdictions, 50% to 80% of the cost of EC is paid by parents and is significantly higher than the 20% to 25% recommended by the OECD. Many Canadians would prefer that regulated early learning and care services—like other educational experiences for children—be 100% publicly funded such as kindergarten. Setting parent fees involves a complex set of decisions. If the director sets the fees based on what parents can afford to pay, this may not generate enough income to cover the costs of operating the desired program nor compensate excellent staff. Inadequate revenue may result in the staff subsidizing the program through wages that are too low. The simplest way to increase income and achieve a balanced budget is to raise parent fees. Careful consideration must be given to the impact on families in the program. It is important to know the fees of other programs in the community. Know what

Many Canadians prefer that regulated EC services like other educational experiences for children be 100% publicly funded.

the families are willing to pay. Programs may be able to charge more if their program is unique and meets parents' needs.

The Iron Triangle of ECE—Formula for Financial Policy in EC Programs

EC programs budgets, like all budgets, have two sides: the money coming in and the money going out. Balancing these two sides is essential and challenging during times of economic recession. When seeking to balance budgets, EC directors typically focus on the fees—the price charged to parents or received as subsidy from governments. In additions to fees, there are two additional factors which influence income: enrolment and fee collection. These three factors in Figure 9–3 form the iron triangle of EC finance. Paying close attention to all three sides is the key to sound financial management.

Both enrolment and fee collection impact actual per-child costs. If a program is not fully enrolled, the per-child cost increases. If bad debts go up (fees are not being collected), the per-child cost increases. In some cases, a budget gap can be addressed by boosting enrolment and/or lowering bad debt rather than raising fees. The three factors are interrelated. In tough fiscal times, when funders are cutting budgets and parents are squeezed financially, ECE programs often face a difficult choice: keep fees high and risk increased vacancy rates and higher bad debt, or lower fees to boost cash flow. Unfortunately, the right answer is not simple or obvious, and it may vary from center to center based on the services offered and the families served.

The iron triangle is a simple formula for a complex issue. It can be a helpful way to stay on track, to remember what's important, but should not replace the many steps involved in sound fiscal management.

Wage enhancement grants were received by 43.5% of centres in Canada, but they accounted for less than 6.5% of centre revenue. Most provinces provide government grants to assist with integrating children with special needs. The government in Quebec implemented a major policy to make child care more affordable for parents. In Quebec, parents pay a $7-per-day fee and the government covers the remaining costs.

Fundraising   Increasingly, early childhood programs are seeking ways to expand financial resources beyond parent fees and government grants. Although many directors appreciate the

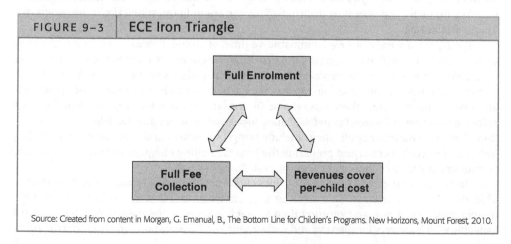

| FIGURE 9–3 | ECE Iron Triangle |

Full Enrolment

Full Fee Collection

Revenues cover per-child cost

Source: Created from content in Morgan, G. Emanual, B., The Bottom Line for Children's Programs. New Horizons, Mount Forest, 2010.

need for fundraising, they often lack experience and an understanding of professional techniques necessary for executing a successful campaign. Before involving the program in fundraising, it is important to consider the amount of work required. Fundraising is usually regarded as a trivial revenue source; and in most cases, parents end up being the donors. It may be more effective to just raise fees!

These activities must have the full support of the operators and the commitment of dedicated volunteers. The quality of this commitment will define the scope of the fundraising campaign. When launching a fundraising effort, the purpose for the funds must be identified. It is easier to generate support for building an outdoor playground than to raise funds for general operating expenses. In fact, raising funds for operating expenses is strongly discouraged and even viewed as dangerous; fundraising cannot always be sustained, and operating funds need to be reliable. However, carefully executed, an annual fundraising campaign may generate ongoing financial support for capital and special expenditures, the true benefit may be in community awareness and cohesion.

Financial Record Keeping

After creating a balanced budget, it is important to employ an effective system for keeping track of income and expenses. The director is responsible for overseeing or preparing this information, generally with an accountant's assistance. The director informs everyone authorized to make purchases of the budget limitations. Early childhood educators, cooks, and housekeeping staff must know the allowable monthly expenditures for budget categories for which they are responsible.

Directors who have had little or no experience with record keeping can improve their financial management skills by taking courses and using information resources available through websites (such as those listed at the end of the chapter). They may employ a local accounting firm that specializes in child care services. Whatever strategy is used, it is essential for the director to be familiar with accounting methods and terminology. Most accounting or computer packages provide monthly balance and income statements. Computer-generated reports can be revised readily so that the most current information is available. Accounting entries recorded by the program should include all income and expenditures regardless of the source. The entries should reflect all financial transactions and be recorded at appropriate intervals (daily, weekly). Poor record keeping result in inaccurate information on which to base key financial and operating decisions. This can result in questions about the program's financial standing.

The right software can save administrative time, enabling directors to spend more time with families and staff and observing the program. Programs are used to monitor financial transactions (e.g., income and expenses, fee payments, payroll, tax payments). Monthly billings, payroll, and funder reporting are among the management tasks which are more efficient as with automated processes, and these tasks should be considered when selecting the right financial software program. Additional benefits include increased accuracy and availability of information. Relevant computer applications include budget templates and systems for maintaining individual payroll records and preparing the payroll, writing cheques and making receipts, recording daily transactions, and reviewing cash flow.

Ongoing tracking necessary for all businesses are **accounts receivable** and **accounts payable**, described below. In addition to using a system for payroll that tracks the hours worked, deductions, rate of pay, and vacation time for each employee, there are computer program available which are very inexpensive and well supported that posts both expenses and deposits.

These categories should be tracked monthly, quarterly, and annually to determine whether or not the developed budget is on target. Directors of similar programs can provide their advice on experience with financial software programs. A number of EC organizations offer software programs and support.

- *Accounts receivable.* Accounts receivable are all monies owed to the program that have not been paid. It is important that directors review accounts receivable on a regular basis. Many collection problems stem from not acting soon enough to collect overdue debts. Accounts receivable records keep track of any payment received, generally on a weekly basis. The director needs to know who is not paying and why. There will always be a few uncollected fees, primarily from those families who withdraw their children without warning, perhaps owing payment for several days. However, prompt attention to those families who are behind in payments can reduce the **bad debt** expense (a bad debt is a receivable that will never be collected). A weekly report should list families by name and the amounts that they owe in an accounts receivable software program.

- *Accounts payable.* These are the records of bills or invoices that have been received by the program for goods and services received but not yet paid. When a bill is received, it should go in a folder in date order. In general, record invoices as accounts payable when received so that they can be reflected in the monthly expenses. It is essential to develop accurate record keeping systems. Once a bill is paid, mark the invoice with the cheque amount, date, and number and note any partial payments.

Financial Policies and Procedures
Salary Schedules

A program director must invest limited resources wisely in order to create and maintain a high quality organization. Even with a limited budget, there are some ways programs can improve performance. Although people don't gravitate to the early childhood field for its financial benefits, even the most committed staff will become discouraged when they do a great job and are paid less than staff in other programs. Some early childhood organizations conduct salary surveys and make them available to members. Some provinces have determined provincial salary scales such as Manitoba and Prince Edward Island.

Administration of salaries is not a simple mechanical procedure. It is a direct expression of the values of an organization. When hiring a staff member, a program is paying for time, expertise, and/or results. If the program is paying for time, the hiring premise may be paying for a warm body to fulfill ratio requirements over a period of time. Consequently, compensation levels only need to attract and retain staff who meet minimum legal requirements. When the program is paying for expertise, individuals who are knowledgeable and practised in early childhood are hired with the expectation that they will perform significantly better than persons without professional education and experience. The salary scale may also reward them for continuing acquisition of knowledge and skills such as a higher pay for an individual who has completed additional training such as working with a child with special needs. If the program is paying for results, the assumption is that what really matters is who performs well on the job, and effective performers are rewarded. When setting a salary scale that reflects performance, it is recommended to give a combination of **cost-of-living adjustment (COLA)** and merit raises to acknowledge individual efforts.

Family Fee Policies

Programs for young children are expensive. Although families seldom pay the full cost of care, EC programs represent a large portion of the family budget—particularly for middle- and low-income families. In setting parent fees, directors must consider market prices, what parents can afford, or are willing to pay. For many families, quality EC programs are simply not affordable. There is a tremendous variation in the rates programs charge. These variations reflect regional cost-of-living factors, age of the child, family incomes, parents' willingness to pay, and outside financial support. As noted earlier, the OECD recommends families paying a maximum of 25% of program costs.

Collecting fees—in full and on time—is essential. Fees only become revenue when they are collected. An EC program can have a budget that balances on paper, but the enrolment may fall below projections. Successful EC directors stay on top of fee collection; they have clear policies, are firm and consistent with families, thorough and prompt with billing, and on top of paperwork. Fee collection can be time consuming unless systems are in place to streamline and automate the process. Making electronic funds transfer is the norm for fee payment and an effective way to strengthen fee collection.

When determining fee policies, directors should consider the following points:

- *Fee levels.* Set realistic fee levels. The fee charged should be based on what it costs to provide a level of quality that the program believes in. If the fees are set to be comparable with those fees of other programs in the community charge, they may not be high enough to cover costs. Some directors keep their fees too low because they fear that parents may not be able to afford higher fees. By doing so, they are dooming the program to a mediocre level of quality. It is best to base the fees on what is required to provide a quality learning program.

- *Parents must be aware of fee policies.* At intake, the director carefully reviews key policies on withdrawals, absences, late pickups, and late payments so that parents clearly understand in advance what the rules are. Many programs require a parent to sign a statement or contract agreeing to these policies.

- *Charging for absences.* Program policies can include lengthy and complicated explanations for why parents are charged when their child is absent. Staff must be paid regardless of whether children are present or not, and so fees must be paid regardless of attendance. When setting policies for absences, programs must strive for a balance between the program's need for financial stability and being sensitive to the needs of families.

- *Payment terms.* Programs require fee payment in advance. Currently, most programs collect on a monthly basis, which keeps the number of collections to a minimum and gives the program greater flexibility in managing cash flow. In some communities, parents cannot afford to pay a month in advance. Therefore, some programs collect on a weekly basis. Some programs prefer to receive payments by automatic bank account deductions, and some even have policies against receiving payments in cash. Some programs permit payments by credit card.

- *Late fee payments.* It is important to confront the problem early and work out solutions that meet the program's needs as well as those of the families. Encourage families who are experiencing financial difficulties to let the director know as soon as possible about problems they may have with fee payments. Work out a schedule of payments that will help the family and increase the likelihood that the payments are eventually made.

- *Late pickups.* This issue poses a problem for the child as well as the staff. Most programs realize that being totally inflexible regarding lateness imposes even more pressure on families who are living stressful lives. Impress upon parents the importance of calling the program if they are going to be late so that the child knows why and so that staff can plan their departure times. In endeavouring to implement family-friendly policies, some programs allow up to two late pickups per year before any financial penalty is allotted. The newsletter *Caregiver Connection*, published by Western Canada Family Child Care Association of BC, cautions that if a staff member is paid directly for late fees owed, she or he is not covered by Worker's Compensation for the time period. This is because a late fee is not treated as taxable income. The association recommends that the program bill the parent directly and pay the staff through regular methods. Whereas others recommend that parents pay staff directly as it is the staff and not the centre that is inconvenienced by late pickups.

- *Withdrawal policies.* Most programs outline specific procedures for withdrawing a child. These are designed to give the program adequate notice so that it can collect any fees due from the outgoing family and find a new child to fill the vacancy. In addition, programs spell out specific policies for temporary withdrawals for a family vacation or illnesses. Everything must be paid for. For example, if a program allows for two weeks' vacation, this means higher fees throughout the year to cover this lost revenue. One strategy is placing an absent child on a priority waiting list so that the child can fill the first available vacancy when she or he is ready to return.

It is important that the program set fee policies that can be enforced consistently. Directors should also consider the following points regarding fee policies:

Ensure that policies are clearly written and sensitive. Programs want to set family-friendly policies that convey respect for parents. When creating financial policies, assume good intentions on the part of parents. Their perspective should be taken into account. Policies ought to be stated in a straightforward, non-judgmental fashion. Avoid using a negative, legalistic tone. Policy writers should keep policies simple and have wording reviewed by parents.

Provide help to parents. Provide parents with information on where and how to apply for fee subsidies and/or information on receiving tax credits.

It takes thoughtful planning to set fee policies that are flexible enough to accommodate the needs of parents yet firm enough to protect the program from financial hardship.

EC PROGRAM FINANCIAL HEALTH FUNDAMENTALS

1. Enrolment of program is at capacity, with a waiting list in place.
2. Fees are based on the full cost of care.
3. Family fees are paid on time.
4. Program's bills and taxes are paid on time.
5. A cash reserve can cover operating expenses between one to three months.
6. Employ an adequate budgeting process.
7. Arrange for access to sufficient financial expertise.

Sources: M. Brower and T. Sull, "Five Fundamentals of Financial Health," in *Managing Money: A Center Director's Guidebook.* (Redmond, WA: Child Care Information Exchange, 1997); Additional suggestions made by Phil Cowperthwaite, 2010.

Collecting Parent Fees

Collecting parent fees is becoming increasingly challenging. Fee collection efforts can be hampered by a slow domestic economy; many families are finding it difficult to make ends meet each month. Fee collection will only get more difficult if the economy continues to stagnate. The most effective fee collection strategies are preventative. It is important for programs to act before unpaid fees become overwhelming for parents and families are unable to catch up. Following are a few preventative measures that may help:

Document and Communicate Policies and Rules
Does everybody involved in the collection process know the centre's policies and rules regarding debt monitoring and collection? Parents, the supervisor, and the board of directors all play key roles in fee collection, and it is important that these roles are documented and well understood. The basic collection policies for parents should be specified in the parent handbook/website. These policies include:

- frequency of payments (weekly, monthly)
- interest and other penalties, if any, to be levied on late payments
- method of payment (postdated cheques, cash, certified cheques in the event of NSFs)
- conditions resulting in withdrawal from the program

Parents should be made aware of the policies during the initial enrolment interview. Policies must be clearly outlined and documented to ensure that neither the board nor the supervisor is put in the position of having to make up rules as they go along. Consequences resulting from non-payment should be clearly communicated to be fair to parents and staff/board members. It is not suggested that policies and rules always be rigidly enforced. Rather, that clear written policies help make difficult situations more manageable and help reduce nasty surprises. Policies should also be set for the roles of the supervisor and the board. Policies should cover:

- responsibility for billing parents
- communication of fee increases
- maintenance of the accounts receivables
- information to be reported to the board
- action to be taken when fees outstanding are 30, 60, or 90+ days overdue
- steps to be taken if the receivables are due from board members or staff

Deviations from the policies should be discussed at the board level on a situation-by-situation basis and documented in the board minutes.

Building Financial Stability for Programs

Early childhood organizations tend to be small. Small businesses often do not have the financial stability or expertise necessary to take advantage of many financing strategies. Some EC programs form collectively to access a management services organization, where a group of programs consolidate administrative costs and operations. These organizations may function as purchasing alliances for insurance and benefits, perform other functions such as facilities management, and represent programs in contract negotiations. Another model is an administrative services organization, which is an entity that serves as a bridge between insurers and early childhood programs. Many insurers do not find it cost-effective to insure individual service organizations of less than 10 employees, which is the size of many early childhood programs. Administrative service organizations may perform a variety of functions, including enrolment of children in the program, eligibility determination for fee subsidy, finding providers for families, claims for staff benefits, payment of salaries, and other tasks. Finally, other small settings have developed joint marketing programs to gain new clients or take advantage of purchasing opportunities that may be too expensive for one program alone. These kinds of partnerships can help small programs look, act, and feel larger.

Shared Services

In many parts of Canada, early care and education (ECE) services are delivered by the private sector—in nonprofit and for-profit centers as well as thousands of home-based businesses. Most of these providers are very small, and many rely solely on tuition revenue. Third-party funding (to fill the price/quality gap) is scarce and often requires detailed accounting as well as compliance with quality standards often viewed as beyond the capacity of many small providers. Most early childhood directors don't have the skills of accountants or business managers; they are experts in child development, focused on the intimate work of educating and nurturing children. With limited resources and personnel to handle both program and administrative functions, both aspects of the program may suffer.

Market challenges and weak business platforms don't just hurt ECE programs, they hurt children and families as well. Without strong fiscal and program management, quality suffers: revenues decline and educators don't get the support they need to effectively guide children's behaviour, implement curricula, or offer additional child and family supports. In fact, some ECEs determine that they cannot continue to work without receiving a living wage. The bottom line is that EC finance isn't just about money; it's also about building an infrastructure and developing new approaches to ECE business management so that staff can focus on child development.

Across the United States, a select group of ECE leaders and funders are pioneering an innovative approach to strengthening the industry—ECE Shared Service Alliances, a community-based partnership model composed of centers and family child care homes working together to share costs and deliver services in a more streamlined and efficient way. By participating in a shared service alliance, EC businesses become stronger, more accountable, more financially sound and efficient, and better equipped to offer affordable, high quality services for children and their families.

Similarly, a group of family child care homes or providers who are not part of an agency can come together in a structure similar to a management services or administrative services organization. Providers can jointly contract for such administrative costs and operations as billing and fee collection, accounting, purchase of equipment and supplies, staff development, transportation, marketing, and so forth. These are but a few of the possibilities.

MARKETING STRATEGIES

Each setting (both centre based as well as individual providers) must pay attention to how it markets its program in order to maximize full enrolment. Families need to know of the program's existence and what kind of educational program is being

(continued)

offered. It is important to research the community, to identify unique features of the setting, to target potential families, and to get your program message out. Your message should inform prospective families of how your services could meet their needs. Things to consider:

- Determine what kind of early childhood supply and demand exists in the community.
- Is child care available for every family that needs it?
- What kinds of early childhood experiences, such as care for infants, are difficult for parents to find?
- Are there certain days or hours of care that are hard to find?
- Are there types of employment that make finding suitable child care challenging?
- Are there types of EC programs for which parents pay more in your community?

Among the considerations when marketing your program:

Project a professional image. Be thoughtful about the name chosen, logos used on internet sites, business cards or pamphlets. View the environment from a potential family's point of view. Is it attractive and welcoming? Does it provide a safe and clean learning environment?

Keep parents informed. Prospective parents are most comfortable with choosing arrangements based on the recommendations of programs from friends. Word of mouth by satisfied parents is the most important. Family resource centres or EC resource and referral services are key services to inform prospective parents of programs. Websites are increasingly being used to keep families informed of program activities.

Develop a high quality program. One of the most important features is having a high quality program that is staffed by professionally educated EC educators.

Marketing is an ongoing process that keeps potential families aware of the presence of the program and knowledgeable about what is being offered.

Family Child Care Budgets

Family child care providers are self-employed business operators. It is important to manage the business aspects of care. Some providers find dealing with the business aspect extremely stressful. Unit 8 of the *Family Child Care Training Program* (CCCF 2000a), "Financial Planning and Management," provides tremendous assistance in learning about budgeting. Some family child care providers follow a strict budget, divided into categories such as food, play materials and equipment, household supplies, administrative supplies, and wages for themselves and others. Consequently, they know exactly how much they have to spend on play equipment each year. If they decide to purchase a playground climber that costs more than their annual play materials budget, they may borrow from another budget category where they expect to underspend.

Other providers have no idea how much they spend each year on specific budget categories, but they have an intuitive sense of their overall budget. They know how much they can afford to spend and stay within budget guidelines. If they do not, they may go out of business. Revenue fluctuates for a variety of reasons, including under-enrolment, ill children, giving a discount to a family with more than one child, or bad debts, where a family leaves without paying the provider. It is wise to follow a budget closely. With this approach, even if the provider changes her plans about what is spent, there will be more financial security from knowing where to cut (or increase income) to make up for unexpected operating expenses. Once the business is operating with greater financial security, the provider can reduce the financial planning by keeping track of monthly expenses and comparing them to average monthly expenses.

Sixty percent of all providers spent between 30% and 59% of their income on child-related expenses such as food and toys (Doherty et al. 2000b). Thus, the net income before taxes of providers is considerably lower than their gross income. However, since they are treated as self-employed persons for tax purposes, on their tax return they can deduct business expenses and a portion of home maintenance costs when calculating the amount of income tax owed. In some communities, some provider annual incomes will be much higher as parents are able to pay competitive fees. For more information on this, check the website hosted by Canada Customs and Revenue Agency at www.ccra-adrc.gc.ca.

The chapter "The Business of Family Child Care" in the Family Child Care Training Program (CCCF 2000a) and Bush (2000) provide additional information on the development of budgets.

FAMILY CHILD CARE BUDGET

INCOME

- Parent fees
- Other

EXPENSES

- Food
- Children's toys and materials
- Field trip expenses
- Advertising
- Office supplies
- Copying
- Computer
- Income for provider
- Professional development
- Membership in professional organizations
- Postage
- Household supplies
- Maintenance and repairs
- Assistant caregiver wages
- Accountant
- Utilities
- Insurance (liability, accident, motor vehicle)

Parent Fees and Subsidy

It is essential that the family child care provider determine the rates parents will be charged before she or he searches for families. In some cases, the agency or licensing office (the office or agency primarily responsible for licensing centres and family child care agencies in individual provinces and territories) may set the rates. As with EC centre-based programs, fees need to be adequate to cover expenses for payments for personnel, food, toys, and equipment. Other factors that should be considered include average rates charged by other providers in the community, the training and experience of the provider, the quality of the program, and the number and ages of children in care. In addition to setting rates, providers should determine when they will review parent fees. This information should be included in the parent contract.

The majority of providers report that the fees charged to full-fee parents have risen over the past three years.

You Bet I Care! notes that, in most jurisdictions, fee subsidy for low-income parents is paid directly to the provider. In the agency model, the agency usually looks after fee subsidy claims for its providers. However, individually licensed providers have to handle this administrative task themselves. Seventy-one percent of licensed providers offered care for at least one child whose parents were receiving subsidy (Doherty et al. 2000b). Administering fee subsidies adds significantly to the individually licensed provider's workload.

Summary

Early childhood programs in Canada have become an important component in the social infrastructure that supports healthy child development, economic security for families, and social cohesion in communities. Handling the finances of these settings is complex. The program should delegate the responsibility for developing and carrying the financial plan to a competent financial director. The overall plan should be carried out by the EC director who has knowledge of accounting and budgeting procedures and, most importantly, an understanding of the requirements of a quality program for children and families.

Providing programs for young children is expensive. A quality program will cost $8000 or more per child per year for children younger than school age. Although families seldom pay the full cost of care, EC programs are a large expenditure in the family budget. To provide a quality program for children, programs must maximize limited resources and work to a plan that lays out the priorities of meeting children's needs. When seeking to balance their budgets, EC directors need to focus on the rate charged to families as well as having full enrolment and fee collection. Paying attention to these three sides of the iron triangle is the key to sound financial management. Most EC directors and family child care providers need more training and expertise in financial matters.

A program's ability to provide high quality services is strongly influenced by the characteristics of the staff—number, qualifications, ability, dispositions, compensation, and stability—and the characteristics of the environment. Each of these aspects is associated with costs and the need for adequate resources. Personnel costs are the largest component of an EC program budget.

Not providing a quality early childhood program passes the burden on to children and families, who ultimately pay the price of a lower quality program. In addition, ever-growing challenges in recruiting and retaining qualified staff are being experienced in a number of communities in Canada. However, like all good investments, an expenditure in quality early childhood programs for children will reap dividends that far outweigh the original cost.

Key Terms and Concepts

Accounts payable,   p. 258

Accounts receivable,   p. 258

Bad debt,   p. 259

Benefits,   p. 250

Budget,   p. 246

Cash flow,   p. 245

Cost-of-living adjustment (COLA),
   p. 259

Fee subsidy,   p. 249

Fixed costs,   p. 249

Incremental budgeting,   p. 248

Maintenance,   p. 249

Operating budget,   p. 246

Operations,   p. 246

Personnel policies,   p. 250

Revenue,   p. 245

Start-up budget,   p. 246

Variable costs,   p. 249

Activities

1. In order to increase awareness of the sources of income for a program budget, make arrangements to interview a director. Gather responses to the following questions:

    - What are the weekly rates for the following age groups: infants, toddlers, preschoolers, school-age children?

    - How much of the total budget is covered by parent fees?

    - What are other sources of funding (operating grants, wage enhancement grants, etc.)?

    - How much time do you spend monitoring spending on a weekly/monthly basis?

2. Investigate how community EC programs pay their employees (i.e., weekly or monthly, hourly wage or salary). Does the program prepare its own payroll, or does it use a service?

3. Review provincial/territorial funding programs available in your region. For which are EC programs eligible? What is the procedure for applying for funds?

4. Develop a detailed budget for a family child care program. Identify what items should be included.

5. Survey three programs in your community to determine the salary ranges for educators. Is there much difference? If so, why do you think there is a difference?

Recommended Reading

Bush, J. *Dollars and Sense: Planning for Profit in Your Child Care Business*. Albany, NY: Delmar, 2000.

Canadian Child Care Federation. *Family Child Care Training Program, Level 3*. Ottawa: Canadian Child Care Federation, 2003.

Copeland, T. *Family Child Care Marketing Guide: How to Build Enrollment and Promote Your Business as a Child Care Professional*. St. Paul, MN: Redleaf Press, 2007.

Morgan, G. and B. Emanual. *The Bottom Line for Children's Programs.* New Horizons, Mount Forest, 2010.

Jack, Gail, *The Business of Child Care: Management and Financial Strategies.* Delmar, NY, 2005.

 ## Weblinks

www.187gerrard.com
Cowperthwaite Mehta

Cowperthwaite Mehta provides administrative services to more than 150 non-profit organizations. This valuable website is designed specifically for community-based not-for-profit child-care centres. It has information on administration and management as well as the following categories: financial management, governance, technology, taxation, and registered charities, as well as child-care-specific information. There is a blog on implications of the Full Day Early Learning initiative in Ontario.

www.earlychildhoodfinance.org
Alliance for Early Childhood Finance

The Alliance for Early Childhood Finance is committed to ensuring that all American children have access to high quality early care and education services and the supports their families need to thrive as parents and workers. The Alliance was established to address the need for deeper, more comprehensive and sophisticated exploration of ECE finance by leading a national conversation, and to engage a wide range of stakeholders from government, business, philanthropy, as well as among the provider community and the families they serve.

They do not believe in a single "best" funding stream or program model. Their view is that ECE can—and should—tap a wide range of funds from many sources and that funds should flow to both programs (via grants or contracts) as well as to families (via portable subsidy in the form of vouchers, certificates, or tax benefits). This website is designed to serve as a library with downloadable copies of reports, memos, PowerPoint presentations, cost modeling spreadsheets, and other tools that we have created for government and non-profit agencies, foundations, and others.

www.cfc-efc.ca/wcfcca
Western Canada Family Child Care Association of BC

This site provides a wealth of information, including links to Child and Family Canada, current British Columbia legislation for operating a family child care home, and a list of resources— both print resources and community groups—for parents and providers.

Advocating for Canada's Children

chapter 10

Objectives

- Outline why advocacy is important.

- Examine the role of the EC educator in advocating for young children, families, and the profession.

- Define types of advocacy.

- Increase awareness of media portrayal of early childhood development.

- Describe the need for public education.

- Identify personal and collective approaches to advocating for early childhood services and the EC workforce.

- Identify the skills needed to promote an awareness of early childhood.

- Appreciating the benefits of collaborating with organizations in addressing issues of quality, compensation, and accessibility.

Why Is Advocacy Important?

The research is clear: The early years matter. Quality early childhood education and care makes a difference for young children. When it is done right, EC benefits families and communities as well as the children themselves. While the potential to change young lives is indisputable, realizing this potential through policies and programs is far from straightforward. A huge gulf exists between the often touted high quality program and the much larger number of barely good enough programs experienced by many children. Until all children in Canada have access to high quality, developmentally appropriate EC experiences and until all EC educators receive the education and financial support they require to ensure their commitment and competence, many advocates are needed to speak out on their behalf. Early childhood educators need to set aside their ambivalence about **advocacy**, work collaboratively with community partners, develop message strategies, and advocate for better resourcing. This chapter examines this public responsibility, suggests strategies to achieve it, and summarizes some advocacy success stories.

Appreciating the Challenges Facing Children and Families

To effectively advocate, educators require firsthand knowledge of the issues facing children, families, and staff. Campaign 2000, an advocacy group highlighted later in this chapter, rates the Canadian government's progress on eliminating child poverty each year. The information is summarized annually in report cards enabling EC practitioners to increase awareness of the issues facing families and children.

Campaign 2000, 2010 national report card shows that two decades after the government of Canada's House of Commons' unanimous resolution "to seek to achieve the goal of eliminating poverty among Canadian children by the year 2000," Canada has far to go to prevent and reduce poverty. The reports' key findings are as follows:

- One in 10 children still live in poverty in Canada today. It's worse for children living in First Nation's communities, where one in four grow up in poverty.

- Children of immigrants, of Aboriginal identity in racialized families, and of those with a disability are clearly at higher risk for poverty. This is often the result of persistent social and economic inequality which threatens social cohesion.

- There are more working poor: 40% of low-income children live in families where at least one parent works full-time year round, up dramatically from 33% in the 1990s.

- Child poverty is persistent across Canada: Rates of child and family poverty (low income cut-offs [LICO] before-tax) are in the double digits in most provinces.

- UNICEF minimum benchmarks recommend that 25% of children under three years and 80% of children aged three to five years should have access to ECEC. Yet, in Canada, there is still only limited coverage—percentage of children for whom a space is available—at only 20.3% for infants to five year olds.

These statistics belie the commonly held view of democracy that social justice provisions should be based on opportunity, that the state, in securing **social justice**, should provide a level playing field where individuals are protected from disadvantages such as poverty. Social justice is concerned with equal justice, not just in the courts, but in all aspects of society. This concept demands that all persons irrespective of ethnic origin, gender, possessions, race, religion, etc. have equal rights and opportunities. There are far ranging ideas about social justice, from the concept of justice as applied in the law, state-administered systems, which label behaviour as unacceptable and enforce a formal mechanism of control. As well there are the more informal concepts of justice embedded in systems of public policy and morality and which differ from culture to culture and therefore lack universality.

The UN recognizes education as a basic right. With research evidence from longitudinal studies and from neuroscience showing that children's earliest experiences being the most significant in determining their future progress in education and later success in life, then to level the field, young children must have access to these optimal EC experiences and a healthy home life.

**EARLY CHILDHOOD PROGRAMS FROM
A SOCIAL JUSTICE PERSPECTIVE:**

- all young children have access to good-quality learning opportunities;

- equal opportunities for all children are a prerequisite for social justice and requires that EC provisions compensate for early disadvantages;

- requires basic equity, a "level playing field," while recognizing that outcomes will vary;

- individuals have freedom to make choices while being protected from the worst effects of poverty and other adversities;

- acknowledges that the early years are the most significant in shaping children's future, and requires ensuring adequate provisions for learning and development.

Source: Siraj-Blatchford, I. and M. Woodhead. Early Childhood in Focus 4; Effective Early Childhood Programs, Bernard Van Leer Foundation, U.K., 2009.

There is a growing demand for EC services. This is being influenced by increased societal value on children's early learning, changing family structures, and labour force challenges. Moving from an array of loosely linked programs to a coherent system of early childhood has been a challenge in Canada. In parts of the country, regulated services are almost non-existent for parents working shifts and irregular hours, or for those needing part-time, seasonal, or emergency care. Specialized services for First Nations children, children with special needs, and other children from diverse backgrounds are often lacking. In some places, long waiting lists for fee subsidy exist alongside full-fee vacancies in established programs. The list of issues is long, and every item poses challenges. Many Canadians have little understanding of these crucial issues; necessary in order to affect government policies. It is critical to increase public awareness. The results will be:

- opportunities for all children to experience optimal early childhood development;

- happier, healthier, and more competent children;

- families who can concentrate on their jobs or studies, knowing that their children are well cared for;

- reduction in the stress many families are experiencing balancing work/family responsibilities by decreasing the number of settings/transitions needed by one family, or reduction in unnecessary travelling time for families;

- siblings who are able to see each other for parts of the day; and

- ultimately a stronger and more competent future workforce.

To increase public awareness and to help children to reach their fullest potential, children and families need adults who will speak out on their behalf—whether it is for better housing and safer communities, or opportunities for high quality EC experiences. This means EC educators have a dual role. First, to be the nurturers of young children providing the stimulating environments and experiences they need to thrive. Second, to translate their knowledge and strong commitment into advocating for these opportunities.

To reach their fullest potential, children and families need educators to speak out on their behalf.

Some important messages to communicate include:

- A child's experiences during the early years have the greatest influence of any time in the life cycle on brain development, learning, behaviour, and health. The quality of children's early years shapes their brain architecture, and affects their health and well-being throughout their lives. It is crucial that we have knowledgeable EC educators and responsive environments to support children's learning. The pathways and connections made in the brain during the early years affect the brain's capacity in future. Investments in early learning support later learning, and lead to greater success in school and throughout life.

- Research confirms that children's success in school and in life is dependent upon much more than expanded academic experiences. Effective EC programs are those in which educators implement developmentally appropriate curricula and assessment practices based on what is known about how children learn best across developmental domains, and they reflect the values and priorities of the children, their families, and the community.

- High quality EC services need to be maintained as well as expanded. The gap between supply and demand is significant. Many Canadians experience frustration and disappointment in their efforts to find suitable early childhood environments for their young child. For their minds to be at ease while they work or study, parents need settings that provide reassurance and inspire confidence. Learning environment that meets the needs of working families continues to be largely unavailable, unaffordable, or unsatisfactory; in some cases, all three problems exist. Even when a quality setting is located for one child in the family, the service may not offer care for the older or younger child in the family. In some situations two—or even three—arrangements are required to meet the needs of one family.

- The education of educators is a major determinant of how well children do in early childhood settings. One of the most important components of high quality programs is education and the ongoing professional development of the staff. Young children learn in different ways than older children. To thrive, young children need strong attachments with educators who:

    - have post-secondary education in early childhood development and are knowledgeable about young children's learning styles and needs;

    - understand the impact that culture, race, ethnicity, language, gender, family environment, and developmental abilities have on learning, and have the knowledge and skills to address the diverse needs of all children; and

    - are adequately compensated and supported in their work.

- High quality early learning and care is particularly important for children living in poverty, children with special needs, recent immigrants, and children in minority communities. These experiences gives them opportunities to develop the foundational knowledge and skills, resilience, and emotional maturity they need to succeed in school and society. It is equally important for children from stable, advantaged families who experience negative effects if programs do not provide responsive, stimulating environments. Family income and support from home is not enough to compensate for poor early learning and care experiences.

- Early childhood programs are envisioned as neighbourhoods of the twenty first century, poised to transform the cultural ills of society through mutually respectful and empowering relationships. Places where social justice exists and that all children and families have the right to expect mutual respect, fair treatment, equal access to resources, and opportunities to learn about others' perspectives.

- Early childhood development is not only a concern of an individual family. It affects the economy and society as a whole. Employers are increasingly aware and, in some cases, attempting to respond to the problems that arise when families are unable to make adequate arrangements for their children.

The Centre for Spatial Economics (2010) found that early learning provides a greater economic benefit for the country's financial health than any other sector. Furthermore, it found that early learning experiences is associated with improved academic achievement and higher future employment earnings. Higher tax revenues are generated by the enhanced employment earnings of parents today and the future earnings of their children. These results make EC a great investment for governments.

Taking on an Advocacy Role

Many early childhood educators see the political arena as a foreign world in which they feel ill at ease and unequipped to participate. They often prefer to leave lobbying and advocacy to the experts. However, EC educators have valuable information to contribute. Early childhood professionals are often in the position of hearing the concerns of parents or noticing a condition that may negatively impact a child's growth and development. Therefore, they have an ethical responsibility to work in partnership with families to create conditions that will foster optimal development for all children. Without the educators's insights and expertise of children and families, elected officials can make uninformed decisions that could have a detrimental impact.

Child advocacy is political or legislative activism—by parents, professionals, or other interested groups—who urge the consideration of social issues affecting children. It is a personal commitment to active involvement in the lives of children, beyond remunerated professional responsibilities, with the goal of enhancing the opportunities for children to achieve optimal growth and development. Early childhood educators have a responsibility to become activists for children and families. Activism does not imply radicalism, only a firm belief in the value of early childhood development and a commitment to influence children's lives for the better.

When educators become child advocates, they move beyond the boundaries of their immediate employment situations into the greater society. They must overcome feelings of powerlessness, which are related to the low value sometimes placed on the profession by the public and lack of public understanding of the importance of early childhood development. There are many misunderstandings about what EC practitioners do. Feelings of powerlessness can also stem from poor compensation. The Child Care Human Resource Sector Council's project on Career Promotions (2009) found that only a few staff felt that their job was respected by the general public. As advocates, early childhood educators must overcome a lack of knowledge of the intricate workings of government and fear of the political process.

There are several additional reasons why EC educators tend to be ambivalent about advocacy. More often than not, individuals entering the field of early childhood see children as the prime focus of their work. They believe curriculum planning and relationships with children are their chief responsibilities. After they begin to work, some recognize that in order to fully understand children, they need to understand the families of these children. That the well-being of children is connected to the well-being of their families, and that this involves some complex issues such as poor housing and poverty. Some may be cynical and believe that political action is fruitless. Others question the use of political forces for child advocacy. Kaiser and Sklar Rasminsky (1999) observed "we may feel safer inside the familiar world of the centre with the children and parents."

It is necessary to incorporate advocacy into one's professional self-image and role, envisioning advocacy as a problem-solving tool. When governments shift priorities, reduce funding, or do not take action, there is a profound impact on the quality of EC service that is provided and long-term consequences for society.

BUILDING A CASE FOR ADVOCACY

Advocates are people who stand up for, speak for, and work to enhance the lives of others who are not able—or not yet able—to speak for themselves. Advocacy is often highly visible and plays out on the local, national, or international stage. But just as often, advocacy is quiet and personal and is immediately noticed by only those most affected. Yet, a seemingly small act of advocacy can create a ripple effect that reaches beyond its immediate purpose, joins with the actions of others, and affects the destiny of many.

Listed below are some of the objectives to which advocacy initiatives may be directed:

- Working for equality and social justice.
- Informing the public about early childhood issues and the impact of public policy on children, families, and communities.
- Increase service capacity, enhance program quality, or demonstrate that a new idea or program type can increase quality or accessibility.

- Strengthen the infrastructure of the field, making early childhood programs of better quality, more accessible, affordable, and equitable.

- Mobilizing families and communities to speak up and speak out for early childhood.

- Encouraging early childhood educators to exercise their democratic right to unionize.

Different Roles: What Type of Advocate Do You Want to Be?

- Some advocates will be **leaders**—people who provide vision, motivate, and keep the advocacy efforts on track.

- Some advocates will be **advisors**—people who share their expertise with the policy makers who are in a position of influence and can bring about change to the status quo.

- Some advocates will be **researchers**—people who can collect data and synthesize research reports into issue briefs and background papers.

- Some advocates will be **"contributors"**—those people who are willing to roll up their sleeves and participate in the nuts-and-bolts work of advocacy, from e-mailing, making phone calls to stuffing letters or marching in front of the provincial government.

- Some advocates will be **friends**—people who do not have the time or resources to participate in every aspect of the planning and implementation of advocacy, yet who care and can always be counted on to help when a push is needed.

Given the urgent need for advocacy for young children and their families, how does an early childhood educator go about this? Three types of advocacy—personal, professional, and informational—are described below.

Personal advocacy can be as straightforward as helping a neighbour understand what you do at your job. The quote "Be the change that you want to see in the world" by Mahatma Gandhi comes to mind when describing personal advocacy. It is vital that early childhood educators understand the important role that they are playing, that they have pride in what they do, and that by providing high quality care in a professional manner they are demonstrating to families the types of experiences that they should expect and demand for their children during the early years. The delivery of poor quality care is the antithesis of personal advocacy. You have to not just be able to "talk the talk" you need to also "walk the walk." It is also based on the way EC educators carry out their daily practice and communicate with others. For example, if someone refers to an EC practitioner as a "babysitter," gently and firmly correct them. Help friends to understand why providing a quality learning program for children costs as much as it does. Enlighten them on the critical importance of the early years for learning; explain how early experiences benefit children.

The more educators learn about the importance of child development and appropriate practices, the more they will resist pressure to accept less than optimal environments in early childhood settings. Keeping informed and making changes to improve children's health and well-being is part of personal advocacy.

Personal advocacy is generally carried out on one's own time. Some employers, such as public institutions, do not support advocacy efforts by employees. In such situations, make it clear that you are speaking as a citizen, not as a public employee.

Professional advocacy is often called "lobbying." Like personal advocacy, its aim is to benefit the profession and the children and families it serves. This type of advocacy attempts to challenge and reform public systems that affect children and families and is directed toward policy development, legislative, administrative, and budgetary processes. Advocacy efforts tend to vary in scope, from addressing the needs of an individual, such as helping a family access services for a child with special needs, to protecting all children. You could work toward something that may benefit the larger community such as a family literacy centre.

One early advocate who tirelessly lobbied all three levels of government to attain universal child care for all Canadian families and children was Pat Schultz. She was a single mother who experienced the difficulties of acquiring affordable child care for her young daughter. She alleged that "even if the rulers sleep a little less comfortably in their beds, then it (advocacy) was worth every minute!" The National Film Board of Canada made a film about her work called Worth Every Minute.

Informational advocacy, or educative advocacy, is directed to raising public awareness of the importance of the period of early childhood and the capacity of high quality programs to strengthen families and provide opportunities for optimal growth and development of young children.

Educators can provide information to families at their own program about cost and benefits of quality early experiences. Some families send their child to a program because of convenience rather than the superb programs offered. They may take quality for granted, or they may assume that because a service is regulated then it is also of high quality. This is not necessarily be true. However, once they have a real understanding of what good ECEC is and its importance for their child's future, they will more likely demand it—both from the program and from the government. Families have a large influence on policy, through their votes and by speaking out. Helping parents become effective advocates for their children is imperative. Whenever issues related to early childhood development are reported in the media, articles should be posted for parents to access as examples of the informational advocacy approach. These communications help foster environments of informed families who can carry these concerns to larger networks.

Developing an Advocacy Agenda

When you commit yourself to being an advocate for the creation of environments that support optimal child development, there is a lot of work ahead. The task isn't simple. The best place to start is in your own program. This next section lays out the steps involved in being an effective advocate.

1. Increase Staff Awareness Regarding Advocacy

At staff meetings, directors and staff can provide regular updates on concerns facing the field, on advocacy campaigns report on meetings attended, and share information and resources. Staff should be encouraged to join professional and advocacy groups. The governing board can be encouraged to contribute to professional development opportunities and/or involvement with early childhood organizations for staff. Directors can inspire and recognize the importance of staff participating. These collective efforts can build bonds among the staff and a sense of solidarity with other concerned people. The action taken by young parents in the Prospects for Young Families in Toronto Project demonstrates the feelings of empowerment that can be achieved by collective action.

Case Study

Prospects for Young Families in Toronto Project

This group worked to improve circumstances faced by young families. Data was collected and compared with information from a similar study conducted a decade ago. Statistics showed that between 1981 and 2001, poverty rates for young families in Toronto jumped by an alarming 56%. During the same period, the median income for these families fell by more than 20%, representing a much larger decline than that of older families. Clearly, decision makers were not hearing what young families needed and ensuring that they got it. The project organizers recognized that parents know what they need to support their children and themselves, and this initiative gave them the opportunity to express their ideas, hopes, and frustrations about how to improve their quality of life. A variety of family structures were represented: single parent families, aboriginal families, newcomer families, same-sex couples, and adolescent parents. Their insights and experiences are a testament to their commitment to building a future for their children. To endeavour to change these patterns, a number of community-based organizations met with 58 young parents (under 35) to see how they were doing socially and economically and to explore their experiences and ideas on:

- improving opportunities for young families
- barriers to employment such as lack of child care, education, and training
- managing the system for those living on social assistance
- finding safe and affordable housing
- accessing adequate and appropriate health care

The families involved with the Prospects for Young Families in Toronto Project were brimming with ideas about how to effect change and are ready to put their energies into action. Many of the recommendations outlined in the project's final report (Wilson 2004) came from the ideas put forward by these families. Several parents who participated in the project are involved with other groups advocating for changes to housing, income security, and child care policies. Some participated in the media conference to release the reports produced by the project and are pressing for action on the recommendations contained in them. Decision makers are listening. In the days following the release of the project's reports, the Mayor of Toronto said he supported one of the key recommendations made by the Prospects report—to convene a "summit on good jobs." There is no doubt that the city's young parents will be watching to ensure that policy makers at all levels of government follow through on these ideas, stop the downward spiral facing them, and improve the quality of life for Toronto's young families.

Michele Lupa, Coordinator

Growing Up Healthy Downtown

(a partnership of multi-service agencies, part of the Family Service Association of Toronto)

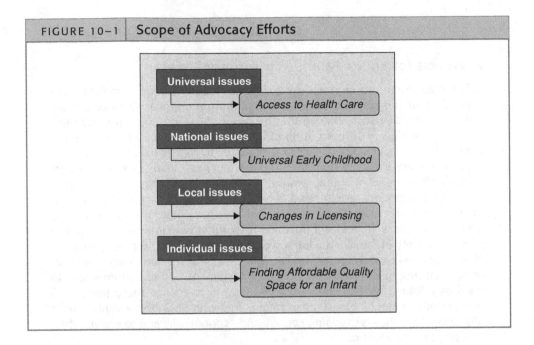

FIGURE 10–1 | Scope of Advocacy Efforts

2. Establish Your Priorities

There are many issues needing attention and it is easy to feel overwhelmed. Any successful advocacy campaign begins with a clear goal. As citizens, we hope and expect that elected officials will do a reasonably good job of governing. However, it has been apparent for some time that there are many unresolved issues related to our chosen field, including health, housing, and child poverty. Figure 10-1 depicts the scope of advocacy efforts from a focus on the individual to those which are universal. Certain issues by their nature are priorities such as child safety. There are times when it is easier or more difficult to make incremental progress. Public policy is development and advanced in the context of political climate, social climate, and the economic environment of the province or Canada. As well, know what are the priorities of the elected officials? This can shape what may shape the setting of your priorities.

In defining the issue, it is important to propose solutions as well as protest problems. It is necessary to identify small, incremental goals. It is less daunting to try to achieve small goals, and results are easier to measure.

Issue 1—What is the impact on families when they don't have access to high quality EC programs? Children, especially those from low-income families, need better access to affordable, high quality EC programs. Many programs are mediocre, offering few opportunities for children to develop the skills and knowledge they need to succeed in school or later in life. Average fees often exceed the cost of attending post secondary programs, and only a small percentage of children eligible for subsidy are being served. This impedes families working or attending school. Families suffer, but more importantly, society suffers. Children are citizens with rights who enrich our communities now. They will also become the workforce and leaders of tomorrow. When children have the opportunity to develop to their full potential, all of society benefits.

Issue 2—What is the connection between educators' salaries and the quality of EC experience that children receive?

Educators who are better compensated tend to stay longer in their jobs. Consequently, they can form consistent relationships with the children and foster in them the emotional stability that they need to learn and grow. Parents also value the consistency and continuity of practitioners. When families experience high turnover, they feel it has a negative impact on children. Too many highly qualified, experienced, well-educated teachers have left the profession because they cannot afford to stay at current wages. Additionally, poor salaries impede the ability of the field to attract the best candidates.

Issue 3—What does an educationally-oriented EC program look like?

A high quality early learning and care program is one that meets the needs of all children and parents, and values educators. In a quality program:

- Children feel accepted and supported by the adults. They form positive relationships with adults and other children, and participate in interesting play-based activities that help them explore the environment, experiment, discover language and ideas, and solve problems.

- Parents feel their involvement, culture, and values are respected. Their children—including children with special needs—have opportunities to learn, play, develop skills, and achieve their full potential.

- Educators are valued and respected. They form cooperative and supportive relationships with colleagues and supervisors. The work environment and working conditions contribute to job satisfaction and pride in their work, and they have opportunities for ongoing learning and career development.

3. Gather the Facts

After an issue has been chosen, it must be presented in a convincing way. Sharing firsthand knowledge about the issues you are working to address builds your credibility. Nothing is more persuasive to a politician than a compelling story that demonstrates the importance of the work. For this, information is needed. Before one can speak confidently and capably about the issues facing families and their children in a changing and demanding society, one must understand the issues and be able to articulate them clearly in one's own mind. One must be aware of the research and gather facts, placing them in a coherent order, and drawing conclusions from them.

You can read about current EC policy issues and about how well solutions are grounded in research in reports such as those put out by organizations such as the Vanier Institute of the Family. They work with other organizations, offering insight and statistics on policy issues that affect young children and families. Become familiar with the many policy organizations that evaluate and analyze EC issues and typically put forward a policy plan or set of initiatives they feel will improve the status of the field.

Advocates should be familiar with key pieces of research and long-term studies and use them in their work. For example, the National Research Council report *From Neurons to Neighborhoods: The Science of Early Childhood Development* has been a touchstone for explaining the importance of children's health, social, and emotional development from birth and the importance of an integration of physical health, emotional development, early screening and interventions, child-adult relationships, and family involvement and education. For advocates and policy makers, *Neurons to Neighborhoods* underscores the importance of promoting children's development, starting prenatally, through resources and policies that provide a range of child and family supports.

A second key piece of research is the HighScope Perry Preschool Study, one of the longest-running studies of early childhood education. Beginning in the 1960s, researchers looked at children from low-income families at high risk for school failure. One group attended a high quality preschool program at ages three and four, while the comparison group did not. Researchers then followed up with both groups of children every year from ages 3 to 40. In 2005, HighScope released the study report, *Lifetime Effects: The HighScope Perry Preschool Study,* demonstrating significant lasting advantages in education, employment, and social outcomes for the children who attended the preschool program over 35 years after the program ended.

Campaign 2000 is a cross-Canada public education movement to build Canadian awareness and support to end child poverty in Canada by the year 2000. Campaign 2000 began out of concern about the lack of government progress in addressing child poverty. Campaign 2000 is non-partisan in urging all Canadian elected officials to keep their promise to Canada's children.

They work to increase public awareness of the levels and consequences of child/family poverty by publishing research on the indicators of child poverty and developing public education resources. Their annual national Report Card on Child Poverty in Canada measures the progress or the lack of progress on eliminating poverty among Canadian children. Discussion papers contain a set of proposals for public policies and social investments based on the life cycle approach to addressing child poverty.

Campaign 2000 is involved in public and government consultations around the issue of child and family poverty and government policy. They lobby all parties in both federal and provincial governments for improved social policies relating to the national child benefit, social housing, child care, labour market supports, community services, and other relevant policy areas.

Build on the deep public concern about this issue by engaging local communities to examine child poverty and children's well-being through presentations, displays, and forums and publications.

Another key organization is the Childcare Resource and Research Unit, which collects, organizes, and synthesizes EC resources and makes them widely available. Their web-based resources include policy developments, demographic fact sheets, information kits, bibliographies, and background papers. (The website address is included later in the chapter.)

A number of organizations, such as the Vanier Institute of the Family and Canadian Policy Research Networks, conduct research on child and family issues. The Vanier publishes comprehensive reports profiling the Canadian family and contemporary issues they face. When using research to guide policy recommendations and make persuasive arguments, it is important to critically investigate the information used.

Educators can subscribe to these organizations' websites and should monitor the media to be aware of current issues and how the issue was reported. By tracking who was interviewed and the names of reporters who cover the issue, one can identify potential allies. Most reporters will gladly listen to an insider's point of view. Once you have shown that you are informed and articulate, they might repeatedly call upon your expertise. It is also important to be familiar with those who have opposing viewpoints. Understanding their arguments helps increase your effectiveness when responding to their concerns. However, it is not enough to get quoted in the news; it must be portrayed in a way that lets policy makers know what they must do to improve the situation. How the story is covered has a huge impact on how the public and policy makers perceive and address it. The publication *Making the Case for Early Childhood Education and Care: A Message Development Guide for Advocates* (Dorfman et al. 2004) provides invaluable information to enable success.

4. Work Collaboratively

The challenges faced in providing optimal development opportunities for children are multi-faceted. They require the involvement and coordination of numerous groups in all levels of government, private sector organizations, and related professions. Policy advocacy can be most effective when groups work together in a coalition. The most powerful coalitions are often those that combine groups that are traditionally not seen as direct stakeholders in the advocacy effort. As noted previously, there are numerous groups that advocate for quality early childhood programs. A climate of deregulation and funding cuts serve as powerful motivators for those concerned with children and families to be involved in public policy. Public policy **advocates** endeavour to change policies, practices, and budgets to make them more responsive to children's and families' needs.

Any advocacy campaign has a greater chance of success when it has a broad base of support. Broadening the base of support to include groups such as health, educational professionals and the business community is essential if widespread public understanding and support for high quality, inclusive EC programs is to be attained. A method of forming a coalition is to identify other groups that have some or all of the same interests. As long as there is some common objective shared by all the groups, the potential exists to form a coalition. In the past decade, the field has gained strong allies such as the Canadian Paediatric Society, the Canadian Teachers' Federation, Family Service Canada, and the National Council on Crime Prevention, to name a few.

The Coalition of Child Care Advocates of BC, the Child Care Coalition of Manitoba, New Brunswick Child Care Coalition, and The Ontario Coalition for Better Child Care are among organizations of interested citizens—parents, early childhood educators, community organizations, and labour organizations who work to increase public awareness. They are non-partisan political action groups working to bring the benefits of early childhood education and care to the attention of the public and policy makers.

They achieve this through:

- Monitoring provincial early childhood policy and legislation.

- Lobbying for changes and improvements.

- Developing policy alternatives for government consideration to improve the quality, accessibility, and management of early childhood services.

- Developing resources and news bulletins on EC policy for use by early childhood education programs, parents, and the general public.

- Conducting public information campaigns through written material, videos, public service announcements, public speaking, and by working with the media.

- Conducting and commissioning research.

- Participating in advisory committees, task forces, community planning bodies, and early childhood development associations.

In Newfoundland and Labrador, the EC community is experiencing many of the same challenges with regard to the EC sector found elsewhere in Canada. Within the sector, many staff are well educated and professional in their work, yet experience low wages, limited benefits, demanding and often poor working conditions, and a lack of recognition for the value of the work they do.

In Newfoundland and Labrador, key stakeholders came together to develop a comprehensive recruitment and retention strategy to support the EC sector. They obtained funding through the Canada-Newfoundland and Labrador Labour Market Development Agreement to research and make recommendations. Key findings were that people were attracted to the work because of the satisfaction and reward of contributing to the early development of children. Consequently, they experienced job satisfaction and commitment. At the same time, many reported that they could not earn a living wage and that often forced them to leave the field.

Their report concluded that "transformational change" is required to build and strengthen the EC workforce and this required that the stakeholders collaborate to reach solutions. The research identified that few professional development opportunities were available that are relevant for administrators, directors, and others in lead positions. Who, although having significant experience, needed to develop the skills and knowledge to provide leadership on human resources. The Early Childhood Education Human Resource Council was created developing a number of strategies including the development of a human resource manual.

These findings mirror those in other communities with investments required to strengthen EC leadership as discussed in Chapter 3 "Leadership and Governance in Early Childhood Programs" as well as the aforementioned importance of collaboration.

Nontraditional Partners to Consider

Since parents are a child's first advocates, they often make good advocates for all children in the community. Organized, parents are a very powerful voice. Parents are also an authentic voice seeking quality child care and school reform. Public officials often treat parents not only as concerned citizens, but also as influential constituents.

Having professionals in other fields such as health or law enforcement as partners shows that your agenda is not motivated by self-interest. Such professionals can provide more data, expert witnesses on a range of topics, and connections to other families and community leaders.

Community- and faith-based organizations, especially those that provide human or social services, often share the same concerns and can strengthen advocacy efforts by such activities as disseminating information through their networks.

Business leaders can be strong allies in advocacy efforts. When business leaders speak, people—especially policy makers—listen. The public's perception is that business leaders understand good investments. They often have political and media contacts that early childhood education advocates have not been able to reach or convince.

Labour unions have taken on issues of pay equity and workplace conditions that intersect with early childhood education concerns. Several unions have a long history of working on public policies to support well funded, quality child care and public schools and paid family leave. They have a history of advocating for better pay, family and medical leave, and other social issues at the state and national level. Unions bring unique skills such as how to organize people, recruiting new members to rallying members around an activity or issue. They conduct polling and focus groups and often have access to media that can enlarge advocacy efforts.

This work can be spearheaded with key organizations such as the Child Care Advocacy Association of Canada (CCAAC) that pursue issues at the federal level and attempt to promote a broad consensus of support within all regions of Canada. Membership includes representatives from education, health care, labour, child welfare, rural, First Nations, Francophone, social policy, anti-poverty, professional, student, and women's organizations.

5. Take Action

A fundamental step in developing an advocacy strategy is to figure out who do we need to target to help us reach our goal. The answer to this question may involve several target audiences. Which jurisdiction does the concern in question fall (federal, provincial, or local)? Pinning responsibility where it belongs can be more complicated than one might expect. Sometimes demands must be presented to two levels of government, such as provincial/territorial and municipal governments. Building allies may involve the MP, MPP or MLA, the media that could help build support for the concern, and other groups that could add strength in numbers. Identify individuals who have responsibility for an issue. You want to build rapport and trust with by becoming a reliable source of information for those elected representatives who are sympathetic to the concerns of children and families. Look at your community and find out how the government structure will enable you to have input into municipal, regional, provincial, and federal decision making on early childhood issues. Keep them informed through sending articles, research that highlights important findings. Extend invitations for them to visit your program or speak at conferences. Of course, ensuring that you vote in elections is an essential step!

CHECKLIST: KEY QUESTIONS WHEN IDENTIFYING A TARGET

Who has the power to solve the problem and pass the desired policy?

Who has the power to influence the target person or institution? (Voters, consumers, taxpayers?)

What is their interest? For example, if the person or institution is elected, they will want to know how many voting parents are in their constituency?

---

6. Enlist More Child Advocates by Informing Others

A key task is to be heard by the right group. Advocates direct their lobbying toward decision makers. Decision makers can range from heads of government to ministers to families to boards of directors. Politicians are decision makers. They need to hear from voters before they will put an issue at the forefront of policy. Policy can be changed through pressure applied by large groups of voters. Task force committees, commissions, and public hearings present opportunities to communicate policy recommendations and respond to government policy initiatives and budget allocations. Position papers and briefs outline each group's perspective and recommendations on a particular issue.

There are a number of ways in which advocates can convey these messages. It is essential to get accurate images of the field of early childhood to the public and government. This requires personal efforts and professional supports.

Membership in a professional and/or advocacy organization provides an effective channel for communication with the public and to government. Many local, provincial, and national groups are actively involved in public education and advocacy efforts, and it is beneficial to be aware of the objectives of these groups and to work with them. (Provincial early childhood organizations are listed in the appendix.)

Individuals you might talk with about your program include legislators, members of the business community, politicians, media representatives, parents, and other professionals.

Write or e-mail the minister responsible for young children, the member of parliament for the riding where you work or reside, your provincial representative (MLA), and/or your municipal councillor. Contact MPs in the Opposition—they long to hear of voter dissatisfaction and welcome ideas, particularly near election time. Describe your program, explaining the service it provides for children and families. Take the opportunity to explain the support you require in order to improve the service. Politicians are interested in knowing the number of children served by the program and their ages. It is useful to have photographs of the children engaged in positive activities. Encourage pre-arranged visits to the program. Include families and staff in presentations.

Remember, no one strategy will work. Each advocacy experience is unique because the people and issues involved vary. Advocates must be prepared to use a variety of techniques and be persistent. Change takes time, and developing any new skill takes time. Some people have special areas of interest. People should take on the jobs they are most comfortable doing. Some will be speakers, others writers, planners, researchers, or envelope stuffers. Each role is necessary and valid.

Using the Power of Social Media for Advocacy

Over 80% of Canadians used the internet in 2009, with three-quarters of them using e-mail every day. These new communication techniques have a powerful influence on the ways people connect with each other. Everyday millions of people log onto social media websites to keep tabs on their friends and to get their daily news fix. Social media websites, like Facebook and Twitter, have become so popular that it's almost unfathomable to not have a Facebook profile. Leading Early Childhood organizations such as the National Association for the Education of Young Children, (NAEYC), the Canadian Child Care Federation (CCCF), and the Child Care Advocacy Association of Canada (CCAAC) are using these sites. The pervasiveness of social media has caught the attention of advertisers as well as, becoming a way for EC advocacy groups, and politicians to reach more people in the shortest amount of time.

Social media enables the user to customize their profile to create the persona they want. EC organizations choose which images to put up, what information to include, what groups to join, and what pages to become fans of. They provide space where they can share their thoughts. Because users generally want to show themselves as "good" people, EC advocacy groups use that intent to gain more public attention. For example, if Julie joins a child advocacy group on Facebook, the information is posted on her profile and on her news feed (a summary of new information from all her friends that is posted on the homepage after logging in). If Julie may have 200 friends who see that she's joined the group and maybe Julie invited some of her friends to also join this child advocacy group. If even just 10 of Julie's friends join the group, the information will show up on their news feed and reach friends that Julie doesn't have. If more than one friend of Julie's joins and her friend, Istvan, who joined the group, on the newsfeed it will say that both Julie and Istvan joined a child advocacy group, which may prompt some people to check out the group and perhaps also join since it seems to be popular with their friends. And the cycle can continue.

The ability to attract hundreds or thousands of people's attention is a great advantage for EC advocacy groups. Although people may want to project a "good" persona online, they generally also want to be "good" people in real life as well. Someone wouldn't join a group unless they believed in its cause and they may have never had a chance to know that the group existed without being a user of social media. Advocacy groups know that in order to get more involvement from people, then they have to make it as easy as possible for them and it doesn't get much easier that a click of a button. Unfortunately, that's also where many people think the advocacy also ends. Once they've joined that advocacy group, they feel like they've done their part to raise awareness. And this is not the case.

Using social media for advocacy can be a double-edged sword. Advocacy groups are able to get their message out into the internet world to millions of people, but trying to get those people to do more than just support their cause by being part of their group is a challenge. Part of the challenge is that there is a fine line between becoming irrelevant and just plain annoying by spamming the members to the point where they unjoin. Facebook users are inundated with groups they could join, and it's challenging for a user to be up to date with the events of any one group unless they received updates on the news feed or messages from the group. If any one group sends too few messages or rarely updates their page, they will be forgotten. Users might not feel as strongly for their cause as they once did, and if they send too many messages/spam or update too frequently, users may end up leaving the group to avoid getting the messages. Either way, it results in the messages not being read and promptly deleted or skipped over. The same problem can occur with Twitter where you microblog in 140 characters or less.

Some people may argue that the internet and social media have created an apathetic society where no one cares strongly about anything. These concerns have plagued advocacy groups in the past. People sign up to become members of a group and don't bother reading the newsletters they're sent in the mail or people can't be bothered to be stopped on the street to sign a petition or listen to the issues. It's especially hard in because everyone has a cause he or she is fighting for. It's difficult for people to decide what is worthy of their time and energy. Some groups have resorted to very sensationalistic tactics in order to get people's attention and, not surprisingly, it works because they get more media attention, but it may also weaken their credibility.

So what can advocacy groups in this technological age do to incite more people to get involved? Is it possible to make participation any easier than a click of a button? Should advocacy groups be satisfied that their cause is getting more awareness with social media? It is difficult to gauge the power of the internet. Advocates cannot remain in the virtual world without conducting additional activities. Advocacy groups must encourage people to participate in grass roots lobbying through many different channels, including social media. They should form coalitions with other groups that are supporting the same causes.

Using Technology to Advantage

- Send a draft blog entry to all bloggers in your membership
- Interview advocates for your podcast
- Start a petition (www.thepetitionsite.com or set up your own)
- Befriend elected officials on Facebook
- Sign up for legislators feeds on Twitter
- Start a poll (Google Survey; Polls Everywhere)

Advocates use social media to influence public perception of components of quality EC.

Source: Photo courtesy of David Hoang

NAEYC's Facebook fan page was created to reach current and potential members, educators, parents, families, and the general public. On their fan page, you'll find the latest announcements and new content and be able to connect around events, photo sharing, and other media.

The Need for Public Education

The concept of EC as a public good and integral part of societal infrastructure appears to be approaching a threshold of acceptance. Policy makers and others who historically expressed little interest in the EC field have begun systems building efforts in many provinces. The actual work of implementing these systems changes requires leadership from the EC field. There are many misconceptions about early childhood education and the needs of Canadian families. Generally, the public does not understand what is involved and therefore do not see the need for specialized professional education. A few continue to believe that a mother's involvement in the workforce will harm her children. Some Canadians question their tax dollars being spent on programs for children and ask why these services are so expensive. There is a need to focus on how early childhood programs help children achieve their full potential and how they benefit the economy by enabling parents to stay in the workforce.

The concerted public and government education effort that is needed to achieve comprehensive, high quality early childhood environments in Canada is hampered, in part, by non-standardized nomenclature in the field. For example, there is little consensus on what we should call ourselves: "early childhood educators," "child care workers," "caregivers," "early childhood professionals," or "providers," to mention a few.

The public's image of EC development needs clarification and improvement. Highly knowledgeable and committed educators are crucial for the delivery of quality programs for children. A very high proportion of staff love the day-to-day aspects of their job. However, the Child Care Human Resources Sector Council's project on Career Promotions (2006) also found poor morale, the potential for high turnover rates, and a lack of awareness of career options.

The perception of being undervalued or not respected contributes to poor staff morale and high turnover and impedes recruitment of new practitioners into the field. There continues to be profound misconceptions about what early learning and care practitioners do. Many current and potential educators are unaware of the potential career paths available in the early childhood sector. As a result, people who would make excellent educators do not consider careers in early learning and care.

There is an urgent need for a public information campaign that ties the increasing evidence of the importance of the early years to recognizing the value of the people who work in early childhood. As discussed in Chapter 1, practitioner education in early child development is linked to high quality care.

Practitioners with appropriate education deserve to receive adequate compensation. It is well known that the compensation that EC professionals receive is the major challenge of the profession. EC professionals' work makes a huge contribution to the economy, and to the well-being and social awareness of future generations. Yet for many ECEs, their remuneration reflects little of this value to society. Instead, early childhood educators have often had their already inadequate salaries frozen. In tracking fees that programs charge to parents and wages they pay to staff members, fees generally have not risen as fast as the cost of living; and accordingly, wages in many cases remain low and may actually be heading in the wrong direction.

The true cost of providing quality EC experiences continues to be poorly understood. Public education campaigns help to garner increased public support for the investment of government funds in early childhood, the education of young children, and adequate remuneration for educators and family child care providers.

The governments of Manitoba, Alberta, and Quebec have each undertaken public education campaigns to attract back educators who have left the field, as well as made attempts to improve compensation to keep more individuals in the field of EC. Newfoundland/Labrador put in incentives such as a $5000 bursary with a two-year return-in-service agreement for new graduates as well as a $1200 bursary to cover the costs of the requisite summer institute for distance education ECE students. As well, campaigns such as the Parade of Promises by Nova Scotia's Child Care Connection NS draw attention to the value of the work itself and the need for improved compensation. The public becomes informed of the wide discrepancies between the responsibilities and skills required to do the job and the compensation levels. In order for these efforts to succeed, all EC educators must make it their business to understand the issues and solutions—more government support and greater public education—and recruit others to join the undertaking.

Framing Media Portrayal of Early Childhood

The internet, television, radio, newspapers, and magazines are powerful influences. An earlier approach to stories in the media was the framing of government support for EC as a necessity and a support to working parents rather than as a child development issue. Consequently, parents rather than children were portrayed as the key benefactors of EC. More recently, the message emphasizes early childhood education as a social benefit for all children, particularly for poor children. Another message is that child care is an economic benefit for parents enabling them to work or study. This serves as a desired message for employers who have access to a broader base of talented employees. For society, good and available early childhood experiences have the ultimate potential of enlarging the tax base and creating more prosperous communities. Robert Fairholm (2009) from the Centre for Spacial Economics found that investing in full-day kindergarten for four- and five-year olds will result in a boost for the government's economy. He had similar findings in the Workforce Shortages project for the Child Care Human Resources Sector Council. In addition to benefitting children, this investment is a job creator and provides a payback through better health outcomes, reduced social costs, and higher future employment earnings. Not only is it important that we keep early childhood in the news, it is critical that we are sending the right message—that high quality child care benefits children, families, and communities.

Strategies to Achieve EC goals

There are many effective strategies that can be used in campaigns from the less intrusive (e-mails or writing letters) to more forceful face-to-face meetings. The most effective campaigns use a variety of strategies. Sometimes, starting small by connecting with your own immediate EC environment has opportunity for success. You have an instant audience of families whose lives are affected. By communicating with your families, you can foster an environment of informed advocate parents who can carry the message to the larger community. Using anecdotes from your program or community is an effective way to build awareness of early childhood concerns. As an educator, you see firsthand the issues that face children and their families. The following questions may help you think about the kinds of information you could provide through public education endeavours:

- How available is regulated child care in your community? Are there waiting lists? Is there a need for care for the children of parents who work shifts? Is care available for children with special needs?

- What percentage of a family's total income is needed for child care? Is funding available to assist families with the cost of child care?

- Do families have access to good information about early childhood services?

- What are the average salaries of educators in your community?

- Are salary levels affecting staff retention and the quality of programs? Are salary levels attracting appropriate candidates to the field?

- Are provincial/territorial licensing standards adequate?

Broaden your audience beyond those directly involved in EC and connect with the larger education and political communities. Speaking with school board members and elected officials about their positions on EC may persuade them to consider issues in new light. It is important to recognize that EC educators can and do make a difference in improving the quality of programs for young children and their families. Only by working diligently together can we hope to continue to change public attitudes toward early childhood and develop appropriate policies that strengthen the field. This change is required to get the critical mass of support needed to provide a comprehensive, high quality EC system that responds to the diverse needs of Canadian families. As you become more aware of the need to take a stand in improving the field, you can continue to add effective strategies to your list.

CHOOSING ADVOCACY STRATEGIES

- Share anecdotes with others about experiences in the program (real stories of children and families) and information about its significance in the community.
- Communicate with elected officials (minister responsible for young children, your MP and MPs in the Opposition, your MLA, and/or your municipal councillor); use the appropriate title, be concise, include what action you would like the member of parliament to take, ask a question; identify the number of families you serve.
- Speak with government staff at both informal and formal meetings.
- Prepare a deputation to policy makers on an issue affecting children, families, and/or staff in your program.
- Write letters to the editor of your local newspaper or popular magazines.
- Write for professional newsletters or journals.
- Get involved in interactive conferences on the internet.
- Provide leadership at workshops or conferences.

Business leaders and politicians have become advocates for early childhood programs, by using the following strategies:

- Increasing their understanding that EC programs have an important educational component for children.
- Talking about investment rather than spending. Early childhood truly is an investment in the future—boosting children's success in school and in future jobs.
- Being specific. Nothing turns off a business person faster than talking in generalities. You need to have a clear proposal with concrete goals and a way to achieve those goals. Be concise and focused, using only the facts you need for a winning case.
- Starting small, and being patient. There's a learning curve to every new venture, and turning a business person/politician into an advocate takes time. It pays to approach people who have already shown an interest in children's issues and then educate them and bring them along.

Summary

This final chapter acknowledges that ECEs witness the impact of social problems that reach beyond families who are poor to parents with moderate incomes. Families from all socio-economic backgrounds are beset by the scarcity of affordable, high quality EC programs. Advocacy and professional empowerment are necessary roles for all EC professionals, and that effective advocacy is informed by holistic knowledge of the child and family, the community, and the field. Effective advocacy develops in partnership with families, and the role of advocate is shared between professionals and family members.

Early childhood educators need to take action to improve EC services so that current and future generations—both families and practitioners—will benefit. The potential of early childhood environments must be communicated. There is a knowledge and skill base needed to carry out advocacy activities, including being informed, active membership in EC organizations, communicating to influence policy makers, using the social media effectively to reach others, and speaking to the media.

Key Terms and Concepts

Advocacy,   p. 269

Advocates,   p. 281

Child advocacy,   p. 274

Informational advocacy,   p. 276

Personal advocacy,   p. 275

Professional advocacy,   p. 276

Social media,   p. 284

Social justice,   p. 270

Activities

1. Identify an organization in your community that is working for better early childhood services. Make arrangements to attend a meeting, interview staff about the goals of the organization, or become a member.

2. If you were given three wishes to bring about changes for children and their families, what would they be? Share your choices with others in the class. Identify priorities from the compiled list. Develop strategies you might use to advocate for these issues.

3. Review daily newspapers to identify statements of public policy related to early childhood development. What are the issues involved? In what ways do you support or disagree with these positions?

4. Review popular publications to assess how often child care is portrayed in the media. What views are held by the general public, and are these views consistent with media portrayals?

5. Invite friends on your Facebook to participate in action for improving a situation for children and families.

Recommended Reading

Dorfman, L., K. Woodruff, S. Herbert, and J. Ervice. *Making the Case for Early Care and Education: A Message Development Guide for Advocates*. Berkeley, CA: Berkeley Media Studies Group, 2004.

Goffin, S. and J. Lombardi. *Speaking Out: Early Childhood Advocacy Toolkit*. Washington, DC: National Association for the Education of Young Children, 2004.

Goffin, S. and V. Washington. *Ready or Not: Leadership Choices in Early Care and Education*. New York: Teacher's College Press, 2007.

Jensen, M. and M.A. Hannibal. *Issues, Advocacy, and Leadership in Early Education*. Needham Heights, MA: Allyn & Bacon, 2000.

Keiff, J. Informed Advocacy in Early Childhood Care and Education: Making a Difference for Young Children and Families, Merrill, 2009.

Robinson, A. and D. Stark. *Advocates in Action: Making a Difference for Young Children.* Rev ed. Washington, DC: National Association for the Education of Young Children, 2005.

Washington, V. and J. Andrews. Children of 2020: Creating a Better Tomorrow, NAEYC, 2010.

Weblinks

The national organizations listed below are among a number of organizations in Canada that provide assistance, publications, and/or technical support to professionals and members of the general public concerned about the well-being of children and families. Weblinks, where available, are included to facilitate accessing further information about publications and services.

www.rightsofchildren.ca
Canadian Coalition on the Rights of Children (CCRC)

The CCRC has a membership of more than 45 non-governmental agencies (NGOs) committed to promoting the rights of children in Canada and abroad. The mandate of the coalition is to ensure a collective voice for Canadian organizations and youth concerned with the rights of children as described in the United Nations Convention on the Rights of the Child and the World Summit for Children declaration. The CCRC was responsible for preparing a report on Canada's compliance with the UN Convention in 1999.

www.childcarecanada.org
Childcare Resource and Research Unit (CRRU)

The Childcare Resource and Research Unit (part of the Centre for Urban and Community Studies, University of Toronto) focuses on early childhood education and care policies and resources. Its mandate is to promote universally accessible and high quality settings in Canada. CRRU provides public education and policy analysis and publishes papers and other resources on child care policy, which are available online.

www.campaign2000.ca
Campaign 2000

Campaign 2000 is a non-partisan, cross-Canada coalition of more than 70 national, provincial, and community organizations. Its mandate is to raise awareness of and support for the 1989 all-party House of Commons resolution to eliminate child poverty in Canada by the year 2000. This non-partisan group urges all Canadian elected officials to keep their promises to children. It publishes an annual report card on child poverty in Canada and organizes events to aid public education and advocacy.

www.frp.ca
Canadian Association of Family Resource Programs

This is a national organization whose mission is to promote the well-being of families by providing national leadership, consultation, and resources to those who care for children and support families.

www.childcareadvocacy.ca
Child Care Advocacy Association of Canada

This organization promotes comprehensive, high quality non-profit child care programs. It provides focus and leadership to social policy activists, labour groups, women's organizations, and the early childhood community through ongoing campaigns designed to view child care as a cornerstone of progressive family policies; the right of all children to access a child care system supported by public funds; and a child care system that is comprehensive, inclusive, accessible, affordable, high quality, and non-profit.

Appendix

Provincial Legislative Offices, Regulations, and Early Childhood Organizations

Alberta

Department Governing Early Childhood Programs

Alberta Education
www.education.alberta.ca/home

Provincial Organizations

Alberta Association for Family Day Home Services
Alberta Association for the Accreditation of Early Learning and Care Services
www.aelcs.ca/

The Alberta Association of Services for Children and Families (AASCF)
www.cfc-efe.ca/ecdapei

British Columbia

Department Governing Early Childhood Programs

Ministry of Education
http://www.bced.gov.bc.ca/earlylearning

Provincial Organizations

Early Childhood Educators British Columbia (ECEBC)
http://www.ecebc.ca/

Coalition of Child Care Advocates of British Columbia
http://www.cccabc.bc.ca/

Western Canada Family Child Care Association of British Columbia
www.cfc-efc.ca/wcfcca

Westcoast Child Care Resource Centre
http://www.wstcoast.org/

Manitoba

Department Governing Early Childhood Programs

Manitoba Education
http://www.edu.gov.mb.ca/edu/

Provincial Organizations

Manitoba Child Care Association, Inc.
http://www.mccahouse.org/

Child Care Coalition of Manitoba
http://childcaremanitoba.ca

New Brunswick
Department Governing Early Childhood Programs

Department of Education
http://www.gnb.ca/index-e.asp

Provincial Organizations

Early Childhood Care and Education NB
New Brunswick Child Care Coalition
http://www.nbccc-csgnb.ca/

Newfoundland and Labrador
Departments Governing Early Childhood Programs

Department of Education
http://www.ed.gov.nl.ca/edu/earlychilhood

Department of Child, Youth and Family Services
http://www.gov.nl.ca/cyfs

Provincial Organizations

Association of Early Childhood Educators of Newfoundland and Labrador (AECENL)
www.aecenl.ca

Family and Child Care Connections
http://www.familyandchildcareconnections.com

Northwest Territories
Department Governing Early Childhood Programs

Department of Education, Culture & Employment
http://www.ece.gov.nt.ca/divisions/earlychildhood

Territorial Organizations

Currently there are no active child organizations in the NWT.

Nova Scotia
Department Governing Early Childhood Programs

Department of Education
http://www.ednet.ns.ca/

Provincial Organizations

Certification Council of Early Childhood Education of Nova Scotia
http://www.cccns.org/cert/home.html

Child Care Connection NS
http://www.cccns.org/

Nova Scotia Child Care Association
http://www.cccns.org/NSCCA/home.html

Nunavut
Department Governing Early Childhood Programs

Department of Education
http://www.edu.gov.nu.ca/

Territorial Organizations

Currently there are no active child organizations in Nunavut.

Ontario
Department Governing Early Childhood Programs Ministry of Education

www.edu.gov.on.ca/earlylearning

Provincial Organizations

Association of Early Childhood Educators, Ontario (AECEO)
http://www.aeceo.ca/
http://www.cfc-efc.ca/aeceo/

Ontario Coalition for Better Child Care
www.childcareontario.org

Home Child Care Association of Ontario
http://www.hccao.com/

Prince Edward Island
Department Governing Early Childhood Programs

Department of Education and Early Childhood Development
www.gpei.ca/education

Provincial Organizations

Early Childhood Development Association of PEI
http://earlychildhooddevelopment.ca

Quebec
Department Governing Early Childhood Programs

Ministère de l'Education, du Loisir et du Sport
http://www.mels.gouv.qc.ca/

Ministère de la Famille et des Aînés
http://www.mfa.gouv.qc.ca/

Provincial Organizations

Association de l'éducation préscolaire du Québec
www.aeceq.ca

Saskatchewan
Department Governing Early Childhood Programs

Ministry of Education
http://www.education.gov.sk.ca/

Provincial Organizations

Saskatchewan Early Childhood Association
http://www.skearlychildhoodassociation.ca/

Yukon Territory
Department Governing Early Childhood Programs

Department of Education
http://www.education.gov.yk.ca/

Territorial Organizations

Yukon Child Care Association
www.cfc-efc.ca/ycca

Glossary

Accountability   To be responsible for one's actions, reporting to funders.

Accounts payable   Bills to be paid by the program.

Accounts receivable   All monies owed by a person or organization to the program that have not been paid.

Accreditation   Type of quality control for programs, building on quality, regulations and licensing standards; often involves self-study and validation by outside professionals.

Adult:child ratio   The number of children for whom an adult is responsible, calculated by dividing the total number of adults into the total number of children. A "high" ratio means there are fewer children per educator; a "low" ratio means there are more children.

Advisory board   An advisory board suggests policies and procedures or provides information to those who administer the program; it has no power to enforce its recommendations.

Advocacy   Lobbying for a cause. In the field of early childhood, the cause may be services for children and families, recognition of quality services, or improved compensation and working conditions for early childhood **educators**.

Advocates   Individuals or groups speaking out on behalf of others. Advocates pursue or define a program believed to be in the best interest of children and families.

Affordability   The ability of parents to pay for programs; the costs of providing a quality program.

Allergies   Physiological reactions, such as asthma, hives, or hay fever, to environmental or food substances. Allergies can affect or alter behaviour.

Altruism   The work is service-oriented and child-focused—not for financial rewards.

Annual General Meeting (AGM)   A yearly meeting of shareholders of a corporation or members of a non-profit organization, especially for holding elections and reporting on the year's events.

Anti-bias curriculum   A method of presenting curricula that helps children to understand and respect differences, such as race, gender, culture, and/or physical ability.

Auspice   Refers to the type of governance structure that operates a program. In Canada, EC services operate under the auspices of **non-profit** or **for-profit** (commercial) organizations and **corporations**, municipalities, or schools.

Bad debt   An **accounts receivable** item that will never be collected.

Belonging   The experience of security, inclusion, respect, and competence by children, parents, and staff.

Benefits   All the money and in-kind insurance, vacations, and other benefits offered to an employee over and above wages. There are both mandatory benefits, such as the Canada Pension Plan and Employment Insurance, and voluntary benefits, such as extended health and dental programs or paid recreational programs.

Best practices   Professional **standards**, elements, and principles that guide the education of early childhood **educators**. The basic principles include: encouraging active learning, addressing individual needs, recognizing different learning styles, providing hands-on learning experiences, and designing an environment in which children are responsible for their own learning.

Board of directors   A policy-making board that holds the ultimate responsibility for **non-profit** programs; also known as "governing board."

Budget   A statement of goals for one year stated in financial terms.

Bylaws   Rules made by a body subordinate to a legislature; rules made by an organization for its members describing such things as how a **corporation** will do its business, its power structure, and how power may be transferred.

Career ladder   A way to describe a continuum of **professional development**. Each rung represents predetermined criteria for advancement to a new step, objective, or opportunity for **educators** to take on new roles.

Career lattice   Incorporates multiple, interlocking **career ladders** providing for the multiple roles and settings within the **early childhood profession**. Each step requires greater preparation, involves increased responsibility and compensation, and allows movement laterally.

Cash flow   The movement of cash used to operate a business or organization; cash inflow compared with cash outflow.

Centre   A group program licensed by the province or territory.

Certification   Professional recognition of an individual's **competency** to practice within a given occupation. This process recognizes that the individual has met the established occupational **standards** of knowledge, skills, and abilities needed to perform required tasks. The term "credentialling" may also be used.

Child advocacy   Political or legislative activism by **parents**, **educators**, or other interested groups who urge the consideration of social issues affecting children.

Child-centred   An educational philosophy that facilitates children selecting activities themselves.

Child development   The process of change in which the child comes to acquire more and more complex levels of moving, thinking, feeling, and interacting with people and objects in the environment. Development involves both a gradual unfolding of biologically determined characteristics and the learning process. Children's development is holistic and inter-dependent, including physical health and well-being, as well as intellectual, language, emotional, and social growth. It is embedded in the contexts of family, culture, and society.

Children with special needs   Children whose development and learning do not follow typical patterns. These children may need modifications to their environments and in their caregiver's style of interaction.

Clarity   The extent to which policies, procedures, and responsibilities in an early childhood setting are defined and communicated.

Code of ethics   A document that maps the dimensions of the **early childhood profession**'s collective social responsibility and acknowledges the obligations individual **educators** share in meeting the profession's responsibilities.

Colleague   Any other adult working in the program as well as professionals from the community.

Collective agreement   A negotiated agreement between an employer and employees' representatives (union) outlining the rate of pay and conditions of employment.

Collegiality   The extent to which staff work together as equals, co-operating rather than competing with one another.

Conflict of Interest   A situation in which an individual has a personal, financial, or other professional interest or obligation which gives rise to a reasonable apprehension that the interest or obligation may influence the member in the exercise of his or her professional responsibilities. Actual influence is not required in order for a conflict of interest situation to exist. It is sufficient if there is a reasonable apprehension that there may be such influence.

Conflict resolution policy   A written statement informing employees that they have the right to express complaints and a right to expect the employer to review and respond to the complaint.

Continuing competence   The state of being adequately qualified or able to meet agreed-upon **standards of practice** relevant to the profession.

Continuity   The way and degree to which aspects of a program relate to one another for the benefit of the children. The term can also refer to strategies among programs to communicate with each other.

Contract   A legally binding agreement, either written or oral, entered into by two parties. To be legally enforceable, a contract must have something offered by one party, accepted by the other party, and agreed upon "consideration."

Corporation   A legal entity with certain powers and responsibilities; a group of individuals who voluntarily join together under the law to form a **for-profit** or **non-profit** enterprise.

Cost-of-living adjustment (COLA)   A change in salary based on the government cost-of-living index.

Culture   The understandings, patterns of behaviour, practices, and values shared by a group of people. The children, families, and staff in an early learning and care setting may identify as belonging to more than one culture.

CPE   Centre de la petit enfance. The primary administrative structure for regulated child care in Quebec. These are not-for-profit, community-based organizations administered by parents that provide both centre-based care for children newborn to age 4 and regulated family child care.

Criminal reference check   A review of provincial or federal databases to determine if a job applicant has any outstanding criminal charges, criminal charges in front of the courts, or any criminal history.

Curriculum   The sum total of experiences, activities, and events that occur within an inclusive environment designed to foster children's development, learning, and well-being.

Decision making   The degree of autonomy given to the board or staff and the extent to which they are involved in program-wide decisions.

Developmentally appropriate   An approach to working with children where early childhood educators use their knowledge of child development to create learning environments and experiences that match the individual child's developing abilities and stimulate their interests, understanding, and emerging skills.

Director   An individual administering, supervising, and managing an early childhood service, including group child care centres, **family child care** programs, nursery schools, and family resource programs. The director is usually responsible for overall administration and **supervision** of staff and, in some situations, may work with the children.

Diversity   Differences and uniqueness that each person brings to the early learning setting, including values and beliefs, culture and ethnicity, language, ability, education, life experiences, socio-economic status, spirituality, gender, age, and sexual orientation.

Early childhood education   Professional practice which includes the assessment and promotion of the well-being and holistic development of children through the planning and delivery of inclusive play-based learning and care programs within the context of diverse family, school, and community groups.

Early childhood education and care   All programs and services for children and families, including group child care, **family child care**, kindergarten, family resource programs, and primary grades. This term is used by the Organisation for Economic Co-operation and Development (OECD).

Early learning environment   An environment focused on relationships among children, parents, and early childhood professionals that provides care, nurturing, and education as a complex and coherent whole, with the goals of fostering children's holistic development and well-being. It includes schedules, routines, physical environment, interactions, activities, and experiences.

Early childhood profession   The group of individuals who have acquired the pedagogical knowledge necessary to provide quality care and education to young children. Pedagogical knowledge is an organized body of knowledge forming the basis of the profession's **occupational standards** and influencing the concept of **best practice**. It includes core principles, relevant subject matter, theories of child development, and related methodology.

Early childhood setting   A setting other than a child's home in which care and education is provided for the child by a person who is not a member of the child's immediate family.

Ecological model   A framework for viewing childhood development that takes into account the various interconnected contexts within which an individual exists—for instance, the family, neighbourhood, and community.

Educator   An adult who works in the field of early childhood, including early childhood educators, family child care providers, family resource personnel, and resource and referral personnel.

Employee records   A collective term for all records containing information about employees and their employment.

Equity   An inclusive approach to practice which creates an early learning environment that recognizes, values, and builds on the diversity of each child and family.

Ethical dilemma   A moral conflict that involves determining appropriate conduct when an individual faces conflicting professional values and responsibilities.

Ethics   Moral principles; the study of right and wrong, duty and obligation. Ethics involves critical reflection on morality.

Ex-officio member   A person who, although not a member of the board of directors, always attends board meetings by virtue of her or his office or status.

Exosystem   According to ecological theory, that part of the environment includes the broader community—government, media.

Family   A group of children and adults who are related by affection, kinship, dependency, or trust, such as single-parent families, same-sex families, multi-generational families, and foster families.

Family-centred   A philosophy encompassing all aspects of family involvement and acknowledging the family as the focal point of care.

Family engagement   This approach emphasizes concepts that are continuous, reciprocal, and strength-based. It recognizes that all families are involved in their children's learning and well-being in some way.

Family child care   Care in a private home by a non-relative. This type of care is sometimes referred to as "home child care."

Family child care agency   The organization responsible for overseeing the individual home and ensuring the implementation of government **regulations**.

Family child care provider   One who offers care in her or his own home to a small group of children. In most provinces, care is limited to six or fewer children. Other terms also used include "caregiver" and "**practitioner.**"

Family involvement   Expands the focus beyond the child by providing education and social services to the entire family.

Fee subsidy   Financial assistance from the government to help **parents** with low incomes pay for child care fees.

First Ministers   The premiers of Canada's provinces and territories.

Fiscal monitoring   Standards associated with funding.

Fixed costs   Those expenditures that tend to stay constant in the short term.

For-profit   An organization run with the aim of making a profit (although in reality it may not); a for-profit organization may be a sole proprietorship (i.e., one individual owns the business), **corporation**, partnership, or co-operative. Any profits may be distributed to investors or reinvested in the program.

Goal consensus   The degree to which staff agree on the goals and objectives of the early childhood development program.

Governance   Refers to general and legal oversight of the operation. It relates to consistent management, cohesive policies, processes and decision rights for a given area of responsibility.

Governing body   The group or person (**board of directors**, owner, parent/advisory committee) legally responsible for the actions of the program.

Grievance procedure   A process to be followed by an employee to settle a dispute, generally identifying who to contact.

Group size   The total number of children in a group.

Human resources (HR) policies   A set of written guidelines covering employer–employee relations. Policies describe conditions of employment and may include job descriptions, advancement opportunities, and procedures for termination of employment, conflict resolution, and so on.

In-service training On-the-job training that adapts material or topics to meet the needs of a particular group. Workshops or seminars are conducted at the workplace.

Inclusion An approach to practice in early learning and care settings where all children are accepted and served within a program and where each child and family experiences a sense of belonging and no child or family is stigmatized or marginalized. Inclusion means to bring people in, rather than to exclude them—in thought, word or deed.

Incremental budgeting Relying on information contained in the budget for the prior year.

Informational advocacy Efforts to raise public awareness of the importance of early childhood and the benefits to children and families.

Innovativeness The extent to which an organization adapts to change and encourages staff to find creative ways to solve problems.

Leadership The broad plan of facilitating a program to clarify and affirm values, set broad goals, articulate a vision, and chart a course of action to achieve that vision.

Legislation Rules defined by government; the laws under which organizations operate.

License A permit given to operators that meet the minimum requirement set by government.

Licensed program A facility that has been assessed to ensure that it provides a minimum quality of care so that children are not harmed.

Licensing A process of applying **standards** or rules (Acts, **regulations**, or guidelines) to a facility to determine whether or not the licensee provides a minimum quality of care so that children are not harmed.

Macrosystem According to ecological theory, the broadest part of the environment that includes cultural, political, and economic forces.

Maintenance Major expenditures on the physical plant: painting, alterations, repair.

Management Refers to the day-to-day work required to achieve the program's vision and to make it a reality.

Mentor Someone who can serve as a role model to help less experienced staff members gain new skills and knowledge.

Mentoring A nurturing process wherein a more experienced practitioner serving as a role model teaches, encourages, and counsels a less experienced staff member to promote the individual's professional and/or personal development.

Mesosystem According to ecological theory, the linkages between family and the immediate neighbourhood or community.

Microsystem According to ecological theory, that part of the environment that most immediately affects a person, such as the family, child care setting, school, or workplace.

Mission statement A statement to clientele and the public at large stating the nature and purpose of the organization. This term may be used instead of "**philosophy**."

Mixed-age groupings See **multi-age groupings**.

Monitoring Official observation after licence issuance to determine ongoing or continued compliance with **licensing** requirements.

Multi-age groupings Placing children who are at least a year apart in age into the same playgroup.

Non-profit An organization not involved in making a profit. A non-profit organization is a legal entity that is intended to break even. It cannot issue dividends; it is required to invest any excess revenues in the program.

Nutrition Encompasses both the quality and quantity of food consumed for healthful living.

Occupational standards Skills, knowledge, and abilities needed to perform competently in the workforce and the **standards** that identify, describe, and measure the abilities individuals must possess. These standards form the basis for the **accreditation** and **certification** processes within the **early childhood profession**.

Operating budget Used when programs become operational and annually thereafter.

Operations   Recurring day-to-day activities involved in the upkeep of a facility, including cleaning and sanitation.

Organizational climate   Collective, rather than individual, perception of the staff regarding the culture, atmosphere, and conditions in the workplace.

Organizational structure   Framework for administration and daily operation of early childhood services, including the process and procedures used in decision making and the handling of information. Components of the organizational structure include sponsorships, provincial/territorial **regulations**, funding, and **parent involvement**.

Parent   Any adult who has the primary responsibility for the child. The term is intended to be inclusive and to encompass not only biological and adoptive parents but also legal guardians and foster parents.

Parent conferences   One-on-one meetings between early childhood **educators** and **parents** to discuss a child's progress and resolve problems.

Parent involvement   Parents sharing in the education and care of their children through participation in activities in the early childhood program.

Pedagogy   An educational approach that reflects a deliberate process of cultivating development and learning.

Performance appraisal   A process to assess how well the staff is meeting the program standards, fulfilling their job responsibilities and contributing to the realization of the program vision, reaching the program goals, and meeting the program objectives.

Personal philosophy   One's beliefs and attitudes related to **early childhood education**; one's ideas about how children learn and how caregivers interact.

Personal advocacy   Involves talking with acquaintances about the importance of early childhood development.

Personnel policies   (currently referred to as **human resources policies**) A set of written guidelines covering employer–employee relations. Policies describe conditions of employment and may include job descriptions, advancement opportunities, and procedures for termination of employment, conflict resolution, and so on.

Philosophy   A statement of beliefs reflecting one's value system. It is often based on theory and guided by research.

Play-based pedagogy   An educational approach which builds upon a child's natural inclination to make sense of the world through play, where early childhood educators participate in play, guiding children's planning, decision-making and communications, and extending children's explorations with narrative, novelty, and challenges.

Policy   A course of action that guides decisions.

Prior Learning Assessment and Recognition (PLAR)   Formal process for determining equivalent academic credit for college-level knowledge and skills acquired through a variety of past learning opportunities, both formal and informal.

Probationary period   The period of time at the beginning of a new employment relationship, usually three to six months.

Procedure   A series of steps to be followed, usually in a specific order, to implement policies.

Process quality   Refers to interactions; the provision of **developmentally appropriate** activities; caregiver consistency; parent involvement; and warm, nurturing, sensitive caregiving.

Professional advocacy   Efforts to challenge and reform public systems that affect children and families. This type of **advocacy** is also known as "lobbying" and is directed toward legislative, administrative, and budgetary processes.

Professional development   Participation in activities such as courses, conferences, and workshops; a process of continuous learning for the purposes of enhancing an individual's competencies and/or professionalism by enhancing their skills and knowledge based on current research and pedagogical development in the field.

Professional ethics   The moral commitments of a profession. Professional ethics require reflective thinking about the profession's responsibilities, values, and practices that extends and enhances the personal morality that **educators** bring to their work. Professional ethics concern the kinds of actions that are right and wrong in the workplace and help individuals resolve the moral dilemmas that they encounter in their work.

Professional judgment   Assessing events and estimating consequences of decisions and actions based on specialized knowledge.

Professionalism   A fluid experience that is ongoing—never ending. Education, knowledge, and experience inform practice, ever reshaped by the unfolding incoming flow of new knowledge and experience. Through ongoing reflective-practice, what is known is re-examined, reconfigured, and refined. From this perspective, professionalism is envisioned as a constant state of becoming.

Public good   A service whose consumption is not decided by the individual consumer but by the society as a whole, and which is financed by taxation. Public goods (and services) include economic statistics and other information, law-and-order enforcement, national parks, etc. No market exists for such goods, and they must be provided to everyone by the government.

Ratio   See **adult:child ratio**.

Rating scale   An instrument for assessing specific skills or concepts based on some qualitative dimension of excellence or accomplishment.

Reflection   A natural process that facilitates the development of future action from the contemplation of past and current behaviour.

Reflective practice   A style of teaching that is based on questioning what one is doing and why; on thinking how theory is translated into practice and how practice informs theory, is to enter into a way of working.

Registration   A process that requires **family child care providers** to certify that they have complied with **regulations** and maintain records.

Regulations   The rules, directives, statutes, or standards that prescribe, direct, limit, or govern early childhood programs.

Resource and referral programs   These community organizations provide a variety of services, such as a volunteer registry of care providers, lending libraries, training for caregivers, and access to liability insurance.

Resource teacher   An individual who assists early childhood **educators** with the **inclusion** of **children with special needs** into **early childhood settings**.

Revenue   Income received by the program, including parent fees, government grants, and funds raised.

Social policy   primarily refers to guidelines and interventions for the changing, maintenance, or creation of living conditions that are conducive to human welfare. Thus, social policy is that part of public policy that has to do with social issues.

Social justice   is concerned with equal **justice**, not just in the courts, but in all aspects of society. This concept demands that all persons irrespective of ethnic origin, gender, possessions, race, religion, etc. have equal rights and opportunities.

Staff:child ratio   See **adult:child ratio**.

Staff development   A broad term that refers to all processes that encourage employees to engage in professional growth and development.

Stakeholders   Individuals or groups that have an investment in a particular system or organization. In early childhood, the stakeholders include the children, parents, **educators**, **directors**, **licensing** inspectors, government, funding agencies, advisory bodies, policy makers, and students.

Standards   Degrees of excellence along a continuum, with some regulations only specifying baseline standards for acceptability below which a program's quality is unacceptable (possibly leading to criminal sanctions) and other regulations indicating excellent quality.

Standards of practice   Benchmarks, or points of reference, against which occupations and the proficiency of people in those occupations are measured or assessed. These standards are also known as **occupational standards**.

Start-up budget   One-time-only costs that are incurred prior to starting a program.

Structural quality   Variables that can be regulated, including **adult:child ratio**, **group size**, and the education and training of practitioners.

Supervision   The process of communicating performance expectations and supporting individual staff members to fulfill their job responsibilities and to reach their full potential during the performance of their jobs.

Support staff   Anyone working under a **director** in an early childhood program who is not directly involved with the children, including clerical, cooking, and cleaning personnel as well as home visitors and others involved in a supervisory capacity.

Task orientation   The emphasis placed on good planning, efficiency, and getting the job done.

United Nations Convention on the Rights of the Child   An agreement to do what is best for children that has been endorsed by almost every country in the world.

Values   The qualities or principles individuals believe to be intrinsically desirable or worthwhile.

Variable costs   Those expenditures that increase as the number of children served increases.

Work environment   The physical and social environment in which work takes place. It includes how people are treated, how they feel, and how they relate to each other, plus the conditions under which work is done: health and safety; supervision, accountability, and opportunities for personal and professional development; and communication, conflict resolution, and problem solving.

Zero-based budgeting   Requires that each expenditure be newly calculated.

Bibliography

Abbreviations

NAEYC National Association for the Education of Young Children CCCF Canadian Child Care Federation

Albrecht, P. 2002. *The right fit: Recruiting, selecting, and orienting staff.* Lake Forest, IL: New Horizons.

Ali, M., P. Corson, and E. Frankel. 2009. *Listening to Families: Reframing services.* Toronto: Chestnut Publishing.

American Academy of Pediatrics and American Public Health Association. 2011. *Caring for our children: National health and safety standards—Guidelines for early care and education programs,* 3rd ed. Washington, DC: Author.

American Academy of Pediatrics and American Public Health Association. 2002. *Caring for our children: National health and safety standards—Guidelines for out of home programs.* 2d ed. Washington, DC: Author.

Avataq Cultural Institute. 2004. *Unikkaangualaurtaa—Let's tell a story.* Montreal: Avataq Cultural Institute.

Bachmann, K., and J. MacBride-King. 1999. *Is work-life balance still an issue for Canadians and their employers? You bet it is!, Work-life balance series no. 1.* Ottawa: Conference Board of Canada.

Baker, M. 1995. *Canadian family policies: Cross-national comparisons.* Toronto: University of Toronto Press.

Ball, J. 2008. *Promoting equity and dignity for Aboriginal children in Canada. Aboriginal quality of life, IRPP choices, 14(7).* Montreal: Institute for Research on Public Policy.

Barnett, W.S. 2003. *Better teachers, better preschools: Student achievement linked to teacher qualifications. Preschool policies matter, 2.* New Brunswick, NJ: Rutgers University, National Institute of Early Childhood Research.

BC Aboriginal Child Care Society (BCACCS). 2004. *Elements of quality child care from the perspectives of Aboriginal peoples in British Columbia, draft standards.* Vancouver: BCACCS.

Beach, J., J. Bertrand, and G. Cleveland. 2004. *Our child care workforce, from recognition to remuneration: A human resources study of child care in Canada.* Ottawa: Human Resources Development Canada.

Beach, J., J. Bertrand, B. Forer, D. Michal, and J. Tougas. 2004. *Working for change: Canada's child care workforce. Labour market update study.* Ottawa: Child Care Human Resources Sector Council.

Beach, J., and J. Bertrand. 2000. More than the sum of the parts: An early childhood development system for Canada. Occasional Paper 12. Toronto: Childcare Resource and Research Unit, Centre for Urban and Community Studies, University of Toronto.

Beach, J., M. Friendly, C. Ferns, N. Prabhu, and B. Forer. 2009. *Early childhood education and care in Canada 2008.* Toronto: Childcare Resource and Research Unit.

Beach, J. 2010. *Environmental scan for the coalition of child care advocates of British Columbia.* Coalition of Child Care Advocates of British Columbia, Vancouver.

Bennett, J. 2008. *Early childhood services in OECD countries: Review of the literature and current policy in the early childhood field.* UNICEF.

Bennett, J., and P. Moss. 2006. Toward a New Pedagogical Meeting Place? Bringing Early Childhood into the Education System. Briefing paper for a Nuffield Educational Semina.

Bennett, J., and M. Neuman. 2004. Schooling for early childhood? Early childhood major challenges: review of early childhood education and care policies. *Prospects* XXXIV (4).

Berk, L.E., and A. Winsler. 1995. *Scaffolding children's learning: Vygotsky and early childhood education.* Washington, DC: NAEYC.

Bernhard, J., M. Lefebvre, G. Chud, and R. Lange. 1995. *Paths to equity: Cultural, linguistic, and racial diversity in Canadian early childhood education.* Toronto: York University.

Best Start Expert Panel on Early Learning. 2006. *Early learning for every child: A framework for Ontario early childhood settings.* Ministry of Children and Youth Services.

Best Start Expert Panel on Quality and Human Resources. 2007. *Investing in quality: Policies, practitioners, programs, parents: A four point plan.* Ministry of Children and Youth Services.

Bird, A.E. 2005. *Learning on the front line.* Unpublished manuscript, Ontario Institute for Studies in Education, University of Toronto.

Boise, P. 2010. *Go green rating scale for early childhood settings.* Minnesota: Redleaf Press.

Boutte, G., D. Keepler, V. Tyler, and B. Terry. 1992. Effective techniques for involving "difficult" parents. *Young Children* 47 (3): 19–22.

Bredekamp, S., and C. Copple, eds. 1997. *Developmentally appropriate practice in early childhood programs,* rev. ed. Washington, DC: NAEYC.

Bronfenbrenner, U. 1979. *The ecology of human development.* Cambridge, MA: Harvard University Press.

Bronfenbrenner, U. 1986. Ecology of the family as a context for human development: Research perspectives. *Developmental Psychology* 221: 723–742.

Bronwell, B. 2000. *Taskforce on rural child care and early education.* Guelph, ON: Ontario Federation of Agriculture.

Bush, J. 2000. *Dollars and sense: Planning for profit in your child care business.* Albany, NY: Delmar.

Caldwell, B. 1987. Advocacy is everybody's business. *Child Care Information Exchange* (March): 29–32.

Campaign 2000. *2010 Report card on child poverty in Canada.* Toronto: Campaign 2000.

Campaign 2000. 2004. *One million too many: Implementing solutions to child poverty in Canada: 2004 report card on child poverty in Canada.* Toronto: Campaign 2000.

Canada. 1994c. *Canadian child care in context: Perspectives from the provinces and territories.* Ottawa: Statistics Canada.

Canada. 1996b. *National longitudinal survey of children and youth: Growing up in Canada,* by D. Keating and F. Mustard. Ottawa: Statistics Canada.

Canada. 1999b. *A national children's agenda: developing a shared vision.* Ottawa: Human Resources Development Canada/Federal-Provincial-Territorial Council of Ministers on Social Policy Renewal.

Canada. 1999c. *Preschool children: Promises to keep.* Ottawa: National Council of Welfare/ Public Works and Government Services Canada.

Canada. 2001b. *Federal/provincial/territorial early childhood development agreement:*
Report on government of Canada activities and expenditures 2000–2001. Ottawa: Government of Canada.

Canada. 2003. *Using your home for day care.* Ottawa: Revenue Canada/Canada Customs and Revenue Agency. Available online: www. ccra-adrc.gc.ca.

Canada. 2011. *Eating well with Canada's Food Guide.* Ottawa: Ministry of Health.

Canadian Index of Wellbeing. 2010. *Caught in a time crunch: Time use, leisure and culture in Canada.* Available online: http://action.web. ca/home/crru/rsrcs_crru_full.shtml?x=129853.

Carter, M., and Curtis, D. 2010. *The visionary director: A handbook for dreaming, organizing, and improvising in your center,* 2d ed. St. Paul, MI: Redleaf Press.

CCCF. 1991b. *National statement on quality child care.* Ottawa: Author.

CCCF. 2000a. *Family Child Care Training Program, Level 1.* Ottawa: Author.

CCCF. 2000b. *Partners in quality: Tools for practitioners in child care settings.* Ottawa: Author.

CCCF. 2000c. *Partners in quality: Tools for administrators in child care settings.* Ottawa: Author.

CCCF. 2001a. Convention on the rights of the child. In *Research connections Canada,* vol. 7. Ottawa: Author.

CCCF. 2004. What's in a name? Discussion paper. E. Elaine Ferguson, author; Lana Crossman and Anne Maxwell, eds. Ottawa: Author.

CCCF and CICH (Canadian Institute of Child Health). 2001. "Supporting Breastfeeding in Child Care," resource sheet No. 57 from the "Nourish, Nurture and Neurodevelopment Resource Kit," *Neurodevelopmental Research: Implications for caregiver practice, on nourishing and nurturing the child's brain for optimal neurodevelopmental health.* Ottawa: Author.

Child Care Human Resources Sector Council (CCHRSC). 2006. *Career promotions and recruitment strategy.* Ottawa: Author.

Child Care Human Resources Sector Council. 2009. *A portrait of Canada's early childhood and care workforce.* Ottawa: Author.

Canadian Day Care Advocacy Association (CDCAA) and Canadian Child Day Care Federation (CCDCF). 1992. *Caring for a living: A study on wages and working conditions in Canadian child care.* Ottawa: CCDCF.

Canadian Institute of Child Health (CICH). 2000. *The health of Canada's children: A CICH profile,* 3d ed. Ottawa: Author.

Canadian Pædiatric Society. 2008. *Well beings: A guide to promote the physical health, safety and emotional well-being of children in child care centres and family day care homes,* 2d ed. Toronto: Creative Premises Ltd.

Canadian Standards Association. 2003. *Children's play spaces and equipment.* Mississauga, Ontario: Author.

Canadian Standards Association. 2007. *Children's play spaces and equipment.* Mississauga, Ontario: Author.

Carneiro, P., and J. Heckman. 2003. *Human capital policy.* IXA DP No. 821. In: J. Heckman and A. Frueger, *Inequality in America: What role for human capital policy?* Chicago, IL: MIT Press.

Caruso, J., and M. Fawcett. 1999. *Supervision in early childhood education: A developmental perspective,* 2d ed. New York: Columbia University, Teachers College Press.

Chandler, K. 1988. Accreditation: One route to professionalism. Presentation at the annual conference of the Alberta Association for Young Children.

Chandler, K. 1994. Voluntary accreditation and program evaluation: Background paper. Ottawa: CCCF.

Chandler, K. 1997. What do we know about ECE training in Canada? Background paper for Steering Committee of Early Childhood Care and Education Training in Canada. Ottawa: Association of Canadian Community Colleges and CCCF.

Chandler, K. 1999. Professional development. In *Research connections Canada,* vol. 3. Ottawa: CCCF.

Chandler, K. 2001. The director's role in staff development. *Interaction* (CCCF) 15 (2): 18–20.

Chandler, K., and P. Hileman. 1986. Professionalism in early childhood education. Association for Early Childhood Education Newsletter.

Child Care Advocacy Association of Canada (CCAAC). 2004. *From patchwork to framework: A child care strategy for Canada.* Ottawa: Author.

Child Care Employee Project. 1990. *Taking matters into our own hands: A guide to unionizing in the child care field.* Berkeley, CA: Author.

Child Care Human Resource Sector Council. 2010. *Occupational standards for early childhood educators.* Ottawa: Author.

Child Care Human Resources Sector Council. 2009. *A portrait of Canada's early childhood and care workforce.* Ottawa: Author.

Child Care Human Resources Sector Council. 2009. *Recruitment and retention challenges and strategies: Understanding workforce shortages in ECEC.* Ottawa: Author.

Child Care Human Resource Sector Council. 2006. *Occupational standards for child care administrators.* Ottawa: Author.

Child Care Resource and Research Unit. 2006. *Canadian early learning and child care and the convention on the rights of the child.* Toronto: Centre for Urban and Community Studies, University of Toronto.

Children's Services Division. 2004. *Operating criteria for child care centres providing subsidized care in Toronto,* rev. ed. Toronto: Community Services, Children's Services Division, City of Toronto.

Children's Services Division. 2009. *Operating criteria for child care centres.* Toronto, Ontario: Author.

Chud, G., and R. Fahlman. 1995. *Honouring diversity with child care and early education: An instructor's guide.* Victoria: British Columbia Ministry of Skills, Training and Labour.

Cleveland G., and M. Krashinsky. 1998. *The benefits and costs of good child care: The economic rationale for public investment in young children.* Toronto: Childcare Resource and Research Unit, Centre for Urban and Community Studies, University of Toronto.

Cleveland G., and M. Krashinsky. 2001. *Our children's future: Child care policy in Canada.* Toronto: University of Toronto Press.

Cleveland, G., B. Foyer, D. Hyatt, and M. Krashinsky. 2007. The Economic Perspective on the Current and Future Role of Non-profit Provision of Early learning and Child Care in Canada. Toronto.

Colker, L. 2008. *Twelve characteristics of effective early childhood educators.* Washington, DC: NAEYC.

Cooke, K., et al. 1986. *Report of the task force on child care.* Ottawa: Supply and Services.

Cowperthwaite, P., and R. Mehta. 1996. *The art of budgeting.* Available online: Cowperthwaite Mehta Chartered Accountants, not-for-profit administration web page: www.187gerrard.com.

Culkin, M., ed. 2000. *Managing quality in young children's programs: The leader's role.* New York: Teachers College Press, Columbia University.

Curtis, D. 2010. *What's the risk of no risk?* Redmond, WA: Child Care Information Exchange.

Derman-Sparks, L., and the ABC Task Force. 1989. *Anti-bias curriculum: Tools for empowering young children.* Washington, DC: NAEYC.

Doherty, G. 1999. *Elements of quality. In Research connections Canada,* vol. 1. Ottawa: CCCF.

Doherty, G. 2000a. Issues in Canadian child care: What does the research tell us? Part 5, Funding child care. In *Research connections Canada,* vol. 5. Ottawa: CCCF.

Doherty, G. 2000b. Standards for quality child care programs; Standards of practice for administrators/directors. In *Partners in quality: Tools for administrators in child care settings.* Ottawa: CCCF.

Doherty, G. 2003. *Occupational standards for child care practitioners.* Ottawa: Canadian Child Care Federation.

Doherty, G., and B. Forer. 2004. Unionization and quality in early childhood programs. In *Research connections Canada: Supporting children and families,* vol. II. Ottawa: Canadian Child Care Federation, 33–52.

Doherty G., D. Lero, H. Goelman, A. LaGrange, and J. Tougas. 2000a. *You bet I care! A Canada-wide study on wages, working conditions, and practices in child care centres.* Guelph, ON: Centre for Families, Work and Well-Being, University of Guelph.

Doherty G., D. Lero, H. Goelman, J. Tougas, and A. LaGrange. 2000b. *You bet I care! Caring and learning environments: Quality in regulated family child care across Canada.* Guelph, ON: Centre for Families, Work and Well-Being, University of Guelph.

Dorfman, L., K. Woodruff, S. Herbert, and J. Ervice. 2004. *Making the case for early care and education: A message development guide for advocates.* Berkeley, CA: Berkeley Media Studies Group.

Early Childhood Education. 2000. *Best practices for cooks.* Toronto: George Brown College, Faculty of Community and Health Sciences.

Ekos Research Associates. 2000. *National survey of children's issues: Final report.* Prepared for the Strategic Policy Communications Branch: Human Resources Development Canada.

Elora Partnership. 2004. *Home child care accreditation initiative research and demonstration of an accreditation system for home child care providers in the province of Ontario.* Available online: www.familydaycare.com/elora_partnership.html

Environics Research Group. 2006. *Canadians' attitudes towards national child care policy.* Ottawa: Author.

Esbensen, S.B. 1987. *The early childhood education playground: An outdoor classroom.* Ypsilanti, MI: High/Scope Press.

Essa, E. 2011. *Introduction to early childhood education,* 6th ed. University of North Texas: Pearson.

Fairholm, R. 2009. *Literature review of socioeconomic effect and net benefits—Understanding and addressing workforce shortages in early childhood education and care project.* Ottawa: CCHRSC.

Fairholm, R. (Centre for Spatial Economics) 2010. *Early learning and care impact analysis.* Atkinson Centre for Child Development.

Feeney, S. 1987a. Ethical case studies for NAEYC reader response. *Young Children* 42 (4): 24–25.

Feeney, S. 1987b. Ethics case studies: The working mother. *Young Children* 43 (1): 16–19.

Feeney, S., and N.K. Freeman. 1999. *Ethics and the early childhood educator: Using the NAEYC code.* Washington, DC: NAEYC.

Feeney, S., and N.K. Freeman. 2005. *Ethics and the early childhood educator: Using the NAEYC 2005 code 2d ed.* Washington, DC: NAEYC.

Feeney, S., B. Caldwell, and K. Kipnis. 1988a. Ethics case studies: The aggressive child. *Young Children* 43 (2): 48–51.

Feeney, S., S. Riley, and K. Kipnis. 1988b. Ethics case studies: The divorced parents. *Young Children* 43 (3): 48–51.

Fennimore, B. 1989. *Child advocacy for early childhood educators.* New York: Teachers College Press, Columbia University.

Ferguson, E. 1997. *Child care administration credentialling: A work in progress.* Halifax, NS: Child Care Connection.

Ferguson, E., and T. McCormick Ferguson. 2001. *Maximizing child care services: The role of owners and boards.* Halifax, NS: Child Care Connection.

Ferguson, E., K. Flanagan-Rochon, L. Hautmann, D. Lutes, A. Masson, and D. Mauch. 2000. *Toward a best practices framework for licensing child care facilities in Canada*. Halifax, NS: Child Care Connection.

Friendly, M. 1994. *Child care policy in Canada: Putting the pieces together*. Don Mills, ON: Addison-Wesley.

Friendly, M. 2004. Strengthening Canada's social and economic foundations: Next steps for early childhood education and care. *Policy Options* (March).

Friendly, M., and S. Prentice. 2009. *About Canada: Childcare*. Halifax, NS: Fernwood Publishing.

Friendly, M. 2006. *Canadian early learning and child care and the Convention on the Rights of the Child. Occasional Paper 22*. Toronto: Childcare Resource and Research Unit.

Friendly, M., G. Doherty, and J. Beach. 2006. *Quality by design: What do we know about quality in early learning and child care, and what do we think? A literature review*. Toronto: Childcare Resource and Research Unit, University of Toronto.

Galinsky, E. 1990. Why are some parent/teacher partnerships clouded with difficulties? *Young Children* 45 (5): 2–3, 38–39.

Galinsky, E. 1999. *Ask the children: What America's children really think about working parents*. New York: Families and Work Institute.

George Brown College. 2000. *Best Practices for Child Care Cooks*. Toronto: George Brown College.

Gestwicki. C. 1999. *Developmentally appropriate practice: Curriculum and development in early education*. Albany, NY: Delmar.

Goelman, H., G. Doherty, D. Lero, A. LaGrange, and J. Tougas. 2000. *You bet I care! Caring and learning environments: Quality in child care centres across Canada*. Guelph, ON: Centre for Families, Work and Well-Being, University of Guelph.

Goffin, S., and V. Washington. 2007. *Ready or Not: Leadership choices in early care and education*. New York: Teacher's College Press.

Goffin, S., and J. Lombardi. 2004. *Speaking out: Early childhood advocacy toolkit*. Washington, DC: NAEYC.

Goss Gilroy Inc. 1998. *Providing home child care for a living: A survey of providers working in the regulated sector*. Ottawa: CCCF.

Government of British Columbia. 2010. *Speech from the throne*. Victoria: Government of British Columbia, pp. 19–20.

Government of New Brunswick. 2010. *Overcoming poverty together: New Brunswick's economic and social inclusion plan*. St. John, NB: Author.

Government of Prince Edward Island. 2010. *Securing the future for our children: Preschool excellence initiative*. Charlottetown, PE: Author.

Greenman, J. 2005. *Caring spaces, learning places: Children's environments that work*. Redmond, WA: Exchange Press, Inc.

Harms, T., and R.M. Clifford. 1998. *Early childhood environment rating scale*. rev. ed. New York: Teachers College Press, Columbia University.

Harms, T., and R.M. Clifford. 2004. *Family home day care environment rating scale*, rev. ed. New York: Teachers College Press, Columbia University.

Harms, T., D. Cryer, and R.M. Clifford. 1990. *Infant/toddler environment rating scale*. New York: Teachers College Press, Columbia University.

Harms, T., E. Jacobs, and D. White. 1995. *School-age environment rating scale*. New York: Teachers College Press, Columbia University.

Hayden, J. 1996. *Management of early childhood services: An Australian perspective*. Wentworth Falls, NSW, Australia: Social Science Press.

Heath, C., and D. Heath. 2010. *Switch: How to change things when change is hard*. New York: Broadway Books.

Hendrick, J., and K. Chandler. 1996. *The whole child*. 6th Cdn. ed. Scarborough, ON: Prentice Hall Canada.

Hepburn, S. et al. 1995. Cost, quality, and child outcomes in child care centres: Executive summary. Denver, CO: University of Colorado.

High/Scope Educational Research Foundation. 1998. *High/Scope program quality assessment instrument (PQA)*. Ypsilanti, MI: High/Scope Press.

Holland, M. 2004. "That food makes me sick!" Managing food allergies and intolerances in early childhood settings. *Young Children* (March): 42–46.

House of Commons Standing Committee on Human Resources, Skills and Social Development and the Status of Persons with Disabilities. 2010. *Federal poverty reduction plan: Working in partnership towards reducing poverty in Canada*. Ottawa: Author.

Human Resources Development Canada. 2003. *Multilateral framework agreement on early learning and child care*. Available online: socialunion.gc.ca/ecd-framework_e.htm.

Irwin, S. 2009. *SpeciaLink early childhood inclusion quality scale*. Wreck Cove, NS: Breton Books.

Irwin, S., D. Lero, and K. Brophy. 2000. *A matter of urgency: Including children with special needs in child care in Canada*. Sydney, NS: Breton Books.

Jensen, J., and R. Mahon. 2001. *Bringing cities to the table, child care and intergovernmental relations*. Ottawa: Canadian Policy Research Networks.

Johnson, J., and J.B. McCracken, eds. 1994. *The early childhood career lattice: Perspectives on professional development*. Washington, DC: NAEYC.

Johnson, K.L., D.S. Lero, and J. Rooney. 2001. *Work-life compendium 2001: 150 Canadian statistics on work, family, and well-being*. Guelph, ON: Human Resources Development Canada and the Centre for Families, Work and Well-Being, University of Guelph.

Jorde Bloom, P. 1997. *A great place to work: Improving conditions for staff in young children's programs*. rev. ed. Washington, DC: NAEYC.

Jorde Bloom, P. 2000. *Circle of influence: Implementing shared decision making and participative management*. Lake Forest, IL: New Horizons.

Jorde Bloom, P. 2002. *Making the most of meetings: A practical guide*. Lake Forest, IL: New Horizons.

Jorde Bloom, P. 2003. *Leadership in action: How effective directors get things done*. Lake Forest, IL: New Horizons.

Jorde Bloom, P., M. Sheerer, and J. Britz. 2002. *Blueprint for action: Achieving center-based change through staff development*, 2d ed. Lake Forest, IL: New Horizons.

Jorde Bloom, P., A. Hentschel, and J. Bella. 2010. *A great place to work: Creating a healthy organizational climate*. Lake Forest, IL: New Horizons.

Kaga, Y., J. Bennett, and P. Moss. 2010. *Caring and learning together: A cross-national study of integration of ECE and education within education*. Paris: UNESCO.

Kaiser, B., and J. Sklar Rasminsky. 1999a. The child care supervisor as child care advocate. *Interaction* (CCCF) (Winter).

Kass, J., and B. Costigliola. 2003. *The union advantage in child care: How unionization can help recruitment and retention.*. Halifax, NS: Child Care Connection NS. Available online: Child Care Advocacy Association of Canada, Home Page, Archives: www.child_careadvocacy.ca/archives/archives03b.html.

Keating, D., and C. Hertzman, eds. 1999. *Developmental health and the wealth of nations*. New York: Guildford Press.

Kontos, S., C. Howes, and E. Galinsky. 1996. *Does training make a difference to quality in family child care*. New York: Teachers College Press, Columbia University.

Kruse, S.D., and K.S. Louis. 2009). *Building strong school cultures: A guide to leading change.*Thousand Oaks, CA: Corwin.

Kyle, I. 2000. *Quality in home care settings: A critical review of current theory and research*. Guelph, ON: Centre for Child Care Excellence.

Lally, R. 1995. The impact of child care policies and practices on infant/toddler identity formation. *Young Children* 51 (1): 58–67.

Marotz, L., and A. Lawson. 2007. *Motivational leadership in early childhood education*. Clifton Park, NY: Thompson, Delmar.

Mayfield, M. 2001. *Early childhood education and care in Canada: Contexts, dimensions, and issues*. Toronto: Prentice Hall.

McCain, M.N., and J.F. Mustard. 1999. *Early years study: Reversing the real brain drain*. Toronto: Government of Ontario.

McCain M.N., J.F. Mustard, and S. Shanker. 2007. *Early years study 2: Putting science into action*. Toronto: Government of Ontario.

McLean, C. 1994. *Regulations, standards and enforcement*. Ottawa: CCCF.

Miller, K. 1999. *Simple steps: Developmental activities for infants, toddlers and twos*. Toronto: Gryphon House.

Ministry of Education. 2010. *Ideas into action for school and system leaders: Promoting collaborative learning cultures: Putting the promise into practice*. Ontario Government.

Mahon, R., and J. Jenson. 2006. *Learning from each other: Early learning and child care experiences in Canadian cities*. Toronto, ON: City of Toronto.

Morgan, G., and B. Emanual. 2010. *The bottom line for children's programs*. Mount Forest, Ontario: New Horizons.

Moss, P. 1994. *Quality targets in services for young children: Proposals for a ten-year action plan*. Brussels: European Commission.

Moss, P., and J. Bennett. 2006. Towards a new pedagogical meeting Place? Bringing Early Childhood into the Education System. Nuffield Education Seminar.

Musson, S. 1999. *School-age care: Theory and practice.* Don Mills, ON: Addison-Wesley.

NAEYC. 2006. *NAEYC code of ethical conduct for early childhood program administrators.* Washington, DC: Author.

NAEYC. 1995. How many ways can you think of to use NAEYC's code of ethics? *Young Children* 51 (1): 42–43.

NAEYC. 1998a. *Accreditation criteria and procedures of the National Academy of Early Childhood Programs,* rev. ed. Washington, DC: Author.

NAEYC. 1998b. NAEYC position statement on licensing and public recognition of early childhood programs. *Young Children* 53 (1): 43–50.

National Association of Child Care Resources and Referrals. 2010. *The economy's impact on parents' choices about child care: Parents' perceptions of child care in the United States.* Arlington, VA: Author.

National Association of Friendship Centres. 2009. *Urban aboriginal poverty and social exclusion survey.* Ottawa: Author.

National Institute for Early Education Research (NIEER). 2010. *Children's activity and movement in preschools study.* Vol. 8, No. 1.

Nolan, M. 2007. *Mentoring, coaching and leadership in early childhood care and education.* Clifton Park, NY: Delmar.

Oates, J. 2010. *Supporting parenting, early childhood in focus.* The Hague, The Netherlands: Bernard Van Lear Foundation.

OECD (Organization for Economic Cooperation and Development). 2006. *Starting strong II: Early childhood education and care.* Paris: Education and Training Division, OECD.

OECD. 2001. *Starting strong: Early childhood education and care.* Paris: Education and Training Division, OECD.

OECD. 2004. *Early childhood education and care policy: Canada, country note.* OECD Directorate for Education.

Ontario. 1996. *Early childhood education program standards.* Toronto: Ministry of Education and Training/College Standards and Accreditation Council.

Ontario College of Early Childhood Educators. 2010a. *Principles for the code of ethics.* Toronto: Author.

Ontario College of Early Childhood Educators. 2010b. *Principles for the standards of practice.* Toronto: Author

Pascal, C. 2009. *With our best future in mind: Implementing early learning in Ontario.* Toronto: Government of Ontario.

Penn, H. 2000. How do children learn: Early childhood in a global context. In H. Penn, ed., *Early childhood services: Theory, policy, and practice.* Buckingham, UK: Open University Press.

Pimento, B., and D. Kernsted. 2010. *Healthy foundations in child care,* 4th ed. Toronto: Nelson.

Prentice, S. 2004. *Time for action: An economic and social analysis of child care in Winnipeg.* Winnipeg, MB: Child Care Coalition of Manitoba.

Prentice, S. 2008. Rural child care in Manitoba: New economic evidence. *Municipal Leader* (Spring): 26–29.

Reiniger, A., E. Robinson, and M. McHugh. 1995. Mandated training of professionals: A means for improving reporting of suspected child abuse. *Child Abuse and Neglect* 19: 63–70.

Rhomberg, V. 2000. Nourishing with the brain in mind: Professional development for cooks in early childhood settings. *Interaction* (CCCF) 14 (3).

Rimer, P., and B. Prager. 1998. *Reaching out: Working together to identify and respond to child victims of abuse.* Toronto: Nelson.

Robinson, A., and D. Stark. 2005. *Advocates in action: Making a difference for young children,* rev ed. Washington, DC: National Association for the Education of Young Children.

Rohacek, M., G. Adams, and E. Kisker. 2010. *Understanding quality in context : Child care centres, communities, markets and public policy.* Washington. DC: Urban Institute.

Rood, J. 1998. *Leadership in early childhood,* 2d ed. New York: Teachers College Press, Columbia University.

Ruopp, R., H. Travers, F. Glantz, and C. Coelen. 1979. *Children at the center: Final report of the national day care study,* vol. I. Cambridge, MA: Abt Associates.

Safe Kids Canada. 1997. *Child's play: A playground safety guide for daycares, schools and communities.* Toronto: Safe Kids Canada.

Saifer, S. 2005. *Practical solutions to practically every problem: The early childhood teacher's manual,* rev ed. St. Paul, MI: Redleaf Press.

Sargent, P. 2002. *Real men or real teachers? Contradictions in the lives of men elementary school teachers.* Harriman, TN: Men's Studies Press.

Schaeffer, S. 2001. *Understanding research: Top ten tips for advocates and policy-makers. Fact sheet.* Washington, DC: National Association of Child Advocates.

Schom-Moffat, P. 1992. *Caring for a living: National study on wages and working conditions in Canadian child care.* Ottawa: CCCF and Canadian Day Care Advocacy Association.

Schweinhart L.J., H.V. Barnes, and D.P. Weikart. 1993. *Significant benefits: The High/Scope Perry Preschool Study through age 27.* Ypsilanti, MI: High/Scope Press.

Sciarra, D.J., and A.G. Dorsey. 2002. *Leaders and supervisors in child care programs.* Albany, NY: Delmar.

Sciarra, D.J., and A.G. Dorsey. 2003. *Developing and administering a child care center,* 5th ed. Albany, NY: Delmar.

Shimoni, R., and J. Baxter. 2008. *Working with families: Perspectives for early childhood professionals,* 4th ed. Don Mills, ON: Pearson Addison-Wesley.

Shonkoff, J., and D. Phillips, eds. 2000. *From neurons to neighborhoods: The science of early childhood development.* Washington, DC: National Research Council.

Shore, R. 1997. *Rethinking the brain.* New York: Families and Work Institute.

Siraj-Blatchford, I., and M. Woodhead. 2009. *Early childhood in focus 4; Effective early childhood programs.* Milton Keynes, UK: Bernard Van Leer Foundation.

Spodek, B., O. Saracho, and D. Peters, eds. 1988. *Professionalism and the early childhood practitioner.* New York: Teachers College Press, Columbia University.

Spodek, B., O. Saracho, and D. Peters, eds. 1990. *Early childhood teacher preparation.* New York: Teachers College Press, Columbia University.

Statistics Canada, Social and Aboriginal Statistics Division. 2006. *Women in Canada: A gender-based statistical report.* 5th ed. OttaMinister of Industry. Catalogue no. 89-503-XPE.

Stevenson, M.F. 1995. *Fundraising for early childhood programs: Getting started and getting results,* rev. ed. Washington, DC: NAEYC.

Talen, T., and P. Bloom. 2005. *Program Administration Scale (PAS).* Washington, DC: NACA.

Tertell, E., S. Klein, and J. Jewett, eds. 1998. *When teachers reflect: Journeys toward effective, inclusive practice.* Washington, DC: NAEYC.

Torjman, S. 2008. *Poverty policy.* Ottawa: Caledon Institute. Available online: www.caledoninst. org/Publications/PDF/720ENG.pdf

Toronto. 2001. *Operating criteria for child care centers providing subsidized care in Metropolitan Toronto.* Toronto: Metro Community Services, Children's Services Division.

No Real Choice on Child Care. Toronto Star, January 11, 2011, http://www.thestar.com/opinion/editorials/article/919339--no-real-choice-on-child-care

Townson, M. 1986. *The costs and benefits of a national child care system for Canada.* Halifax: DPA Group Inc.

UNICEF. 2000. *The state of the world's children 2000.* New York: UNICEF Publications

Van der Gaag, J., and T. Jee-Peng. 2001. *The benefits of early childhood development programs: An economic analysis.* Washington, DC: World Bank Publication. Available online: www. worldbank.org/children.

Vanier Institute of the Family. 2010. *Families count: Profiling Canada's families.* Ottawa: Vanier Institute of the Family.

Waldfogel, J. 2005. *Expert roundtable on child development: Families, work arrangements, and child development.* Ottawa: Social Development Canada.

Washington, V., and J. Andrews. 2010. *Children of 2020: Creating a better tomorrow.* Washington, DC: NAEYC.

Westcoast Child Care Resource Centre. 2001. *Towards partnership/Vers un partariat: Multi-language resources for families in child care/ Ressources multilingues pour les familles ayant un enfant en garderie.* Vancouver: Westcoast Child Care Resource Centre.

Whitebook, M., L. Sakai, E. Gerber, and C. Howes. 2001. *Then & now: Changes in child care staffing, 1994–2000, technical report.* Washington, DC: Center for the Child Care Workforce.

Whitebook, M., C. Howes, and D. Phillips. 1990. *Who cares? Child care teachers and the quality of child care in America. Final report of the National Child Care Staffing Study.* Oakland, CA: Child Care Employee Project.

Willer, B., ed. 1990. *Reaching the full cost of quality in early childhood programs.* Washington, DC: NAEYC.

Willer, B. 1994. A conceptual framework for early childhood professional development. In *The early childhood career lattice: Perspectives on professional development,* edited by J. Johnson and J.B. McCracken. Washington, DC: NAEYC.

Wilson, B. 2004. *Community voices: Young parents in Toronto speak out about work, community services and family life.* Toronto: Community Social Planning Council of Toronto and Family Service Association of Toronto.

Wilson, L. 2010. *Partnerships: Families and communities in Canadian early childhood education,* 3rd ed. Toronto: Nelson.

Woodhead, M., and J. Oates. 2007. *Transitions in the lives of young children. Early childhood in Focus no. 2* , The Hague, Bernard Van Leer Foundation.

Woodhead, M., and J. Oates. 2010. *Culture and learning, early childhood in Focus no. 6,* The Hague, Bernard Van Leer Foundation.

Woodhead, M. 1996. *In search of the rainbow: Pathways to quality in large scale programs for young children,* Practice and reflections, no. 10, The Hague, Bernard Van Leer Foundation.

Workers Health and Safety Centre. 1999. *Health and safety module for child care workers in Ontario.* Don Mills, ON: Workers Health and Safety Centre.

Worotynec, S. 2000. The good, the bad and the ugly: Listserv as support. *CyberPsychology and Behavior* 3(5): 797–809.

Yankelovich, D. 2000a. *What grown-ups understand about child development: A national benchmark survey.* Washington, DC: Zero to Three.

Yankelovich, D. 2000b. *Parents speak: Findings from focus group resources on early childhood development.* Washington, DC: Zero to Three.

Index